• BEN JONSON •

BEN
JONSON

A Life

DAVID RIGGS

HARVARD UNIVERSITY PRESS

CAMBRIDGE, MASSACHUSETTS

LONDON, ENGLAND

1989

Publication of this book has been aided by a grant
from the Hyder Edward Rollins Fund.

This book is printed on acid-free paper, and its binding
materials have been chosen for strength and durability.

Library of Congress Cataloging-in-Publication Data

Riggs, David.
Ben Jonson : a life / David Riggs.
p.   cm.
Bibliography: p.
Includes index.
ISBN 0-674-06625-1 (alk. paper)
1. Jonson, Ben, 1573?–1637—Biography.
2. Authors, English—Early modern, 1500–1700—Biography.
I. Title.
PR2631.R54 1989
822'.3—dc19   88-13984
[B]   CIP

Designed by Gwen Frankfeldt

To my mother
and the memory of my father

Acknowledgments

To thank everyone who helped in the preparation of this book would require a preface of gargantuan proportions; so I will confine myself to a few obligations that loom especially large.

Jonas Barish, Harry Levin, and Norman Rabkin encouraged me to undertake a biography of Jonson and helped me obtain the fellowship that provided a year in which to begin writing it. The earliest version was composed at the Huntington Library during the summer of 1981 and at the Stanford Humanities Center during 1981–82. Both of these institutions have my warmest thanks. I am especially grateful to Ian Watt, the former director of the Humanities Center, for his unstinting support at every stage of this project and for his painstaking critique of my first draft. The existence of this biography is largely due to his guidance and encouragement. I owe thanks as well to Wesley Trimpi and Ronald Rebholz for their careful reading of that early draft; to John Bender, Martin Evans, John Leone, and Steven Orgel, who also read it and gave me invaluable advice about how to transform a biographical handbook into a readable narrative; and to the anonymous referee who supplied an extensive and penetrating commentary on the manuscript that I submitted to the Harvard University Press in 1985.

Three years later another group of expert readers gamely offered to peruse the final draft while it was being readied for publication. J. B. Close, Ian Donaldson, Lydia Fillingham, Eric Mallin, Michael Warren, and Robert Watson made scores of improvements, ranging from the placement of commas to crucial matters of fact and interpretation, on very short notice. Ron Davies, who typed the revised manuscript, added many suggestions of his own and saw to it that all of these last-minute revisions found their way into the finished product.

Colleagues and friends guided me through fields of study that were unfamiliar and answered questions that I scarcely knew how to frame. Herant Katchadourian reconstructed the story of Jonson's early life from the perspective of a trained psychoanalyst; I have gratefully incorporated many of his insights into my text. Paul Seaver introduced me to the urban landscape of Elizabethan London, uncovered new information about Jonson's relationship to the Bricklayers' Guild, and shed light on his citation for recusancy in 1606. Kevin Sharpe shared with me his vast knowledge of Jacobean and Caroline court life, commented on all of the book in draft, and made countless suggestions in conversation. Margaret Davis Aiken volunteered many shrewd observations about the earliest likenesses of Jonson and Shakespeare. Ira Livingston generously assisted me in obtaining the illustrations that appear in these pages.

Finally, I should like to thank Robert Polhemus, George Dekker, and Albert Gelpi, the three colleagues who chaired the Stanford English Department while I was writing this book. They met all of my requests for research assistance and gave me a teaching schedule that made it possible to continue writing when I was not on leave. My greatest and quite unpayable debt is to Sue, Elaine, and Matt. They welcomed Ben Jonson into our household—even after it became apparent that he had come for an extended stay—and cheerfully endured all the stresses and strains of long authorship.

Contents

Westminster and the western part of the City of London. Detail from the map of London in Georgius Braun and Franz Hogenberg, *Civitates orbis terrarum*, 1572.

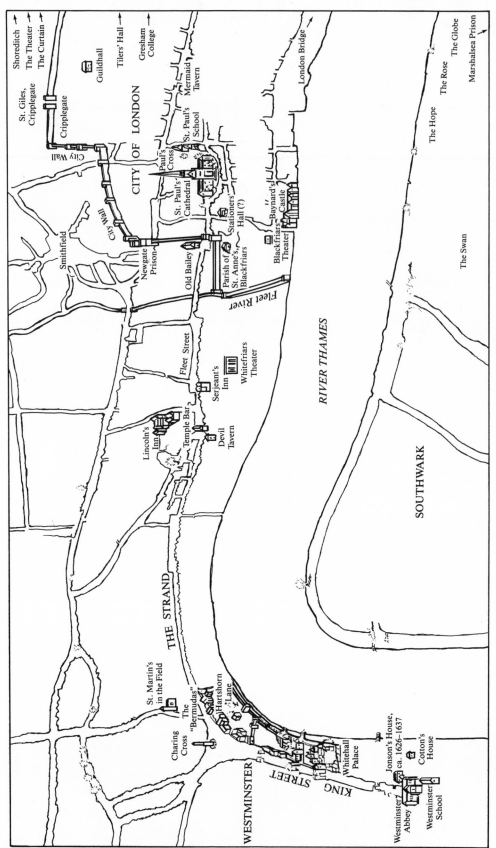

Sites associated with Ben Jonson's life.

· BEN JONSON ·

All references to Jonson's work are to the text in *Ben Jonson,* 11 vols., ed. C. H. Herford, Percy Simpson, and Evelyn Simpson (Oxford, 1925–1952), abbreviated as "HS" in the text and notes. I have silently modernized *u, v, i, j,* and scribal contractions. Extended passages in italics have been changed to roman type. Titles of works are in modern spelling. The abbreviations listed below are also used throughout, followed by line number, poem number, or poem and line numbers.

Ep	*Epigrams*
Conv	*Ben Jonson's Conversations with William Drummond of Hawthornden*
Disc	*Timber; or, Discoveries Made upon Men and Matter*
For	*The Forest*
Und	*The Underwood*
UV	*Ungathered Verse*

Prologue

Some people regarded Ben Jonson as a scoundrel; others took him for a sage. There was ample basis for both views. A biographer who concentrated on contemporary gossip, satires, court records, and private correspondence could easily conclude that Jonson was a notorious reprobate and public nuisance: a drunken, swaggering, murderous sponge who gained his livelihood by writing libelous plays and flattering poems, and routinely attacked his friends behind their backs. His admirers have sought to discredit such charges on the grounds that Jonson was the innocent victim of his enemies' malice. At the age of forty-seven, however, in the course of extended private conversations with William Drummond, the Laird of Hawthornden, Jonson spoke quite openly about his drinking bouts, petty animosities, killings, womanizing, and criminal record. But the autobiographical passages in Jonson's published work, and tributes and memorabilia written by his friends, tell a very different story; a biographer who took these portrayals at face value could just as easily conclude that Jonson was a discreet and scholarly man who treasured his solitude and the society of a few intimate companions. He portrays himself as a "modest" individual, "known only to that *Few* which are truly able to know him," as his friend John Selden put it; his poetry and criticism mirror the same qualities of plainness, moderation, and sober rationality that inform his everyday existence. He discourages readers from inquiring too closely into his personal life by insinuating that there is not much to know about it. He has *"ever trembled to thinke toward the least prophanenesse"*; his project, both in his writing and his life, is to curb extravagance.[1]

Taken separately, these two protagonists can only perpetuate sterile controversies about the nature of the "real" Jonson; taken in conjunction, they offer a remarkable opportunity to study the interplay of reckless self-assertion and rationalistic self-limitation in a single life. Jonson is like a prudent businessman who periodically feels an irresistible urge to go to the racetrack. Just as one would expect, he loses everything he owns by the end of the day; within a few months, however, Jonson is wealthier, and more prudent, than ever. The oscillations between defiant risk taking and sober retrenchment are less drastic after he reaches his mid-thirties, but the pattern persists until the end of his life.

My objectives are to keep both sides of Jonson's personality in perspective and to reconstruct the individual who negotiated between these extremes. In this biography, therefore, I analyze Jonson's behavior from two complementary points of view. When he is acting like a professional artist making practical choices, I adopt the outlook of a social historian. In these sections of the book, my aims are to reconstruct his social and intellectual milieu; to describe the conditions within which he produced his plays, poems, and masques; and to relate his writing to his personal circumstances at any given moment. When Jonson's behavior resists this kind of explanation, I seek out a psychological one. These parts of my narrative are frankly speculative and treat the ramifications of his childhood experience, the enactment of persistent neurotic impulses, and the therapeutic functions of his writing.

The two strands of my argument converge in the analyses of Jonson's plays. In writing his satirical comedies for the London stage, Jonson simultaneously released his pent-up aggressions and reconstituted himself as a man of letters, a leading figure in the literary avant-garde of Renaissance England. When his enemy Inigo Jones complained to Jonson that "no ill thou couldst so taske dwells not (in thee) / and there the store house of your plotts wee see," he spoke more wisely than he knew (HS, XI, 385). In the last analysis, I argue, Jonson's writings reveal the malcontent troublemaker, astute careerist, and literary artist to be one and the same person.

The dominant motifs of Jonson's professional life are social and literary ambition. Between his early twenties and his mid-forties the upward trajectory of his career is breathtaking: forsaking his apprenticeship in the Bricklayers' Guild, he was by turns a journeyman actor touring the provinces, an innovative playwright trying to reach both a popular audience and an educated readership, a court poet to the household of King James I, the first English dramatist to bring out his works in folio, and a royal pensioner whose verse manuscripts circulated among a select circle of gentlemen and ladies. By the time of his death two decades later he had become the most celebrated poet of his age, a man who outshone even Shakespeare and Donne in the eyes of his contemporaries. Since his career coincides with the rise of the literary profession in England, his personal success story takes on the characteristics of a cultural phenomenon: in following his rise we are also witnessing the emergence of authorship as a full-time vocation.

Jonson not only prevailed over external obstacles that were built into the fabric of his society; he also overcame psychological disabilities that would have doomed a lesser man either to oblivion or to extinction at an early age. The record of his misadventures rivals the story of his success and is too long to be explained away on the grounds that he was a victim of circumstances, or lived in a more boisterous age than our own. Contemporary sources reveal that he killed two men for no apparent reason, went to prison on three separate occasions, was "almost at the Gallowes" (*Conv*, 249) and wore the brand of a convicted murderer on his thumb, enjoyed sleeping with other men's wives (but not with single women), sired one or more illegitimate children, was paraded through the streets of Paris in a drunken stupor, and narrowly escaped having his ears and nose mutilated after collaborating on a play that lampooned King James I. In his thirty-third year, his own mother was on the verge of bringing his life to an end and acquired a dram of "Lustie strong poison" (*Conv*, 281–282) for that purpose. This turbulent personal history goes back to the formative stages of Jonson's career and indicates that the course of his development was far more checkered than he cared to admit in public. The facade of a swift and sure ascent to Parnassus concealed a maze of personal and professional crises; the man who encouraged the reading public to view him as a model of even-tempered rationality had a foul mouth, a violent temper, and could be recklessly self-indulgent.

The progress of Jonson's literary career reflects his growing ability to cope with these inner demons and to achieve a degree of the self-mastery that he prized so highly. The key to psychological health, it is now widely believed, lies in the adaptive styles that enable individuals to resolve inner conflicts in a constructive fashion. If Jonson's instinctual drives were unusually fierce, his repertory of defense mechanisms was correspondingly rich and effective. Humor, which Freud regarded as "the highest of these defensive processes" because it "scorns to withdraw the idea bearing the distressing affect from conscious attention,"[2] was the main catalyst in his personal and professional growth. When Jonson's wayward impulses led him to commit overtly antisocial acts, he placed his future in jeopardy; but when the same psychological disorders found expression in his stage comedies, they became a source of strength and launched the professional career that ultimately secured his future.

Although he continued to exhibit the same disabilities throughout his life, the mature artist discovered a wealth of creative uses for them. His greatest comedies, *Volpone* and *The Alchemist,* are replete with adaptive devices that transform the dross of lust and aggression into the gold of artistic creation. That he consciously grasped the analogy between his experience and his art is more than we can say, but his continuing preoccupation with alchemy, sublimation, mock encomia, self-transformation, and the psychopathology of the bodily humors suggests that he was at least intuitively aware of it.

The most rigid of Jonson's defenses was reaction formation, which can be defined as behavior that is "diametrically opposed to an unacceptable instinctual impulse." The autobiographical passages in his critical dialogues, prefatory letters, prose jottings, and poems repeatedly insist on the changeless purity of his inner self, even when the factual record belies such assertions. Although self-transformation is the most compelling aspect of his biography, the actual experience of growth and change left him unsatisfied; his ultimate, and unrealizable, ambition was to transcend his origins, to preserve the product of growth while discarding the process. Karen Horney characterizes the compulsion to triumph over one's own past as *"the drive towards a vindictive triumph."* This project "may be closely linked to the drive for actual achievement and success," she writes, but "its chief aim is to put others to shame, or defeat them through one's very success." Its "motivating force," she continues, "stems from impulses to take revenge for humiliations suffered during childhood." [3]

A simple, yet revealing, example of Jonson's tendency to efface his origins is the spelling of his last name. The title pages of the first three printed works that bear his name all refer to him as "Johnson." Since he carefully prepared these texts for the printer, and was quite finicky about such matters, we can be reasonably sure that this spelling, which also appears in all the early manuscript copies of his poems, was the one he employed for the first thirty years or so of his life. In his thirty-second year, however, he switched to "Jonson," and when he reprinted the three earlier texts in the 1616 *Works* he expunged his name from their title pages. "Johnson" thus became a nonperson, and the question of why he chose to adopt the anomalous spelling that set him apart from his contemporaries has never even been posed.

Turning to the matter of his ancestry—the usual starting point for a biographical narrative—we find another instance of retrospective self-fashioning. The first three court records that allude to his social status variously describe him as a "player," a "yoman," and a "bricklayer and citizen of London," phrases which indicate that he was not of gentle birth. In his thirty-third year, however, a fourth court record refers to him as "Armiger," a gentleman entitled to bear the heraldic arms of his ancestors. This document does not indicate who the ancestors were, but many years later, during his conversations with Drummond, Jonson remarked that "his grandfather came from Carlisle and he thought from Anandale to it, he served King Henry 8 and was a Gentleman."[4] Although this gentlemanly forbear gave the erstwhile bricklayer a crucial link to an earlier generation of landed gentry, he is a relative latecomer in the chronicle of Jonson's own life. At some point between the third and fourth appearances in court, around the time when he changed the spelling of his name, Jonson persuaded the Herald's Office that he was descended from the Johnstones of Annandale and purchased the right to bear their hereditary coat of arms. Ben Johnson, the journeyman bricklayer, disappeared in the wake of Ben Jonson, the courtier's grandson.

However instrumental these maneuvers may have been in furthering Jonson's career, or fortifying his self-esteem, they provoke precisely the kind of speculation they were meant to discourage. Jonson inadvertently calls attention to the side of himself that he wants to conceal; the adult's eagerness to rearrange his past arouses our curiosity about the child who came before him.

PART
ONE

Coming of Age
in Elizabethan
England

• CHAPTER ONE •

Beginnings

Ben Jonson was born in obscure circumstances. Evidence gathered from the later years of his life indicates that his birthday fell on June 11, 1572, but no contemporary record of that event has survived, nor have the names of his father, his mother, any siblings, or the place of his birth. He told Drummond that his father "losed all his estate under Queen Marie, having been cast in prison and forfaitted" and "at last turn'd Minister." With his untimely death, the family descent continued into the childhood of Ben, "a Ministers son" who "was Posthumous born a moneth after his fathers decease." [1]

Jonson made no reference whatever to the first seven years of his life except to say that he was "brought up poorly." His seventeenth-century biographers were unable to discover anything about his infancy, but they did glean a couple of facts about his early adolescence. "When a *little child*," Thomas Fuller reports, "he lived in *Harts-horn-lane* near *Charing-cross*, where his Mother married a *Bricklayer* for her Second husband." [2] Charing Cross stood just north of the royal city of Westminster and a mile west of the walled City of London. The village of Charing did not have a substantial "middle" class of artisans and merchants: this part of the urban population lived, by and large, within the city walls. It was rather a residential area containing both the town houses of the courtiers who attended the Queen at Westminster and a sizable contingent of the urban poor, who dwelt in the alleyways behind the mansions that fronted on the Strand. The occupants of Hartshorn Lane, which ran from the Strand down to the Thames, included a bricklayer named Robert Brett among their number and if, as seems likely, he was Jonson's stepfather, the boy

Bricklayer and other manual laborers. From Wynkyn de Worde, *Robert the Devil,* ca. 1510. Although Jonson "could not endure" his stepfather's trade, he was apprenticed to it and joined the Tilers' and Bricklayers' Company in 1599.

escaped the plight of the very poor. Brett was a reasonably prosperous artisan who helped pay for renovations at the parish church of St. Martin in the Fields in the mid-1590s, and was Master of the Tilers' and Bricklayers' Company at the time of his death in 1609. The sewage ditch that ran along the premises of Brett's cottage seems to have been the distinctive feature of the neighborhood where he and his family resided. During Jonson's lifetime, Hartshorn Lane would become one of the major sewage canals in the greater London area. Nevertheless, Jonson's stepfather managed to transform this liability into an asset: a lease granted in 1586 mentions "the little garden lately made over the sewer by Roberte Brette." [3]

Jonson was surrounded, then, by extremes of poverty and wealth from the earliest years of his life. The walk from Hartshorn Lane to the parish school at which he began his education ran through the lower part of St. Martin's Lane, where he traversed the "Bermudas," a maze of alleyways that had been turned into the urban equivalent of the Bermuda straits by the pimps, whores, gamesters, and "roaring boys" who accosted unwary passers-by; past the Royal Mews, which had served as the monarch's

Dryden?

stables and tilting yard since the time of Henry VIII; and on into the fashionable church of St. Martin in the Fields.[4]

At some point after he reached the age of seven, a "friend"—the first of his many patrons—secured him a place at Westminster School. Whoever this benefactor was, he did Jonson an immense favor. The journey to his new school transported the bricklayer's stepson from a workman's cottage into the central locus of power and prestige in Elizabethan England. The daily walk to Westminster took him up Hartshorn Lane, down the Strand, through the Holbein gate and the King's Street gate (two of the main entrances to the royal palace at Whitehall), down King's Street, under the High Tower, through the cluster of buildings surrounding Westminster Abbey, and on into the school itself. Westminster was one of the elite academies of Tudor England, "the most fashionable school in the country" by Lawrence Stone's reckoning. The quality of the education, the native abilities and family connections of the other students, and the physical location of the school itself gave the young scholar an enormous head start on the ladder of patronage and preferment. The proper name of the school, taken from the old name of the cathedral, was the Royal College of St. Peter's, and the crown continued to take an active interest in its fortunes. Whereas the religious observances at St. Paul's, its counterpart in London, were relatively free of ceremony and ritual, those at St. Peter's, in keeping with Queen Elizabeth's own preferences, remained "more after the medieval fashion of schools than in line with the German models." The Queen herself attended the school play at Christmas and occasionally visited the premises while classes were in session.[5]

Tudor monarchs endowed schools like Westminster in the hope of creating an elite corps of educated gentlemen whose ultimate purpose was to serve the prince in the country or at the court. A hundred years earlier, a mastery of the intellectual disciplines Jonson encountered at Westminster would have marked him out as a future cleric. But during the intervening century continental educators like Vives and Erasmus, and their English counterparts Eliot and Ascham, had made a classical education available to prospective members of the lay ruling class; for such training, they argued, offered the surest grounding in the arts of government. "Learning needs rest," Jonson noted in his commonplace book, "Soveraignty gives it. Soveraignty needs counsell: Learning affords it."[6] The idea was familiar, but it had an immediate, and visible, relevance at Westminster, where the monarch was close at hand. Jonson's subsequent portrayals of himself as a learned poet whose learning entitled him to a place at court will seem less pretentious if this background is kept in mind. The path that led from Hartshorn Lane to Westminster School had Whitehall for its eventual destination.

View of Westminster in the sixteenth century by H. W. Brewer. From Herbert A. Cox, *Old London Illustrated*, 1923. On his way to school Jonson entered the precinct of Westminster Abbey through the High Tower (upper right corner). The school was located in the monastic buildings to the left of the abbey (upper left center).

Beginnings

The student body at Westminster School was a mixture of students on scholarship and boys whose parents could afford to send them there. The forty Queen's Scholars were poor (children who stood to inherit more than ten pounds were ineligible for these awards), had their expenses paid by the school, lived with the dean or master, and were encouraged to compete for scholarships to Oxford or Cambridge. Some of the fee-paying students lived nearby with their families, while others came from the country and boarded with relatives who lived in the neighborhood. Jonson fell into none of these categories. As a working-class child from Charing, whose fees were temporarily subsidized by a "friend," his situation was quite anomalous: at the end of the day his path led back to the bricklayer's cottage on Hartshorn Lane. What E. Pearlman calls the "twin themes of social disability and social pretense" that pervade Jonson's adult life were inscribed on the map of his childhood experience. Whatever psychological costs this arrangement entailed, it also meant that the range of Jonson's childhood experience was broader than that of his fellow students. If his time at Westminster provided him with a formal education, his familiarity with the street life of the "Bermudas" put him in touch with the criminal types who would people his greatest comedies. At the height of his career, Jonson would characterize "the Streights or the *Bermuda's*" as a place of education "where the quarelling lesson is read . . . The Lecturer is o' the one side, and his Pupils o' the other."[7]

The school did provide him with a means of breaking the tie to Hartshorn Lane, for Westminster was the only grammar school to award its scholarships on the basis of an academic competition. The school statutes stipulated that prospective scholars were to be examined every year for two days "in grammar, the humanities, and writing." The examinations or "challenges," as they were called, emphasized Latin grammar. In the course of this ordeal, candidates moved ahead of one another by catching their rivals out on difficult constructions and fine points. After spending his adolescence in an environment where advancement depended on grammatical precision, Jonson would continue to insist upon the importance of correct speech throughout his life. "*Language* most shewes a man," he wrote, "speake that I may see thee." His famous cavil at a seemingly inconsistent sentence in Shakespeare's *Julius Caesar* ("Caesar did never wrong, but with just cause") is only the best known of many such instances. He chided contemporary audiences for applauding playwrights who were careless in this regard ("such impropriety of phrase, such plenty of *soloecismes,* such dearth of sense, so bold *prolepse's,* so rackt *metaphor's*"). Within his plays, grammatical sloppiness in a character's speech is an infallible sign of moral and intellectual weakness, and the same rule applied to society at large: "Wheresoever, manners and fashions are corrupted, language is. It imitates the publicke riot."[8]

The curriculum at Westminster, like that of any Tudor grammar school, was almost exclusively devoted to the study of Latin. The boys were required to parse, memorize, and translate about a hundred lines of Latin every week; Jonson must have worked his way through at least five hundred pages of poetry and prose in this manner. By the time he left Westminster, he had committed substantial portions of Cato, Terence, Ovid, Virgil, Cicero, and Horace to memory. His firsthand knowledge of Greek was probably limited to Lucian, the one Greek author who was to have a major influence on him.[9]

Jonson's teacher at Westminster was William Camden, one of the leading schoolmasters of Elizabethan England. In his epigram to this "most reverend head, to whom I owe / All that I am in arts, all that I know" (*Ep*, 14.1–2), Jonson portrays his mentor as a surrogate father, and Camden was ideally suited to play this role in his student's life. To begin with, he was an eminent linguist whose Greek grammar went through seven editions in Jonson's lifetime. Just as important, Camden understood the ways in which learning could serve the state. During Jonson's years at Westminster, Camden completed *Britannia; or, A Chorographical Description of England, Scotland, and Ireland*, the first of his major works, and saw its original, Latin edition through the press in 1586. The *Britannia* reconstructed the history of Roman Britain, and demonstrated its continuing relevance to the England of Elizabeth I, by providing a "chorographical description" of the British Isles. Chorography is the classical genre of geographical narrative, deriving from Ptolemy and Strabo, which recounts the history of a region by giving a systematic description of its principal sites. By bringing his vast erudition to bear on the archaeological and linguistic materials that he uncovered during his county-by-county treks across the British Isles, Camden showed that modern England still retained much of its Roman heritage and thus shared a common ancestor with the European family of nations.

Britannia proved to be an enormously popular book. The Latin text went through five editions by 1600, and an English translation by Philemon Holland appeared in 1610. Camden's example was instrumental in shaping his pupil's vision of an England where the classical world was vividly present in wood nymphs, river gods, architectural forms, and curious etymologies. Jonson was himself gathering material for a chorographical poem about Scotland during the walking trip that took him to the home of William Drummond. More than any poet of his day, Camden's pupil had "an uncontrived sense of the immediacy of the Roman past," writes Richard Peterson, "which was not something far removed, but, as his master demonstrated, directly underfoot, an archaeological layer of England's history which could be mined poetically as Jonson was to mine the English language for Latin cognates and roots."[10]

William Camden, after Marcus Gheeraerts the Younger, ca. 1622. Jonson's schoolmaster at the end of his life. The book in the foreground is Philemon Holland's translation of Camden's *Britannia* (1610).

Camden introduced his survey of the counties of England by proposing to "shew with as much brevity as I can who were the ancient inhabitants, what was the reason of the name . . . and lastly, who have been dukes or earls of them since the Norman Conquest." The passages commending the illustrious nobility of every county, including men and women who were Camden's own contemporaries, gave yet another dimension to the *Britannia*. His laborious investigations into family genealogies made him the great Elizabethan authority on titles of honor, and because of this capacity for making fine social distinctions he was uniquely qualified to determine a person's social rank. His appointment to the College of Heralds as Clarenceux King at Arms in 1597 was the logical outcome of his scholarly labors. As King at Arms, Camden had the official responsibility for determining a person's social worth; he, along with the heralds he supervised, had the authority to grant the coat of arms that identified a man as a gentleman in the status-conscious society of late Elizabethan England.[11] Jonson's continuing preoccupation with the question of true versus spurious nobility, his sense of himself as a poet who conferred rank and dignity on worthy contemporaries, and the skill with which he navigated the upper strata of the aristocracy, all reflected his master's concerns.

As an antiquarian and philologist, Camden believed that "the reason of the name" frequently contained additional layers of meaning that held the clue to a person's true identity. "Plato will have [etymologies] admitted," he remarked in a paper delivered around 1600, "if there be a consonancy and correspondency between the name of the thing and thing named." Jonson would proceed along these lines in his court masques and in the collection of laudatory epigrams that he published at the height of his career. When he puns on the Latinate senses of Sir Horace Vere's name ("vere," "vir"), or exhibits a red cliff to signify the Radcliffe family, he is following his teacher's example.[12]

Many of Camden's associates became Jonson's friends as well. In approximately 1586 Camden, together with his old Westminster pupil Robert Cotton, and the lawyers James Ley and Henry Spelman, founded the Society of Antiquaries. Although the society disbanded shortly after the death of Elizabeth, Cotton's library continued to provide a focus and a resource for persons pursuing research into English and continental antiquities. Jonson would make use of this library throughout his life. This connection also kept him in contact with other scholars, such as his Westminster schoolmate Hugh Holland, and the antiquaries John Selden, Edmund Bolton, and Richard Carew, all of whom belonged to the circle of Camden and Cotton.[13] Here again, Camden provided his pupil with more than a formal education: he furnished access to a community of learned men that widened Jonson's horizons throughout his career.

The schoolmaster and antiquary was even further ahead of his time than he could have foreseen. When Jonson subsequently hailed him as the man "to whom my country owes / The great renowne, and name wherewith shee goes," he referred to the fact that Elizabeth's successor, James VI of Scotland, styled himself King of *Britain* in order to promote the union of England and Scotland. *Britannia,* as Jonson suggests, helped pave the way by establishing the legitimacy of the Roman name. Nor was it merely a question of nomenclature: the notion that Great Britain was a single entity, descended from the Roman Empire, and destined to revive the glories of Augustan Rome, would form the centerpiece of royal iconography during the early years of James's reign, when Jonson was establishing his reputation at the new court. In keeping with his classicizing, neo-Augustan tendencies, Camden opposed Puritanism, "favoured a cautious and pacific foreign policy and disliked apocalyptic enthusiasm"; here, too, Jonson would remain faithful to his schoolmaster's principles.[14]

Although Jonson's connection with Westminster proved invaluable during the years ahead, he failed to win a scholarship during his own time there. The wording of his remarks to Drummond ("he was put to school by a friend . . . after taken from it") indicates that he was "taken from" grammar school before finishing his course of studies, whereas Queen's Scholars completed the entire curriculum; he did not proceed to university, as Queen's Scholars ordinarily did; and his "master" Camden was in fact second master while Jonson was enrolled at Westminster, and only taught the younger students (HS, I, 3). Jonson's reminiscences thus imply that he never advanced beyond his fourth form year, and left school in 1588 or 1589, around the age of sixteen.

Upon leaving Westminster, Jonson was "put to ane other Craft." He left Drummond to guess what the other craft was, but numerous contemporary allusions make it clear that he took up his stepfather's trade of bricklaying. Both Aubrey and Fuller say that he helped build a wall at Lincoln's Inn, and the account books of the inn show that Robert Brett, the bricklayer who lived on Hartshorn Lane, was employed to erect a wall there in 1590 and 1591.[15] This information squares with Jonson's own account, which has him going straight from Westminster to a manual trade.

But Jonson "could not endure" his stepfather's craft and joined the English army stationed in the Netherlands, perhaps when the garrison was strengthened in 1591. This was not a prudent decision. The pay of a common soldier was virtually equivalent to the seven pence a day earned by a bricklayer's apprentice; a soldier's chances of surviving to collect his pay

An English army on the march. From John Derricke, *Image of Ireland*, 1586. Jonson probably marched among the ranks of the common infantrymen who are carrying pikes, swords, and daggers in the right foreground.

were scarcely better than even; and if he did return, he was likely to be crippled for life. To judge from Jonson's reminiscences, he joined the army for psychological, rather than material, reasons. "In his service in the Low Countries," he recalled, "he had in the face of both the Campes killed ane Enemie and taken opima spolia from him." [16] Once Jonson had killed his man, he returned home "soone"—the wording of Drummond's notation suggests that he did not serve out his time—presumably because he had accomplished what he set out to do.

This episode is the first sign of Jonson's extraordinary aggressiveness and, as such, clamors for a little explanation. The visible and proximate causes of Jonson's anger lie in the circumstances of his childhood. In the distant background (if he was aware of it) there was the knowledge that he had been deprived of his familial estate and gentlemanly status by a series of unlucky accidents. Other deprivations lay closer to home. His father had abandoned him before he was born; his mother had transferred a share of her affection to the bricklayer whom she married while Jonson was still a young child; he had been separated from his surrogate father Camden without being allowed to complete his course of studies at Westminster. This young man bore a heavy load of resentment. The military campaign in the Low Countries provided him with an opportunity to renounce his stepfather's trade and express his wrath with impunity. Although his behavior was reckless, he was already beginning to find constructive uses for his rage. On the field of battle, the bricklayer's stepson could take by violence something that he felt had been unfairly denied him. Bedecked with his *opima spolia,* the day laborer became the hero of a chivalric passage at arms conducted on foreign fields.[17]

The young Jonson also carried on an active sex life, and this too took him beyond the pale of ordinary adolescent behavior. "In his youth," he remarked to Drummond, "he was given to Venerie. he thought the use of a maide nothing in comparison to the wantonness of a wife and would never have ane other mistress." Why did the young Jonson have a fixation on sleeping with married women rather than maidens? There is, of course, no reason to suppose that wives are more wanton than their single counterparts. Wives differ from maidens because they have husbands and thus introduce a third party into the transaction; when Jonson slept with married women he was committing an aggressive act against the spouses whom he had displaced. Not surprisingly, his reminiscences about these exploits have to do with injured husbands rather than wanton wives. After telling Drummond about a picture in which Ahasuerus, the biblical prototype of the victimized husband, comes across "Haman courting Esther in a Bed," he added that "he himself being once so taken the Good man said, I would not believe yee would abuse my house so." Another "man made his own wife to Court him, whom he enjoyed two yeares erre he knew of it, and one day finding them by chance Was passingly delighted with it." In a less salacious variation on this theme, he recalled that "one day being at table with my Lady Rutland, her husband coming in, accused her that she keept table to poets, of which she wrott a letter to him which he answered My Lord intercepted the letter, but never challenged him."[18]

Although Jonson evidently outgrew the need to play the adulterer in real life, this scenario never lost its hold on his imagination, for it recurs with obsessive frequency in his comedies: in play after play, a deluded or jealous husband looks on while his wife has, or is about to have, an affair with an unattached gallant. The mature dramatist invariably associates sexual excitement with cuckoldry; conversely, relationships between single men and women tend to be utterly devoid of emotion, even when they lead to marriage.

The most plausible explanation for Jonson's preoccupation with cuckoldry lies, once again, in the tangled circumstances of his childhood. His own family life had been disrupted by his stepfather at an early age; when he reached late adolescence he exacted revenge against the heads of other households. The original transgressor in this retaliatory cycle entered the Jonson family at a time when Ben was "a little child" (HS, XI, 508) who had no apparent rival for his mother's affection. The bricklayer's appearance there, to judge from what happened afterward, was a traumatic event for the boy. Although he concealed his stepfather's existence even from Drummond (from whom he concealed very little), their conversations indicate that he "could not endure" working for him and joined the army because it was the only viable alternative to his apprenticeship. But the need to redress the original grievance, and to even the score with the man who had successfully competed for his mother's love, continued to rankle. In the illicit liaisons of Jonson's youth it is the displaced young man who captures the lady's affection while his rival, her husband, assumes the part of the humiliated onlooker.

Jonson made a significant break with this destructive cycle on November 14, 1594, when he married one Anne Lewis at the parish church of St. Magnus the Martyr. The church stood near the corner of Thames Street and New Fish Street, at the head of London Bridge, so Anne would have come from the City of London. He probably felt a strong romantic attachment to her at the time of their wedding. Elizabethan men normally put off marriage until they were sufficiently well established to set up an independent household: the average age of a bridegroom was above twenty-six. Jonson's decision to marry at twenty-two, when he was only halfway through his apprenticeship, was a rash act. Apprentices were legally bound to remain single until they had served out the full seven years of their term. Jonson's marriage to Anne Lewis brought his affiliation with the Bricklayers' Guild to an end and severed the vocational tie that bound him to his stepfather. But he was also entering into a new and potentially constructive relationship with his spouse. Instead of pursuing other men's wives, he could now begin a family of his own. Anne became pregnant the following summer and delivered their first son, Ben, in the spring of 1596.[19]

The termination of Jonson's apprenticeship presented an opportunity for constructive change in his professional life as well. By the time his first son was born he had entered a profession that was less reputable, but potentially more rewarding, than either soldiering or bricklaying: he became an actor. This change of vocation would not have been feasible between June 1592 and June 1594, when the playhouses were closed because of the plague. But they were open again in the summer before Jonson's marriage, and he probably entered the theatrical profession around that time. Thomas Dekker, an unfriendly witness, later alleged that Jonson had taken "mad Hieronimoes part"—the leading role in Thomas Kyd's *The Spanish Tragedy*—"to get service among the Mimickes" and had "ambled (in a leather pilch) by a playwagon, in the high way" with a company of strolling players. The players were probably the Earl of Pembroke's Men, who had Kyd's play in their repertory and who are known to have been on tour in 1595–96. Not long thereafter, in the first half of 1597, Pem-

Village Scene with Outdoor Theater, by Jan Brueghel the Elder, ca. 1600. As a traveling player Jonson had to compete for attention. While the villagers in the background perform a rustic dance, the well-dressed spectators in the foreground pay more attention to one another than to the actors.

broke's Men were performing at the Swan, the London theater that Francis Langley had recently erected on the Bankside, and Jonson was in their employ.[20]

At first glance, his decision to leave his wife and son to become a touring player seems to be a heartless act, and toward the end of his life he apparently did come to feel some regret about it. At the time, however, he may well have believed that his new occupation would serve his family's interests. A journeyman actor drew the same pay as a bricklayer's apprentice, and if the journeyman were skillful enough to become a "sharer" in the profits of his company, he could take home between 2½ and 3½ shillings per day—far more than Jonson could ever have earned laying bricks. Moreover, he was well qualified for his new profession: he was highly literate, had a superb memory, was a practiced swordsman, and had received some training in music while at Westminster School.

Hieronimo discovers his dead son Horatio. Detail from the title page of Thomas Kyd, *The Spanish Tragedy*, 1615. Dekker taunted Jonson over the scene in which "thou ranst mad for the death of Horatio."

All that the fledgling actor lacked, it appears, was talent. Jonson was not one of the five actor-sharers who contracted with Francis Langley in the Winter of 1597 to perform at the Swan. According to Dekker, Jonson put "up a Supplication to be a poore Jorneyman Player," but could "not set a good face upon't."[21] Under these unpromising circumstances he decided, in the early months of 1597, to try his hand at yet another occupation: he became a playwright.

When Jonson began writing for the London playhouses, he took up a profession that had not existed at the time of his birth. "Before the accession of Elizabeth, and even halfway through her reign," writes Gerald Bentley, "English drama was almost wholly amateur."[22] Strolling players, who performed moralities and interludes wherever paying audiences were to be found, had long since introduced professional acting to Tudor England, but the men who furnished the players with scripts did so only as a sideline. They held down regular livings as clergymen, schoolmasters, scholars, musicians, lawyers, printers, or simply as

Sketch of the interior of the Swan Theater by Johannes de Witt, ca. 1596, as copied by Aernout van Buchel. The Swan, where Jonson's first two plays were performed, resembled the other public playhouses that stood on the outskirts of the city. De Witt's drawing shows a large, unroofed amphitheater with three tiers of galleries and a rectangular stage that extends onto the floor of the arena.

retainers in great households. They were called upon to write plays for special occasions; the texts that they produced might find their way into the repertory of the common players or even achieve the immortality of print. But there was no regular market for dramatic scripts, and the notion of writing plays as a full-time occupation lay beyond the realm of possibility.

By 1597, the year of Jonson's debut, the stage had become one of the major growth industries of Elizabethan England. The erection of regularly established London playhouses, commencing with the Theater in 1576, made it feasible, for the first time in English history, to earn a living by writing for the stage. The social and economic factors that brought about this change are straightforward enough. During the Elizabethan era a vast and unprecedented number of Englishmen migrated to the London area, and the players found it advantageous to establish semipermanent residences there.[23] Once they did so, however, they were obliged to expand their repertory to suit the needs of the new urban consumers. The older groups of common players were touring professionals who took their wares from town to town. As long as the players were relocating on a more or less continuous basis, they could get by with a minimal number of scripts. Hitherto they had gone to the audience; henceforth, they had to get the audience to come to them on a weekly, and ideally a daily, basis. Once the actors moved into the London playhouses, they encountered an unprecedented, and seemingly insatiable, demand for new plays.

The urban audience included a substantial number of repeat visitors who required a continuously varied menu of dramatic entertainments. The typical life span of a new script, Bernard Beckerman calculates, was about two weeks, with double admission prices on opening day. The very factor that made the new playhouses so lucrative—their sheer size—made a steady supply of new plays an economic imperative. Stephen Gosson, writing in 1582, reported that "the Palace of pleasure, the Golden Asse, the Oethiopian historie, Amadis of Fraunce, the Rounde Table, baudie comedies in Latine, French, Italian, and Spanish" had already "beene thoroughly ransackt to furnish the Playe houses in London." Alfred Harbage estimates that the two acting companies based in London during the year 1595, the Admiral's Men and the Lord Chamberlain's Men, together averaged about 2,500 paying customers a day, or 15,000 a week. At the same time, by Harbage's reckoning, the total number of London theatergoers was well under 40,000. The only way to attract such a large fraction of the urban audience, day in and day out, was to vary the repertory. In satisfying this demand, the acting companies created a new profession.[24]

When Jonson entered the picture, the new occupation was an accomplished fact; the meaning of this fact, however, was anything but established, and it remained a matter of acute controversy for much of his lifetime. The earliest entries in the *Oxford English Dictionary* under "dramatist" and "playwright"—the modern, normative terms for the new occupation—are cited from texts published in 1678 and 1687, a century after the contentious era in which the first generation of practitioners made their way. The emergent author of 1597 inhabited a very different world. He was entering a marketplace that lay open to all comers and was crossed by heated professional rivalries. Jonson, who employed the word "playwright" as a term of abuse (*Ep,* 49, 68, 100), enthusiastically participated in these rivalries and, by so doing, fashioned an artistic identity that he would preserve throughout his long and productive career.

The controversy about the status of the new professional playwright in England turned on class distinctions that were deeply embedded in Tudor society. "All the people which be in our contrie be either gentlemen or of the commonality," according to the prominent Elizabethan schoolmaster Richard Mulcaster. "Gentlemen, or the comon sort of Nobilitie," Camden explained, "bee they, that either are descended of worshipfull parentage, or raised up from the base condition of people, for their vertue or wealth." The commonality consisted of "marchaunts and manuaries" (manual laborers).[25] The first generation of playwrights had no set place in this two-tiered hierarchy, and their new livelihood proved exceedingly difficult to classify. Was it a fit pursuit for a gentleman? Or was it essentially a craft? Put simply, these questions pertained to the writers' social origins. An actor turned playwright was likely to be branded a base "mechanical"; a university man who sold his work to the players could still claim that he had been bred a gentleman. But such distinctions quickly dissolved in the fluid ambience of the playhouse. Robert Greene, a Cambridge graduate, felt that he had compromised his status as gentleman by entering the employ of his social inferiors. Shakespeare, the "upstart crow" whom Greene affected to look down upon, was the son of a Stratford glove maker, but he labored so prodigiously as both an actor and a playwright that by 1596 he was able to purchase a coat of arms and a landed estate in Stratford-upon-Avon.

The question ultimately hinged upon one's view of the work itself. A professional entertainer who earned his living by turning out scripts in response to the demands of the marketplace still wore the appearance of a skilled artisan. His place in the social hierarchy was akin to that of a craftsman (Mulcaster's "manuarie"), or of a tradesman who dealt in speeches and plots; but a lettered poet who improved the moral condition of his times by holding popular errors up to ridicule could claim that he was practicing a liberal art. His status was akin to that of a schoolmaster, a university don, or a counselor to the commonwealth at large.

The recruits to Jonson's new profession fell into two distinct groups, and these closely mirrored the class distinctions repeatedly invoked by contemporary writers. There was a cadre of artisan playwrights that included both professional actors and men affiliated with what Harbage aptly calls the literate crafts: scriveners, clerks, and stationers. And there was a cadre of university graduates who had been educated for work in the Church or government service and took up playwriting as a kind of alternative career. Schoenbaum's *Annals of English Drama* gives the names of some twenty individuals whose work was offered to the new London audience between Jonson's birth and the year of his debut. Eliminating three men whose professional affinities are unknown (Thomas Lupton, Henry Porter, and William Haughton), one arrives at a group that is pretty evenly divided between the literate artisans and the university men. The first playwright to appear among the artisan cadre is George Walpull (1576; the date of the writer's first known play is given in parentheses after each name), clerk of the Stationers' Company from 1571 to 1575. He is followed by Robert Wilson (1581), a premier actor of the 1580s who was singled out by two contemporary witnesses for his "extemporall witte," and Richard Tarlton (1585), a famous jester from the 1580s. The entry of Thomas Kyd (1587), the son of a London scrivener, into the theatrical profession probably occasioned Thomas Nashe's scathing reference to "shifting companions" who "leave the trade of *Noverint* [scrivener] whereto they were born and busie themselves with the indeavours of Art." Anthony Munday (1587) was another stationer's apprentice who subsequently took up playwriting. William Shakespeare (1591) was still performing important roles for his company at the turn of the century. Thomas Heywood (1596) acted in London from 1590 to 1619 and wrote a splendid *Apology for Actors* published in 1612. Ben Jonson (1597), finally, was a journeyman actor who played the part of Hieronymo (Kyd's most famous character), and was later ridiculed on the London stages for having played it badly.[26]

Stephen Gosson (1577), the first of the university men, attended Corpus Christi, Oxford, from 1572 to 1576, and soon turned from writing plays to writing pamphlets attacking the stage. George Peele (1581) took his Oxford M.A. in 1579; John Lyly (1584) received the same degree in 1575. Christopher Marlowe (1587) held an endowed scholarship that provided for six years' residence at Corpus Christi, Cambridge, where he took his M.A. in 1587. Thomas Nashe (1587), who was writing for Pembroke's Men in the spring of 1597, was a contemporary of Robert Greene and Marlowe at Cambridge, where he received his B.A. in 1586, and probably remained until 1588. Greene (1587), another scholarship boy, had received his M.A. by 1583, at which time he was residing in Clare Hall. Thomas Lodge (1588) went to Trinity College, Oxford, took his B.A. in 1577, and commenced his legal education, at Lincoln's Inn, in the following year. George Chapman (1596) is said to have attended university, but there is no documentary evidence to prove it; let him stand as an anomaly. Finally there is the many-sided Ben Jonson, former student at Westminster School, who years later would be made "Master of Arts in both the Universities by their favour," he explained to Drummond, rather than by "his studie" (*Conv*, 252–253).

The ambivalent status of the new profession conformed, with uncanny precision, to the mixed circumstances of Jonson's early life. He was a bricklayer's stepson who worked at that craft after leaving school and a journeyman actor who was struggling, in 1597, to get a foothold in that profession. Yet the same man was also the grandson of the Scottish courtier who had served King Henry VIII and the son of a minister of the gospel. As an alumnus of Westminster School he could number scholars, jurists, and courtiers among his acquaintances.

The dominant voices on the current literary scene had much advice to offer someone in Jonson's position. Elizabethan critics, lacking any sense of playwriting as an autonomous profession, and mindful of the class distinction between the artisans and the scholars, repeatedly stressed the superiority of the latter group. "Players," wrote Geoffrey Fenton, "corrupt good moralities by wanton shewes and playes: they ought not to be suffred to prophane the Sabboth day in such sports, and much lesse to lose time on the dayes of travaile." But "comicall and tragicall showes of schollers in morall doctrines, and declamations in causes made to reproove and accuse vice and extoll vertue," he went on, "are very profitable." The scholarly attack on the players began in earnest when Stephen Gosson, the first of the university graduates turned playwright, published a pamphlet attacking his erstwhile colleagues and dedicated his treatise to the great humanist and courtier Sir Philip Sidney. Gosson made the tactical blunder of censuring playing *and* poetry in one fell swoop. Sidney responded by writing his celebrated *Apology for Poetry* and devoting the bulk of it to establishing the value of poetry as a humanistic endeavor. Yet Sidney had nothing but contempt for the current generation of player-poets, and his account of them, midway through his digression explaining "why England (the mother of excellent minds) should be grown so hard a stepmother to poets," pointedly reinforced the fundamental distinction between poets, the culture heroes of liberal humanism, and their foils, the hapless player-poets. In a treatise that sets out to defend every conceivable variety of poetry, the actor's handiwork affords a unique instance of failed literature, incorporating absurdities that even "the ordinary players of Italy will not err in." [27]

In the same spirit, Thomas Nashe informed the "Gentleman Students of Both Universities" that "every mechanical mate abhors the English he was born to," a state of affairs he attributed to "the servile imitation of vain-glorious Tragedians, who contend not so seriously to excell in action, as to embowell the cloudes in a speech of comparison, thinking themselves more than initiated in Poets immortality, if they once get *Boreas* by the beard."[28] The unkindest cut of all was Robert Greene's notorious attack on Shakespeare, the "upstart crow" who stole his feathers from the university men. Greene's gibe already sounded petty in 1591, and with the benefit of hindsight it looks monumentally obtuse: for the great achievement of Shakespeare and his fellows, as critics have recognized since the time of Dryden, was to synthesize the twin heritages of popular stagecraft and formal learning. Nevertheless, the men who forged that synthesis (and Jonson was surely one of them) were working at a time when these traditions were in a state of keen opposition. Jonson, who came to see merit in the elitist critique of Shakespeare and believed that he had found a better way of writing plays, had no way of knowing that the chief playwright for the Lord Chamberlain's Men would one day be hailed as the peer of Homer and Virgil or that he himself would lead the way in celebrating Shakespeare's greatness. His initial belief "that Shaksperr wanted Arte" (*Conv*, 50), no less than his confidence in his own superior artistry, bears the indelible stamp of rivalries that were in their full vigor when he took up his new profession. If he began his theatrical career among the artisans, he soon perceived that the stage offered him an opportunity to make his way back, to claim a place to which his birth and education had entitled him.

The gentlemen playwrights virtually disappear during the mid-1590s. Philip Henslowe, manager of the Lord Admiral's Men, mentions in his diary over twenty new authors who found work in this period, and only two or three of these had university degrees. The first hint of a resurgence among their ranks comes in a letter from Nashe to his "worshipfull good freinde Mr. William Cotton," written early in the autumn of 1596. Nashe explained that he had stayed in town during the tedious vacation months because of "an after harvest I expected by writing for the stage & for the presse," and by the summer of 1597 he had completed part of a play for Pembroke's Men. But Nashe had second thoughts about this venture and abruptly departed to Yarmouth, where he wrote *Nashe's Lenten Stuff* during Lent of 1598. In the course of that book he refers approvingly to "that witty Play of *the Case is altered*," a comedy that he had evidently encountered before leaving London the previous summer. Since Nashe and Jonson were both associated with Pembroke's Men at that time—the one as a playwright, the other as an actor—the first performance of this, Jonson's earliest known play, can be dated in the first half of 1597.[29]

At first glance, the young actor who wrote *The Case Is Altered* appears to be a new recruit, albeit a curiously sophisticated one, to the ranks of the artisan playwrights. He borrowed his main plot from Plautus's *The*

Thomas Nashe, artist unknown. From Gabriel Harvey(?), *The Trimming of Thomas Nashe,* 1597. Jonson's collaborator was notorious for his vitriolic satires. In this pamphlet attributed to his bitterest enemy, he is wearing fetters.

Captives and his subplot from the same author's *Pot of Gold,* neither of which had yet been translated into English. His adaptation of these materials falls within the genre of romantic comedy that Shakespeare was cultivating so successfully at this time, and it incorporates all the features that normally went into this kind of play: lost children, mistaken identities, trials of friendship, discourses on courtesy, and a studiously conventional recognition scene, together with the obligatory farcical subplot that classicizing critics like Sidney found so distasteful. But even though Jonson committed himself to a plot that called for vibrant displays of romantic love and a long, tearful reunion, he was either unwilling, or unable, to show his characters experiencing joy and delight. The result is a comedy that promises more than it delivers. No fewer than five men, notes Anne Barton, are in love with the heroine, yet she has only thirty-seven lines to speak in the entire play. The climactic recognition scene is so perfunctory that it reads like a parody:

> *Chamount* Then now no more my *Gasper,* but *Camillo,*
> Take notice of your father: gentlemen,
> Stand not amazd; here is a tablet,

With that inscription, found about his necke
That night, and in *Vicenza* by my father,
(Who being ignorant, what name he had,
Christned him *Gasper*) nor did I reveale
This secret till this hower to any man.
    Count   O happy revelation! o blest hower!

As Barton comments, the flatness of the writing in this passage suggests that Jonson "found it difficult temperamentally to yield himself to those age-old tricks by which comedy, flying in the face of things as they are, proceeds to resurrect the dead, pretending that all losses are restored and sorrows end." [30]

It is the farcical subplot of *The Case Is Altered* that holds the first inklings of Jonson's comic genius. The scenes of low comedy center upon Jaques de Prie, an old miser, and his stepdaughter Rachel. Where the protagonist of Jonson's source merely happens to have a beautiful daughter, his counterpart in *The Case Is Altered* has abducted his supposed child from a noble household many years before the play begins. This preliminary theft adds a new dimension to the miser's character: in Jonson's version he becomes a wicked stepfather—the villain of an archetypal family romance. If Jonson withholds assent from the conventional happy ending wherein the lost child recovers her birthright, his imagination positively luxuriates in the perversity of this miserly stepfather. Midway through the play, fearing that the suitors have "smelled" his gold, Jaques (pronounced "jakes" and hence a pun on "privy") enters "*with his gold and a scuttle full of horse-dung*," and attempts to put them off the scent. In the most grossly scatological scene in all of Elizabethan drama, he proceeds to "hide and cover" his hoard with manure, crawling around on all fours and triumphantly asking, "Who will suppose that such a precious nest / Is crownd with such a dunghill excrement?" (III.v.S.D., 14–15). Later, fearing that he has been robbed, Jaques calls for his mastiff Garlic and examines the suspect's hands, arms, legs, and hair for telltale traces of "durt." Finding none, he again kneels down on stage, removes the manure that covers his treasure, and rapturously inhales the odor of his gold: "O how sweet it smels" (IV.viii.70).

No literary source can account for the rampant, unalloyed obscenity of these scenes, but they are perfectly comprehensible in terms of Jonson's *gestalt*. The money-grubbing foster parent who holds a genteel child in thrall is a fantasy version of his stepfather. When Jaques comes onstage carrying his scuttle full of horse dung, he resembles nothing so much as a bricklayer bearing a load of odorous mortar; Jonson had presumably watched his stepfather carry scuttles of manure when Brett constructed the little garden over the sewer on Hartshorn Lane. The torrent of scatological abuse that he directs at this figure expresses his feelings of resentment toward the man who married his mother and tried to make a bricklayer out of him.

The expressly anal character of this material calls to mind Edmund Wilson's well-known theory about Jonson's personality. Noting the recurrence of such imagery in Jonson's writing (and there is a great deal of it), and fastening upon certain of his character traits (pedantry, a tendency to hoard up knowledge, obstinacy, irascibility), Wilson concludes that Jonson is "an obvious example of a psychological type which has been described by Freud and designated by a technical name *anal erotic.*"[31] The scatological material in *The Case Is Altered* confirms the value of Wilson's hypothesis but also calls attention to its built-in limitations. The roots of the anal-erotic personality, according to Freud, lie in the infant's failure to progress beyond the anal stage of development, when he learns to control his bowels, and into the Oedipal stage, when he forms a relationship with his father. The circumstances of Jonson's childhood would have made it difficult for him to manage this transition, for his real father had died before he was born and his stepfather evidently was absent during his early infancy. The scenes in which Jaques builds his cache of manure appear, then, to be the work of a man who suffers from the very malady that Freud describes: since Jonson never proceeded through the stage at which the child learns to cope with intergenerational conflict, when he fantasized about stepfathers, he instinctively regressed to the anal stage and soiled his foster parent with excrement.

Yet it is inadequate simply to conclude that Jonson "was" an anal-erotic personality who never shed the obsessive behavior patterns associated with this psychological type. The author of *The Case Is Altered* had infantile wishes, but he had also found a creative way of gratifying those wishes. Composing a comedy is an adaptive, rather than a neurotic, act; like Robert Brett, Jonson had discovered how to turn manure into a valuable commodity. When he projected his compulsions onto the alien figure of the miserly stepfather, they took on a new meaning. The humorous side of the miser's behavior, which is immediately apparent to the audience but never to Jaques, lies in the substitution of gold for excrement: the adult fingering his coins is a civilized descendant of the child hoarding up his own waste products. While Jonson imaginatively participates in this fantasy, he also conveys a powerful sense of revulsion toward the object of his satire. Moreover, his reaction against the skinflint was perfectly genuine: in his own life, Jonson erred on the side of prodigality rather than miserliness. Drummond found him "carelesse either to gaine or keep," and everything we know about his financial affairs bears out that judgment.[32]

Drummond also believed that Jonson was "oppressed with fantasie, which hath ever mastered his reason, a generall disease in many poets." When Jonson wrote for the stage, however, he entered a public arena where he could share his fantasies with others. His savage mockery of the miserly stepfather aptly expressed the outlook of the younger sons, dis- placed gentlemen, unemployed graduates, and free-spending courtiers who made up a sizable fraction of the playhouse audience. Although it is no longer performed, *The Case Is Altered* made a favorable impression on the playwright's contemporaries. Nashe singled it out for commendation; a young Oxford graduate named Charles Fitzgeoffrey wrote, and later published, a Latin epigram in praise of it; four extracts were included in an anthology of contemporary writing that appeared in 1600; and a quarto text of the entire play was printed in 1609.[33] By the spring of 1597 Jonson's case was altered—the failed actor had become a skilled novice playwright, had tentatively identified his audience, and had attracted the attention of his colleague Thomas Nashe.

In the spring of 1597, Nashe too was writing a comedy for Pembroke's Men, but he did not proceed rapidly enough to suit the company. "I having but begun but the induction and the first act of it," he recalled, "the other foure acts without my consent, or the least drift of my drift or scope, by the plaers were supplied, which bred both their trouble and mine to." Nashe was "terrified" by the finished product, so much so that he was "glad to run from it" to Yarmouth, where he spent the following year in seclusion. Although Nashe refers to "the plaers," the legal proceedings that ensued upon the first performance of *The Isle of Dogs,* as the play was called, mention only one collaborator. "One of them," according to the minutes of Queen Elizabeth's Privy Council, "was not only an Actor but a maker of parte of the said Plaie," and this actor turned playwright was Ben Jonson.[34]

The Isle of Dogs has not survived, but its title, Nashe's hurried depar- ture for Yarmouth, and the fact that it was promptly suppressed, indicate that it was an exceedingly subversive play. Popular tradition held that the Queen kenneled her royal hounds on the Isle of Dogs, a narrow spit of land that lay just across the river from Greenwich, where Elizabeth held court for much of the year 1597. The place name would have lent itself to a satire on canine courtiers. Nashe was famous for his witty lampoons of contemporary life, and the late Elizabethan craze for "biting" satires, the natural outlet for the disaffected scholar playwright, was just getting underway. There was undoubtedly a market for such a play, but the Queen's Privy Council looked askance at mordant commentaries on the times, and Nashe decided that the risk was too great. Jonson, who had less to lose, stepped into his place.

The council reacted to the staging of *The Isle of Dogs* in the summer of

1597 with a calculated display of power. On July 28 the Lord Mayor and Aldermen of the City of London asked the Privy Council to issue orders "for the present staie & final suppressinge of . . . Stage plaayes, aswell at the Theatre, Curten, and banckside, as in all other places in and abowt the Citie." The city's request was not all that unusual, but the council's response was extraordinary. For once, they did issue orders, also dated July 28, stipulating "that not onlie no plaies shalbe used within London or about the citty or in any publique place during this time of sommer," but also that "those play houses that are erected and built only for suche purposes shalbe plucked downe, namelie the Curtayne and the Theatre nere to Shorditch or any other within that county." On August 15 the council sent out yet another letter, explaining that they had "caused some of the players to be apprehended and comitted to prison," including Jonson, the "maker of parte of the said plaie." The council now instructed its agents to ask the malefactors "what is become of the rest of theire fellowes that either had theire parts in the devisinge of that seditious matter or that were actors or plaiers in the same" and "also to peruse soch papers as were fownde in Nash his lodgings." Jonson told Drummond that when his "judges could gett nothing of him to all their demands bot I and No, they placed two damn'd Villains to catch advantage of him, with him, but he was advertised by his keeper" and remained silent. Despite Jonson's recalcitrance, a third letter, dated October 8, instructed the Keeper of the Marshalsea "to release Gabriell Spencer and Robert Shaa, stage-players, out of prison, who were of lat comitted to his custodie," together with "the like waarant for the releasing of Benjamin Johnson."[35]

The letters of July 28 and August 15 made it appear as though the council had decided to level a devastating blow at the London players and playhouses, but this impression is highly misleading. Although the July 28 letter seems to mandate the permanent suppression of professional theater in the metropolitan area, the additional stipulation that "there be no more plaies used in any publique place within three miles of the citty untell Alhalloutide next" suggests that what the council really had in mind was a temporary restraint lasting until November 1. In the meantime, Philip Henslowe, the business manager of the Admiral's Men, took advantage of the commotion by entering into business agreements with several members of Pembroke's Men, Ben Jonson among them. This move simultaneously strengthened Henslowe's hand and crippled the rival company that had recently set up shop at the Swan. After the dust finally settled, the main beneficiaries turned out to be the Queen and her Privy Council and the two companies that her councilors patronized. When playing resumed, the Queen's Master of the Revels issued licenses to the Lord Chamberlain's Men and the Lord Admiral's Men, the two companies that wore the livery of her Privy Councilors, but did not issue a license to Pembroke's Men. The crown thus made abundantly clear its readiness to impose heavy sanctions upon any company that incurred its displeasure, even while ensuring that the two companies responsible to its ministers of state enjoyed the status of a protected monopoly. The events of 1597, Glynne Wickham concludes, mark a watershed in the history of the English stage. Previously, the theater business was fundamentally independent in character; henceforth, the court would increasingly make it an object of scrutiny, patronage, and control.[36]

Ben Jonson, who had ventured to complete the offending script in the first place, got a firsthand view of the council's priorities. When the crown took offense at *The Isle of Dogs,* he went to prison in disgrace. After his release the following autumn, he immediately found work with Henslowe, who in turn owed his continued prosperity to the goodwill of the Privy Council and the Revels Office. The manager of the Admiral's Men had by then decided that Jonson could be of use to him: did he also help the offending playwright secure his release? By a curious coincidence, Jonson made his first appearance in Henslowe's books on the very day that the council issued its ambiguous orders for the restraint of plays. On July 28, the manager of the Admiral's Men loaned "Bengemen Johnson player" the sum of four pounds and entered the receipt of three shillings nine pence. Why Henslowe advanced him the four pounds, and what Jonson did to repay the three shillings nine pence, is unclear. But subsequent entries in Henslowe's *Diary* reveal that "Benjamin" was writing plays for the Admiral's Men throughout most of 1598 (HS, XI, 307–308).

By the end of 1597, then, Jonson had completed the transition from actor to writer and had begun to move away from the ranks of the artisan playwrights and into those of the gentleman poets. Several years later, Thomas Dekker, speaking on behalf of the players, taunted him by recalling his ill-fated start with Pembroke's Men: "When the stagerites banisht thee into the Ile of Dogs, thou turn'dst Ban-dog (villainous Guy) and ever since bitest."[37] In plain prose, Dekker alleged that the actors ("stagewrights," with a pun on stagirites, or Aristotelians) excluded Jonson ("Guy") from their fellowship and made him into a snarling satirist, and he has been one ever since. If, as Dekker implies, there was bad blood between Jonson and the players who "banisht" him into *The Isle of Dogs,* the events that ensued in the wake of that play can scarcely have made them feel any more kindly toward one another. Pembroke's Men's reward for putting on Jonson's second play was the imprisonment of some members, the dissolution of the company, and permanent exclusion from the greater London area. The ill feeling was apparently mutual. Barely a year after his release from Marshalsea prison, Jonson would kill Gabriel Spencer, one of the actors who went to prison with him in the summer of 1597. Although Jonson's lifelong antipathy to actors, and his determination to define himself as a man of letters rather than a playwright, were foreseeable from the circumstances of his early life and from the nature of the opportunities that beckoned in the mid-1590s, personal hostilities came into play as well.

· CHAPTER TWO ·

The Comedy of Humors

After his release from Marshalsea prison on October 8, 1597, Jonson returned to the vicinity of Charing Cross. Later that autumn, when the churchwardens at St. Martin in the Fields levied their parishioners for funds to renovate the interior of the building, his name appeared, along with that of Robert Brett, among the list of contributors.[1] The focus of his professional life, however, now lay with the Admiral's Men, who performed at the Rose Theater on the south bank of the Thames.

The manager, Philip Henslowe, was his only visible source of financial support during the following year. On December 3 Henslowe gave Jonson an advance of twenty shillings "upon a boocke which he showed the plotte unto the company which he promised to [deliver] at cryssmass next." On January 5 Henslowe lent him five more shillings, but this meager sum was not even enough to make ends meet. On April 2, 1598, Jonson borrowed ten pounds from an actor named Robert Browne and signed a note promising to repay the full sum by May 27. When the debt came due, he failed to repay any of it, and Browne repeatedly dunned him during the months that followed. On August 18 Henslowe paid out another six shillings "to bye a Boocke called hoote anger sone cowld of mr porter mr cheattell and bengemen Johnson," but Jonson's share of this paltry advance cannot have done much to alleviate his wants.[2]

The novice playwright was confronting the hard economic realities of his profession. Elizabethan dramatists had to turn out scripts very rapidly if they hoped to earn a decent living. Henslowe paid his writers, or more often teams of writers, an average of six pounds for a new script. At that rate, Jonson would have had to produce a play every five months simply to improve on the fifteen and a half pounds per annum that he had earned as a bricklayer's apprentice. It was certainly feasible to write three or more plays a year. Thomas Dekker, who entered Henslowe's employ in 1598, had a hand in forty-four plays between 1598 and 1602. Thomas Heywood, another contemporary of Jonson's, referred to some "two hundred and twenty, in which I have had either an entire hand, or at least a maine finger" at the close of his forty-year career.[3] Although Jonson's reputation for being a slow writer has been vastly exaggerated, he was not facile enough to succeed in a system that prized quantity over quality to this extent. And unlike Shakespeare, who averaged two and a half plays a year during the 1590s, he could not supplement his income either by acting or by drawing a share of his company's earnings.

The drawbacks of trying to gain his livelihood by writing for the Admiral's Men had become clear to Jonson by the summer of 1598. After ten months in Henslowe's employ he had earned a total of thirty-one shillings, and he was ten pounds in debt to Robert Browne. Having neither the facility nor the inclination to compete with the likes of Dekker and Heywood, he decided to follow in the footsteps of the "university wits" of the 1580s. He would use the stage to display his superior ingenuity and classical education, hoping to catch the eye of a powerful patron or to gain employment at court.

Jonson's use of classical sources in *The Case Is Altered* caught the eye of at least one contemporary reader. Charles Fitzgeoffrey's epigram on Jonson's first comedy playfully accuses him of stealing his material from Plautus ("you have certainly pilfered these artful plays, which you continue to sell as your own, from the serene heavens"); acquits him after hearing testimony "that those dramas were actually yours and that you constructed them not secretively but delightfully"; and solicits Jonson's pardon: "I am silent with shame, you have conquered me, Johnson, with Apollo as judge and patron" (trans. from HS, XI, 370). The scenario of Fitzgeoffrey's epigram, which may well be the earliest criticism of Jonson, will recur frequently in the seventeenth-century assessments of him. He is accused of plagiarizing the classics; he is acquitted on the grounds that he has improved upon the originals.

When Jonson later reflected on the course of his literary career, however, he singled out *Every Man in His Humour,* the play that he completed in the summer of 1598, as "the first" of "the fruits." The impetus for his new comedy was George Chapman's *Humorous Day's Mirth,* a play that had captivated London audiences during the previous year. The entries in

Henslowe's *Diary* show thirteen performances of *An Humorous Day's Mirth* in 1597 alone and an unprecedented average receipt of fifty-three shillings per performance.[4] Jonson doubtless hoped to capitalize on the phenomenal popularity of this play, and his own comedy of humors mirrors Chapman's in several important respects.

Chapman's hero is a "philosophicall scholar" who amuses himself by outwitting a succession of affluent boobies. This plot formula clearly had a powerful appeal for Jonson (a frustrated scholar in his own right), for it crops up not only in *Every Man in His Humour* but in his next three comedies as well. Yet Jonson's treatment of this material is very different from Chapman's. In *An Humorous Day's Mirth* the conflict between scholar and fool is relatively superficial. Since the hero and his dupes all belong to the aristocratic world of the court, there is no hint of any class conflict: the scholar ultimately seeks to reform rather than to humiliate his victims, and once he achieves this goal, the distance between the protagonist and his dupes effectively disappears. Jonson, however, set out to sharpen the opposition between wit and folly wherever he could. Young Lorenzo, his scholar-hero, is not a courtier but an unemployed man of letters, "Of deare account, in all our Academies" (I.i.13), who—like Jonson—has chosen folly as his peculiar field of study.

The issue of Young Lorenzo's vocation frames the play. At the outset of the drama his father complains that he is wasting his time on "idle *Poetrie*"; at the close the aspiring young writer delivers a lengthy oration in defense of poetry. The play itself, like all of Jonson's early comedies after *The Case Is Altered,* is a youthful poet's essay in self-definition. Defying his antipoetic father, Young Lorenzo and his friend Prospero spend their day seeking out a representative assortment of fools and putting them through their paces. Old Lorenzo understandably regards this pastime as the height of idleness, but for a writer in the neoclassical tradition it is precisely the business of the comic poet to identify and display folly. "Only thus much is now to be said," in Sidney's summary definition: "Comedy is an imitation of the common errors of our life, which [the poet] representeth in the most ridiculous and scornful sort that may be, so as it is impossible that any beholder can be content to be such a one." To laugh at fools is not a form of folly; it is the antithesis of folly. "If a lover enters the theater," Lucian remarks, "he is restored to his right mind by seeing all the evil consequences of love."[5] In reacting to the spectacle of witless buffoonery, reason becomes conscious of its innate capacities.

The originality of *Every Man in His Humour* lay in the claim to rigor and comprehensiveness implied by its title. Jonson's play does not merely recount a humorous day's mirth; it provides a general anatomy of human folly. Neoclassical critics, influenced by Aristotle's oft-cited pronouncement that comedy depicts men "worse than the average . . . not as regards any and every sort of fault, but only as regards one particular kind, the Ridiculous,"[6] were uniformly agreed that affectation and stupidity were the special province of the comic poet. Jonson accepted this dictum and all its implications. The comic poet was a supremely rational being—poised, aloof, indifferent to the vagaries of the marketplace—and his work portrayed precisely the opposite sort of person: nervous, self-absorbed, totally susceptible to the tug of novelty and fashion. Yet neoclassical theorists also emphasized that the butts of stage comedy should be *model* eccentrics, representative deviations from a norm that any educated person could recognize. On the face of it, this is a paradoxical proposition: what is meant by a "normal" oddity, or a "typical" curiosity?

In sorting out this puzzle, Jonson harked back to the older, medical sense of the word "humor," and discovered, in the psychology of the Galenic tradition, a coherent taxonomy of eccentric behavior patterns. The Greek physicians had originally conceived of the erring humors as a way of accounting for divergences from the ideal of perfect health. In a sound constitution, the four humors (bile, phlegm, choler, and blood) are perfectly blended and, hence, untraceable. When a humor transgresses its proper boundaries, however, it generates systemic disruptions: for example, a livid complexion accompanied by a burning fever means that the choleric humor has overflowed its normal channels. It now combines the outward characteristics of a substance (size, color, movement) with the inner vacuousness of a symptom. Galen and his followers, who included the vast majority of sixteenth-century physicians, maintained that all such disorders could be accounted for by a single code, or "semiotica . . . which part doth judge by signes, and tokens, what the diseases are, and what be their natures . . . and whether they may be cured easely, and in short time, or whether they be hard to be cured, and must be cured in longer time, or whether they cannot be cured at all."[7]

Galen divided the spectrum of human eccentricity into four humors, but Jonson adopted the simpler, and equally commonplace, bipolar scheme based on psychological disorders associated with choler and blood. While choler manifests itself in excessive anger, the sanguine humor, if carried to extremes, can lead to incontinent or perverted sexual desire. These two stereotypical obsessions, which correspond to the irascible and concupiscent temperaments, are the foundation of Jonson's comedy of humors. On a purely verbal level, they are personified by Captain Bobadilla, the braggart warrior, and Matheo, the plagiarizing love poet. These "two Signior Out-sides" (V.iii.355) do not even experience the passions they mimic but rather piece out their affectations with scraps of verse filched from *The Spanish Tragedy,* Marlowe's *Hero and Leander,* and Samuel Daniel's *Delia.*

These characters are symptomatic of an era in which, as Jonson complained in the Induction to his next play, the very meaning of the word "humor" had abruptly broadened from its older sense of a pathological type and had come to include the transitory mood, the fad, and the fashionable affectation.[8] Jonson emphasizes the hollowness of these characters by playing them off against Giuliano, the quarreler, and Thorello, the *jaloux*, who at least have the saving grace of bona fide obsessions. "A tall man," as Prospero remarks of his brother Giuliano, "is never his owne man til he be angry" (IV.iii.9). These humors are in turn superseded by Young Lorenzo, the rational version of the poet-lover, and his friend Prospero, the duellist-tactician who keeps his irascible qualities under control. Together the two gallants form a composite image of the whole self. Doctor Clement, the merry magistrate who presides over the trial in act V, represents the playwright's highest ideals. By dressing him up in his old military gear and having him compose verses extemporaneously, Jonson gives him the symbolic trappings of a universal man: he is both a soldier and a poet.

Just as Galen's semiotics furnished Jonson with a complete set of character types, Galen's pathology supplied the basic outline of his comic plot. When a humor enters a state of flux, it encroaches upon the neighboring organs, which then absorb the humor, grow distended, and either burst or—if the outcome is successful—reject it. The physicians refer to this process as "coction"—a kind of slow, physiological cooking. Once the body has expelled the indigestible waste products that cannot be assimilated into a wholesome organism the erring humors return to a state of equilibrium. The same principles apply to the working out of a comic narrative. Jonson assembles a variety of characters who exhibit symptoms of the humoral disorders. They overflow into houses and rooms that are too constricted to contain them, just as the pathological eccentrics who people *Every Man in His Humour* crowd into Thorello's house, fortifying their choler with tobacco and their lust with wanton verses until they burst the bounds of propriety. Thrust into the streets, the humors abandon their normal family ties and merge into fluid syndicates of irate and erotic types. The humors feed on delusions of grandeur, but all their victories are Pyrrhic, for the bigger a disorder becomes, the harder it is to satisfy. Having outgrown the limits of domestic order, they recklessly transgress the limits of civil rule and their collapse follows swiftly and inevitably. As the distempered humors die of their own excess, their healthy counterparts (Prospero, Young Lorenzo, and Hesperida) compose themselves into a new and harmonious mixture. The braggart warrior and the plagiarizing sonneteer are analogous to the unwholesome remnants that the body rejects during the final stage of the therapeutic process: when Doctor Clement formally expels them from the concluding feast, the cure is complete.[9]

The place of the humors in classical psychology is akin to that of the unconscious in modern psychoanalysis. They manifest themselves in obsessive patterns of behavior that run the gamut from tiny verbal slips to overtly antisocial acts. From a pathological standpoint, these quirks are equivalent to symptoms: when the treatment is finished, the symptoms disappear. For purposes of analysis, the sanguine and choleric humors correspond to those wellsprings of desire and aggression that Freud called the love instinct and the death instinct. If a joke has overt intentions, Freud maintains, they can always be categorized as either smutty or hostile.[10] The access of clarity that ensues when the joke is over corresponds to the movement from disturbance to tranquillity that brings stage comedy to its familiar close. Jonson's comic heroes carry out the function traditionally assigned to the "eye" of reason or the superego, the "watching institution" of psychoanalysis: for the greater part of the play they observe the erring humors, carefully noting their follies but always keeping them at a safe distance. Doctor Clement, finally, assumes the role of the professional physician or analyst. His scrupulous cross-examination of various witnesses to the day's events and his careful sifting of their tangled reports enables him to produce a complete diagnosis and to specify the appropriate remedies. When he burns Matheo's plagiarized verses and invests Young Lorenzo (Jonson's alter ego) with his magisterial robes, the poet's triumph is complete.

Yet Young Lorenzo pays a price for his superiority. Although he takes all the prizes at the end of the play, he is too insipid to arouse any real enthusiasm. David Garrick delighted eighteenth-century theatergoers with his recreation of the jealous husband, Thorello, and Dickens toured England giving his rendition of the braggart warrior, Bobadilla. Young Lorenzo is far too bland to warrant this kind of attention. Part of the problem lies in the medical theory from which Jonson drew his idea. Since health consisted in the total absence of eccentric symptoms, a healthy, humorless individual was perforce a man without qualities. The parallel concept of the four elements stipulated that someone in whom all the elements were perfectly blended could achieve the extraordinarily rich character that Shakespeare ascribes to Brutus, in whom the elements were "so mix'd" that "Nature might stand up / And say to all the world, 'This was a man.'" But the inner logic of humoral medicine stubbornly equated normality with an absence, with the elimination of eccentricities. The ideal man of Galenic medicine has a curiously passive, even priggish, demeanor. Thus, Jonson's sketch of Criticus, who has the "most perfect and divine temper" of all his heroes, continually calls attention to what the protagonist is *not:* "He is neither too phantastikely melancholy, too slowly phlegmaticke, too lightly sanguine, or too rashly cholericke, but in all, so composde and order'd, as it is cleare, *Nature* went about some ful worke, she did more then make a man, when she made him." [11]

Young Lorenzo shows no emotion whatever until the closing scene, when his father accuses him of squandering his youth on poetry—his only real passion. He replies to this attack with a long and rhapsodic oration in defense of the poet's vocation. "Indeede if you will looke on Poesie, / As she appears in many," Young Lorenzo concedes, "Patcht up in remnants and olde worne ragges, / Halfe starvd for want of her peculiar foode, / Sacred invention," then his father's objections are understandable. But if Old Lorenzo will view "poesy" in her ideal state, "Attired in the majestie of arte, / Set high in spirite with the precious taste / Of sweete philosophie," he will recognize "how proud a presence doth she beare" (V.iii.318–333 *passim*).

Young Lorenzo was articulating young Ben Jonson's aesthetic creed. The main topics of this oration—the ethereal nature of poetry, its need for a refined audience, the abuses of bad poets, the vulgarity of the popular audience, the deplorable state of contemporary letters—recall the professional rivalry between players and poets discussed in the previous chapter. The same scenario appears in the writings of the first generation of gentlemen playwrights, the prefaces to Chapman's early poems, Sidney's *Apology for Poetry*, George Puttenham's *Art of English Poesy*, and the critical pronouncements that crop up in Jonson's early plays. The cryptic phrases that Jonson inscribed on the title page of his copy of Puttenham's treatise imply an attitude to poetry that borders on religious awe. The medial, "Introite: Nam hic dii sunt" ("Come in, for the gods are here"), is the counsel that Heraclitus reputedly gave to guests who hesitated to enter his kitchen. A second, "Abrahamus Christum, Joh 8," refers to the biblical account of Christ's relationship to Abraham: did Jonson mean that the poet (Jonson) stands to his precursor (Puttenham) as Christ does to Abraham? A third inscription, "Ut Cervus Fontem Psal. 42," alludes to the opening simile of the forty-second psalm: "As the hart panteth after the water brooks, so panteth my soul after thee, O God." [12]

What, then, does the analogy between Jonson and Young Lorenzo reveal about the poet who conceived it? *Every Man in His Humour* creates the impression that its author was aloof, rational, and fanatically devoted to the pursuit of his craft. And so, in some measure, he was. His ideal self-image would be unintelligible to us if he had not exhibited some of the same characteristics in his everyday life; both Dekker and Marston allude to those characteristics (or pretensions) in their lampoons of him.

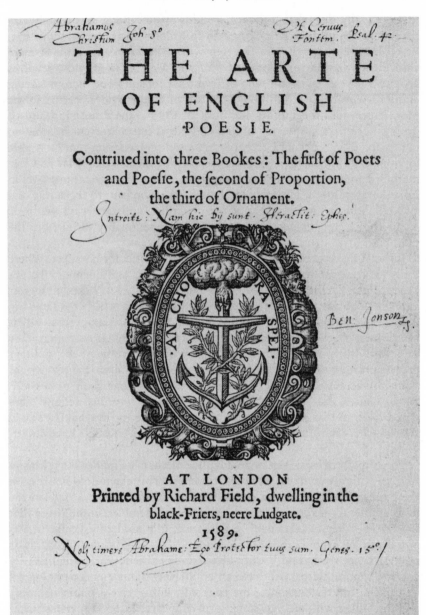

THE ARTE
OF ENGLISH
POESIE.

Contriued into three Bookes: The firſt of Poets
and Poeſie, the ſecond of Proportion,
the third of Ornament.

AT LONDON
Printed by Richard Field, dwelling in the
black-Friers, neere Ludgate.
1589.

Title page of George Puttenham, *The Art of English Poesy*, 1589, with Jonson's
annotations. The Latin inscriptions proclaim the sacredness of the poet's vocation.

It is equally clear that Jonson, for all his protestations, was acutely vulnerable to the humors he pilloried so relentlessly. By his own admission, he took a peculiar relish in sleeping with other men's wives: is it mere coincidence that the sexual comedy in *Every Man in His Humour* revolves around a jealous merchant who believes that Jonson's poet-hero is having an affair with his wife? Although the act of adultery never occurs in the play, it pervades the fantasy life both of the paranoid husband and of Young Lorenzo's suspicious father. Indeed, these characters become so preoccupied with Young Lorenzo's supposed philandering that he is able to elope with the merchant's sister-in-law. The illicit wishes that had formerly led Jonson to commit adultery were satisfied on a vicarious level in his comedy of 1598. His alter ego reduces the merchant to the status of a cuckold, wins his independence from his father, and carries off the bride of his choice, yet remains a paragon of bland rationality throughout the play.

Jonson's comedy of humors also provided an outlet for his anger. Where the young infantryman had vented his wrath on "ane Enemie," the apprentice playwright leveled his fire at parodic images of his own aggressiveness. Captain Bobadilla is a former soldier who wields his rapier in public, and so (as we shall soon see) was Jonson. As these verbal salvos found their marks (Italian fencing instructors, garrulous veterans), they provoked fresh quarrels in their turn. When members of the military profession took offense at Jonson's portrait of the captain, the playwright pointedly reminded them of his own service in "Your great profession; which I once, did prove: / And did not shame it with my actions" and dared them to disagree with him: "He that not trusts me, having vow'd thus much, / But's angry for the Captaine, still, is such" (*Ep*, 108.6–7, 9–10).

The comedy of humors was an adaptive mechanism that enabled Jonson to cope with his own lust and aggressiveness. This claim does not rest on the handful of evidence presented thus far; it must stand or fall on the body of literary texts and personal anecdotes assembled in the pages that follow. The "key to certainty," in the words of a modern psychiatrist, "is not depth of examination but redundancy"; and Jonsonian comedy is nothing if not redundant.[13] Until he passes his fiftieth year, virtually every comedy that he writes will have an adulterous triangle and pathological quarrelers; in every instance, the cuckolds will receive a public shaming and the bullies will undergo some form of incarceration. The personifications of clear-eyed sanity will grow more introspective and even cynical in the years ahead, but they too will persist, secure in the knowledge of their own superiority.

Viewed in the context of these long-range patterns, the ideal of aloof rationality takes on a new meaning: Jonson embraced it, one surmises, because he could not come to terms with his own disorderly impulses in any other way. The same economy of chaotic energy and ironclad restraint underlies his lifelong search for "correct" models of writing and his life-long deference to the authority of classical authors. Although his belief in the power of reason was real and important, it only tells half the story. The same man who read Drummond a lecture on Horace's *Art of Poetry* also wanted his host to know that he had "consumed a whole night in lying looking to his great toe, about which he hath seen tartars & turks Romans and Carthaginions feight in his imagination." Drummond concluded that he was "oppressed with fantasie" (*Conv*, 322–324, 692).

As Alvin Kernan remarks, Jonson's "rigid classicism, moral authoritarianism, and stout insistence upon form and realism seem as much desperate defenses raised against disaster as rational aesthetic positions freely chosen."[14] Humor and sublimation, the most potent weapons in Jonson's armory of defenses, are the least desperate of adaptive styles; but reaction formation, which prompts the user to steer a course that runs precisely counter to the very passions he is trying to control, is by definition a far less flexible mechanism. Its reversal of the subject's needs precludes their direct expression or acknowledgment and thus leaves the user in a state of continuing frustration.

Every Man in His Humour was in the repertory of the Lord Chamberlain's Men by September 20, 1598, when Sir Tobie Matthew wrote to Dudley Carleton of a German visitor who had lost two hundred pounds "at a new play called Every Man's Humour." Jonson's decision to take his new play to the premier acting company of his day suggests that he regarded it as superior to the work he had been doing for Henslowe. Unlike the Admiral's Men, Shakespeare's company boasted a major playwright among its ranks and garnered most of the invitations to perform at court. Shakespeare himself performed in Jonson's comedy. Since the play was "sundry times publickly acted," the production must have been at least moderately successful, although probably no more than that.[15] The play performed in 1598 did not win anything like the acclaim that had greeted Chapman's *Humorous Day's Mirth* or even Jonson's *The Case Is Altered*.

Jonson, however, never wavered; the form that he devised in 1598 would resonate across the length and breadth of his professional life. Puttenham, in a passage that Jonson underscored and embellished with approving marginal squiggles, had argued that "if Poesie be now an Art, and of al antiquitie hath beene among the Greeks and Latines, and yet were none, untill by studious persons fashioned and reduced into a method of rules and precepts, then no doubt there may be the like with us." [16] Jonson came to see that he had written a play that satisfied these criteria.

Although a century later critics found Jonson's brand of comedy too reductive for their tastes, contemporaries were impressed by the elegance of his reduction. It allowed him to preserve the familiar character types and the intricate plots of ancient comedy, while discarding the secondary, and by his lights alien, tradition of Hellenistic romance. Yet Jonsonian comedy was entirely hospitable to the native tradition of jestbooks, allegorized morality plays, and popular farce. By applying the humoral types to the current scene, he was able to fashion a universalized, yet flexibly topical, "image of the times." In 1598 he set his sights on pretentious fencing masters and sugary sonneteers; shortly thereafter he contrived a classicized comedy of humors organized around the complementary figures of Horace and Ovid, the ancient masters of satire and love poetry; in 1610 the focus would shift to militant Anabaptists and a genteel gourmand; four years later he juxtaposed an irascible urban magistrate to a greasy pig woman; in 1626 he satirized the aggressive popular press and the winsome Lady Infanta Clara Pecunia, Infanta of the Mines. Times changed, but the basic lineaments of the form remained intact. It is easy to see why contemporaries hailed him as the "great refiner of our Poesie, / Who turns't to gold that which before was lead" (HS, XI, 431). No English playwright had ever conceived of such a model.

Not even Shakespeare. Despite the elite bias in favor of topical satire and abstract design, the popular Elizabethan audience stubbornly clung to its preference for familiar tales, and Shakespeare gave them what they liked. Critics of the popular stage repeatedly berated playwrights for recycling material lifted from well-rubbed anthologies like *The Palace of Pleasure, Ethiopian History, Amadis of Fraunce,* and the Arthurian cycles, all cited by Gosson in 1582. Jonson's gibe at the popular acclaim for "some mouldy tale, / Like *Pericles*" (HS, VI, 492) reiterates Gosson's criticism. To weigh the accuracy of this assessment one need only ponder the contents of Geoffrey Bullough's *Narrative and Dramatic Sources of Shakespeare.* Bullough's eight roomy volumes are an anthology of the most familiar stories in sixteenth-century literature—stories that were very widespread, often on an international scale, well before Shakespeare turned to them. When he wrote about the Plantine twins, Romeo and Juliet, the famous victories of Henry V, or Hamlet's revenge, he dealt with known and marketable quantities. The material had already been shaped by earlier authors, and because such stories were virtually synonymous with ideas of genre, Shakespeare's audience would have known what to expect, even if it did not always get what it expected.

Jonson's comedy bears little resemblance to the popular novels, romances, old plays, and histories that were the common coin of Elizabethan and Jacobean drama. For the most part, there are no narrative or dramatic sources for Jonson's comedies. *The Case Is Altered,* written just a year before *Every Man in His Humour,* is the exception that proves the rule: Jonson would never again borrow a fully developed plot from another author. Within the annals of Jonsonian scholarship, the only real analogue to Bullough's compilation is the massive three-volume commentary that concludes the Oxford edition of his works. These dense glades of annotation reveal the astonishing, and quite unprecedented, richness of allusion that Jonson achieved within the compass of his own method. His primary categories are the humors, the ageless types of human folly. He makes them weighty and convincing by drawing upon a truly encyclopedic range of sources: classical satires, symposia, courtesy books, coney-catching pamphlets, *commedia dell'arte,* moralities, ethical treatises, character books, medical texts, jestbooks, and almanacs. His source materials are usually catalogues or anatomies rather than serial narratives. Jonson alludes to them, quotes them at length, and occasionally borrows a jest or a device, but he never tries to extract a plot from them. Indeed, Jonson's whole idea of plot, as Jonas Barish shows, hinges on the premise that there is no inherent order in the materials that come to an artist; instead, the sense of wholeness and closure depends upon the playwright's "freedom to improvise in any way at any moment." [17]

Shakespearean narrative ordinarily unfolds across extensive stretches of time and space, and these project what is crudely, but fairly, called the "Elizabethan World Picture." As the world falls apart, storms rage, night falls, winter descends; as the wheel turns, storms clear, truth comes to light with the dawn, and winter turns into spring. Lovers run off into the forest, madmen wander on the heath, outcasts find a world elsewhere, but journeys end in lovers' meeting. Longing for a return to those golden days, literary historians have often castigated neoclassical plot conventions on the grounds that they were an aberrant intrusion of academic "rules" into an inherently "free" field of discourse. But the range of conventions available to any artist is limited by his intellectual milieu. Of course Shakespeare's artistry is extraordinarily free and imaginative, but it was also a disciplined mimesis of the late medieval cosmos. He alone among the major contemporary dramatists had mastered a system of correspondences that permitted the continuous synchronization of fictional situation and natural setting.

Jonson found this convention preposterous: "Wee owe no thankes to *Rivers,* that they carry our boats; or Winds, that they be favouring, and fill our sailes . . . For these are, what they are, *necessarily.*" He founded his own dramaturgy on the classical unities. The eight-hour day and the fixed Vitruvian *scaena* simultaneously preempted the old narrative scheme and instituted a new one in its place. Things could no longer unfold in the natural order because the old temporal rhythms were excluded *a priori* from the representational scale of drama. The *Corpus Christi* play, the staged romance, and what we ordinarily think of as "Shakespearean" drama could not survive under these conditions; but by the same token, Jonson, Molière, and Racine became possible.[18] Jonson's way of representing human behavior foreshadows the methodology of Baconian science. Instead of seeking out cosmological or theological causes, he assembles a collection of representative samples and generalizes about their common properties.[19] *Every Man in His Humour* is an anatomy rather than a story; its goal is to achieve a normative analysis of abnormal behavior.

• CHAPTER THREE •

Angry Young Man

The Lord Chamberlain's Men performed *Every Man in His Humour* at the Curtain Theater in the north London suburb of Shoreditch, their temporary home while the Globe Theater was under construction. By this time the Jonsons had probably moved to the parish of St. Giles, Cripplegate, which was adjacent to Shoreditch. Jonson was in the vicinity of the Curtain on September 22, shortly after the debut of *Every Man in His Humour,* when he encountered Gabriel Spencer, a former member of Pembroke's Men. The meeting had a tragic outcome. According to the jury that subsequently indicted him for manslaughter, Jonson

> made an assault with force and arms &c., against and upon a certain Gabriel Spencer, when he was in God and the said Lady the Queen's peace, at Shorediche in the aforesaid county of Middlesex, in the fields there, and with a certain sword of iron and steel called a Rapiour, of the price of three shillings, which he then and there had in his right hand and held drawn, feloniously and willfully struck and beat the same Gabriel, then and there with the aforesaid sword giving to the same Gabriel Spencer, in and upon the same Gabriel's right side, a mortal wound, of the depth of six inches and the breadth of one inch, of which mortal wound the same Gabriel Spencer then and there died instantly.

In recounting this incident to Drummond, Jonson linked it to the passage at arms in Flanders, where he had "killed ane Enemie and taken opima spolia from him." He alleged that Spencer, "whose sword was 10 Inches longer than his" had "appealed [him] to the fields"—that is, challenged

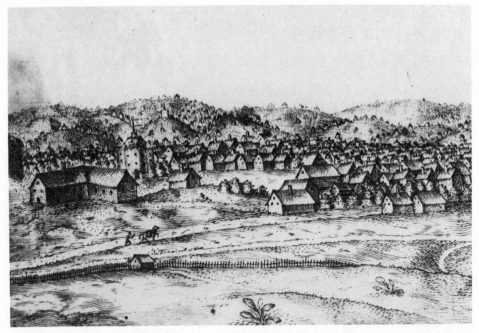

The Theater and the Curtain. Detail from "The View of the City of London from the North towards the South" in the manuscript journal of Abram Booth, ca. 1597–1599. Flags mark the rooftops of two playhouses in the north London suburb of Shoreditch. On the left is the Theater. The smaller structure on the right is the Curtain, where the Lord Chamberlain's Men performed *Every Man in His Humour* in 1598.

him to a duel—and had wounded him in the arm. The jury, however, determined that he, not Spencer, was the aggressor in this affair, and Jonson pleaded guilty to their indictment. Philip Henslowe made no mention of a duel when he alluded to Spencer's death in a letter to his son-in-law Edward Alleyn, dated September 26. "I have loste one of my company whiche hurteth me greatley," he wrote, "that is gabrell for he is slayen in hoges den fylldes by the hands of benge[men] Johnson bricklayer." Three years later Dekker accused Jonson of "killing a player." Spencer's past does bear out Jonson's claim that the conflict was forced upon him; not two years previously, he had killed a goldsmith's son when the boy threatened to throw a candlestick at him.[1] But the very idea of a "duel" between a bricklayer and an actor, neither of whom was entitled to bear arms, is a contradiction in terms.

Jonson, who now found himself in Newgate prison, had crossed the line that separates youthful recklessness from criminal wrongdoing. He had already killed a man in the Low Countries, mainly, to judge from his own account, for the sport of it; just a year before he had landed in jail for his coauthorship of *The Isle of Dogs;* now "he was Emprisoned and almost at the Gallowes." In the midst of this dire predicament, he once again acted rashly. While awaiting his sentence, he converted to Roman Catholicism "by trust of a priest who Visited him in Prison." The motives that prompted him to take this extraordinary step are hard to fathom. The Catholic faith was an outlaw religion in Elizabethan England. Catholics who declined to attend Anglican services incurred a fine of twenty pounds a month and if they were unable to pay it their property was confiscated. They could not hold public office. It was a felony to receive a priest and thus, *de facto,* a felony to take the sacrament from him. Catholics were subject to arbitrary imprisonment and excruciating tortures at the hands of their captors; those suspected of plotting against the crown could expect to have their intestines removed in public. While confined to the Marshalsea prison during the previous summer Jonson had been interrogated by Richard Topcliffe, the Protestant Grand Inquisitor, so he was familiar with the methods employed by government agents. Moreover, the timing

Fencers with rapier, sword, and dagger. From J. Swetnam, *The Schools of Defence,* 1617. Jonson killed Gabriel Spencer with a rapier, the longer of the two weapons wielded by the fencer on the left. Its narrow pointed blade and cup hilt made it particularly effective as a thrusting weapon in private quarrels.

of his conversion was uncannily poor. The Franco-Spanish peace treaty of 1598 increased the likelihood that England and Spain would go to war, and the English authorities promptly began to execute greater numbers of their Catholic countrymen.[2] Jonson's decision is the more puzzling in that his family history reveals no traces of Catholicism: no childhood memories were tugging at his conscience. Nor, finally, can his conversion be ascribed to the anonymous priest's powers of persuasion. Jonson was only in Newgate for two weeks and he took his new religion "by trust."

What inspired such trust? During the brief interval when he was almost at the gallows the question of where he would spend eternity took precedence over any temporal considerations. A man about to be hanged need not be overly concerned with the statutes against recusancy. An Anglican minister could have heard his confession and given him the sacrament, but since the Church of England, in accordance with the teaching of Luther, held that the individual believer had to take responsibility for his own salvation, the minister could not assure Jonson that God had forgiven him. But the Catholic priest who converted him had the power, by right of apostolic succession from Christ Himself, to absolve him of his sins. Unlike his Protestant counterpart, the priest would not have required Jonson to feel remorse over his crimes as such or to believe that God had pardoned him; fear of punishment—the lowest form of contrition—was sufficient grounds for absolution.

Jonson "was a man of almost ungovernably violent passions," Pearlman comments, "but a man who was also in need of external control. By killing, Jonson brought down the law upon himself; in prison, under stress, he accepted religion as an act of trust in a figure of authority."[3] Yet in deferring to the priest he was also committing a fresh act of defiance, for his Catholicism made him an outlaw in the eyes of the state. When Jonson submitted to the higher power embodied in the priest, he did not resolve the problem of his insurgency; he compounded it.

Jonson was arraigned at the Justice Hall in the Old Bailey on October 6. After confessing to the crime of manslaughter, he took advantage of an archaic legal custom and pleaded benefit of clergy. This form of plea went back to the early Middle Ages, when the only persons who knew how to read were clerics. As originally conceived, it gave any man who could prove that he was literate the right to have his case tried in the bishop's court; by Jonson's day it had become a loophole for educated male felons. If the magistrate were willing to entertain his plea, any first offender who could translate at sight from a Latin Bible was entitled to go scot-free. Jonson was lucky enough to come before a sympathetic judge, and after translating his "neck verse," he was released from custody.

Even so, he did incur two serious penalties. First, the court confiscated everything he owned—and the form of the indictment indicates that he did possess some property. Second, his thumb was branded with the letter "T" (for Tyburn, where he would have been hanged) in order to prevent him from pleading benefit of clergy a second time. It is curious that none of Jonson's enemies ever refer to that "T" in their many lampoons of him. Did he cut away, or burn out, the branded flesh? Or did he hold his hand in such a way that no one saw it?[4]

Jonson walked out of the Old Bailey utterly destitute, a branded felon whose religion would continue to identify him as a criminal. He decided not to make matters worse by refusing to attend Anglican services, but instead chose, like many Elizabethan Catholics, to wait until a new sovereign was on the throne (HS, I, 220). He also withdrew from the stage for the first few months after his release. On October 23 Henslowe gave Chapman four shillings as partial payment for completing "a tragedie of benegemens plotte." This "plotte" may have been what Jonson had shown Henslowe the previous December, when he had promised to finish it "at cryssmas next." In any event, the commission had now gone to Chapman, and Jonson had no further transactions with Henslowe until late in the following summer (HS, XI, 307–308).

Instead, he abruptly resumed his old trade of bricklaying. Between October 6, 1598, and January 31, 1599, Jonson managed to become a member of the Worshipful Company of Tilers and Bricklayers. For a man in his circumstances this was not a simple task. He and his former master had to present themselves before the Bricklayers' Court of Assistants and explain why Jonson had broken his apprenticeship in 1594, when he married Anne Lewis. After satisfying the court on that account, the master had to pay the guild a sum of money (perhaps as much as three pounds) to "redeem" Jonson's apprenticeship. After meeting these conditions, and paying the company clerk three shillings four pence for recording his freedom, the fledgling journeyman went to the Guildhall, paid yet another fee, and became a Citizen of London. On St. Mark's Day (April 25), the clerk made the following entry in the Tilers' and Bricklayers' Company Quarterage Book: "4d. Benjamin Johnson—3s.4d." The initial figure of four pence refers to the quarterly payment that was regularly levied on members of the company. The additional three shillings four pence probably refers to the fee that Jonson paid the clerk when he entered the company.[5]

By becoming a member of the guild, Jonson gained the right to contract for wages as an independent artisan. He may well have believed, at this disastrous juncture in his life, that his old craft held the key to his economic survival, but the obstacles in his path were formidable. At the end of January, his creditor Robert Browne, still intent upon regaining the ten pounds that he had lent Jonson the previous April, had him arrested for debt, tried, and committed to Marshalsea prison (HS, XI, 572). We do not know how long he languished there, or who furnished the ten pounds that secured his release (Brett? Henslowe?), but the stark reality of his poverty was plain enough. Jonson obviously lacked the means to set up shop as a master bricklayer. True, he could now sell his labor whenever and wherever he chose, but a journeyman's wage of nine pence a day was scarcely any better than the seven pence a day he had earned as a mere apprentice.

At approximately this time—when they could least afford it—the Jonsons began having more children. The three-year hiatus between the spring of 1596, when their first son, Ben, arrived, and the early months of 1599, when Anne became pregnant once again, is sufficiently long to warrant a little attention. Perhaps the Jonsons deliberately limited the size of their family during this interval by the practice of *coitus interruptus,* then the commonest means of birth control. This course of action would have suited their troubled financial situation. That option ceased to be available, however, after Jonson's conversion to Roman Catholicism in October of 1598. Then, as now, the Catholic Church forbade its members to employ any form of contraception whatsoever. Like their modern counterparts, some parish priests honored this prohibition more in the breach than in the observance; but English priests were trained at Douai and Louvain, which were strongholds of neo-Augustinian orthodoxy, and they adhered to the letter of the Church's teaching on the subject of birth control. Moreover, if the moralizing "Epode" that Jonson published two years later bears any relationship to his actual beliefs at this time, the new convert had adopted an inflexibly austere moral standard. The speaker of the "Epode" insists, in good Augustinian fashion, on making an absolute distinction between carnal and spiritual love; a virtuous individual, he concludes, will make no concessions whatever to his fleshly appetites, "And to his sense object this sentence ever, / *man may securely sinne, but safely never.*" [6]

Once Jonson became a Catholic, sexual love was permissible only for the purpose of procreation. And he and Anne did procreate: Joseph, their second son, was baptized at the parish Church of St. Giles, Cripplegate, in December of 1599, and Mary, their first daughter, probably came a year or so later. The names of these two children suggest a new-found spirit of religious enthusiasm. The biblical Joseph and Mary were the perfect stepfather and mother; by naming his children after these exemplary parents, Jonson could simultaneously affirm his piety and create the ideal family he had been deprived of as a child. At the same time, he was giving out hostages to fortune. His two children could hardly be expected to remedy the deficiencies of his own childhood, or to fulfill the extravagant hopes implied by their names. An Elizabethan father was lucky if his children survived to adulthood. One child out of two died before reaching his or her fifth birthday, and the odds of an infant's surviving until the age of fifteen were only one out of three.[7]

The Tilers' and Bricklayers' Company Quarterage Book does not mention any subsequent payments from Benjamin Johnson. In the summer of 1599 the journeyman bricklayer was again writing for the London stage. By August 10 he and Dekker had finished part of a domestic tragedy called *Page of Plymouth* and received an advance of forty shillings. Three weeks later, Henslowe paid another forty shillings to a syndicate of writers, Jonson and Dekker among them, who were at work on a play called *Robert II, King of Scots*. At the end of September, Henslowe advanced Jonson still another twenty shillings "in earneste of a Boocke called the scottes tragedie" (HS, XI, 308). Since Jonson relegated these plays to oblivion, it is natural to infer that his early tragedies were hackwork. Nevertheless, they did catch the eye of two contemporary critics. In 1598 Francis Meres had numbered Jonson among "our best for Tragedie," and a year later John Weever saluted the "embuskin'd *Johnson*" who "doth retaine / So rich a stile, and wondrous gallant spirit" (HS, XI, 362). But tragedy held little appeal for him at this point in his life. By the autumn of 1599, he was preoccupied with *Every Man out of His Humour,* the "comical satire" that he was writing for the Lord Chamberlain's Men.

Weever alleged that Jonson's poverty made him turn to satire. In a pamphlet published two years later, he informed him that "*opus* and *usus* [need and want] put you to such a pinch, that you made sale of your Humours to the Theater" (HS, XI, 363). Weever had a point. The material circumstances of Jonson's life, to say nothing of his criminal record and his religion, made him a likely candidate for the role of the angry satirist. But Jonson's straitened personal circumstances also typified a larger cultural rift in late Elizabethan England. By the end of the 1590s the most talented poets of his generation had already formed an informal literary protest movement, and he shared many of their grievances.

The young men who turned to satire in the waning years of the reign were the products of an educational system that was turning out graduates at a rate that greatly exceeded the number of suitable posts. At the beginning of her monarchy Elizabeth had expanded the size of the student body at Oxford and Cambridge in order to meet the urgent need for an educated Protestant ministry. Stone estimates that admissions to the two universities tripled between 1560 and 1590. By the last decade of the sixteenth century, however, the demand for new Bachelors of Arts had long since been satisfied, and the surplus graduates, many of whom congregated in London, made up a small but highly visible group of discontented intellectuals. Lodge, Nashe, Harington, Hall, and Marston fell into this category, as did Donne, although he withheld his satires from publication during his lifetime. Elizabeth's monarchy was now beset by a number of nagging problems. The Queen's failure to resolve the succession crisis, or to end the lingering war with Spain and the Irish revolt, or to remedy the ongoing price inflation, the spread of monopolies, and the recurrent grain shortages, aggravated the unemployed graduates' sense of disillusionment. Although Jonson lacked a university degree, his Westminster education had exposed him to the same cycle of expectation and frustration, and he had already collaborated with Thomas Nashe on *The Isle of Dogs,* a play that exemplified the mood of the new satirists.[8]

Men in positions of authority recognized that such persons constituted a threat to the commonwealth. It is a cause "of Seditions and Troubles," Bacon observed, "when more are bred scholars than preferment can take off." Lord Ellesmere later surmised that "learning without living doth but breed traitors." By the spring of 1599, the Privy Council had decided that the situation was out of hand. On June 1 John Whitgift and Richard Bancroft, the Archbishop of Canterbury and the Bishop of London, respectively, issued a list of scurrilous books to be burned by the common hangman and decreed "that no satires or epigrams be printed hereafter."[9]

Seven of the poets who published satires or epigrams between 1593 and 1601 (Davies, Goddard, Guilpin, Lodge, Marston, Owen, and Harington), or about half the total number of published satirists, belonged to the community of law students and barristers at the Inns of Court. Jonson later dedicated *Every Man out of His Humour* to the Inns of Court, noting that "when I wrote this *Poeme,* I had friendship with divers in your societies; who, as they were great Names in learning, so they were no lesse Examples of living. Of them, and then (that I say no more) it was not despis'd." A list of members who are known to have been on friendly terms with him, and who resided at the Inns of Court during the late Elizabethan era, would include Richard Hoskins, Richard Martin, Sir John Salusbury, Benjamin Rudyerd, Thomas Overbury, John Beaumont, and Thomas Bond of the Middle Temple; Francis Bacon and Henry Goodyere of Gray's Inn; Sir John Harington, Christopher Brooke, and John Donne of Lincoln's Inn; and John Selden and Francis Beaumont of the Inner Temple. Hoskins and Martin appear to have been especially close to Jonson during these years. Hoskins's son Bennet told John Aubrey that he had asked "Mr Johnson to adopt him for his Sonne": "no said he I dare not, 'tis honour enough for me to be your Brother. I was your Fathers sonne; and t'was He that polished me." When Jonson was threatened with prosecution in 1601, Richard Martin, to whom he dedicated another of his early comedies, came to his rescue.[10]

The men who "polish'd" Jonson and furnished him with "examples of living" had a proclivity for reckless raillery and abuse. Philip Finkelpearl aptly characterizes both Hoskins and Martin as "troublemakers, more or less serious disciplinary problems, and not merely as youths." Like many of their fellow students, they shared in a "group tendency toward physical abuse and the untimely exhibition of wit." Martin twice led gangs of students from the Middle Temple into the neighboring streets, where they "broke the ordinance by making outcries, forcibly breaking open chambers in the night and levying money as the Lord of Misrule's rent." After being expelled and reinstated, Martin took a leading role in the Templar's infamous Christmas Revels of 1597–98. His mockery of John Davies on that occasion was apparently so vicious that Davies attacked him with a wooden club shortly thereafter—a crime for which Davies was, in turn, expelled and imprisoned. Hoskins, Jonson's adoptive "father" and another key figure in the revels of 1597–98, had been forced to resign his fellowship at Cambridge after a "bitterly satyrical" commencement address there. Both men prided themselves on their raillery and saw no reason to apologize for it. Jonson's friend Benjamin Rudyerd admiringly remarked of Martin that "fortune never taught him to temper his own wit or manhood." When Hoskins's public mockery of King James I finally landed him in the Tower of London (Martin narrowly escaped the same fate), he was unrepentant to the last and wrote to his wife Benedicta, "for my part I had rather dy with witt then live without it." By 1599, Jonson had assumed this stance. When Dekker dared him to "sweare not to bumbast out a new Play, with the olde lynings of Jestes, stolne from the Temples Revels," he was calling attention to an affinity that Jonson himself later acknowledged.[11]

The Bishops' Order of June 1, 1599, put the aspiring satirist in a precarious position. He had already been imprisoned for his share of *The Isle of Dogs* and could scarcely afford another setback at this point in his life. Unlike his mentors at the Inns of Court, Jonson did not have an independent income to fall back on; but he did have a classical education, and he knew that the great satirists, comedians, and moralists of antiquity had faced the same dilemma in which he now found himself. At some point in the year 1599—to judge from his later reminiscences— he commenced a careful study of those forebears.[12]

This was a major undertaking for an impoverished minor playwright, and it marks a significant milestone in Jonson's intellectual development. By the time he wrote his comedy of 1599, he had obtained access to a good private library and taken careful notes on whatever he believed would be relevant to the work that he had in hand. This daily program of reading and note taking would eventually transform the boy who left school at sixteen into a man of vast erudition; its immediate effects are widely apparent in *Every Man out of His Humour*. His first two comedies hardly ever allude to classical or to modern European authors, and the few such allusions that do occur (to Terence, for example, or to the first few lines of the *Aeneid*) could easily be the product of his grammar school education. His third comedy, by contrast, makes reference to Plautus, Terence, Persius, Horace, Juvenal, Cicero, Seneca, Plutarch, Lucian, and Caelius Firmanius Symposius among the ancients, and Erasmus and Castiglione among the moderns (HS, IX, 394–482). Jonson was not simply acquiring erudition for its own sake; his display of learning was a defensive measure. As the author of a new satirical comedy (the printed text was the first to use the word "satire" in its title since the ban of June 1), he ran the risk of being haled before the authorities for the third time in three years. He tried to minimize that risk, and to disarm potential accusers, by showing that he had not exceeded the license granted to classical authors.

Jonson formulates this line of defense in the Induction to the play and in eleven separate scenes in which a chorus of critics debates the merits of his work. When Asper, the "presenter" of Jonson's satire, is warned that his "humour will come ill to some," he responds with an erudite lecture on the meaning of the word "humour." Cordatus, who plays the part of the author's "friend," repeatedly points out that his play is no more offensive than comparable works by Aristophanes, Plautus, Terence, and the other ancient comedians: "If we faile / We must impute it to this onely chance, / *Arte* hath an enemy call'd *Ignorance*." Asper and Cordatus are also familiar with the ancient discussions of the license permitted to comic writers. In the course of their colloquy they draw upon Plato's remarks about the therapeutic effects of laughter, Aristotle's distinction between buffoonery and wit, Horace's claim that ancient comedy had grown more refined with the passage of time, and Martial's contention that it was allowable to attack vicious "types" so long as living individuals were not explicitly named. Although Jonson does not follow his ancient exemplars blindly, they too were innovators in their day: "I see not then," Asper concludes, "but we should enjoy the same licence, or free power, to illustrate and heighten our invention as they did." [13]

Jonson marshals such an elaborate array of defenses in his Induction that one begins to wonder if he is not protesting too much. Is the play really as harmless as its author and his model spectator would have us believe? Shorn of its critical apparatus, *Every Man out of His Humour* is a vitriolic satire on contemporary English life. Jonson heaps abuse on all of the malcontent scholar's favorite targets—the grain hoarder, the vainglorious knight, the uxorious merchant, the coquettish city wife, the foppish courtier, the affected court lady—and he is positively savage when the time comes to bring them "out" of their humors. One man's dog is poisoned onstage, a second man hangs himself, a third discovers his wife in the arms of his friend, a fourth is carried away to prison, and a fifth has his mouth sealed up with wax after being beaten. These scenes look like the work of the man who was clapped into the Marshalsea prison for *The Isle of Dogs* just two years previously. But whenever Jonson's satire grows intolerably corrosive, the chorus of critics comes to his rescue. When, for example, the grain speculator unsuccessfully tries to commit suicide in the midst of a throng of jeering farmers, an accusatory spectator solemnly objects that "the intent and horror of the object, was more then the nature of a *Comoedie* will in any sort admit." "What thinke you of PLAUTUS in his *Comoedie*, called *Cistellaria*," the ever-obliging Cordatus replies, "where he brings in ALCESIMARCHUS with a drawne sword ready to kill himselfe, and as hee is e'ne fixing his brest upon it, [is] restrain'd from his resolv'd outrage, by SILENIUM and the bawd: is not his authoritie of power to give our *Scene* approbation?" (III.viii.83–92). Jonson's "friend" reminds the audience that the grain hoarder is only a character in a play: not the flesh-and-blood entrepreneur who was provoking real riots in the late 1590s, but an illusion sanctioned by a long and august literary tradition. The framing scenes insist on the fictional status of Jonson's play; they notify the would-be censor that this is art, and high art at that, rather than life.

This comic interplay between uncontrollable rage and bookish erudition makes artistic capital out of Jonson's authorial self-division. Asper corresponds to the "public" Jonson—the donnish scholar-poet who aspires only to please the "attentive auditors" that "come to feed their understanding parts." At the end of the Induction, when Asper leaves the stage to put on the costume that he will wear during the play, there is a momentary breakdown of authorial control. During this hiatus, the Prologue refuses to speak his part and the author's enemy, Carlo Buffone, comes onstage bearing a cup of wine. Carlo announces that although Jonson "keepes a good philosophicall diet, beanes and butter milke" at home, he gets drunk whenever he goes out in public: "Hee will take you off three, foure, five of these, one after another . . . and then . . . he sailes away away withall, as though he would worke wonders when he comes home." The buffoon is Jonson's shadow self, "a violent railer" who "will sooner lose his soule then a jest." Drummond characterized Jonson in the same terms ("given rather to losse a friend, than a Jest"); and Aubrey's account of Jonson's drinking and working habits ("he would tumble home to bed; and when he had thoroughly perspired then to studie") is identical to Carlo's.[14]

Asper then reappears, attired as the desperately impoverished scholar Macilente ("emaciated"), and the author regains control of his text. Macilente, who is consumed by envy of his well-fed neighbors, corresponds to the "private" Jonson—the displaced intellectual who has recently lost all of his property and commenced a rigorous program of self-education. Where Asper, the classicizing poet, symbolizes the creative pole of Jonson's imagination, Macilente, the malcontent scholar, evokes its destructive capacities, and it is he who does the dirty work of bringing the poet's *bêtes noires* out of their humors.[15]

Macilente's own future remains very much in doubt at the end of the play. He begins to move up the social hierarchy in act III, when the merchant Deliro becomes his patron; but this sudden shower of prosperity also robs him of his reason for being. He can hardly sustain the posture of a malcontent scholar when he is attired in the silken finery of a courtier. Jonson was ambivalent about the whole issue of Macilente's future—so much so that he could only resolve his ambivalence by summoning a *deus ex machina*. At the conclusion of the first performance at the Globe Theater in the autumn of 1599, a boy actor dressed as Queen Elizabeth appeared on stage, and Macilente, who had now resumed the identity of Asper, the author in the play, greeted "her" with a flowery compliment: "Envie is fled my soule, at sight of her, / And shee hath chac'd all black thoughts from my bosome." In the midst of his Epilogue, however, Asper abruptly likens his load of envy to a river of excrement flowing toward the Queen:

> And as our cities torrent (bent t'infect
> The hallow'd bowels of the silver *Thames*)
> Is checkt by strength, and clearnesse of the river,
> Till it hath spent itself e'ene at the shore;
> So, in the ample, and unmeasur'd floud
> Of her perfections, are my passions drown'd.

This is a backhanded and confusing compliment. The extraordinary image of London's sewage canal (Asper's humor) "bent t'infect / the hallow'd bowels" of the Thames (Queen Elizabeth) hints that the Queen is both the ultimate object of Asper's envy and the only person who can resolve it. Small wonder that the Globe audience "seem'd not to rellish" this afterpiece and refused to countenance a repeat performance of it. Jonson, however, was undaunted, and when *Every Man out of His Humour* was per-

Elizabeth I with Time and Death, posthumous, artist unknown. To the left of Elizabeth, Time has fallen asleep. To the right Death looks over her shoulder. Two putti are about to bestow an immortal crown.

formed at court during the Christmas season of 1599–1600, the company restored the original conclusion.[16]

Whether Elizabeth paid any attention to this curious afterpiece, and what she made of it if she did, remains a mystery. If Jonson actually did hope to win the Queen's favor, he had chosen an improbable way of doing so. Asper's Epilogue does, however, afford a plausible image of Jonson's own mixed emotions at the moment when he made his initial bid for royal patronage. As Jonson reduced his protagonist to a state of childlike dependence on this remote and forbidding mother, infantile resentments (he had spent his own childhood in a tenement that stood adjacent to a rivulet of "our cities torrent") flooded his imagination and took on the childlike aspect of excrement—just as they had when he depicted the miserly Jaques de Prie. Yet if Jonson could be taken into the "ample, and unmeasur'd flood" of the Queen's maternal bounty, his pent-up malice would dissolve forever.

· CHAPTER FOUR ·

Search for Patronage
and the Poet's Quarrel

Although *Every Man out of His Humour* won the approval of the "happier spirits in this faire-fild Globe," Jonson's own connections with the stage were increasingly tenuous. Prior to *Every Man Out* he had adopted the manner of an educated, classicizing playwright; in 1599 he went a step further and made common cause with a select group of "pure and apprehensive eares" whose "voices speake for our desert" (HS, III, 604). He was now searching for an elite audience that could free him from his dependence on the stage, and this quest led him out of the public playhouses.

His first, tentative break with the established acting companies came in the autumn of 1599. He had no further dealings with Henslowe for a period of two years; he did not write another play for the Lord Chamberlain's Men until 1603. Instead, he sought other venues for his work. He brought out quarto editions of his plays, began to write nondramatic poetry for prospective patrons and patronesses, and penned two comedies for the Children of Queen Elizabeth's Chapel Royal, who began performing at the Blackfriars Theater around the turn of the century.

Since all of these ventures commenced between the autumn of 1599 and the autumn of 1600, at a time when Jonson had just begun the program of reading and note taking that would ultimately bear fruit in his *Discoveries,* they appear to be the result of a conscious choice. Having achieved a *succès d'estime* on the public stage, he now conceived of himself as a man of letters rather than a professional playwright. In order to realize that conception, he had to obtain the support of individual patrons, and patronage was the common denominator of all his new undertakings. The quartos were intended to attract the attention of educated readers at the legal academies, the universities, and the royal court; the nondramatic verse appealed directly to persons in a position to help him; and the comedies written for the Children of the Chapel Royal were performed before an audience largely composed of the literary and social elite.

Although this strategy was well conceived, it was open to question on several counts. Jonson was the impoverished stepson of a London bricklayer, yet he aspired to a place in a noble household; he had made his mark as a satirist, yet he wanted to be taken into the establishment; he had been educated as a humanist, yet he coveted the office of a court entertainer; he was a fiercely independent individual, yet he was putting his services at the disposal of his social superiors. There were no easy resolutions to these problems—Jonson would grapple with them for the better part of his life. Yet the main thrust of his solution was straightforward enough: Jonson projected his own code of values onto his prospective patrons. He complimented them because they shared his disregard for the external marks of wealth and status, his disdain for courtly foppery, his relish of classical letters, his appreciation for the fine points of literary craftsmanship, and his commitment to an unostentatious manner of life. In short, he congratulated them for conforming to his own self-image. Jonson could thus be at once deferential and assertive; but since his addressees were far less straitlaced than he made them out to be, he also made himself vulnerable to the charge of being a priggish social climber who deserved to be ridiculed for his pretensions.

A printer named William Holme entered *Every Man out of His Humour* on the Stationers' Register on April 8, 1600. Jonson's sale of his manuscript to Holme was highly unorthodox. Elizabethan playwrights normally transferred exclusive control over their manuscripts to the acting companies that purchased them. Although neither the writers nor the actors were entitled to take out copyrights—that privilege was restricted to printers who belonged to the Stationers' Company—the acting companies had a strong vested interest in keeping their playhouse manuscripts out of print. As long as the actors retained sole possession of the author's manuscript, anyone who wanted to see the play performed, or to become familiar with its contents, had to come to their playhouse. Once a sizable number of theatergoers had read a play, its novelty, and hence its commercial value to the players, was drastically reduced. When an acting company did sell a playhouse manuscript to a printer there were mitigating circumstances: performances had been discontinued because of the plague, one of the actors had already conveyed a pirated text to an unscrupulous printer, or the play's popularity had diminished. When Jonson sold his copy of *Every Man out of His Humour* to Holme within a year of its successful debut, he was claiming, in effect, that the author continued to own his work after the players had purchased a copy of it.[1]

Jonson carefully oversaw the publication of his first quarto, taking the opportunity to insert various material superfluous to the acting version. His title page explicitly appealed to an audience of educated *readers*, offering them "*more than hath been Publickely Spoken or Acted.*" Contrary to normal practice, this title page omits any reference either to the acting company or to stage performances. Instead, it stresses the superiority of the printed text "AS IT WAS FIRST COMPOSED" and before it was adapted to the exigencies of the playhouse. Although Latin mottoes, such as the ones Jonson borrowed from Horace, frequently appeared on the title pages of nondramatic poetry, they were hardly ever used to characterize plays acted in public. The first of the three mottoes comes from the epistle (I.ix) in which Horace, writing to his patron Maecenas, defends himself against the charge that he has slavishly followed his Greek exemplars: "I walked not where others trod." Just as Horace revived the spirit of Greek satire in a Roman setting, Jonson has reinvigorated his classical models in modern England. The other two Latin tags allude to the famous passage in the *Ars Poetica* where Horace compares poetry to painting. Jonson was stating his preference for the meticulously crafted work that makes a better impression "if you stand nearer" and will always please "though ten times called for." His own works, by the same token, will show to better advantage in the study than on the stage; his precise craftsmanship will bear the test of many rereadings.[2]

He stipulated that *Every Man out of His Humour* be sold at William Holme's bookshop at the gateway of Sergeant's Inn, in the immediate vicinity of the Inns of Court. Holme would not have paid him more than a pound or two for *Every Man out of His Humour*, but Jonson could count upon the author's customary allotment of twenty or thirty free copies, and this was a valuable commodity. Elizabethan authors usually tried to sell these volumes at inflated prices to their friends and acquaintances. Given the popularity of Jonson's new comedy, and the range of his contacts within the legal community that resided near Holme's shop, he could easily have garnered several pounds or more in this fashion. Over seventeen hundred law students and barristers lived within a mile or so of Sergeant's Inn and belonged either to the Inns of Court or to the Inns of Chancery. About 40 percent of these held the rank of "peer esquire," and four-fifths of the remainder styled themselves "gentlemen"; all could afford to pay a minimum fee of forty pounds per year for room, board, and tuition. Jonson chose his clientele wisely: *Every Man out of His Humour* went

The Comicall Satyre of

EVERY MAN,
OVT OF HIS
HVMOR.

AS IT WAS FIRST COMPOSED
by the Author B. I,

Containing more than hath been Publickely Spo-
ken or Acted.

VVith the feuerall Character of euery Perfon.

Non aliena meo preſſi pede | ✳ ſi propius ſtes
Te capient magis | ✳ & decies repetita placebunt.

LONDON,
Printed for *William Holme*, and are to be ſold at his Shop
at Sarjeants Inne gate in Fleetſtreet.
1600. 2 3

Title page of Jonson's *Every Man out of His Humour*, 1600. Descriptive phrases notify readers that the printed text of the play is superior to the version that was performed on the stage.

through three editions in the year 1600, a feat unequaled by any play since John Lyly's *Campaspe* in 1584.[3]

Jonson had suddenly become a well-known author. Within a period of nine months, about fifteen hundred copies of *Every Man out of His Humour* found their way into the hands of the reading public. The Lord Chamberlain's Men, who wanted to protect their own interest in *Every Man in His Humour,* tried to prevent him from publishing it as well and entered a "blocking registration" at the Stationers' Company on August 4; but their efforts were unsuccessful, and Jonson's printer secured the copyright to his earlier comedy of humors on August 14, 1600.[4] Meanwhile, extracts from his published and unpublished work appeared in *Belvedere; or, The Garden of the Muses* (1600) and Robert Allot's *England's Parnassus* (1600), two anthologies of contemporary English poetry. The opening pages of Nicholas Breton's *Melancholic Humours* (1600) displayed Jonson's tributary verses. Trivial though it is, the last of these accomplishments indicates how far he had come since 1598: Jonson had now supplanted George Chapman as the leading "humorist" of his day. Just as important, he could now present copies of his published work to prospective patrons and patronesses.

By this time, Jonson had made a conscious decision to seek support from a variety of potential benefactors. Apart from his verse tribute to Thomas Palmer's *Sprite of Trees and Herbs* (*UV,* 1), which may go back to 1598, Jonson's earliest datable poems fall between November 1599 and October 1600. His acrostic epitaph on Margaret Radcliffe, one of Queen Elizabeth's ladies-in-waiting, was probably written between her death on November 10, 1599, and her burial twelve days later. An "Ode to James, Earl of Desmond" was finished by October 1600, when part of the poem appeared in *England's Parnassus.* At about the same time he sent manuscripts of his "Proludium" and "Epode" to Sir John Salusbury. Both works subsequently appeared, along with contributions from Chapman, Marston, and Shakespeare, in Robert Chester's *Love's Martyr* (1601), a collection of poems dedicated to Salusbury and his wife. Chester also published the "Ode *Enthousiastikē*" [Enthusiastic], the first of several poems that Jonson addressed to Lucy, Countess of Bedford. On New Year's Day of 1600, he presented Sir Philip Sidney's daughter Elizabeth, Countess of Rutland, with a verse epistle (*For,* 12) prophesying that

> all, that have but done my *Muse* least grace,
> Shall thronging come, and boast the happy place
> They hold in my strange *poems.*

The most conspicuous of these addressees are the Countesses of Rutland and Bedford. It is impossible to say how he became acquainted with these two titled ladies, but both of them belonged to the parish church at St. Martin in the Fields, where Jonson had been a communicant prior to his conversion. The epistle to Lady Rutland mentions the "timely favours" that her friend and neighbor Lady Bedford had already done for him, so it seems that Jonson's solicitations had borne some fruit by January 1600. Yet the epistle also insists that the impoverished poet is indifferent to material rewards. The world, he concedes, esteems verse less than gold, "But let this drosse carry what price it will / With noble ignorants": with Lady Rutland, he knows, "my offring will find grace." The poetic legacy she has inherited from her father, Sir Philip Sidney, is "worth an estate, treble to that you have." [5]

Like Macilente, his scholar-hero of 1599, Jonson was ambivalent about worldly success. He rejoiced in the support of these wealthy noblewomen, but he also insisted that his motives were wholly altruistic. He yearned to be an insider even as he struggled to preserve his aloof independence. Whether by accident or design, he pinned his hopes on persons who were currently out of favor and thereby allowed himself to suppose that they shared his contempt for wealth and status. The Earls of Bedford and Rutland, and perhaps Sir John Salusbury, were followers of the Earl of Essex, whose standing at court had taken a disastrous and permanent turn for the worse in the autumn of 1599. Thomas Palmer had been deprived of his Oxford fellowship because of his Catholicism, and continued to be persecuted after retiring to his estate in Essex. The Earl of Desmond, another fellow Catholic, had spent his entire adult life in prison. The noble addressees of 1599–1600 were currently disenfranchised, yet they hovered, like Jonson, on the periphery, waiting for their luck to change. [6]

The return of the Children of the Chapel Royal to the Blackfriars Theater offered access to yet another kind of elite audience. The Children belonged to the singing school of Queen Elizabeth's chapel and had contributed to Tudor court drama throughout the sixteenth century. It was only in 1576–77, when Richard Farrant leased a private building in the Blackfriars district of London and turned it into "a continual house for plays" put on by the Children that the boys' companies became an autonomous theatrical enterprise. Nevertheless, the Chapel Children were still attached to the royal household, and they continued to perform under conditions that nurtured the illusion of genteel amateurism. While the adult companies played in vast open-air amphitheaters, situated in outlying suburbs where the urban authorities were powerless to restrain them, the Chapel Children performed in an enclosed room of a private dwelling located in the fashionable London neighborhood of Blackfriars. The smaller house, with its confining roof and artificial lighting, held the promise of "gracious silence, sweet attention, / Quicke sight, and quicker apprehension." Geographically, but *not* legally, the Blackfriars district was inside the City of London, and the company thus enjoyed access to the well-heeled London audience together with freedom from the municipal authorities.[7]

Throughout their history, the children's companies maintained assumptions about the relationship of writer to actor that were markedly different from those that prevailed at the public playhouses. The writers were masters and the actors were schoolboys. The masters had literary skills, which were the fruits of their superior education; the boys had mechanical skills, acquired through set drills and rehearsals. Here, then, was a hierarchy of actor and writer that fit neatly into the established orders of Elizabethan society, a true "poet's theater" in which the actors confined themselves to the business of acting. The university-educated playwrights who came to the fore during the 1580s—Peele, Lyly, Marlowe, and Nashe—had all written for the children's companies. It was to be expected that their successors—John Marston, George Chapman, and Ben Jonson—would follow suit when the companies reopened, after a nine-year hiatus, at the turn of the century. The spectators at Blackfriars were not merely paying customers; many of them were prospective patrons as well. The location, ticket prices, and dramatic traditions of the Blackfriars Theater made it the natural haunt both of the lawyers, to whom Jonson dedicated *Every Man out of His Humour,* and of the court, to whom he dedicated *The Fountain of Self Love; or, Cynthia's Revels,* the comedy he was writing in 1600.

The Prologue to *Cynthia's Revels,* which the Chapel Children performed in the autumn of 1600, informs the Blackfriars audience that Jonson's muse "shunnes the *print* of any beaten path / And proves new wayes to come to learned *eares.*" The pun on "print" speaks volumes about Jonson's intentions. Since his prospective patrons are physically present in the well-heeled Blackfriars audience, he does not need to approach them via the usual medium of the printed dedication. These were spectators who could comprehend and reward his muse in one and the same gesture: "The garland that she weares, their hands must twine, / Who can both censure, understand, define / What merit is."[8]

Jonson was also aiming for another performance at court: Queen Elizabeth (Cynthia) had scheduled a remarkably full season of court festivities (revels) for the holiday season of 1600–1. Jonson not only knew about the Queen's plans; he also knew or thought he knew why she had taken this step, and he shared this knowledge with the audience, explaining to them that "DIANA (in regard of some black and envious slanders hourely breath'd against her, for her divine justice on ACTEON, as shee pretends) hath here . . . proclaim'd a solemne revells." "Acteon" was the Earl of

Essex, whose notorious intrusion into Queen Elizabeth's bedchamber the previous autumn, coupled with other offenses, had brought Elizabeth's "divine justice" (house arrest, dismissal from all offices of state) down upon his head. The Queen's "solemne revells" of 1600–1 were, as Joseph Loewenstein argues, "a display of flamboyant magnificence designed to demonstrate her inviolability in the face of the slight but persistent popular allegiance to Essex." Jonson did not merely, or even primarily, write the play for the Blackfriars clientele; he was also offering the Queen his services as a maker of court entertainments. Its alternative title anticipates a change in status both for the author and his hero. Jonson hoped to move from the lowly medium of stage comedy (*The Fountain of Self Love*) to the more exalted sphere of the court masque (*Cynthia's Revels*).[9]

The play flaunts Jonson's ambitions at every turn. Criticus, his well-educated but impoverished protagonist, seeks preferment at court but is crowded out of the limelight by a horde of "mimiques, jesters, pandars, parasites / And other such like prodigies of men" (III.iv.20–21) who treat the Queen's proclamation as an invitation to unbridled self-indulgence. When Criticus takes his case to Arete (Virtue), a member of the Queen's inner circle, she advises him to

> Thinke on some sweet, and choice invention, now,
> Worthie her serious, and illustrous eyes,
> That from the merit of it we may take
> Desir'd occasion to preferre your worth.

In other words, he is to write a masque, and shortly thereafter, Arete commissions Criticus to prepare one for Cynthia's Revels. When Cynthia finally appears, accompanied by the stately measures of "Queen and Huntress, Chaste and Fair," Criticus's triumph is assured: upon the performance of this, the first of his court masques, the impecunious young poet immediately joins the Queen's personal entourage. Dekker flatly accused the author of writing himself into the part, and Jonson, whose strategy was identical to that of his hero, never denied the accusation. Indeed, he had the printer publish a separate sheet inscribed with the author's *envoi* "To CYNTHIAS fayrest *Nymph*," Lady Bedford, the living counterpart of Arete. Another inset leaf, bearing the inscription "Alumnus olim, aeternum Amicus," went to William Camden, who had become King at Arms at the College of Heralds just three years earlier.[10]

There were flaws in Jonson's strategy, and these are apparent even on the fantasy level of *Cynthia's Revels*. He clung to the fiction of an altruistic patroness who was indifferent to the allure of wealth and fashion, but the man who had spent his formative years in the royal city of Westminster knew perfectly well that anyone of consequence in Elizabeth I's court was adept in extravagant self-display. Jonson's Prologue declares that the play "affoords / Words, above action: matter, above words," and Criticus maintains this antitheatrical stance throughout: as a plain-living scholar he regards the courtiers' preoccupation with visual effects—mirrors, cosmetics, gestures, articles of clothing—with utter revulsion; but *Cynthia's Revels* is itself a richly theatrical work of art. Moreover, the court masque, at which that "fine dancing dame" Lady Bedford excelled, was the most spectacular pastime of them all. The contradiction between Criticus's reformist stance and his desire to be employed as a court entertainer seriously undercuts his fantasy of self-improvement: the same fops and buffoons who arouse his disgust throughout the play return in act V to perform his own masque before Cynthia. If the typical masquer is a sybaritic and conceited fop, it hardly makes sense for Criticus (or Jonson) to want to write masques; nor, finally, does Cynthia intend that he should do so. At the end of the play the Queen gives Criticus and Arete the job of correcting the morals of her court: "To you two / We give the charge; impose what paines you please: / Th' incurable cut off, the rest reforme." [11]

Jonson's chances of obtaining such a post were exceedingly remote. To appreciate just how precarious his standing at court actually was, one need only consider the fate of *Cynthia's Revels*. The Master of the Revels apparently decided that the Queen would like the play, and it seems to have been performed at court on Twelfth Night of 1601. But there is good reason to believe that the court audience disliked Jonson's comedy. In the second act of *Cynthia's Revels*, Criticus's page Mercury declares that "pride, and ignorance" are "two essentiall parts of the courtier." A year later a character in Dekker's *Satiromastix* mocked Horace (Jonson) "because thy sputtering chappes yelpe, that Arrogance, and Impudence, and Ignoraunce, are the essentiall parts of a courtier." At the conclusion of Dekker's play Horace is made to swear that "when your Playes are misselikt at Court, you shall not cry Mew like a Pusse-cat, and say you are glad you write out of the Courtiers Element." [12]

The motto on the title page of *Cynthia's Revels*, which also appears on the 1601 quarto of *Every Man in His Humour,* is yet another indication that the play had failed to win Jonson any supporters at court: "Quod non dant Proceres, dabit Histrio. / Haud tamen invideas vati, quem pulpita pascunt." ("The actor will provide what the nobles are unwilling to give; Yet you should not scorn the poet whom the stage feeds"). Jonson took his motto from lines 90 and 93 of Juvenal's seventh satire, where the satirist complains that the failure of the Roman nobility to support poetry has forced writers to depend on actors. "You can get from a stage-player what no great man will give you: why frequent the spacious ante-chambers of the Camerini or of Barea?" The performances at Blackfriars and the court looked as if they might offer a way out of this dilemma, for they brought the poet face to face with the very class of persons whose neglect had compelled him to write for the stage. But Jonson's hopes proved ill-founded. Despite the efforts he had mounted during the previous two years, he too had failed to break his dependence on the actors.

The performances and quartos of 1599–1601 transformed Jonson into a public figure, but the status of this figure remained very much in doubt. Dekker's allegation that his plays were "misse-likt at court" suggests that Jonson had failed to win friends there; moreover, he had made at least one new enemy. Early in 1601, John Marston decided that Jonson's pretensions deserved to be ridiculed in public.

It is hard to say who struck the first blow in the quarrel between Marston and Jonson.[13] According to Drummond, Jonson "had many quarrells with Marston . . . the beginning of them were that Marston represented him in the stage." It is true that Marston's *Histriomastix* (1599) depicts the career of one Chrisoganous, a high-minded and scholarly dramatist who aspires "to feed the hearings of judiciall ears," and the resemblances between this character and Jonson are plain enough. But Marston presents Chrisoganous in a highly favorable light, so *Histriomastix* hardly affords the basis for a quarrel. Jonson, however, did take an audible smack at Marston when he took a number of esoteric words from the latter's published works and put them in the mouth of a foolish character in *Every Man out of His Humour* who roundly declares that

> whereas the *Ingenuitie* of the time, and the soules *Synderisis* are but *Embrions* in nature, added to the panch of *Esquiline,* and the *Inter-vallum* of the *Zodiack,* besides the *Eclipticke line* being *opticke,* and not *mentall,* but by the *contemplative & theoricke* part thereof, doth demonstrate to us the *vegetable circumference,* and the *ventositie* of the *Tropicks,* and whereas our *intellectuall,* or *mincing capreall* (according to the *Metaphisicks*) as you may reade in PLATO's *Histriomastix* . . .

Marston actually employed this vocabulary (synderisis, panch of esquiline, eclipticke, and mincing capreall have all been traced to his published work), so he is undoubtedly the object of Jonson's ridicule.[14]

Why did Jonson have at Marston? Anyone who resorts to barbarisms like the ones cited above could be said to invite mockery, but the stylistic issues raised by Marston's fustian had a special import for Jonson. Marston, despite his contentions to the contrary, employed the coarse and bombastic diction associated with the "harsh" satirists of antiquity: Lucilius, Persius, and Juvenal. On the title page of *Every Man Out,* Jonson had already declared his allegiance to Horace, who had championed the opposing ideal of urbanity and simplicity. His parody of Marston was a bit of one-upmanship about the proper style of satire: Jonson was playing Horace to Marston's Lucilius, and notifying his rival that he was the better satirist of the two.

Jonson had now given Marston at least one reason to go on the attack, and other motives gradually came into play as well. At some point in this imbroglio, Jonson "beat" Marston and "took his Pistol from him." He also wrote three satirical epigrams on Marston, whom he dubbed "Playwright"; if, as is likely, these were circulating in manuscript, they must have aggravated the tension between the two men. In *Satiromastix* Dekker accuses Jonson of composing "bitter Epigrams" on his enemies and circulating them "amongst the gallants in severall coppies." One of these epigrams openly taunts Marston on his thrashing at the hands of Jonson:

> PLAY-WRIGHT convict of publike wrongs to men,
>> Takes private beatings, and begins againe.
> Two kindes of valour he doth shew, at ones;
>> Active in's braine, and passive in his bones.

Finally, Marston regarded the character of Hedon, the "light voluptuous reveller" who prances his way through *Cynthia's Revels,* as a satire upon himself. This last grievance looks trivial at first, but it lies, as David Kay has shown, at the heart of the quarrel between Jonson and Marston.[15]

Both *Every Man out of His Humour* and *Cynthia's Revels* insist upon a fundamental opposition between the penurious scholar and the well-heeled gallant, and both plays depict the scholar's unequivocal triumph over the courtier. When Jonson's plays were "misse-likt at Court," he asserted that he wrote "out of the Courtier's Element." Marston, the scion of landed gentry and something of a reveler in his own right, would have found these sneers offensive. There was, moreover, the related question of whether or not scholar-satirists like Asper and Criticus really belonged in private theaters that were intended to provide entertainment for gentlemen of leisure. Marston's answer to that question is pretty well implied by the title of *What You Will,* his counterblast to Jonson, which one of the children's companies performed early in 1601. Marston's Induction, which in other respects parallels the Induction to *Every Man out of His Humour,* stresses at the outset that pleasure is prior to "rules of art," and the play that follows upholds the ideal of the courtly amateur.

The resemblances between Lampatho Doria, the butt of Marston's ridicule, and Jonson's public spokesmen, Asper/Macilente and Criticus, are too close to be merely coincidental. Lampatho's name conveys the story of his life. "Lampe," his nickname, connotes bookishness; "dor" was an all-purpose word for inept fools. In *Cynthia's Revels,* the learned Criticus gives the dor to the would-be courtier Amorphous; in *What You Will,* the gallant Quadratus gives the dor to Lampatho Doria, the bookish fool. Like Asper/Macilente, Criticus, and Ben Jonson, "Lampe" has led the life of a poor scholar engrossed in "*Aquinas, Scotus,* and the musty *sawe* Of anticke *Donate,*" but it all comes to naught: "I fell a railing, but now soft and slow, / I know, I know naught, but naught do know." Like Jonson, Lampe tries to court a great lady in verse, but his clownish attempts at love poetry only confirm that he is "a meere Scholler, that is a mere sot." When the Duke finally asks, "What sport for night?" Lampe replies, "A Commedy, intitled *Temperance.*" But the Duke, a thoroughgoing voluptuary, has no patience with the kind of philosophical comedy that had appealed to the austere Cynthia: "What sot elects that subject for the Court / What should dame Temperance do heere? away!"[16]

Marston directed his fire at Jonson's self-image, and his criticism was straightforward enough. Jonson had used the figure of the scholar-satirist to mount an attack on the courtly amateurs; Marston thought that he had gone too far and repaid him in kind. In the early months of 1601, when Jonson was mulling over his response to *What You Will,* he learned that he had another enemy to contend with as well. Dekker had now begun writing *Satiromastix,* which would be performed by both the Children of St. Paul's Cathedral and the Lord Chamberlain's Men early in the following autumn. Dekker and the adult actors had their own motives for attacking Jonson. *The Isle of Dogs* and the killing of Gabriel Spencer still rankled with Dekker; and the sneers at "popular applause" and "fomie praise, that drops from common jawes" in the Prologue (13–14) to *Cynthia's Revels* did not win Jonson any friends among the Lord Chamberlain's Men. He put a further strain on his relationship with the adult actors when he revised *The Case Is Altered* for the children. The refurbished text of his early comedy features a prolonged and gratuitous lampoon of Anthony Munday (wryly dubbed "Antonio Balladino"), a prominent playwright for the Admiral's Men, and heaps scorn on the "rude barbarous crue" who frequent "the common *Theaters*" (II.vii.68, 40).

In *Poetaster,* completed well in advance of *Satiromastix,* Jonson took up a complex set of professional rivalries. He wanted both to resolve the quarrel with Marston to his own advantage and to settle his accounts with Dekker in advance (he wrote the play in fifteen weeks). In keeping with these dual objectives, he devised a plot that has two distinct lines of action. Acts I, II, and IV tell the story of Ovid's love affair with Julia, the daughter of Caesar Augustus, and its unhappy denouement; acts III and V focus upon the complementary figure of Horace, together with his friends, enemies, and patrons.

The Ovidian material supplied Jonson with the case history of a courtly poet who falls from grace and thus harked back to the conflict between courtier and satirist that looms so large in *Every Man Out, Cynthia's Revels,* and Marston's *What You Will.* But Jonson also took the opportunity to qualify his previous criticisms of the courtier poets. If Ovid must endure the penalty of banishment, his companions Tibullus and Propertius, who dance to the same tune as he, remain admirable figures. Even after Ovid's disgrace, Horace says that his offense was nothing more than "innocent mirth, / And harmelesse pleasures, bred, of noble wit." Ovid goes astray when he and the Emperor's daughter Julia become involved with a circle of sleazy urban social climbers that includes Albius the jeweler, his philandering wife Chloe, and the aspiring courtier Crispinus (alias John Marston). When Caesar discovers Ovid and his daughter slumming with these middle-class voluptuaries at one of their vulgar parties, the poet's doom is sealed. Jonson's snobbery does not inspire much confidence, but he did capture the atmosphere of Marston's milieu. A contemporary diarist and law student named John Manningham noted that Marston "daunct with Alderman Mores wives daughter, a Spaniard borne, fell into a strang commendacion of hir witt and beauty. When he had done, shee thought to pay him home, and told him shee though[t] he was a poet. ''Tis true,' said he, 'for poets faine, and lie, and soe did I when I commended your beauty, for you are exceeding foule.'" This incident occurred during the holiday season of 1600–1, just when Jonson was mulling over his portrayal of the poetaster.[17]

The banishment of Ovid portends a wholesale alteration of cultural values. In purely literary terms he is analogous to the elegiac poets and Petrarchan sonneteers who came to the fore in the early 1590s and were on the wane by 1600. On the social landscape of late Elizabethan England, his counterparts were men like Essex and Southampton, the courtly libertines who fell from grace in the year of Jonson's play. On the curve of Jonson's own development, the banishment of Ovid bore out his inclination to cultivate satire, comedy, epigram, and epistle (the classical genres of the plain style) and to put the mellifluous verse forms of the great Elizabethan poets behind him. In the "Proludium" that he wrote to preface his "Epode" of 1601 he pondered the value of the Ovidian elegy and found it wanting: "An elegie? no, muse; it askes a straine / to loose, and Cap'ring, for thy stricter veine" (*For,* 10.1–2).

Henceforth, Jonson would remain unstintingly loyal to Ovid's friendly rival Horace.

The Horatian material in *Poetaster* provides the case history of a satirist under attack and so looks ahead to the imminent blast from Demetrius (alias Thomas Dekker) and his allies. But since Dekker, the bad satirist, had yet to show his hand, he was harder to characterize than Marston. Jonson decided to focus instead upon the company he kept. Demetrius is hand in glove with Histrio, the player whose company has "hir'd him to abuse HORACE, and bring him in, in a play" (III.iv.323); with the philistine Captain Tucca, who scorns "*humours, revells,* and *satyres,* that girde, and fart at the time" (III.iv.190–191), but nevertheless offers to help prepare the lampoon; and with Lupus the Tribune, who is both a censorious urban magistrate and an unscrupulous informer.

Although Jonson did not know what Dekker had in store for him, he did have firsthand experience with the shady confraternity of hired informers, *agents provocateurs,* and government officials who lurked about the London theaters. In 1597 some such person had supplied the government with information which led officials to conclude that *The Isle of Dogs* was a play "contaninge very seditious and sclandrous matter." Jonson's conversion to Roman Catholicism doubtless deepened his antipathy to spies; since informers received the property of recusants whom they reported to the authorities, government spies were always on the lookout for Catholics. Horace's adversaries adopt essentially the same methods that Jonson's had employed some three and a half years previously. First, they inform upon Ovid; then, after Horace berates them for doing so, they break into his lodgings, discover an emblem that can be construed as injurious to Caesar, and take it to the emperor.

The fiasco of 1597 became, in Jonson's reimagining, an unmitigated triumph. He sets the stage by beginning the fifth act with two scenes showing Caesar to be an enthusiastic and discerning patron of writers. The Emperor welcomes the courtier poets, Gallus and Tibullus, together with the satirist Horace, to his court; he questions the three about Virgil; he listens to the great heroical poet recite a passage about Rumor from his *Aeneid.* This portrayal of the Augustan literary milieu closely follows the one given by Horace himself in his famous epistle to Augustus (*Epistles,* II.i). In the epistle Horace maintains that Roman poets should emulate the exalted civic poetry of Greece, and he sees himself, together with his friends Varro and Virgil, and their patrons Maecenas and Augustus, as ushering in the golden age of Roman letters. He repudiates overly crude writers, including Plautus, who write for the popular stage, and he praises Caesar for patronizing Virgil. The last act of *Poetaster* restates Horace's position, which had now become the ideal of Sir Philip Sidney and Ben Jonson.

The abrupt intrusion of Histrio, Tucca, Demetrius, and Crispinus, and their pathetic attempts to libel Horace by accusing him of libel, establish Horace's superiority by displaying the shabby opportunism of the players for all to see. When Caesar tells Horace to set the appropriate punishments for his adversaries, Jonson's fantasy of self-vindication is complete. He now holds the post of official moralist to the Imperial Court, just as Criticus had; his enemies (Marston, Dekker, and the players) are at his mercy, and he proceeds publicly to shame them.

In taking Horace for his model Jonson chose a poet whose life closely resembled his own. Horace's father was a freed slave; Jonson was a bricklayer's stepson. Both men received an education that set them apart from other members of their social class, and after completing their education, both served in the army for a brief period of time. Horace's poetry brought him into contact with important men; Jonson's "strange poems" had already brought him into contact with the Countesses of Bedford and Rutland. Jonson's early poems were "strange" because he was experimenting with two forms—the ode and the epistle—that were still unfamiliar to English readers; these were, however, Horace's favorite genres. Both men were the leading satirists of their era. In the Induction to *Every Man out of His Humour,* Jonson had already surveyed Horace's development, which evolved from harsh invective to genial commentary on contemporary mores. Jonson had not yet found his Maecenas or obtained the material rewards that enabled his Roman counterpart to lead a life of relative ease, but Horace had shown the way.[18]

The choice of Horace's genres over Ovid's was a significant step for Jonson. *The Underwood,* a collection of his verse that remained unpublished until after his death, includes a number of amatory poems that have never been convincingly dated. Several are elegies, and four (*Und,* 38–41) resemble Donne's elegies so closely that scholars have questioned Jonson's authorship of them (*Und,* 39, is now assigned to Donne or alternatively Roe). The similarity of these poems supports the hypothesis that the two men exchanged poems in manuscript, and since the "Proludium" and *The Poetaster* both indicate that Jonson decided to renounce the elegy around the turn of the century, he may well have written these poems before then. Although Jonson would write elegies in the future, he nonetheless remained true to his public stance and kept them out of print during his own lifetime.

The Horatian career pattern limited Jonson's choices in another respect as well. Horace expressly declined to write heroic poetry, and he repeatedly disclaimed any interest in the high style associated with the so-called greater genres of epic and tragedy. If Jonson proposed to follow in his master's footsteps, he too would have to confine himself to satire (broadly interpreted to include stage comedy), epistle, epigram, and ode. Horace confronted the implications of his own choice in a verse form called the *recusatio* ("refusal"). A *recusatio* evokes the style and content of a poem the author refuses to write. At the beginning of the sixth ode in book I, for example, Horace tells Agrippa that he will be "heralded by Varius, a poet of Homeric flight," rather than by Horace: "No such deeds, Agrippa, do I essay to sing nor the fell anger of Peleus' son, who knew not how to yield, nor the wanderings o'er the sea of the crafty Ulysses, nor the cruel house of Pelops." By the time Horace has completed his little pastiche of epic conventions, the ode is essentially finished. The *recusatio* is a deeply paradoxical genre. Because the centerpiece of these poems is always a sample of the genre that Horace disavows, he gives the reader the impression that he really could write (for example) epic verse if he chose to. He disclaims any interest in it, yet he finds it attractive; he sees through Varius's box of tricks, yet he deftly weaves them into his own poem; he declares that he is not competing with his rival, yet he clearly feels the need to do so. In the end, he wins the competition by withdrawing from the contest just before it begins in earnest.[19]

Jonson had already begun to experiment with the *recusatio* by 1601. The "Proludium" (*For,* 10) that he sent to Sir John Salusbury announces that he will not write elegiac poetry ("An elegie? no, muse; it askes a straine / to loose, and Cap'ring, for thy stricter veine") and then tantalizes the reader with a dozen lines of splendid elegiac verse. This paradoxical combination of disclaimer and imitation crops up repeatedly in *Poetaster.* Jonson disavows Ovid, yet he retells the story of Ovid and Julia in the lovers' own words. The two lovers part in a balcony scene strongly reminiscent of *Romeo and Juliet*—again, Jonson lays claim to the very model he is repudiating. In the last act, he brings Virgil on stage, has him recite forty-two lines of the *Aeneid* in Ben Jonson's new English translation, and then abruptly halts the recital. Having briefly displayed his mastery of the high style, Jonson brings his real hero, Horace, back to the center stage. The whole performance is a staged *recusatio.* Jonson hints that he could write in the style of Ovid, or Shakespeare, or Virgil, if he felt inclined to do so; but he does not.

His attempt to create the impression that he really was (as the playwright Henry Chettle wrote in 1603) "the English Horace," while Dekker and Marston were mere hacks, was so successful that one tends to overlook the basic similarities between the poet and the poetasters. Just eighteen months before, Jonson had collaborated with Dekker on *Page of Plymouth* and *Robert II, King of Scots.* Both men lived in the parish of St. Giles, Cripplegate, both had served in the Low Countries during the early 1590s, and both had recently been imprisoned. Jonson and Marston had so much in common that an informed observer, looking at the two men in 1601, might have supposed they were mirror images. They were the two prominent figures in the satirical movement of the late 1590s; they both set out to free satire from "those strict and regular formes, which the nicenesse of a few (who are nothing but forme) would thrust upon us," and they both agreed with Horace that the satirist was, nevertheless, obliged to preserve a measure of decorum. They both embraced stoicism; they both wrote for Henslowe; they both contributed poems to Chester's *Love's Martyr*. They borrowed liberally from one another's works. Finally, Marston seems to have intended *Histriomastix,* the play that lurks at the origin of the *poetomachia,* as an expression of solidarity between himself and Jonson.[20]

A contemporary observer would also have surmised that two men who resembled one another so closely were bound to quarrel. The Elizabethan theory of social order rested on the assumption that two individuals will behave peaceably if—and only if—they can assign each other to a graduated social hierarchy. Bacon opens "Of Seditions and Troubles" with the caution that "tempests in state . . . are commonly greatest when things grow to equality; as natural tempests are greater about the *Equinoctia.*" Shakespeare states the thesis even more concisely in the famous oration on degree in *Troilus and Cressida:* "Take but degree away, untune that string, / And hark what discord follows." As Jonson himself would later observe,

> the peacefull *gods*
> In number, always, love the oddes;
> And even parts as much despise,
> Since out of them all discords rise.

Anthropologists have observed variations of this paradigm in a wide variety of cultural settings. René Girard has argued that this crisis of "No Difference," as he calls it, is fundamental to the creation of social hierarchies. Like the mythological "enemy twins," men who are identical to one another fight in order to establish the differences that can serve as the basis of a new social order.[21]

Girard's theory is applicable to Jonson's life, particularly in light of what rapidly became a remarkable history of violent quarrels. Consider, by way of illustration, a hypothetical reconstruction of that history. The first of the quarrels occurred between Jonson and the anonymous "Enemie" whom he slew in his late teens. Prior to this encounter he and the Spanish infantryman were two common soldiers, the humble prototypes of Old Hamlet and Old Fortinbras; afterward Jonson bore away *opima spolia,* the token of his superior virility, as if he were Roman valor personified. The second killing came in the autumn of 1597, around the outset of his literary career. He and Gabriel Spencer had been fellow actors for about two years. They toured the provinces together in 1595–96, they performed at the Swan in the spring of 1597, they both went to Marshalsea in the summer of that year, and they both worked for Henslowe later in 1597–98. On September 22, 1598, Jonson encountered his old colleague at precisely the moment when he was trying to establish a new and different identity as a man of letters; the two men quarreled violently and Spencer, the actor, fell at the hands of Jonson, the poet-in-the-making. Later in his career he would characterize this encounter as a duel, an initiation rite that confirmed his status as a gentleman.

In 1599 he found a new enemy twin in the person of John Marston, the other leading satirist of the day. In the hopes of forging an alliance, Marston publicly complimented Jonson in *Histriomastix;* Jonson responded by publishing a burlesque of Marston's diction, and the quarrel was underway. At some point in the course of it, he again resorted to physical violence, beating Marston and taking his pistol from him. Luckily for Marston, however, Jonson now bore a felon's brand; instead of killing his enemy he sublimated his aggressive energies in his art, just as he had done in his three earlier comedies. *Poetaster* appropriates the *opima spolia* of classical satire while leaving Marston himself unharmed. Three years later the two men would be friends again.

Nevertheless, the aggressive thrust of Jonson's satire came to the attention of the authorities, just as it had in 1597. An informant complained to Chief Justice Popham about *Poetaster,* and Jonson again faced the prospect of corporal punishment in the earlier part of 1601. But Richard Martin, the lawyer, interceded on his behalf, and Jonson emerged unscathed (HS, IV, 201).

Dekker, however, was still to be heard from. Jonson's second antagonist now found himself in the strategically desirable position of the wounded party. Although he subsequently acknowledged that "*the more noble* Reprehension" would have focused on "*his* mindes Deformity," he leveled his fire at Jonson's "*fortunes, and condition of life,*" excusing himself on the grounds that his enemy had done likewise.[22] Dekker saw precisely where his adversary was vulnerable. Jonson had laboriously created a personal myth that set him above his rivals; Dekker countered that the real Ben Jonson was a sleazy hack who in no way corresponded to Horace, his ideal self-image.

Jonson had self-consciously upheld the dignity of the poet's profession. His contention that the poet's function was to serve the Prince and commonwealth lay at the heart of his quarrel with the courtly amateurs, who saw poetry as one of several accomplishments that made up a complete gentleman; it marks the one point at which he diverged significantly from Sidney and Puttenham, who upheld the ideal of the "courtly makers,"

Wyatt and Surrey. Dekker put his adversary back into the prosaic world of the workaday commercial writer, and thus stood Jonson's ideal on its head. In the opening act of *Satiromastix; or, The Untrussing of the Humorous Poet* (1601), Horace appears *"sitting in a study behinde a Curtaine, a candle by him burning, bookes lying confusedly,"* immersed in the grubby round of commissions that bring in his meager livelihood. Dekker, who had acquired a copy of Jonson's ode to James, Earl of Desmond, depicts the priest of Apollo in the throes of meeting a deadline:

> O me thy Priest inspire.
> For I to thee and thine immortall name,
> In—in—in golden tunes,
> For I to thee and thine immortall name—
> In—sacred raptures flowing, flowing, swimming, swimming:
> In sacred raptures swimming,
> Immortal name, game, dame, tame, lame, lame, lame.

In many of his early poems (such as the Desmond ode, "And Must I Sing?" the "Epode," the Epistle to Lady Rutland) Jonson depicts himself as a man rapt with the love of truth; in Dekker's lampoon he exhibits the matter-of-fact professionalism of a thoroughly commercial artist. He writes "in a most goodly big hand"; he has prefabricated acrostics and odes among his wares; he peddles love letters; and he furnishes poesies for rings, knives, and handkerchiefs to his gallant, but illiterate, companion Asinus Bubo. He has even devised a system of form letters for communicating with admirers and prospective patrons. Horace will write anything for money: for two shillings he turns out a love letter for the inarticulate Welshman Sir Rees ap Vaughan; when Sir Rees's bald rival Sir Adam Prickshaft gets the upper hand, Horace obligingly supplies his hirsute patron with an oration in praise of hair. Jonson's epigram "To Fine Grand" suggests that Dekker's caricature contained some measure of truth. The epigram is an invoice demanding that Fine Grand pay Jonson for services rendered:

> *In-primis,* GRAND, you owe me for a iest,
>   I lent you, on meere acquaintance, at a feast.
> *Item,* a tale or two, some fortnight after;
>   That yet maintaynes you, and your house in laughter.
> *Item,* the *babylonian* song you sing;
>   *Item,* a faire *greeke* poesie for a ring:
> With which a learned *Madame* you belye.
>   *Item,* a charme surrounding fearefully
> Your *partie-per-pale* picture, one halfe drawne
>   In solemn cypres, the other cob-web-lawne.

> *Item,* a gulling *imprese* for you, at tilt.
>> *Item,* your mistris *anagram,* i' your hilt.
> *Item,* your owne, sew'd in your mistris smock.
>> *Item,* an *epitaph* on my lords cock,
> In most vile verse, and cost me more paine,
>> Then had I made 'hem good, to fit your vaine.

The speaker in Jonson's epigrams is of course a literary artifact, but he frequently bears a strong resemblance to the author himself—witness "To Playwright." The difference between Dekker's lampoon and Jonson's self-caricature is largely a matter of tone. The butt of *Satiromastix* fawns on his patron; Jonson calls Fine Grand to a reckoning: "Fortie things more, deare GRAND, which you know true, / For which, or pay me quickly', or Ile pay you."²³ Nevertheless, Jonson does insinuate that the creator of Asper, Criticus, and Horace had himself plied the trade of a poetaster.

The hackwork that Horace executes for his employers is harmless enough. It is Horace's epigrams, satires, and lampoons that gall Crispinus and Demetrius, and they take it upon themselves to teach him a lesson. They taunt him with his beginnings as a failed actor and suggest (plausibly enough) that he turned to satire because he needed an outlet for his aggressiveness: "Art not famous enough yet, my mad *Horastratus,* for killing a Player, but thou must eate men alive?" (IV.ii.61–62). They put him in the category of jesters, like Carlo Buffone, who cadge free meals at taverns by relating unsavory stories about their friends. Horace's final humiliation comes in act V, when Demetrius and Crispinus take their erstwhile tormentor to court attired as a satyr. Needless to say, Dekker's ideal court is very different from the ones that Jonson had portrayed in *Cynthia's Revels* and *Poetaster.* King William Rufus, the waggish monarch in *Satiromastix,* is a jaded womanizer who readily agrees when his courtier Crispinus proposes that they flay the satyr of his shaggy skin. Slight though it is, Dekker's ending reasserts the courtier's superiority to the satirist and so counters the main drift of Jonson's comical satires. He was reiterating, in a nastier way, the message of *What You Will.*

At the climax of his ordeal, Horace gazes into a portrait of his Roman namesake and listens while his enemies mercilessly rehearse the differences between the fake Horace and the real one:

> Thou hast such a terrible mouth, that thy beard's afraide to peepe out: but looke, heere you staring Leviathan, heere's the sweete visage of *Horace* ... *Horace* did not skrue and wriggle himself into great Mens familiarity, (impudentlie) as thou doost ... *Horace* had not his face puncht full of Oyletholes, like the cover of a warming pan: *Horace* lov'd Poets well, and gave Coxcombes to none but fooles; but thou lov'st none, neither Wisemen nor fooles, but thy selfe: *Horace* was a goodly Corpulent Gentleman, and not so leane a hollow-cheekt Scrag as thou art. (V.ii.250–263)

‹ 82 ›

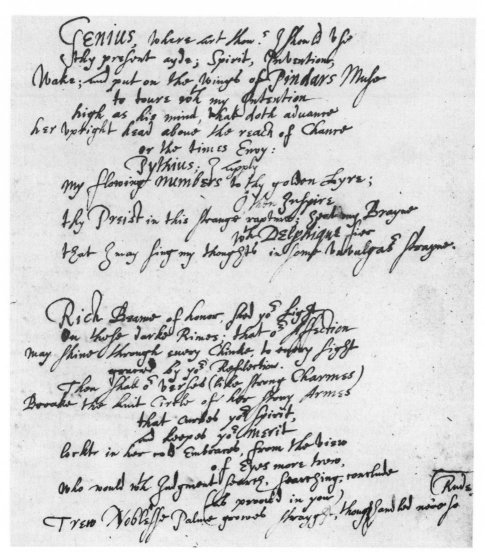

Autograph manuscript of Jonson's "Ode to the Earl of Desmond," ca. 1600, ll. 1–23. Dekker alleged that Jonson wrote his verses "in a most goodly big hand" so that his patrons would find them easy to read.

Most of the other items Dekker singled out for mockery—Jonson's bricklaying, acting, travails over *The Isle of Dogs*, conviction for murder, poverty, and prickly self-esteem—can be corroborated from other sources; there was doubtless some truth in this ugly caricature as well. How else could it have raised a laugh? Jonson had identified with Horace in order to differentiate himself from Dekker and Marston; Dekker stressed the differences between Horace and the historical Ben Jonson. He scored a number of palpable hits. Despite the brilliance with which he conducted his side of the quarrel, Jonson failed to win a clear-cut victory. He had defined a role for himself, but his ability to fill that role was still open to question.

The Cambridge undergraduates who wrote *The Return from Parnassus, Part II* (1601–2), a burlesque of current theatrical gossip, were under the impression that Shakespeare had launched a counteroffensive against his younger rival. At one point in the play, Will Kemp, a leading actor in the Lord Chamberlain's Men, remarks that "our fellow *Shakespeare*" has given Jonson "a purge that made him beray his credit" (HS, XI, 364). No one has ever explained what "Kemp" was talking about, but since Shakespeare was working on *Twelfth Night; or, What You Will* during the latter part of 1601, if there was a "purge" it is presumably to be found in that play. Marston had inaugurated the Poet's Quarrel with *What You Will*, the first play to lampoon Jonson in public. Later that year, the title of *Twelfth Night; or, What You Will*—apart from *Henry VIII* no other play by Shakespeare has an alternative title—invited theatergoers to associate *Twelfth Night* with *What You Will*.

The ones who registered the association would have noticed that both plays were based on a popular Italian comedy called *The Deceived*—Manningham recognized that this was the source for *Twelfth Night*—and that all three told a similar story. In the main plot, a noble suitor pursues a reluctant gentlewoman; in the subplot, a crew of courtly mischief makers play practical jokes on a graceless social climber who tries to compete with the Duke for the gentlewoman's affections. Marston assigned the latter role to Lampatho Doria, alias Ben Jonson; Shakespeare gave it to Malvolio, a surly ill-wisher who has a number of traits in common with the twenty-nine-year-old Ben Jonson. He is too thin-skinned to endure a little harmless raillery ("To be generous, guiltless and of free disposition, is to take those things for bird-bolts that you deem cannon-bullets"); he courts a noble lady in the hope that she will magically transport him out of the middle-class world to which he properly belongs; he has read Pythagoras, but thinks "nobly of the soul" and does not believe that "the soul of our grandam might happily inhabit a bird"; he uses the word "element" in an affected manner ("you are idle shallow things; I am not of your element"); he has been "made the most notorious geck and gull / That e'er invention play'd on." Only a coterie audience could have appreciated jokes of this kind, and *Twelfth Night* is the only play by Shakespeare known to have had such an audience. The Middle Temple, which had recently readmitted John Marston to its ranks, commissioned a special performance of *Twelfth Night; or, What You Will* in their Great Hall on February 2, 1602.[24] By this time, however, Jonson was discovering a new role for himself, and a new use for his talent.

• CHAPTER FIVE •

Early Tragedies

Jonson's family suffered a dreadful series of calamities between his twenty-ninth and thirty-first birthdays. Although it is impossible to say precisely when the first blow fell, there is reason to believe that Anne Jonson gave birth to their first daughter, Mary, early in 1601 and lost her later that year.

The sole source of information about Mary Jonson is the epitaph "On My First Daughter" that her father wrote on the occasion of her death "at six moneths end." Brief though it is, the poem enables us to form some notion of this girl's fleeting existence. Since "On My First Daughter" is an exercise in Mariolatry, it can be dated after Jonson's conversion to Catholicism in October 1598. The first child that the Jonsons conceived after his conversion was Joseph, who was born early in December 1599. Joseph was baptized in an Anglican church, but no record of Mary's christening has survived; perhaps her parents had a Catholic priest administer the rite in secret. In any event, the interval between the arrival of their second and third children had to be relatively brief. According to the epitaph, Mary was "the daughter of their youth." Ben and Anne Jonson had separated from one another by the winter of 1602–3, and they remained apart for at least a year, and probably for several years.[1] The "youth" of their marriage was over by that time; the "daughter of their youth" had come and gone; and her bereaved father, who passed his thirtieth birthday in 1602, had begun to feel the ache of mortality.

This sequence of events helps explain an extremely puzzling change in Jonson's professional life. In the autumn of 1601 he abruptly set the mask of Horace aside and turned his attention to tragedy, the genre he had abandoned two years previously. On September 25 Henslowe paid him an advance of two pounds for "adicians in geronimo" (additions to Kyd's *Spanish Tragedy*). He completed this work by June 22, 1602, when Henslowe paid him the extraordinary sum of ten pounds to write a tragedy called *Richard Crookback*. At about the same time he was composing an "Apologetical Dialogue" for the 1602 quarto of *Poetaster*. The "Apologetical Dialogue" is essentially a reprise of the Poet's Quarrel, a final attempt to assert Jonson's innocence of the "*sundry impotent libells*" that had recently been directed at him. In his concluding speech, however, the "Author" suddenly declares that he "will trie / If *Tragoedie* have a more kind aspect. / Her favours in my next I will pursue." This is not merely a professional issue for him; on the contrary, a vision of tragedy has been welling up in his soul:

> There's something come into my thought,
> That must, and shall be sung, high, and aloofe,
> Safe from the wolves black jaw, and the dull asses hoofe.[2]

Up until now Jonson had kept all of his tragic verse out of print, apart from three unplaced passages that appeared in Allot's *England's Parnassus*. In 1602, however, Thomas Pavier offered the reading public *The Spanish Tragedy . . . Newly Corrected, Amended, and Enlarged with New Additions of the Painter's Part, and Others, As It Hath of Late Been Divers Times Acted*. The notion that Jonson actually wrote these "new additions" has not sat comfortably with modern scholars, and much evidence has been marshaled to show that he did not do so. But the arguments against Jonson's authorship are not compelling, and Anne Barton has recently offered a persuasive defense of Jonson's claim to them. All of the passages added to Kyd's text focus on the allied themes of premature death and parental bereavement, and these were subjects close to Jonson's heart. The remarkable story of Queen Elizabeth's maid of honor Margaret Radcliffe, who lost four of her brothers within a period of months and then ended her "maiden modest dayes" by starving herself to death in the autumn of 1599, had already inspired his earliest datable poem. When he decided to revise *The Spanish Tragedy*, Barton argues, Jonson seized upon the opportunity to explore the psychology of parental grief: he selected five moments when Kyd's protagonist Hieronimo bemoans the untimely death of his son Horatio, and these were the "adicians in geronimo" that appeared in the Pavier quarto.[3] And they were only the beginning: the next two years of Jonson's life are replete with dead children. He would compose at least two more poems about them; he would undertake two tragedies in which they assume prominent roles; and he would encounter one of them in a nocturnal vision. Although he declines to say what it is that has "come into my thought" at the close of the "Apologetical Dialogue," he leaves a conspicuous trail of evidence, and all of it leads back to the figure of a dead child.

This flood of empathy requires some explanation. Jonson lived in an age when infant mortality was extremely common and seldom remarked upon. A parent who knows that his child will probably die before reaching maturity may well be reluctant to form a strong attachment. Jonson felt otherwise. His abiding preoccupation with boys and girls who perish in their youth becomes understandable when one recalls that his own child-hood—or at least the image of it that he carried in his adult mind—was an unhappy one. Like Dickens, he could identify with lost children because he too had known misfortune at an early age. But why did this latent empathy with the dead child stir his imagination during the autumn of 1601? The best available explanation is the death of Mary Jonson.

At about the same time, Dekker was reminding him of the per-formances in which "thou ranst mad for the death of Horatio" (HS, XI, 366). When Jonson decided to revise Kyd's play, the lines that had formerly evoked this florid display of grief lingered in his prodigious memory. Trying to improve upon them, however, was a formidable task. To judge from the taut, sententious passages entitled "Murder," "Peace," and "Gold" that appear over Jonson's name in *England's Parnassus,* his early tragic verse lacked the emotional range of Thomas Kyd's; but the lamentations of Hieronimo are what one Elizabethan actor would call "a part to tear a cat in," and Jonson's additions had to be pitched on the same emotional register. He could hardly expect to carry out Henslowe's com-mission without challenging Kyd on his own ground.

Jonson had been preoccupied with the issue of artistic rivalry during the earlier half of 1601. In *Poetaster* and the "Proludium" (*For,* 10) he had disclaimed any interest in either the high style of epic and tragedy or the middle style of the elegy, but couched his declinations in a form (the *re-cusatio*) that allowed him to try his hand at the very genres he was reject-ing. When he decided to write the additions, his latent wish to compete with the tragedians who wrote for the popular playhouses, and to appro-priate their techniques, came to the fore.

Hieronimo's defining trait, and the basis of his popularity with the Eliz-abethan audience, is his madness. As the bereaved father plunges into in-sanity, he rises to a kind of eerie lucidity; he is unable to stop talking, yet he achieves a stunning economy of phrase. In his effort to duplicate this effect Jonson created a Hieronimo who is even crazier than the hero of the original version. Kyd lets the protagonist's insanity develop gradually;

Jonson has him go stark raving mad the moment he discovers his son's body. Kyd's Hieronimo craftily conceals his knowledge of the murderer's identity until he is in a position to act upon it; Jonson's Hieronimo confronts him at the earliest possible moment. In the Third Addition Hieronimo's plight suddenly takes on an uncanny resemblance to Jonson's personal situation. For no apparent reason Jonson's Hieronimo lists all the disadvantages of having an unwanted son and contrasts this hypothetical boy to the beloved child he has lost: "What is there yet in a son? He must be fed, / Be taught to go, and speak."[4] Kyd's text offers no basis for this tirade, but it is relevant to Jonson's own circumstances. He had two sons: Ben, who was now five years old, and Joseph, the two-year-old boy whom he had sired at the behest of the Catholic Church, and who had to be "fed / Be taught to go, and speak" while his impoverished father was writing these very lines.

In the Painter's Scene, his *pièce de résistance,* Jonson altered the time and space of Kyd's play and displayed his mastery of the earlier playwright's representational medium. Prior to the "additions" Jonson had adhered to the classical unities of time and space: the action of his plays always occurs within the twelve-hour day and man-made space prescribed by neoclassical theorists. The Painter's Scene, however, takes place at night (Kyd had set it in the daytime) in the arbor where Hieronimo's son was murdered. Jonson's Hieronimo immediately insists that this time and this place must bear the responsibility for his son's death. He blames the moon for not shining on the night of Horatio's death; he rails against the tree that

> grew, and grew, and bore and bore,
> Till at the length
> It grew a gallows, and did bear our son.
> It bore thy fruit and mine: O wicked, wicked plant.   (68–71)

Although this section of the Painter's Scene occupies just fifty-four lines, it utilizes dramaturgical effects that Jonson had never employed before. Like Kyd and Shakespeare, he was invoking the great analogy between the human microcosm and the natural macrocosm. At the same time Hieronimo's madness allowed Jonson to withhold judgment on the validity of that analogy. A rational man might not blame his son's misfortune on the moon or the trees, but a madman could seize upon these discarded images and infuse them with meaning.

Jonson was not content merely to take over Kyd's techniques; he also wanted to demonstrate his superiority to his predecessor. The latter part of the Painter's Scene was intended both to expand and to replace the analogous section of *The Spanish Tragedy.* In Kyd's version a second be-

reaved father beseeches Hieronimo, who is a judge, to bring *his* son's mur-
derers to justice. This second father is too distraught to speak, so he hands
Hieronimo a written petition, and Kyd's hero instantly perceives that his
silent, grieving double represents "the lively image of my grief" more truly
than his own words can ever do:

> If love's effects so strives in lesser things,
> If love enforce such moods in meaner wits,
> If love express such power in poor estates.
> . . . . .
> Then sham'st thou not, Hieronimo, to neglect
> The sweet revenge of thy Horatio?

Kyd's Hieronimo poses a question about representation: what expressive
medium most adequately renders the pain that accompanies the loss of a
child? By way of answer he alleges that the second father's visual representation of grief is superior to his own verbal one. His meditation on this
theme caught the attention of Shakespeare, whose Hamlet reiterates Hieronimo's point in the "rogue and peasant slave" soliloquy that occurs
immediately after the Player's Scene in *Hamlet* (1601). After watching the
First Player perform, Hamlet soliloquizes on the power of the tragedian's
acting and exclaims against his own verbosity: "Is it not monstrous that
this player here"—whose cause is nothing compared to his—has "Tears
in his eyes, distraction in his aspect / A broken voice" while Hamlet
"Must, like a whore, unpack my heart with words."[5] This scene would
also have lingered in Jonson's memory, for it occurs immediately after the
discussion of the Poet's Quarrel among Hamlet, Rosencrantz, and Guil-
denstern.

At the outset of the quarrel, in the Prologue to *Cynthia's Revels,* Jonson
had proclaimed that his own drama "affoords / Words, above action: matter, above words." In rewriting the encounter between the two fathers he
preserves the underlying question about representation, but his answer to
that question is diametrically opposed to the one given by Kyd and Shakespeare. Jonson turns the second father into a painter, a professional maker
of images. Despite the fact that the painter too has a murdered son, it
never occurs to Jonson's Hieronimo that the artist's inarticulate grief could
be the "lively image" of his own; instead, he repeatedly challenges his
double to produce an adequate *visual* representation of paternal grief:
"Draw me like old Priam of Troy, crying, 'The house is a-fire, the house
a-fire, as the torch over my head.' Make me curse, make me rave, make
me cry, make me mad, make me well again, make me curse hell, invocate
heaven, and in the end, leave me in a trance—and so forth." Jonson's
Hieronimo challenges the painter to depict "matter" without words, to

render scenes that could only be represented in language, and to execute commissions that could only be carried out by a poet.[6] Hieronimo's unacknowledged antagonists are the predecessor dramatists, Kyd and Shakespeare: Jonson was claiming that his "words" were superior to their "action."

On June 22, 1602, Henslowe paid him ten pounds "in earneste of a Boocke called Richard crockbacke & for new adicions for Ieronymo" (HS, XI, 308). The tragedy of King Richard III satisfied the criteria that were now uppermost in Jonson's mind. It included the most famous case of infanticide in English history, it featured a whole chorus of grieving parents, and it gave him an opportunity to imitate, and improve upon, Shakespeare's *Richard III*—just as Shakespeare had improved upon the work of his predecessor, the anonymous author of the *True Tragedy of Richard III*. Unlike the comedy of humors and the comical satires, Jonson's new project put a premium on imitation and competition rather than "strangeness" and originality. Ten pounds was an extraordinarily large advance for a new play, but Henslowe was acquiring a remarkable property. Jonson's *Richard III* promised to add an entirely new dimension both to the Poet's Quarrel and to the competition between the Admiral's Men and their rivals at the Globe.

Later that year, Pavier acquired the "additions" but declined to publish the author's name on the title page. This arrangement gave Jonson everything he wanted. On the one hand, he collected a pound or two from Pavier and put himself in a position to gauge the public response to his new work. On the other, he did not compromise the role of "Horace" that he had so painstakingly constructed during the previous three years, and he kept his personal tragedy safe from the wolf's black jaw and the dull ass's hoof. Or so he hoped. Marston inserted a parody of the Painter's Scene into the 1602 quarto of *Antonio and Mellida*, presumably because he knew, or suspected, that Jonson had written it. Marston had no discernible motive for attacking the anonymous master who has so often been credited with the "additions," but he did have a strong animus against Jonson and wanted to deny him the mantle of Kyd and Shakespeare.

Jonson's experience, no less than his writing, took on a somber cast during the months ahead. Salomon Pavy, a thirteen-year-old boy who had acted in *Cynthia's Revels* and *Poetaster*, died in July 1602, and Jonson commemorated his passing in his epitaph "Upon Sall Pavy, a Boy of 13 Years of Age and One of the Company of the Revels to Queen Elizabeth." Like many of the Chapel Children, Salomon Pavy had been kidnapped by Nathaniel Giles, the Queen's choirmaster, who forcibly abducted him into the company at the age of ten. The children and their parents had no legal redress—the boys were impressed on the authority of the Queen—and Jonson took an interest in their welfare. He told Drummond that Nathan Field, who had held a scholarship at St. Paul's when at the age of nine he was seized by Giles and his henchmen, "was his Schollar": "He had read to him the Satyres of Horace & some Epigrames of Martiall." Young Pavy, who had been "apprentice to one Peerce" when he was kidnapped, was not so well educated, and must have spent much of his tenth year learning to read and memorize long passages of dramatic dialogue. In the Induction to *Cynthia's Revels* Jonson has Pavy play the part of Sall, a mischievous, good-humored boy who prides himself on his newly acquired ability to read and pointedly addresses himself to the literate Blackfriars spectator "that hath hope to bee saved by his booke"—just as Jonson himself had once been saved.[7]

"Upon Sall Pavy" eulogizes a *puer senex* who spent his childhood pretending to be an adult. Jonson depicts his untimely death as a kind of cosmic joke: Sall played the parts of "Old men so Dulie" that "the Destinies thought hime to be one, / He faind so truely." This extravagant compliment disguises (even as it alludes to) the painful truth that hovers around the edges of this epitaph. Sall was old before his time; his life was a performance wherein he was doomed to play a part devised by cynical adults. When the destinies realize their mistake, they try to bring the boy back to life, but it is too late. Because Sall is "much too good for earth, / Heaven vowes to keepe him."[8] This form of consolation, which holds that it is better to die young since heaven is preferable to earth, crops up frequently in Jonson's funereal verse. Its recurrence suggests that he could only come to terms with death by rejecting life and that his piety was inextricably bound with his melancholy.

On February 12, 1603, Manningham heard from his friend Thomas Overbury that "Ben Johnson the poet now lives upon one Townesend, and scornes the world" (HS, I, 30; XI, 576). Manningham's "now" implies that this was still a fairly recent piece of gossip; in all likelihood Ben and Anne Jonson had separated within the previous few months.

The only firsthand account of why this marriage went awry occurs in the conversations with Drummond, where Jonson states that his wife "was a shrew yet honest" (*Conv*, 254). This summary judgment refers, however, to a later separation and does not take Anne's views into account. She had been married to her husband for eight years at the time of their first separation and had been a faithful ("honest") wife to him. When he converted to Roman Catholicism, she was obliged either to abstain from sex with her husband—a man of strong sexual appetites—or to bear more children. She bore two more children, even though Jonson could not adequately support them, and had probably seen one of them die by this time. In the meanwhile, her husband curried favor with two glamorous noblewomen and became totally preoccupied with his own work. In the "Apologetical Dialogue" of 1602 he describes himself as one who spends "halfe my nights, and all my dayes, / Here in a cell, to get a darke, pale face, / To come forth worth the ivy, or the bayes" (233–235). And his wife did not even have the consolation of knowing that her husband was worth the ivy or the bays: thus far, his compulsive work habits had made him into a public laughingstock. Small wonder if Anne grew shrill when her marriage became intolerable.

During the Poet's Quarrel both Marston and Dekker had intimated that Jonson was angling for the patronage of wealthy young men who were new to London and who sought out the company of the *literati*. Robert Townshend, Jonson's earliest identifiable patron, was just such a person. The younger son of a wealthy Norfolk squire, Townshend had matriculated at Hertford College, Oxford, in 1593, and entered Gray's Inn in 1599 at the age of nineteen. His history survives because he enjoyed the company of writers and made it his business to patronize them. Jonson later presented his "noble Freind" with an inscribed quarto of *Sejanus* (1605); John Fletcher would hail him as "the perfect Gentleman" in verses prefixed to *The Faithful Shepherdess*.[9]

Jonson did not remain with Townshend for long, however. In the spring of 1603 he departed from London, leaving his wife and children behind, and moved to Robert Cotton's country estate at Conington in Huntingdonshire. He told Drummond that he was residing there "when the King came in England, at that time the Pest was in London." This chronology is somewhat unclear. Queen Elizabeth died on March 24 and her successor, King James VI of Scotland, literally "came in England" on April 6, when he entered the border town of Berwick-upon-Tweed. But the "Pest," or bubonic plague, did not arrive in London until the beginning of May, just as James was completing his own journey to the capital. Either or both of these occurrences could easily have motivated Jonson's departure from London. Perhaps he set out for Conington at the end of March because he wanted to join forces with Cotton, who was intimately involved in the plans for the Jacobean succession; perhaps he foresaw the coming of the plague (as many Londoners did) and decided to leave the city before it arrived.[10]

Visitations of the plague in England were generally confined to congested urban areas, particularly London. Any city dweller who had access to a country house could be virtually certain of escaping the disease by vacating the town. The mortality bills for the great epidemic of 1665, to

Broadsheet of city dwellers fleeing from the plague, 1631.

cite an extreme case, list over 100,000 Londoners but do not include a single magistrate, courtier, or wealthy merchant. Members of the lower classes were forbidden to leave the city; they had no choice but to remain there and die.[11] During a major epidemic, like that of 1603, mortality rates could run higher than 50 percent in the crowded London parishes, such as St. Giles, Cripplegate, that lay adjacent to the city walls.

The journey to Conington opened up a chasm between Jonson and his family. But even though he left them behind, he had not put them out of his mind. Shortly after his arrival at Cotton's house "he saw in a vision his eldest sone (then a child and at London) appear unto him with the Marke of a bloodie crosse on his forehead as if it had been cutted with a sword." The seven-year-old boy "appeared to him he said of a Manlie shape." Jonson was dreaming about the plague. Whenever a member of an urban family contracted the disease, public officials locked the house, imposed a quarantine on everyone who lived there, and nailed a red cross to the door. A watchman was then instructed to make sure that no one left the premises until forty days after the last trace of infection.[12] In Jonson's dream the red cross (the "day residue" of Freudian dream analysis) was transposed from the door of the house in London onto the boy's forehead "as if it had been cutted with a sword." Jonson's "vision" occurred at the time of young Ben's seventh birthday, and this reminder of the boy's growing up helps account for his son's appearance in manly shape, the second striking feature of the dream. The child he had left behind had metamorphosed into a fully grown young man, old enough to take Jonson's place in the household he had abandoned.

Yet the "bloodie cross" indicated that the boy would not outlive his seventh year. The paradoxical combination of the mortal wound and the manly shape suggests that the wielder of the sword was punishing Jonson's eldest son for his effrontery in coming of age so rapidly—that is the tacit logic of the dreamer's account. Jonson himself subsequently resolved this paradox by reasoning that the youth in his vision was "of that Grouth that he thinks he shall be at the resurrection" (*Conv*, 271–272). The bloody cross, in this interpretation, signifies that Christ will be merciful to the lad who bears it. But the immediate psychological impact of this vision cannot have been so consoling. The dream fused the dreamer's wish to abandon his family—just as his father had abandoned him—and his guilt over the gratification of that wish into a single harrowing image.

His old master Camden had also come to Conington, and "in the morning he came to Mr. Camdens chamber to tell him" about his dream. Camden "persuaded him it was but ane appreehension of his fantasie at which he should not be disjected," but for once Camden was wrong: "In the mean time comes there letters from his wife of the death of that Boy in the plague" (*Conv*, 266–270). Jonson's epitaph "On My First Son" conveys his response to this dreadful news:

> Farewell, thou child of my right hand, and joy;
>   My sinne was too much hope of thee, lov'd boy,
> Seven yeeres tho'wert lent to me, and I thee pay,
>   Exacted by thy fate, on the just day.
> O, could I loose all father, now. For why
>   Will man lament the state he should envie?
> To have so soone scap'd worlds, and fleshes rage,
>   And, if no other miserie, yet age?
> Rest in soft peace, and, ask'd, say here doth lie
>   BEN. JONSON his best piece of *poetrie*.
> For whose sake, hence-forth, all his vowes be such,
>   As what he loves may never like too much.   (*Ep*, 45)

Jonson begins by confessing that his "sinne was too much hope"—he had presumed that Ben would live to reach manhood. He drives this moral home by recalling the ancient truism which holds that we are not given our lives but instead are "lent" them for an unspecified period of time. The four-line section that begins "O, could I loose all father, now" seeks an alternative to the psychology of hope. If Jonson could "loose all father now" and stop feeling like one, he might see that Ben is fortunate to have escaped the "worlds, and fleshes rage."

But of course, he cannot free himself of paternal affection, and this quatrain concludes by grimly anticipating the misery of age. That prospect does not, however, overcome Jonson's faith in his life's work, for in the closing section he invites the boy to speak from the grave and "say here doth lie / BEN. JONSON his best piece of *poetrie*." The poet's gift of utterance brings Ben back into the present, where the pun on the Greek meaning of "poetry" ("making") links the vocations of fatherhood and art. Even so, Jonson's "best piece of *poetrie*" is a *memento mori*; it teaches him to resist the allure of "too much hope." His final vow "that what he loves may never like too much" voices his resolve to free himself from affective ties that had become unbearable to him. The verb "to like" has the seventeenth-century sense of "to please" in the last line of "On My First Son," and Jonson employs it to make an exacting distinction: he will continue to love, but he will not take too much pleasure in what he loves.[13]

Readers who encounter this famous poem in an anthology of English verse usually assume, with good reason, that they are listening to a bereaved father trying to shed his attachment to a lost child. But Jonson also had to cope with his anxiety over the other members of his family. His wife Anne and (presumably) his three-and-a-half-year-old son Joseph were still incarcerated in the house with the red cross nailed to the door, and their plight was truly desperate. The bubonic plague was transmitted by infected fleas who carried the bacillus from one person to another. Contemporary physicians were unaware of this fact and thus did not realize that the mandatory quarantine, far from combatting the spread of the plague, greatly increased the likelihood that the members of the victim's family would be bitten and contract the disease themselves. It is impossible to be certain about what happened to Joseph Jonson, but the statistics offer little basis for optimism. In a typical London parish, one out of every three infants died during plague years. Over twenty-four hundred of the approximately three thousand persons who resided in St. Giles, Cripplegate, died between July and December of 1603.[14] A three-year-old boy, locked in a house where the plague had already struck, was exceedingly vulnerable. There is, finally, no evidence to suggest that Joseph survived the year 1603. Jonson, who entered the world as a fatherless child, in all likelihood was now a childless father.

During the months that followed the death of his first son, Jonson found himself in a grotesquely ironic situation. The gravest personal tragedy of his life coincided with the greatest professional opportunity he had ever known. The accession of King James I was a godsend for men who had sought, but failed to win, advancement during the previous regime. Whereas the flow of patronage had virtually dried up during the last years of Elizabeth's reign, the new King showered offices and honors upon his new subjects, particularly during "the first three years that were as Christmas." On May 11, 1603, for example, James knighted Jonson's friends Sir Robert Townshend and Sir Robert Cotton, as we must now call them, along with one hundred and thirty other lucky gentlemen, in a single session on his journey south from Scotland.[15]

His connections with Cotton and Camden would have proved especially valuable during this interval. Cotton's patron Henry Howard had been secretly corresponding with James since 1601 in order to lay the legal groundwork for the Scottish succession. When the Queen died in March, Howard immediately commissioned a defense of the Scottish claim. Within days Cotton produced a tract defending the antiquity of James's claim to the English crown and justifying his right to style himself "Emperor of Great Britain."[16] Jonson thus found himself among the intellectual avant-garde of the new monarchy during the very weeks when he was mulling over his own contributions to the accession-year literature.

His vow to remain detached from "what he loves" spoke to his professional as well as his personal circumstances: there was scarcely time to worry about Anne and Joseph, or to mourn for Ben, under these circumstances. His first commission to entertain the new royal family arrived soon after his first son's death. Queen Anne and Prince Henry were scheduled to arrive at Sir Robert Spencer's Althorp estate on June 20, and when they did so, Jonson's *Particular Entertainment of the Queen and Prince Their Highnesse at Althorpe* had already been written, delivered, and rehearsed. We do not know who helped him obtain this, the first of his many Jacobean commissions, but it is worth noting that his patroness Lady Bedford, who had journeyed to Edinburgh in order to solicit the new Queen's favor, was already Anne's favorite lady-in-waiting. Anne Clifford, who met up with the royal party a couple of days before their arrival at Althorp, noted in her diary that the Countess was by now "so great a woman with the Queen as everybody much respected her." [17]

The *Althorpe Entertainment* does little more than recapitulate the motifs that Jonson's Elizabethan predecessors had used on such occasions. As the Queen and Prince strolled through the grounds of Spencer's estate, they encountered a woodland Satyr, Queen Mab, and a consort of elves, all of whom welcomed them with speeches written by Jonson. The voice of the frustrated court poet breaks through only once, when the Satyr compliments Spencer for holding himself aloof from the corrupt court of Elizabeth I: the country squire has never acquired the arts of bribery and flattery "though this lately were some matter / To the making of a courtier." "Now," however, Spencer can go to court, "Since a hand hath governance, / That hath given those customes chase" (180–181, 184–185). Jonson doubtless hoped to follow him there. Although the artistic importance of a work like the *Althorpe Entertainment* is negligible, private entertainments were extremely attractive from an economic standpoint. The texts were never more than a few hundred lines, and the fees could run as high as twenty pounds—or forty pounds, if the occasion were a court masque.

Such commissions were particularly important to Jonson at this time since he was now unable to earn a living by writing plays. The Privy Council had closed the theaters after Queen Elizabeth's death on March 24, and the prohibition stayed in effect because of the plague. It was anyone's guess when the playhouses would reopen: they had remained closed for almost two years during the epidemic of 1592–1594.

By the spring of 1603, Jonson had either completed or abandoned *Richard Crookback*. One can only speculate about the fate of this play. It could have been performed, but not published, like the other scripts that he had sold to Henslowe; he may have set it aside in March, when the Admiral's Men stopped giving performances; or perhaps he could not equal, let alone improve upon, Shakespeare's *Richard III,* and abandoned the project. By the summer of 1603 (and probably earlier than that) he and a collaborator had begun work on a new tragedy entitled *Sejanus His Fall.* The collaborator wrote a "good share" of the original, acting version of *Sejanus,* but when Jonson subsequently published it, he declined either to identify him or to include any of his work, explaining that "I have rather chosen, to put weaker (and no doubt lesse pleasing) of mine own, than to defraud so happy a *Genius* of his right, by my lothed usurpation." The man who inspired this tribute was presumably a friend of the author's, a skillful playwright and a classical scholar who shared Jonson's intricate knowledge of the reign of the Emperor Tiberius. The only contemporary author who answers to that description is George Chapman, and his claim to the lost "share" of *Sejanus,* however tentative, is stronger than anyone else's.[18]

Just a year previously, Jonson had been on the verge of writing a tragedy derived from the popular dramatic tradition; now he was once again seeking out an alternative to the native heritage of Kyd, Marlowe, and Shakespeare. In the Preface to the printed text he advised his readers that he had followed the "offices of a tragic writer" prescribed in chapter 6 of Aristotle's *Poetics:* "truth of Argument" (plot), "dignity of Persons" (character), "gravity and height of Elocution" (diction), and "fulnesse and frequencie of Sentence" (thought). Jonson pointedly omits spectacle, the last of Aristotle's requirements, and this omission follows logically from the Painter's Scene of 1602. In the course of revising *The Spanish Tragedy* Jonson proclaimed the impossibility of finding visual equivalents for tragic experience; shortly thereafter, when he set out to write his own imitation of classical tragedy, he found that "spectacle" was the one office of a tragic writer that he did not care to discharge.

He also dampened the emotional impact of his verse. In the "additions" he had successfully imitated the heavily accented blank verse line of Marlowe and Kyd. The verse style of *Sejanus* runs to the other extreme. Individual lines repeatedly disintegrate into discordant phrases that are barely controlled by submerged symmetries of syntax and meter; the recurrent breaks in the movement of the verse continually draw attention to "the space, the space / Betweene the brest, and lips" (III.96–97) that becomes the staging ground for lies and deception. In the "additions," which were completed around the time of his first daughter's death, Jonson had tried to put a passionate feeling of grief into words; in *Sejanus,* the emotion of grief is constricted, concealed, and suppressed.

The absence of pageantry and rhetorical bravura reinforced the "argument" that he found in his historical sources. The spectacular moments of Elizabethan tragedy—those challenges, battles, triumphs, weddings, coronations, and funerals that so delighted the common spectator—magnified the importance of the individuals involved and thus lent their deeds a luster that exceeded the confines of brute historical necessity. The assassination of *Julius Caesar,* as recounted in Shakespeare's tragedy, holds dire and unforeseeable consequences, yet it was still, as Brutus claimed, a deed that would echo down the corridors of time. History held no such consolations for the luckless men and women who lived out their days under Tiberius Caesar.

Earlier Elizabethan playwrights had concentrated on the glorious history of the Roman Republic; but Sir Henry Savile's rendering of Tacitus, completed by Richard Greneway in 1598, carried the story forward well into the reign of Nero and thus gave Jonson's immediate contemporaries a radically different perspective on the legacy of Rome. The individual achievements that had loomed so large in earlier accounts could now be seen within a cycle of organic rise and fall that revealed their futility. The reign of the Emperor Tiberius was the turning point in this historical catastrophe. During the earlier part of his reign Tiberius retained at least the semblance of a good ruler and, like his predecessor Augustus, sought to preserve the traditional authority of the senate. But in his ninth year, Tacitus writes, Tiberius lapsed into tyranny: "And the cause and beginning of this change lay with Aelius Sejanus."[19]

The rise of Sejanus, as Jonson imagines it, coincides with the triumph of the patronage system over familial ties. *Sejanus* is the tragedy of a patron and client who systematically eliminate all opposition to their network of alliances. Their opponents, the Germanicans, hark back to the era of Cato, Cassius, and Brutus, the activist Republican patriots; yet they remain frozen in the posture of stoic apathy. The purity of their virtue hinges on their refusal to participate in a corrupt world; even though they are lawful heirs of the earlier emperors, they will not oppose their adversary with his own weapons. The kind of resistance that had still been valid in the semifeudalized world of the late republic has slipped out of reach in the early empire: "*Brave* CASSIUS *was the last of all that race*" (I.i.104).

The Germanicans are reminiscent of the younger Jonson who wrote the comical satires and the "Epode." They too believe that "Not to know vice at all, and keepe true state, / Is vertue, and not *Fate*" (*For,* 11.1–2). Because they are excluded from the political process and will not actively resist the Emperor, their only outlet is speech. Like Asper, Criticus, and Horace, they deliver a moralizing commentary on the times; like Jonson in his late twenties, they are harassed by the spies, informers, and kangaroo courts that the imperial state uses to silence its enemies. But Jonson no longer holds out any hope that the moralists will ever succeed in reforming anyone or that a just ruler will someday hear their plea; they are merely grist for the mill of the imperial court. As John Sweeney remarks, the "passing of the Germanicans is a failure of Jonson's satiric voice, at least as a tool of social reconstruction." [20]

If the Germanicans recall the ideals of Jonson's late twenties, the crimes of Tiberius and Sejanus hint at the tragedies of his early thirties. Both men are destroyers of children; both take a grotesque delight in disrupting the natural cycle of generation. Tiberius, who countenances the poisoning of his own son, murders the young out of sheer perversity. The Emperor keeps "a slaughter-house, at *Capreae;* / Where he doth studie murder, as an arte," and to this butcher's shop he brings "boys, and beauteous girles tane up, / Out of our noblest houses." When their parents and friends try to protect these innocent victims, the children are "ravish'd hence, like captives, and, in sight / Of their most grieved parents, dealt away / Unto his *spintries, sellaries,* and slaves." This war against the young expresses Tiberius's grandest desire, which is to create a world shorn of successors: "While I can live, I will prevent earths furie: / *Emou thanontos gaia michthētō pyri* [When I am dead, let fire overwhelm the earth]." Sejanus, who severs sexuality from procreation and vows to father "a race of wicked acts," is his ideal deputy. Where the Emperor kills for sport, Sejanus murders the young for reasons of ambition. Beginning with Tiberius's son Drusus, he tries to carve his way to the throne by murdering as many of the Emperor's rightful heirs as he can lay his hands upon, and his success is staggering:

> I, that did helpe
> To fell the loftie Cedar of the world,
> GERMANICUS; that, at one stroke, cut downe
> DRUSUS, that upright Elme; wither'd his vine;
> Laid SILIUS, and SABINUS, two strong Okes,
> Flat on the earth; besides, those other shrubs,
> CORDUS, and SOSIA, CLAUDIA PULCHRA,
> FURNIUS, and GALLUS, which I have grub'd up;
> And since, have set my axe so strong, and deepe
> Into the roote of spreading AGRIPPINE;
> Lopt off, and scatter'd her proud branches, NERO,
> DRUSUS, and CAIUS too, although re-planted.

Jonson had found the classical counterpart of Richard Crookback, a man whose legacy and boast is a blasted family tree. At the close he is succeeded by yet another child-killer, the "wittily, and strangely-cruell MACRO," who begins his reign by delivering Sejanus's innocent daughter to "the rude lust of the licentious hang-man" to be raped and then "strangled with her harmlesse brother." [21]

The writing of *Sejanus* enabled Jonson to ponder the loss of his own children from a safe distance. He wove literally hundreds of allusions to Tacitus, Suetonius, Dio Cassius, Pliny, Juvenal, and Seneca into the text of *Sejanus,* and he inserted citations to nearly all of them on the margins of the 1605 quarto. The references discouraged the reader, and perhaps Jonson as well, from connecting the play to the author's own situation. Yet the stark outlines of a wish that he had acted upon, and of losses he had suffered, can be discerned across the *cordon sanitaire* of historical distance. When Tiberius substitutes the bond of patron and client for that of parent and child, he inaugurates a transvaluation of Roman mores that relieves the father of any obligation to nurture his offspring and sacrifices family on the altar of self-interest. During the months when he was writing *Sejanus* Jonson's own experience was moving along a similar axis. When he left his wife and children in Cripplegate and rode north to join Cotton and Camden, he too was elevating the claims of patronage over those of parenthood; by the following autumn he had, in all likelihood, lost the last of his own three children. Jonson, however, had committed no crime. His abandonment of his wife and children was the act of a man who responded to the pressures of circumstance in an understandable way; the death of his two sons was a stroke of fate for which he bore no responsibility. *Sejanus* was a repudiation that reaffirmed Jonson's own innocence. The story of Tiberius and Sejanus made it possible for him to displace a potentially intolerable burden of anxiety onto a pair of authentic villains. His misfortune was their crime; his tragedy held them accountable to posterity.

PART TWO

A Jacobean
Man of
Letters

• CHAPTER SIX •

The Poet and the King

Jonson's trail grows indistinct during the latter half of 1603. Perhaps he remained at Conington; perhaps he joined the throng of suitors who followed James and his court on their extended progress through southern England. The capital city had turned into a charnel house by the end of the summer. Some thirty-four thousand Londoners, or about a third of the total population, died before the year was out; the absentees did not return until later that winter when the mortality rate finally dropped below the danger point.[1]

Jonson did appear at court during the Christmas season of 1603–4. Although the London playhouses were closed for the duration of the plague, James had taken the Lord Chamberlain's Men under his patronage shortly after his accession (henceforth they became the King's Men) and he brought them to Hampton Court at the end of December. *Sejanus* was one of the plays selected for performance during this holiday season, and Shakespeare himself acted in it—it is his last appearance on the cast list of any play. This was an auspicious moment for Jonson. After all the reversals of the past few years, he at least had the satisfaction of knowing that he enjoyed the respect of the King's Men and, depending on the outcome of the performance, perhaps even of the King himself. But the occasion turned out badly. When the company performed his tragedy, Jonson "was called befor the Councell for his Sejanus & accused both of popperie and treason" by Lord Henry Howard.[2]

Howard and his allies were in a position to do him a great deal of harm. Shortly after coming to power, the King had elevated the old, and predominantly Catholic, Howard family to the status of a major faction in the new regime. The day after James's initial meeting with Sir Robert Cecil, his Secretary of State, the King named Thomas Howard (whom he would soon make Earl of Suffolk) the Lord Chamberlain of his court. He reappointed another Howard, Thomas, Earl of Nottingham and the hero of the Armada, to the post of Lord Steward, the second-ranking office in the royal household. And he gave Suffolk's uncle Lord Henry Howard, who had helped pave the way for the Scottish succession, a seat on the Privy Council; a year later James made Jonson's accuser Earl of Northampton.[3]

Lord Henry Howard's accusation was doubly vexing because he had already taken Sir Robert Cotton into his service and might have been expected to look favorably on Cotton's learned friend Jonson as well. Why did he choose instead to hale him before the Privy Council? The bone of contention was Jonson's "popperie." James took a more lenient view of recusancy than Elizabeth had, and Jonson, like many English Catholics, stopped taking Communion in the Anglican Church in 1603. Lord Henry Howard was pro-Catholic, but he found it expedient to act as though he were a loyal Anglican and therefore made a point of harassing his former co-religionists from time to time. Jonson offered him a convenient target. Howard was also a notoriously vindictive man, and Jonson crossed him at some point in their relationship: he told Drummond that the Earl "was his mortall enimie for brauling on a St. Georges day one of his attenders."[4]

His debut at the court of James I turned out to be an ominous occasion. In addition to the ill-received performance of *Sejanus*, he had to bear the disappointment of standing by while Samuel Daniel prepared the first Jacobean Twelfth Night masque. And here again, he ran afoul of the Howards: on January 6, 1604, he and Sir John Roe, a wealthy young heir from Essex whom Jonson characterized as "ane infinit Spender," were "ushered" from a court masque by Lord Chamberlain Suffolk (*Conv*, 184, 155). Jonson's temper evidently erupted on this occasion, for Roe immediately sent him a verse epistle counseling moderation: "It is no fault in thee to suffer theirs," he wrote, "Forget we were thrust out. It is but thus / God threatens Kings, Kings Lords, as Lords doe us." In consoling his friend, Roe went to the source of Jonson's frustration: "Let for a while the times unthrifty rout / Contemne learning, and all your studies flout" (HS, XI, 371). Such commonplaces came easily enough to Roe, but the unthrifty rout had been flouting Jonson's studies for several years now—it was time for a change.

Under Elizabeth, Jonson had adopted the stance of an uncompromising moralist aloof from the vicissitudes of court life. Now, like anyone who hoped to thrive under the new regime, he had to cultivate a self-image that was pleasing to James and consistent with the mores of the new court. He made a concerted effort to do so during the early months of 1604. Broadly speaking, a poet who sought to catch the eye of the King had two alternatives. He could stress the continuity between the new regime and the old, emphasizing James's Protestantism, his English ancestry, and his readiness to participate in the national heritage of his new subjects. Or he could stress the differences between Elizabeth and James, emphasizing James's determination to make peace with the European nations, his plans to unify England and Scotland, his imperial status as ruler of the British (and not simply English) people, and his associations with the legacy of Roman Britain. Everything in Jonson's background— his classical learning, his Catholicism, his alienation from the previous regime, and his connections with Camden and Cotton—predisposed him toward the latter alternative.

James had previously published two volumes of his own poetry, and Jonson made the affinity between the poet and the King the subject of his early epigram "To King James": "But two things, rare," he wrote to James, "the FATES had in their store, / And gave thee both, to shew they could no more" (*Ep*, 4.3–4). These lines allude to a famous adage in the meditative lyrics that the Roman poet Florus exchanged with the Emperor Hadrian: "Only kings and poets are not born every year" ("*Solus Rex et Poeta non quotannis nascitur*"). The maxim suggests that poetry and kingship, the "two things rare," are dual aspects—the one contemplative, the other active—of a single capacity for rule. Just as the king actively molds and shapes the body politic, "he which can faine a *Commonwealth* (which is the *Poet*) can governe it with *Counsels*, strengthen it with *Lawes*, correct it with *Judgements*, informe it with *Religion*, and *Morals*" (*Disc*, 1034– 37). The phrasing of the epigram tactfully locates the "poetic" phase of James's career in the past ("For such a *Poet*, while thy dayes were greene, / Thou wert, as chiefe of them are said t'have beene"), and hints that Jonson now intends to assume the royal office that James has vacated: "Whom should my *Muse* then flie to, but the best / Of Kings for grace; of *Poets* for my test?" (*Ep*, 4.5–6, 9–10).

James had decided that his own commonwealth would take the form of a renascent British empire. Its prototype was Roman Britain; its modern counterpart, the King believed, would come into being after he had united the kingdoms of England and Scotland. "On the Union," another epigram dating from the beginning of the reign, contrives to "faine a *Commonwealth*" that prefigured the shape of this new monarchy. In his opening address to the Parliament of 1604 James declared, "What God hath conjoined then, let no man separate. I am the husband, and all the whole Isle is my lawfull Wife." The closing words of "On the Union" are a coda to this royal wedding: "The world the temple was, the priest a king, / The spoused pair two realmes, the sea the ring." These lines reaffirmed the

The most High and Mighty Monarck IAMES. by the grace of God.king of Great Brittaine. France, and Ireland .Borne the 19 of Iune .1566. The most excellent Princeſſe ANNE Queene of Great Brittaine. France. and Ireland . Borne the 12 of October .1574 .

Ar to be ſold at the whit horſe in popes head Alley by Iohn Sudbury And George Humble

James I and Anne of Denmark, by Renold Elstrack, ca. 1603. One of several engravings that commemorated James and Anne's accession in 1603. The inscription below styles them imperial rulers of Great Britain, France, and Ireland.

bond of king and poet in a way that was intimately familiar to James; one early manuscript even attributes the poem to James I.[5]

James set forth the distinctive themes of his new monarchy in *Basilikon Doron,* a treatise on kingship that he had published in Latin four years previously. The King issued a revised translation of *Basilikon Doron* early in 1603 and saw his treatise go through an astonishing run of seven editions in the course of that plague-ridden year. Bacon wrote of its "falling into every man's hand, [it] filled the whole realm, as with a good perfume or incense, before the King's coming in." Camden declared that "it was the pattern of a most excellent and every way accomplished king" and found it "incredible what an expectation of himself [James] raised among all men, even to admiration." In the closing words of *Basilikon Doron,* the "British Augustus" adopts Virgil as his ideal poet-counselor and reminds his son Prince Henry of the famous words that Anchises addresses to his son Aeneas in book VI of the *Aeneid:* "This shall be thine art, to ordain the law of peace, to be merciful to the conquered, and to beat the haughty down." Since Camden's *Britannia* was the definitive account of Roman Britain, he was uniquely qualified to make pronouncements about the historical foundations of James's modern empire. At the outset of the new reign, while Jonson was residing with the two of them at Conington, Camden's pupil Cotton had traced the Jacobean succession back to the rulers of Roman Britain. Cotton also seems to have been involved in the planning for James's royal entry into the City of London; and when that event took place on March 15, 1604, after being postponed for nearly a year because of the plague, his friend Jonson was commissioned to prepare the first and last of the seven triumphal arches.[6]

Under Elizabeth, Jonson had played the part of Horace, the genial corrector of morals; under James, he would emulate Virgil, the poet of empire, as well. In his opening speech of welcome, Genius Urbis, who presided over Jonson's arch at Fenchurch, surveyed the prior epochs of British history (Roman, Saxon, Danish, and Norman), and declared that "the greatest, perfectest, and last" age was now at hand. If James listened attentively, he would have heard an echo of the famous lines in Virgil's Fourth Eclogue that herald the dawn of the Augustan era: "The great series of ages is coming into being anew. / The last age of the Cumean song is come." Immediately after these lines in the Fourth Eclogue, Virgil proclaims that "a new generation descends from heaven"; at the analogous moment in the *King's Entertainment,* Genius Urbis turned to Prince Henry, the "springing glory" of James's "godlike race," and went on to pray that "from this branch, may thousand branches more / Shoote o're the maine, and knit with every shore."[7] The blasted family tree in *Sejanus* had epitomized a complex series of failures: the collapse of Rome's imperial dream,

Jonson and Harrison's Arch at Fenchurch. From Stephen Harrison's *Arches of Triumph,*
1604. Divine wisdom, standing in the largest of the niches between the arches, upholds British
Monarchy, the central figure in the facade above, who sits beneath a panorama of London.
The arch is an allegorical image of monarchical rule: sustained by wisdom, the sovereign
supports the city.

the triumph of patronage over family, the destruction of Jonson's own lineage. The "broade spreading Tree" of the *King's Entertainment* was an ample image of hope for the future. It evoked the continuing legacy of Augustan culture, the durability of the Stuart succession, and James's hope of creating a latter-day *pax Augusta* by marrying his heirs to both the Catholic and the Protestant scions of the ruling European dynasties.

As James passed through the city, under the three arches prepared by Jonson's nemesis Thomas Dekker, he encountered a radically different image of his commonwealth. Dekker's *Nova Felix Arabia* Arch in Cheapside identified James with the phoenix, the mythical bird that recreates itself from its own ashes. This icon carried hallowed associations with Elizabeth I and thus emphasized James's continuity with the Protestant, Tudor monarch whom he was succeeding. Dekker's Rustic Arch employed the familiar Elizabethan imagery of the garden state tended by its sovereign husbandman: Sylvanus, the principal speaker, had figured prominently in both *The Princely Pleasures at Kenilworth* (1575) and *The Entertainment at Elvetham* (1591). Finally, Dekker's New World Arch was an "inchanted Castle," and "another Towre of Pleasure" containing "all the States of the land, from the Nobleman to the Ploughman"—once again, a thoroughly medieval image of the commonwealth. Although they appealed to the London populace, these images had no particular relevance to James's plans for the future, nor did they signify any lasting transformation of the state. Dekker's "New World" could just as well have been brought about by the appearance of Queen Elizabeth I. Jonson's, by contrast, focused on the person of James Stuart and exhibited a wealth of novel iconographic material.[8]

Dekker was inviting the King to participate in the folkways of the London citizenry; James, who loathed crowds and prided himself on his erudition, found this invitation impossible to accept. Commentators have frequently noted the difference between the royal entry of 1559, when Elizabeth mingled with the crowds and made impromptu speeches, and that of 1604, which James found a considerable ordeal. One witness complained that the new King "was not like his *Predecessor,* the late *Queen* of famous *memory,* that with a well-pleased affection met her peoples Acclamation." James, he went on, merely "endured the days brunt with *patience,* being assured he should never have another." The traditions of urban pageantry represented by the annual Lord Mayor's shows persisted, and indeed thrived, under James, but these events would henceforth express the viewpoint of an urban community that felt increasingly cut off from the life of the court.[9] By the same token, entertainments designed exclusively for the royal family were to enjoy a remarkable efflorescence during James's twenty-two-year reign. The King's aloofness was a rebuff to Dekker and the London citizenry, but not to Jonson, whose arch at Temple Bar ushered James out of London and into the royal city of Westminster. His neo-Roman iconography created a setting in which James's remoteness from the populace was a virtue, a sign that he had adopted an imperial style of rule.

A few days later, on March 19, Jonson's "Panegyre on the Happy Entrance of James . . . to His First High Session of Parliament" revived the form of address used to honor Roman emperors on state occasions. The shared elitism of the poet and the King, which is implicit in all of the early works that Jonson addressed to James, becomes fully explicit in the "Panegyre." In Jonson's reimagining of James's triumphal ride through London, the people who fill the streets dissolve into a flood of affect: "Walls, windores, roofes, towers, steeples, all were set / With severall eyes." Meanwhile, the poet and the King remain aloof from this commotion. Where ordinary mortals merely saw James riding in state, Jonson beheld the goddess Themis (daughter of heaven and earth) descend from above to instruct the newly crowned King, and listened as she offered James the very advice that the King himself had given to Prince Henry in *Basilikon Doron*.[10] The mythological apparatus of the "Panegyre" barely disguises its real subject, which is the relationship between the King and Counselor. Jonson's view of this relationship is at once assertive and deferential. He is divinely inspired, but the goddess whom he overhears quotes verbatim from James's own writings; he is an absolute monarchist with respect to the people, but an egalitarian with respect to the King, whom he reminds in the tag that brings the poem to a close, "*Solus Rex et Poeta non quotannis nascitur.*"

His services were especially suited to James because Jonson recognized that the new King, who was hardly a model of Roman *gravitas* in his private life, also prized earthy humor and broad repartee. The Scottish court of James VI was far more casual and unkempt than its English counterpart, and James persisted in his unmannerly ways when he came south in 1603. While among his intimates, the man who held himself aloof from the London populace was observed to relieve his bowels on horseback, slobber over his meals, go for weeks at a time without bathing, finger his favorites' codpieces, and abandon urgent state business for the pleasures of the chase. He liked to engage in coarse raillery with members of his entourage, and he expected them to respond in kind. When advised that his loving subjects wished to see him, James "would cry out in Scottish, 'God's wounds! I will pull down my breeches and they shall also see my arse.'"[11]

Jonson got his first opportunity to enter this exclusive little world on May 1, 1604, when his *Private Entertainment of the King and Queen* was performed at the Highgate house of Sir William Cornwallis, a client of Cecil's. In the course of the *Private Entertainment* his leading character, the horned Pan ("rude ynough, though otherwise full of salt"; line 201), reminded James of his loathing for women and his passion for hunting:

> Sure, either my skill, or my sight doth mock,
> Or this lordings looke should not care for the smock;
> And yet he should love both a horse and a hound,
> And not rest till he saw his game on the ground.   (219–222)

In the same spirit, Pan congratulates Queen Anne on her fondness for the bottle:

> Here mistresse; all out. Since a god is your skinker:
> By my hand, I beleeve you were borne a good drinker.
> They are things of no spirit, their blood is asleepe,
> That, when it is offred 'hem, do not drinke deepe.   (225–228)

Everyone knew about James's and Anne's drinking bouts, the King's intemperate love of hunting, and his misogyny; but Jonson was the only one of the aspiring court poets to recognize that the King was more likely to trust and reward a poet who could jest with him about his private follies. Raillery was ultimately a disguised form of compliment: "But still," Pan concludes, "you triumph, in this facilitie, over the ridiculous pride of other Princes; and for ever live safe in the love, rather then the feare, of your subjects" (273–275). In seizing the opportunity to engage in such repartee, Jonson intimated that he too belonged to the royal household.

At approximately this time, the Globe audience was hissing *Sejanus* off the stage. Contemporary allusions indicate that the spectators were not merely bored or put off by the play; they found it deeply offensive. One of Jonson's admirers was appalled to see "the Peoples beastly rage / Bent to confound thy grave, and learned toile" (HS, XI, 317). Years later, he himself recalled that his tragedy "suffer'd no lesse violence from our people here, than the subject of it did from the rage of the people of *Rome*" (HS, IV, 349).

The fate of *Sejanus* gave him still another incentive, if any were needed, to seek preferment at court and private commissions. A man who knew how to frame an address to the King had a valuable commodity to sell. In 1604, the Haberdashers' Company paid Jonson the handsome sum of twelve pounds for a "device, and speech" that were presented before James at the "Lord Mayor's triumphs" (HS, XI, 586). The city companies seem to have employed Jonson in this capacity on numerous occasions during the reign. It is impossible to say how many times they purchased his services, for he relegated all of the work he did for them to oblivion;

but two or three of these commissions would have provided him with an ample yearly income.

B. Jonson His Part of the Kings Entertainment in Passing to His Coronation was registered for publication on March 19, 1604, and appeared, together with the *Althorpe Entertainment* and the "Panegyre," in a quarto published later that year. The published text of the *King's Entertainment* furnished interested readers, including the King, with documentary evidence of the author's erudition. On the printed page, the speeches that had been delivered from his arches are surrounded by reams of scholarly commentary, including citations to all of the ancient and modern texts (such as Camden's *Britannia*) that he had drawn upon. The finished product looked like a Renaissance edition of a classical work. A few years previously, in *Cynthia's Revels,* Jonson had decried the visual quality of Elizabethan courtly spectacles; when he was subsequently commissioned to prepare such a spectacle for James, he arrived at an ingenious compromise with his earlier position. Each of his visual images now appeared to carry a heavy freight of discursive meaning. "The *Symboles* used, are not . . . simply *Hieroglyphickes, Emblemes,* or *Impreses,*" he explained, "but a mixed character, partaking somewhat of all, and peculiarly apted to these more magnificent Inventions." Dekker scoffed at this parade of learning. "Such feates of Activitie are stale, and common among Schollers," he observed, but "the Multitude is now to be our Audience, whose heads would miserably runne a wooll-gathering, if we doo but offer to breake them with hard words." But Dekker's rejoinder played into the hands of his rival, who insisted that his images were so "presented, as upon the view, they might, without cloud, or obscuritie, declare themselves to the sharpe and learned: And for the multitude, no doubt but their grounded judgements did gaze, said it was fine, and were satisfied." [12]

A keen observer of visual signs might have noticed that the author of the *King's Entertainment* had changed the spelling of his own last name by dropping the medial "h" in the first syllable of "Johnson." The new spelling was not a casual aberration: Jonson would employ it in his printed works and private correspondence for the rest of his life. Names meant a great deal to Jonson. Like his master Camden, he was a keen student of etymologies and family nomenclature, and often ruminated on the relationship between names and persons. What prompted him to alter the spelling of his own surname? To begin with, the new spelling proclaimed his uniqueness: there were many Johnsons in Jacobean London, but only one Jonson. In a narrower sense, the change of name set him apart from his real father and his three children, all of whom had been Johnsons. The aggrieved parent who wrote "On My First Son" had wished that he could "loose all father, now"; the altered spelling, which appears in the first occurrence of his name after the death of his sons, reaffirmed that intention. "Johnson" was an inherited name ("son of John") that connoted filial and paternal attachments; "Jonson" was an invented name that implied autonomy.

Jonson had been living apart from his own family—which now consisted only of himself and Anne—for a little over a year at this point. The sole source of information about his whereabouts in 1604 is the following garbled passage from his conversations with Drummond: "To me he read the Preface of his arte of Poesie, upon Horace Arte of poesie, wher he heth ane apologie of a Play of his St Bartholomees faire, by Criticus is understood Done. ther is ane Epigram of Sir Edward Herberts befor it, the [word missing] he said he had done in my Lord Aubanies House ten yeers since anno 1604." Drummond appears to be saying that Jonson wrote his translation of Horace's *Art of Poetry* ten years before *Bartholomew Fair* (1614), in 1604, while residing at the home of Lord D'Aubigny, one of James's Scottish favorites; the missing word in the manuscript would be "translation" or "poem." When he subsequently dedicated *Sejanus* to Aubigny, Jonson recalled that his patron had attended the disastrous debut of that play in the spring of 1604. A year later, in 1605, he publicly alluded to "my Observations upon *Horace* his *Art of Poetry*, which (with the Text translated) I intend, shortly to publish." How long he remained with Aubigny is a matter of conjecture, but when he was cited for recusancy in the spring of 1606, he insinuated that he and Anne were still separated at Easter 1605. So Jonson evidently changed the spelling of his name while he was in the midst of a prolonged separation from his wife.[13]

Esmé Stuart, the Seigneur of Aubigny, was a twenty-four-year-old blood relative of the King's who had come south with him in 1603. Aubigny was such an attractive patron that Jonson may have found it impossible to refuse his hospitality. He had recently joined the Gentlemen of the Bedchamber, an exclusive fraternity of six courtiers who served as James's personal valets. Although the Gentlemen received no stipend and did not hold government offices, they enjoyed day-to-day access to the monarch and held their posts for life. Since James often spent weeks at a time within his private lodgings, where no one could go except for his family and the Gentlemen and grooms who attended him there, Aubigny was perfectly situated to help direct the flow of royal patronage. The Gentlemen of the Bedchamber, all but one of whom were Scots in 1604, have only recently attracted the attention of social historians; as a group, however, they wielded more power than any of James's ministers of state, and Aubigny was thus far more influential than any of Jonson's previous benefactors.[14]

Like many Englishmen, including his friend Cotton, Jonson seems to have discovered genteel Scottish ancestors just at the time when a Scot became King of England. The first of his citations for recusancy, which is dated January 9, 1606, describes him as "Armiger"; he was now a gentleman and legally entitled to bear the arms of his ancestors, the Johnstones of Annandale, whose coat of arms displayed "three spindles or rhombi" (HS, XI, 579; I, 3). While Jonson suppressed the tie to his father, who had lost the family estate, he in turn reaffirmed his connection to the genteel grandfather who had formerly possessed it. Since Camden was Clarenceux King at Arms, Jonson probably did not have to furnish the heralds with documentary proof of his descent from the Johnstones, or even to supply the bribe that was customarily offered in lieu of such proof. This change of status is yet another indication that he had decided to refashion himself in the image of a Jacobean courtier. In the winter of 1604–5 Ben Johnson, the late Elizabethan malcontent, was on the verge of becoming Mr. Ben Jonson, court poet to King James I.

The most sought-after commission of all went to the author of the annual Twelfth Night masque at Whitehall. The text of these entertainments was typically about four hundred lines long; the usual fee was forty pounds. Since the courtiers who participated in and attended the masques were among the most powerful people in England, the potential rewards were vast indeed. If one of them thought well enough of Jonson's work to become his patron, the poet could look forward to such benefits as gifts, monetary stipends, food and lodging for extended periods of time, protection from the law, and last but not least introductions to still other persons in a position to improve his lot. An impressive array of Jacobean lords and ladies did Jonson favors of this kind, and the common denominator of all these associations is the masque. This commission also allowed him to assume the status of a servant to the King, which Jonson clearly coveted. A successful masque writer could aspire to become his majesty's Master of the Revels (Dekker claimed that Jonson had sought this post),[15] and there was always the possibility that James would grant him a royal pension.

The court masque first appeared during the reign of Richard II, and all subsequent versions of it preserve the imagery of an idealized feudal court. The disguised revelers offered service, in the form of dancing and entertainment; the Prince dispensed bounty, in the form of hospitality. Although gifts were sometimes exchanged in the course of these festivities, the two parties did not treat this occasion as a cash-and-carry proposition.[16] The only people to receive gross hire and salary were the peripheral poets, actors, and professional musicians who provided incidental entertainment. The courtiers and the prince clung to the fiction that they were exchanging spontaneous gestures of affection. Nevertheless, pleasing James I was an opportunistic and lavishly financed occupation in which success could be measured in terms of the stakes one carried away. The masquers did not merely dance to delight the King; they danced to make him delighted with them.

Only a certain brand of courtier had the skills required to play this game. As a group, the masquers needed to have the athletic ability, physical stamina, personal beauty, and technical discipline that are the tools of a dancer's trade. The display of gorgeous clothes and jewelry was an integral part of the performance: the dancers often laid out enormous sums for these, and the art of wearing them gracefully had to be mastered as well. Renaissance monarchs valued such attributes highly. For men like Sir Christopher Hatton and the Earls of Leicester and Essex, who danced before Elizabeth, or the Earl of Montgomery and the Duke of Buckingham, who performed for James, personal glamor was the "open sesame" that led to great wealth and office. Stone estimates that Elizabeth, James, and (to a far lesser extent) Charles gave grants and favors worth more than three and a half million pounds in Tudor and Stuart money to the peerage. He also notes that nine peers "hogged no less than 45 per cent" of the total: "Two of the 9, Essex and Leicester, were lovers of the virgin Queen; 3, Montgomery, Somerset, and Buckingham, were lovers of the homosexual King." Moreover, the rate of giving increased by a factor of over thirteen after James's accession in 1603. These were the days, Bishop Hacket recalled, when "the Chief Treasurer was called the Count of Largesse, as the Prince's Revenues served only for Bounty and Largesse." [17]

Other great courtiers, such as Lord Burleigh and Sir Francis Walsingham under Elizabeth, or Salisbury and Sir Francis Bacon under James, stayed away from the dance floor and mastered the skills that were needed to manage the royal bureaucracy. Bacon, for one, viewed the politics of revelry as a costly and childish business. "These things are but toys to come amongst such serious observations," he complained; "But yet," he added, "since princes will have such things, it is better, they should be graced with elegancy, then daubed with cost." As Bacon implies, the masque was an ephemeral pursuit conducted in a setting where ephemera could have important consequences. "These things are but toys" yet "princes will have such things." In the *Althorpe Entertainment*, Jonson had already voiced his own misgivings about courtiers who danced their way to prestige and his hope that James would put a stop to this practice. "I not deny," he says,

> where Graces meete
> In a man, that qualitie
> Is a gracefull propertie:
> But when dauncing is his best,
> (Beshrew me) I suspect the rest.[18]

James would never heed this salutary advice. Jonson's success at making the text of the masque into a vehicle for moral instruction attests to the seriousness of his humanistic ideals, but the agenda was ultimately set by his social betters, and they had other aims in view.

Broadly speaking, the poet was in the employ of King James. James paid, in whole or in part, for most of the court masques, and he was the one who ultimately had to be pleased. In a narrower but equally important sense, the poet was working for the courtiers who performed in these spectacles. Unlike his predecessor Queen Elizabeth, James neither danced in the masques nor took an active role in planning them. Such evidence as survives indicates that someone in his immediate family, or an intimate member of the royal household, usually took the lead instead.[19] Jonson's relationship to these noble dancers replicated, on a smaller scale, their own relationship to King James. The poet was a prospective client; the dancers represented a prospective source of patronage. To succeed in these commissions, Jonson had to harmonize the dancers' self-image, the King's personal iconography, and the occasion at hand. By helping the courtiers to please James, the poet, in turn, could please them.

Fortunately for Jonson, in the autumn of 1604 James asked Queen Anne to organize the Twelfth Night masque. Although Jonson did not have many powerful friends at the new court, he did have two things in common with Anne of Denmark. First, they were fellow Catholics. Second, and more important, his patroness Lady Bedford was the Queen's favorite lady-in-waiting and advised her in the planning of the Queen's masques. During the previous holiday season the Countess had obtained the commission to write *The Vision of the Twelve Goddesses* for Samuel Daniel— a favor that prompted Daniel to thank her for "preferring such a one, to her *Majesty* in this imployment."[20] A year later the commission went to Jonson.

The Queen presented him with a difficult assignment. "It was her Majesties will," he learned, "to have them *Black-mores*" (HS, VII, 169). Since African females, and particularly an African Queen, carried powerful connotations of female autonomy and ethnic diversity, Anne's instructions tacitly challenged the Jacobean myth of male supremacy and imperial rule. Furthermore, the Queen's decision to have herself and her ladies wear blackface, rather than removable vizards, made it impossible to efface this impression by altering their appearance at the conclusion of the performance; and yet the masque was supposed to convey an extended compliment to the King.

The Masque of Blackness contrives to satisfy "her Majesties will" without encroaching on his majesty's prerogative. In its broad outlines Jonson's plot subordinates the Queen's blackness to the King's power to whiten and cleanse. At the outset of the performance Niger, the ladies' father, explains that his daughters had been troubled by "the fabulous voices of some few / Poore brain-sicke men, stil'd *Poets*" who attributed their blackness to the "intemperate fires" of the African sun; but then the ladies saw an apparition of the moon goddess, Aethiopa, who told them of a land "*whose termination (of the* Greeke) / Sounds TANIA,*" where they would find "a greater *Light, / Who formes all beauty, with his sight.*" Their quest had now come to an end, on Twelfth Night of 1605, in the fabled kingdom Brit*tania*, where they stood before the "greater light" (James) whose beams were "of force / To blanch an AETHIOPE, and revive a *Cor's.*"[21] The masquerade of blackness seeking sunlight situates the African ladies in a pretend world where veiled beauty instinctively gravitates toward sovereignty and sovereignty dispels the shadows of ill-repute. As many instances from the reigns of Elizabeth and James make clear, court protocol operated in precisely this manner, just as it does today. To be involved in a bad scandal, as Lady Rich was a year later, meant banishment from the court; but readmittance conferred a clean bill of health. So the brainsick poets had a point: the ladies' blackness did imply that they were "intemperate." James, however, could alter their complexions.

But *The Masque of Blackness* also has a counterplot that defies the brainsick poets and insists upon the beauty of the ladies' native hue. The opening song hails "Faire NIGER" whose "beautious race" proves "that beauty best / Which not the colour, but the feature / Assures unto the creature." If the ladies are "Faire" to begin with, why do they need "a greater light" to whiten them? (Since the court had commissioned a performance of *Othello* in November, this question could easily have occurred to anyone in the Whitehall audience.) What is more, the King never does "blanch" the Ethiopian ladies, nor does it appear that he could have, given the viscosity of the cosmetics they were wearing. Instead, a solitary voice summoned the Queen and her retinue back to sea just "*as they were about to make choice of their men,*" and seaward they went, to be purified, not by the King, but by their own ablutions.[22]

Despite the obligatory tribute to James, the surface impression of license that inhered in the ladies' dark complexions was just as compelling as the King's power to whiten and cleanse. Although there was, Stone concludes, "a tightening up of the sexual *mores* of the nobility and gentry as a whole in the early seventeenth century," nevertheless, "a small minority was moving swiftly in exactly the opposite direction," and that minority was centered in the court of James I, where "the real breakthrough into promiscuity" first occurred. In 1603 Lady Anne Clifford was already convinced that "all the ladies about the court had gotten such ill names that it was grown a scandalous place and the Queen herself was much fallen from her former greatness and reputation she had in the world."[23] Several of Niger's daughters, particularly those who were older, married, and experienced hands at court, had already achieved a fair degree of notoriety in their own right. Penelope, Lady Rich, the "Stella" of Sidney's sonnet sequence, had already left her husband to live with Charles, Lord Mountjoy (Daniel cast her as Venus in *The Vision of the Twelve Goddesses*). Elizabeth, Countess of Derby, had had an affair with Penelope's celebrated brother Robert, the second Earl of Essex, some years earlier. Catherine, Countess of Suffolk, and Audrey, Lady Walsingham, were both said to be mistresses of Robert Cecil. Contemporary gossip does not attribute any such liaisons to Lady Bedford, but she was plainly an opportunistic, physically attractive woman who used her charms to get ahead at court. When

Lucy, Countess of Bedford, miniature by Isaac Oliver, ca. 1605. Lady Bedford's admirers would have aspired to wear such miniatures.

her husband, Edward, came to grief over his part in the Essex uprising of 1601, a contemporary rhymer scoffed that the Earl would be sorely punished "except his fine dancing dame / Do their hard hartes tame." [24]

After watching Anne and her entourage perform in Daniel's inaugural Twelfth Night masque, Dudley Carleton wrote to Chamberlain that the Queen "had a trick by herself for her clothes were not so much below the knee but that we might see a woman had both feet and legs which I never knew before." If Carleton found the Queen's rakish attire a source of wry amusement in 1604, he was scandalized by what he saw a year later. Their apparel was "too light and Curtizan-like for such great ones," he complained: "Instead of Vizzards, their Faces, and Arms up to the Elbows, were painted black . . . *and you cannot imagine a more ugly Sight, then a* Troop of *lean-cheek'd Moors.*" Carleton's remarks attest to the unresolved ambivalence of *Blackness*. Since the ladies never removed their masks, the transformation of blackness into beauty remained incomplete. The social dances between the lady masquers and the assembled courtiers, which ideally would have signified the ladies' reception into the court, struck him as an unseemly hodgepodge. The Spanish Ambassador "took out the Queen [to dance], and forgot not to kiss her Hand, though there was Danger it would have left a Mark on his Lips." [25]

The achievement of *Blackness* was inextricably linked to the assertive gestures that Carleton deplored. The Queen's blackface is part of what Stephen Greenblatt describes as "the process whereby subversive insights are generated in the midst of apparently orthodox texts and simultaneously contained by those texts." [26] Jonson invests Anne and her entourage with a symbolic identity that signifies their autonomy vis-à-vis the King and his court; yet even in departing, the ladies' gaze remains fixed on the throne to which they shall return a year hence: "Back *Seas,* back *Nymphs;* but, with a forward grace, / Keepe, still, your reverence to the place." Anne's transformation into an African queen did not involve a breach of etiquette. As a less straitlaced observer than Carleton might have seen, it was in perfect accord with the courtly ideal of *sprezzatura* that Baldassare Castiglione describes as "a certain nonchalance with regard to what is not essential . . . as when a youth dresses up as an old man yet wears loose attire so as to be able to show his agility." [27] This kind of playful mockery requires a finely honed sense of decorum—of where to stop and what to leave unsaid. Had Jonson pressed the issue of the ladies' sexuality, or alluded to the rumors that surrounded their private lives, he would have had to answer to the Privy Council yet another time. But to portray them as the dark-skinned daughters of Old Niger, bearing symbolic names and "mute Hieroglyphics" appropriate to their real selves, was artful insouciance.

• CHAPTER SEVEN •

Eastward Ho, *Prison, and* Volpone

Despite the disapproval of Dudley Carleton and his friends, Jonson had good reason to feel optimistic about his prospects at the new court. He had an unrivaled grasp of James's public image, and he had attached himself to Anne, the person primarily responsible for planning the Twelfth Night masques. Yet just when the path to royal preferment was clearer than it had ever been, he committed an indiscretion that could easily have ruined his chances at court forever.

In the spring of 1605, Jonson collaborated with Chapman and Marston on a new comedy called *Eastward Ho*. At first glance this play looks innocuous enough. A dissolute knight named Sir Petronell Flash marries the social-climbing daughter of a London goldsmith and cheats her out of her dowry; he then sets sail for Virginia, but his boat is blown off course and capsizes near the Isle of Dogs—the site of the comedy that had landed Jonson in prison eight years earlier. At this point, the collaborators decided to take a large risk. Two anonymous gentlemen suddenly appear on the marshy riverbank. One of them (he is simply called First Gentleman) informs Sir Petronell that he is in the "Ile a Doggs" and dismisses him with this pointed rebuke: "Farewel, farewel, we wil not know you for shaming of you. I ken the man weel, hee's one of my thirty pound knights" (IV.i.173, 177–178). Now the man who had recently instituted the notorious practice of selling knighthoods for thirty pounds was King James, whose court lay just across the river at Greenwich. Were it not for the King's scandalous innovation, Sir Petronell would still be plain Mr. Flash, the goldsmith's daughter never would have married him, and all would be well.

Eastward Ho, *Prison,* and Volpone

Lest anyone fail to grasp the reference to James, First Gentleman turns into a comic Scotsman with a heavy brogue while speaking the line that refers to "his" thirty-pound knights. The fling at James's accent was particularly apt because his Scottish cronies frequently collected the thirty-pound bribes. George Eld, who printed *Eastward Ho,* suppressed still other gibes at the Scots who came south with the King, but one of them managed to survive the first press run. Just prior to their departure for Virginia, Captain Seagull tells Sir Petronell that the New World has no drawbacks whatever, apart from "a few industrious Scots perhaps, who indeed are disperst over the face of the whole earth." The captain goes on to explain that "there are no greater friends to English-men and *England,* when they are out an't, in the world, then they are," and concludes with a sneer at James's plan for uniting the two kingdoms: "And for my part, I would a hundred thousand of 'hem were there, for wee are all one Countreymen now, yee know; and wee shoulde finde ten times more comfort of them there, then wee doe heere." [1]

These passages were, of course, liable to bring the King's wrath down on the heads of the three collaborators, who ran the risk of imprisonment, corporal punishment, and permanent exclusion from the court. The playwrights compounded the element of risk by neglecting to submit the script to Lord Chamberlain Suffolk, who was away from London for most of the summer. Jonson's willingness to take these risks is especially puzzling since he had been trying to make a favorable impression on James for much of the previous year. Why did he jeopardize his chances at this crucial juncture in his career? Speaking for himself and Chapman, he subsequently wrote to Salisbury that "our Fortune hath necessitated us to so despisd a Course." [2] But if he received his usual fees, the masque and the two entertainments he had written during the previous year would have brought in nearly seventy pounds. Why put this source of income at risk for the two or three pounds that he collected for his share of *Eastward Ho?*

Jonson's audacity can be better understood against the backdrop of Jacobean court life. James's court was a staging ground for competing factions, and most of Jonson's prospective benefactors bore a grudge against the Scots. His patroness Queen Anne bitterly resented the clique of Scottish favorites who had usurped her place in James's affections and (at one point) had even taken charge of her children. Beaumont, the French Ambassador, reported that she was quite open about her disaffection. "Consider for pity's sake," he wrote in June 1604, "what must be the state and condition of a prince, whom the preachers publicly from the pulpit assail, whom the comedians of the metropolis bring upon the stage, whose wife attends these representations in order to enjoy the laugh against her husband." The Children of the Chapel Royal, who performed *Eastward Ho*, were servants in the Queen's household; if Anne saw them enact it, she would have enjoyed still another laugh at her husband's expense. Robert Cecil, who was now Earl of Salisbury and the most powerful source of patronage in James's government, found that the tightly knit group of Scottish courtiers in the Bedchamber had drastically limited his access to the King. "I wish I waited now in [Elizabeth's] Presence Chamber," he confided to a friend, "with ease at my board, and rest in my bed. I am pushed from the shore of comfort, and know not where the winds and the waves of a court will bear me."[3] James himself thrived on debate, prided himself on his tolerance, and liked irreverent jokes; he was certainly capable of enjoying the anti-Scottish humor in *Eastward Ho*.

Even if Jonson's reckless streak did come into play, it need not have worked to his disadvantage. As Beaumont's dispatch suggests, James's popularity had begun to diminish, and he was in danger of becoming a public laughingstock. In March 1605, around the time of *Eastward Ho*, Samuel Calvert wrote to Ralph Winwood that "the play[er]s do not forbear to represent upon their stage the whole course of this present time, not sparing either King, state, or religion, in so great absurdity, and with such liberty, that any would be afraid to hear them." One way to silence the voices of dissent was to buy them off. Izaak Walton later wrote that Jonson's royal pension "was well pay'd for love or fere of his raling in verse, or prose, or boeth."[4]

Nevertheless, the butts of *Eastward Ho* had their own interests to defend. The play came to the attention of a Scottish courtier named Sir James Murray, who complained to the King that Jonson had written "something against the Scots in a play Eastward hoe." Marston appears to have fled at this point, but Jonson and Chapman were "hurried to bondage and fetters" without "examininge, without hearinge, or without any proofe, but malicious *Rumor*": "the report was that they should then had their ears cutt and noses."[5]

During his confinement Jonson wrote six letters to powerful courtiers (Suffolk, Salisbury, Montgomery, Pembroke, and two unnamed lords) and one to an unnamed lady. These letters are filled with anxiety about his predicament. He describes himself as being persecuted, polluted, and buried alive; he finds it particularly galling to be imprisoned over something so base as—"the word irkes mee"—"a Play"; he surmises that the absence of any regular judicial process has left him and Chapman "on uneven bases," at the mercy of their enemies, and he implores Pembroke to "be hastie to our succoure." His letter to Pembroke reveals that the Earl had done favors for him in the past, and Jonson felt that he could count on his support during the present crisis. He saw another prospective ally in Pembroke's brother Philip, Earl of Montgomery, the first royal favorite at the new court and the one Englishman who served in the royal Bed-chamber. He was also confident that the unnamed lady, who was probably the Countess of Bedford, would stand by him. But Jonson's backers did not have a seat on the Privy Council or hold any important post in James's government. They were residuary legatees of the old Leicester-Essex faction, men whom James held in esteem but to whom he granted largely ceremonial offices.[6]

Salisbury and the Howards oversaw the daily process of decision making, and Jonson therefore had to entreat their assistance as well. The authors' failure to submit their script to Lord Chamberlain Suffolk before giving it to the actors was an offense "for which," Chapman conceded, "we can plead nothing by way of pardon." Jonson's own letter to a "Most honorable Lord" was probably intended for the Lord Chamberlain. Since he had no prior connection with Suffolk, he simply reminded him that "evrie noble and just man, is bound to defend the Innocent," and complained that he had not been allowed to tell his side of the story: "The Manner of it afflicts me ... being committed hether, unexamined, nay unheard (a Rite, not commonlie denyed to the greatest Offenders) and I made a guiltie man, longe before I am one." He concluded by promising that he would "forbeare to trouble your Lordship till my languishinge estate may drawe free breath from youre Comfortable worde."[7]

Salisbury seems to have been better disposed toward Jonson than Suffolk was. Jonson had already been summoned before the Earl over *The Isle of Dogs*, "which (yet)," he declared, "is punish'd in mee more with my shame, than it was then with my Bondage," and more recently, over *Sejanus*. Salisbury had apparently supported him on both occasions, and it aggravated Jonson that "before I can shew my selfe gratefull (in the least) for former benefitts, I am enforc'd to provoke your Bounties, for more." Quoting from the prefaces to Martial's epigrams and Erasmus's *Praise of Folly*, he insisted that "no Man can justly complain, that hath the vertue to thinke but favorably of himselfe," and asked "whether, I have ever (in any thing I have written private, or publique) given offence to a Nation, to any publique order or state, or any person of honor, or Authority." This defense put the ball back in his accuser's court. In effect, he was asking Sir James Murray whether he actually saw himself and his sovereign mirrored in the anti-Scottish satire of *Eastward Ho*. The charge of libel, he hinted, should really be leveled at his accusers: "My noble Lord, they deale not charitably, Who are too witty in another mans Workes, and utter, some times, their own malicious Meanings, under our Wordes" (HS, I, 194–195).

The final say, however, lay with Lord Chamberlain Suffolk, and in the end he decided to be lenient, perhaps at the instigation of Jonson's patron Lord D'Aubigny. In a subsequent letter to Suffolk, Chapman reports that

Aubigny has told him "that his highnes hath remitted one of us wholie to youre Lordship's favoure; And that the other had still youre Lordship's passinge noble remembrance for his Joint libertie." Chapman thanked the Earl for having "pardon'd and grac't" where he "might justly have punish't." Aubigny's decision to side with the playwrights seriously weakened Murray's case: if James's Scottish cousin, who was equally indebted to the King's largesse, did not take offense at *Eastward Ho,* why should Murray feel that his ox was gored? Jonson felt a profound sense of gratitude toward his benefactor. In his epigram "To Esmé, Lord Aubigny" he calls "*Posteritie* / Into the debt" and reminds readers yet unborn

> How full of want, how swallow'd up, how dead
> I, and this *Muse* had beene, if thou hadst not
> Lent timely succours, and new life begot.[8]

Just as "the Anger of the Kinge is death," in the words of Jonson's letter to Pembroke, so the mercy of the King was redemption. Rejoicing in his deliverance, Jonson "banqueted all his friends, there was Camden Selden and others," after his release. "At the midst of the Feast," when the wine was flowing, "his old Mother Dranke to him and shew him a paper which she had (if the Sentence had taken execution) to have mixed in the Prisson among his drinke, which was full of Lustie strong poison and that she was no churle she told [him] she minded first to have Drunk of it herself" (*Conv,* 278–283). The "old Mother" who displayed her *memento mori* to the assembled revelers is a deeply enigmatic figure. Had she planned to murder her son by secretly poisoning his drink? Or was it to have been a double suicide pact? She exhibited her packet of poison to Jonson's best friends in the midst of offering him a toast: this was a public expression of love, yet it bristles with hostility. She had intended to take her child's life in the belief that a son whose nose and ears had been removed was not worth having. Nevertheless, the *liebestod* of her own projected suicide intimates that she felt a strong attraction toward the child whom she had intended to kill: if he were to be maimed, she would have nothing to live for. Her presence at the banquet, as well as her behavior there, implies that she was an important part of his life; but this anecdote represents the sum total of what he had to say about her. Even so, beneath all these layers of ambiguity Jonson's old mother had a straightforward message to convey. Her appearance at the feast confirmed and publicized the impression that her son's life had hung in the balance during his imprisonment.

At the age of twenty-six Jonson had responded to a threat of death by defying the state and joining the Catholic Church. When a comparable crisis occurred in his mid-thirties, he made a prolonged, and ultimately successful, effort to reach an accommodation with the state. His incarceration in 1605 made it abundantly clear that the price of continued defiance was too great to be borne; at the same time, the advantages of making common cause with James's government were more apparent now than they had ever been. Jonson's letters from prison are full of assurances about his loyalty, his patriotism, and his eagerness to do the state some service. His conduct during the months that followed his release indicates that he had every intention of fulfilling those assurances.

Until this point Jonson's transactions with the Privy Council had always been acrimonious. In the autumn of 1605, however, he was presented with an extraordinary opportunity to show his loyalty to James's government, and he made the most of it. On the night of November 4, a recusant named Guy Fawkes was discovered in the cellar of Parliament House together with thirty-six barrels of gunpowder that he had planned to explode when King James opened a joint session of the Lords and Commons on the following day. Shortly thereafter, Salisbury learned that Jonson had dined with Robert Catesby and Thomas Winter, two of the leading figures in the Gunpowder Plot, just a month previously. On November 7, the council summoned Jonson and asked him to track down a Catholic priest whom they wanted to interrogate about the plot. He complied with their request "upon the first Mention of it," and armed with a commission promising that "he [the priest] should securely come and go," set about his mission. But the Catholic clergymen did not trust him. Jonson could "speake with no one in Person" but instead "receav'd answere of doubts, and difficulties." Writing to Salisbury on the eighth, he brusquely indicted the entire community of English priests and questioned the wisdom of remaining within the Catholic Church: "So that to tell your Lordship plainly my heart, I thinke they are All so enweav'd in it, as it will make 500 Gentlemen lesse of the Religion within this weeke." "For my selfe," he added, "if I had bene a Priest, I would have put on wings to such an Occasion, and have thought it no adventure, where I might have done (besides His *Majesty,* and my Country) all Christianity so good service" (HS, XI, 578; I, 202–203).

Having adopted the Catholic faith "by trust of a priest," Jonson now found himself at odds with the priesthood. Father Thomas Wright, the one Catholic priest with whom he is known to have been on friendly terms prior to the plot, had consistently maintained that English Catholics could, and should, be loyal subjects of the crown; Wright was now interrogating Guy Fawkes at the behest of the council. The refusal of the priests to cooperate with Jonson, however accurate their assessment of their duty, could only strengthen his ties to the government. It was James and Salisbury to whom, at the close of his letter to the Earl, he pledged his loyalty: "I do not only with all readinesse offer my service, but will perform it with

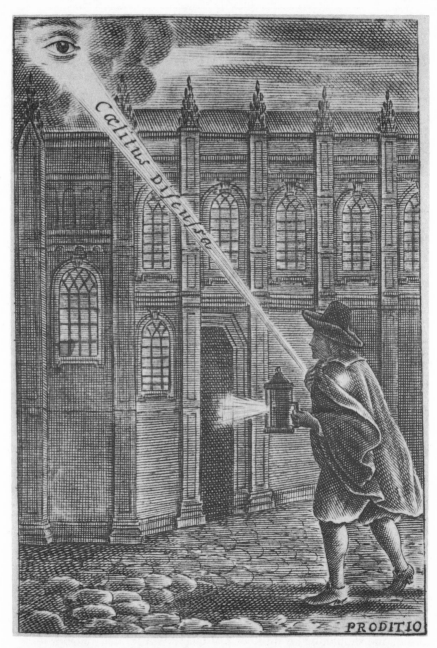

Guy Fawkes Discovered by Providence, 1605. Fawkes is sneaking into Parliament House. The inscription in the ray of light says "Caelitus discussa" (overthrown by heavenly aid). "Proditio" (lower right) means "betrayal."

Detail from *The Execution of the Gunpowder Plotters,* artist unknown, 1606. On the right a conspirator is cut down from a gibbet. The conspirator on the left has had his intestines removed and cast onto the fire. His left leg is about to be immersed in pitch in order to preserve it for public display. The executioner is exhibiting his heart to the crowd. This spectacle helps explain Jonson's decision to cooperate with the authorities.

as much integrity, as your particular Favor, or his Majesties Right in any Subject he hath, can exact."[9]

Jonson could not help the council unravel the plot, but he did express his fealty to James by articulating the King's own view of what had happened. In his speech to Parliament on November 9, 1605, James tried to set the failed assassination attempt in the best possible light. He stressed that those English Catholics "who yet remain good and faithfull Subjects" would not be turned into scapegoats. He maintained that his deliverance from harm was a mark of God's special favor toward himself and reminded the assembled Lords and Commons that God had saved himself and them on "two great and fearfull *Domes-dayes.*" The Gowrie Plot, which had been foiled in 1600, had threatened not only Scotland but England as well, since "ye also by your future interest, should have tasted of my ruine"; the Gunpowder Plot portended an even greater disaster since this "was a destruction prepared not for me alone, but for you all that are here present, and wherein no ranke, age, nor sexe should have been spared." Jonson's epigram "To King James" (*Ep, 35*) carried forward the work of reconciliation. As a law-abiding Catholic, he rejoiced in the knowledge that "we have now no cause / Left us of feare, but first our crimes, then lawes." Like James, he discerned the hand of providence in the King's rescue ("how could we know god more?"), and he too drew a parallel between the earlier and the later attempts on James's life: "First thou preserved wert, our king to bee, / And since, the whole land was preserv'd for thee."[10]

Jonson also needed to settle his accounts with the Privy Councilors who had stood by him when he was accused of libel. During his confinement, he had promised Salisbury that he would sing the praises "of you and yours to Posterity" (HS, I, 196) upon winning his release, and that promise had now fallen due. Since Jonson had, so far as one can tell, refrained from writing poems in praise of important statesmen prior to 1605, he was committing himself to a new and challenging form of verse. The laudatory poem addressed to a powerful patron poses the most difficult of tests for a poet who prides himself on his honesty and independence. How does one celebrate the great man's virtues without lapsing into flattery?

This question takes on central importance in "To Robert Earl of Salisbury," a poem that deals with the problems of writing about Salisbury rather than with the Earl himself. To begin with, Jonson questions the necessity of writing the poem at all, since Salisbury's achievements are self-evident: "What need hast thou of me? or of my *Muse?* / Whose actions so themselves doe celebrate." He answers this question by frankly acknowledging that it is he who needs Salisbury: "'Tofore, great men were glad of *Poets:* Now, / I, not the worst, am covetous of thee." Although he has no hope "Of adding to thy fame; thine may to me, / When, in my booke, men reade but CECILL's name." The implied compliment ("you are so great that nothing I say can make any difference") can also be read as a critique of the complimentary mode ("you are what you are and nothing I say can make any difference"). The ironic reading tacitly challenges the patron to enhance the poet's self-esteem by living up to the terms of the naive reading. Jonson's initial response to the challenge of the laudatory poem is a *recusatio;* he praises Salisbury by declining to praise him.[11]

Despite Jonson's initial wariness his second epigram to King James and the two other epigrams he addressed to Salisbury mark a significant change in his attitude toward the commonwealth. His earlier poems of praise, which date back to the turn of the century, had been addressed to fellow outsiders who preserved their virtue by holding themselves aloof from public affairs. He was still thinking in these terms when he helped

The righte honorable: ROBERT
CECILL Earle of SALISBVRI.
Vicount Cranborne. Baron of
Essingdon, principall secretary
to his Maiestie, Mr of ye Courte
of wardes & liueres, Chancelor of
the vniuersitie of Cambridge,
knyghte of ye noble order of the
garter, and one of his highenesse
most honorable priuye Councell.
SERO
SED
SERIO

Robert Cecil, Earl of Salisbury, by Renold Elstrack, 1605–1608. The tablet on the upper left alludes to the Earldom of Salisbury, which was conferred on Cecil in 1605.

prepare the arches for James's royal entry and wrote the "Panegyre." Even in the midst of a tumultuous civic procession the King remains an essentially private figure, a man preoccupied with abstract virtues that are perceptible only to himself and the poet. In the aftermath of the Gunpowder Plot, however, Jonson came to view James as a national hero who had made God's will visible to his people, and himself as a public poet who spoke for those people—"we," "us"—by singing James's praises. In the second of his epigrams to Salisbury, Jonson can "see / The judgement of the king so shine in thee"; he concludes the third by saying that to praise Salisbury is to praise the commonwealth: "whil'st I meant but thine to gratulate, / I'have sung the greater fortunes of our state." [12]

Over the course of that autumn he wrote patriotic epigrams to William Lord Mounteagle, the Catholic peer who had uncovered the plot, and Sir Henry Cary, the hero of a battle fought in Germany on October 8, 1605. In his epigram "To Thomas Earl of Suffolk," his benefactor of 1605, the criterion of popular approval becomes even more important than that of lineage or rank. Despite Howard's "blood" and "place," he stood "highest then, / When, in mens wishes, so thy vertues wrought, / As all thy honors were by them first sought." It is the ordinary well-wisher, Jonson concludes, who ultimately "proves, that is gods, which was the peoples voice." *Vox populi vox dei:* for a man who had scorned the "fomie praise, that drops from common jawes," it is an extraordinary change of attitude. [13]

By the end of October Jonson was reunited with his wife Anne and attending services in the Anglican Church. The first hint of a reconciliation crops up in a court record dated January 10, 1606, which alleges that the Jonsons "refuse not to Come to divine servis but have absented themselves from the Communion" despite "beinge oftentimes admonished." The *Book of Common Prayer* (1559) decreed that every parishioner had to take Holy Communion on Easter Sunday of every year. The authorities were specifically concerned, then, with the Jonsons' failure to receive the sacrament during the previous spring. On April 26, the day before Easter, when Jonson went before the court to answer this charge, he stated that "bothe he and his wife doe goe ordinarily to Churche and to his own parish Churche and so hath done this halfe yeare." Since the Gunpowder Plot had been foiled a "half yeare" previously, it appears that the Jonsons began attending Anglican services at St. Anne's, Blackfriars—their new parish church—immediately after the exposure of the plot, when anti-Catholic sentiment was running high. The date at which they began living together is harder to pin down; but since Jonson also testified that he was unable to say whether or not his wife had received Communion on Easter 1605, the reconciliation was still a recent occurrence in the autumn of that year. [14]

Hymenaei, Jonson's Twelfth Night masque for 1605–6, combines the themes of marital and political union. The leading motifs of *Hymenaei*—the sacredness of marriage, the triumph of female reason over male passion, the sacrifice of self-interest to the good of the commonwealth—linked Jonson's personal affairs to the life of the state. The purpose of this masque was to solemnize the marriage of Robert Devereaux, the fourteen-year-old Earl of Essex, to Lady Frances Howard, the thirteen-year-old daughter of the Earl of Suffolk. Suffolk and Salisbury had arranged the match in the hope that it would patch up a feud. Four years earlier they had helped bring young Essex's celebrated father to the executioner's block; now they sought to end the quarrel by marrying the young Earl into the family of his old enemies. Although Essex was, in the view of the Venetian Ambassador, "but little the friend of Salisbury, who was the sole and governing cause of the late Earl's execution," he had no choice but to set his enmity aside.[15] This marriage was a transparently public occasion; it proclaimed that the time had come for individuals to subordinate their private interests to the good of the whole.

Hymenaei is a set of variations on this central theme. "The conceit or soule of the mask," wrote the news merchant John Pory, "was Hymen bringing in a bride and Juno pronubas priest a bridegroome, proclaiming that those two should be sacrificed to Nuptial union, and here the poet made an apostrophe to the union of the kingdomes." The "sacrifice" of these two individuals was accompanied by a stunning display of iconographic lore linking the wedding to the great principle of union in all its manifestations. The preliminary capering of eight male dancers (the four humors and the four affections), who "leapt forth to disturb the sacrifice to union," signified the absence of Reason, who alone could unify the little state of man. The descent of Reason and her ladies-in-waiting in the "*two great cloudes, that . . . were seene to stoupe, and fall gently downe upon the earth*" ("not after the stale downright perpendicular fashion, like a bucket into a well," Pory noted appreciatively, "but came gently sloping down") corresponded to the great chain of being that united heaven and earth. The symbolism of the speeches and songs was stupendously complex. Just as James had unified England and Scotland, so the classical wedding rite linked modern Britain with ancient Rome, and English common law with Scottish civil law. Juno, goddess of marriage, was a pun on *uno,* the Latin word for "one," just as every marriage, in this ornate symbolic panoply, reenacted the mystery of the many and the one. King James was the "priest of peace" who united the roles of God and man.[16]

In *Hymenaei* Jonson repeatedly insists that the local interests of disparate individuals must ultimately be incorporated into a symmetrical whole. Yet he must have recognized that these ideological concepts were being used to validate a naked display of power in which one set of individuals (Essex, his mother, and his father's old followers) were coerced into yielding to another (Salisbury and the Howards). This subtext became visible on the following night when fifteen champions of Truth jousted with fifteen champions of Opinion in the *Barriers,* which Jonson wrote as a sequel to *Hymenaei.* Needless to say, the partisans of Truth, who were upholding the cause of marriage (unity), prevailed over those of Opinion, who vied on behalf of the single life (division). Assigning the jousters their parts in these *Barriers* posed some interesting questions of diplomacy: what courtier would willingly wear the livery of Opinion in a contest he was foreordained to lose? Salisbury kept a list of the men assigned to each of the two sides—a clear indication that he was directly involved in the planning for this spectacle. The solution was straightforward. The Howards, along with their relatives, clients, and fellow Catholics, filled out the ranks of Truth (five of the fifteen who fought for the bride bore the Howard name). The majority of those who upheld the cause of Opinion had followed the late Earl of Essex; he had personally knighted at least half of them.[17] To oppose matrimony, on such an occasion, was implicitly to oppose the wedding that had taken place the day before. Some of the jousters doubtless believed in the discredited opinion that they were called upon to defend; but the script relegated them to the losing side. Jonson would not have had anything to say about who fought on which side, but he did write the script, and he would shortly publish the *Barriers,* along with the names of the winners and the losers, in the 1606 quarto of *Hymenaei.*

The younger, Elizabethan Jonson had cast his lot with the defiant malcontents of that era. Although he had not followed the second Earl of Essex, he was close to several Essexians and (loner that he was) had formed no visible ties to any faction at court. By the end of 1605 an older, Jacobean Jonson had joined forces with Salisbury and the Howards and was actively promoting their interests under the banner of "union." Whether we choose to characterize this budding court poet as opportunistic, prudent, or patriotic, it is clear that his relationship to the state had undergone an important change. The Elizabethan Jonson, and especially the author of *Sejanus,* drew a sharp line of division between moral virtue and power; the Jacobean Jonson would consistently equate virtue and power.

The correspondence over *Eastward Ho,* the early epigrams to Jacobean statesmen, and the self-conscious juggling with "truth" and "opinion" in the *Barriers,* all indicate a new willingness to compromise, to see both sides of an issue, and to keep an open mind. At the same time, Jonson was reading (or rereading) Lucian and Erasmus, the great proponents of skepticism and irony. During his confinement in 1605 he either had a copy of Erasmus's *Praise of Folly* at hand or knew the text well enough to quote it from memory in his letter to Salisbury.[18] In the winter of 1605–6 he drew upon *The Praise of Folly* and on Erasmus's translations of Lucian's *Dialogues* while working on *Volpone; or, The Fox,* the play that would finally establish his reputation as a major comic writer.

The Lucianic device that caught the attention of both Erasmus and Jonson was the mock encomium—the oration in praise of "things without honor"—and, more broadly, the foolish orator who tries to seduce the reader into adopting his or her own viewpoint. In Lucian's ninth *Dialogue of the Dead,* for example, Jonson came across Polystratus, a childless old plutocrat who, like Volpone, spends a happy life reaping gifts from legacy hunters and finally bequeaths his fortune to a "pretty boy from Phrygia." Unlike Juvenal and Horace, Lucian never denounces the target of his satire; instead, he lets Polystratus present his case in a highly persuasive fashion. By suspending judgment, Lucian implies that what is deplorable in one context (ethical, familial) may be advantageous in another (economic, aesthetic). The reader, rather than the author, is the person who finally has to choose between these alternatives.[19]

Jonson turned to Lucian at a moment when he was rethinking his entire approach to comedy. After the fiasco of *Eastward Ho*—not to mention the three previous occasions on which he had been accused of slander—outright mockery was no longer a feasible alternative for him. Lucian, the praiser of folly, offered Jonson an oblique, rather than a direct, plan of attack. Lucian does not censure anyone; his protagonists condemn themselves. Erasmus praised him for "reviving the sharpness of old comedy while stopping short of its abusiveness" and concluded that he knew "of no stage comedy or satire which can be compared with this man's dialogues."[20] Jonson had tried to achieve this effect of sharpness without abusiveness in his comical satires, *Every Man out of His Humour, Cynthia's Revels,* and *Poetaster,* but all three plays were fraught with personal animosity, and all struck contemporaries as unduly strident. When Jonson adopted the Lucianic method and discarded the persona of the comical satirist, that problem disappeared.

Consider, for example, the famous opening speech in *Volpone.* The protagonist delivers a stirring oration in praise of gold. He likens its quickening power to that of the sun and contends that it is the ultimate measure of human happiness, "far transcending / All stile of joy, in children, parents, friends." A younger Jonson would have characterized the speaker as a buffoon and (in case anyone missed the point) produced an authorial spokesman to itemize his follies. The author of *Volpone* offers no rebuttal whatever to these all too believable claims, but instead leaves his audience suspended midway between approval and revulsion. Volpone's performance, as Douglas Duncan remarks, is "as theatrically compelling as it is morally outrageous." *Volpone,* he continues, marks a major turning point in Jonson's artistic development: "His lifelong belief that the sensationalism of the theater militated against moral discrimination ceases to inhibit him, and becomes a source of strength, as soon as he starts to write obliquely."[21] Like *The Faerie Queene* and *Paradise Lost, Volpone* forces its readers to work their way through a maze of seductive falsehoods; if they are any the wiser at the end of the play, it is because they have withstood this assault on their moral bearings.

Volpone worships gold because it holds the promise of unlimited self-gratification:

> What should I doe,
> But cocker up my *genius,* and live free
> To all delights, my fortune calls me to?
> I have no wife, no parent, child, allie,
> To give my substance to; but whom I make,
> Must be my heire: and this makes men observe me.
> This draws new clients, daily, to my house,
> Women, and men, of every sexe, and age,
> That bring me presents, send me plate, coine, jewels,
> With hope, that when I die, (which they expect
> Each greedy minute) it shall then returne,
> Ten-fold upon them . . . (I.i.70–81)

The distinctive feature of this household is the absence of any familial ties whatsoever. Since he has no one to leave his "substance" to, Volpone attracts an endless succession of clients who send him "plate, coine, jewels" in the hope of inheriting his fortune. Like *Sejanus, Volpone* depicts a world where the bond of patron and client has supplanted all familial loyalties. Volpone and Mosca, the legacy-hunting magnifico and his clever parasite, are the comic analogues of Tiberius and Sejanus; the same patterns of behavior that arouse disgust in Jonson's tragedy of 1603 become a source of ribald delight in his comedy of 1606. The Fox, who has neither wife, parent, child, nor ally, takes a perverse delight in the ruination of other men's families. He and his parasite, who doubles as Volpone's child and lover, are not content merely to acquire their clients' gold; instead, and at considerable risk, they persuade one man to disinherit his son and another to give the magnifico his wife. Jonson consistently portrays the seducer and his accomplice as colorful and amusing characters, and spectators usually find it impossible to judge them harshly. Bonario and Celia, the disinherited son and the abused wife, are drab by comparison.

Just as Volpone gulls his clients, Jonson gulls his audience; but Jonson's falsehood has the capacity to educate as well as to delude. Where his illusory hero inflicts real injuries, the author provides a vicarious experience of vice that teaches the audience to strengthen its powers of discrimination. The analogy between the author and his leading character is submerged at the outset, but it leaps into the foreground when Volpone, hoping to catch a glimpse of Celia, his client's wife, disguises himself as a mountebank and stations his portable stage beneath her window. The mountebank's lengthy description of his professional life has no particular relevance to Volpone's situation, but it says a great deal about Ben Jonson in the winter of 1606. The key to this personal allegory, as Alvin Kernan has shown, lies in the commonplace analogy between physician and author, or medicine and writing. Read in this light, the mountebank's self-portrait takes on a strikingly biographical dimension. It *"may seem strange,"* he begins,

> that I, your SCOTO MANTUANO [Ben Jonson], *who was ever wont to fixe my banke in face of the publike* piazza [in the centrally located private theaters], *. . . should, now (after eight months absence* [following last summer's performance of *Eastward Ho*], *from this illustrous city of* Venice [London]) *humbly retire my selfe, into an obscure nooke of the* piazza [the Globe Theater] *. . . I am not . . . content to part with my commodities at a cheaper rate, then I accustomed: looke not for it* [admission prices were raised for the earliest performances of *Volpone*]. *Nor that the calumnious reports of that impudent detractor . . . who gave out, in publike, I was condem'd a 'Sforzato to the galleys* [sentenced to corporal punishment], *for poisoning* [slandering] *the Cardinall* BEMBO'S—*Cooke, hath at all attached, much lesse dejected me.*

Just as Jonson had boasted of his superiority to popular playwrights who borrowed their plots from familiar collections of tales and basked in the admiration of the groundlings, Scoto scorns the *"ground* Ciarlitani," that *"come in, lamely, with their mouldy tales out of* Boccacio" to the applause of *"your shrivel'd, sallad-eating* artizans." [22]

Having replied to his detractors, Scoto proceeds to advertise his wares. This part of his oration begins with a disarming show of modesty: *"I have nothing to sell, little, or nothing to sell."* In other words, to quote Duncan's gloss, after "years devoted mainly to cultivating an exalted image of the moral poet at court and at the Blackfriars Theater, his object in coming to the Bankside was not to sell a stern moral message, or indeed to sell anything"—except his play. Like Lucian and Erasmus, he presents himself, with self-deprecating irony, as a writer who merely seeks to provide a little harmless recreation. Yet Scoto/Jonson takes enormous pride in his craftsmanship and boasts that although *"very many have assay'd, like apes in imitation of that, which is really and essentially in mee, to make of this oile; bestow'd great cost in furnaces, stilles, alembeks, continuall fires, and preparation of the ingredients . . . when these practitioners come to the last decoction, blow, blow, puff, puff, and all flies in* fumo: *ha, ha, ha."* Although Scoto never gives away any trade secrets, it is clear from the description of his laboratory that he practices alchemy. Scoto uses the furnaces and alembics to vaporize and distill his raw materials until nothing remains but *"this blessed* unguento, *this rare extraction, that hath only power to disperse all malignant humours."* The alchemical term for this process is *sublimation.* Jonson, the praiser of folly, uses the same method to produce his literary gold. He collects the basest elements of human experience, extracts their essential properties, and creates something extraordinarily precious: a work of art. His mastery of this process has not come easily. *"For my selfe, I alwaies from my youth have indevour'd to get the rarest secrets, and booke them . . . whil'st others have beene at the* balloo, *I have beene at my booke."* But Scoto's apprenticeship is now at an end. Like his bookish creator Ben Jonson, he is *"now past the craggie paths of studie, and come to the flowrie plaines of honour, and reputation,"* where he enjoys the patronage of *"the Cardinals* Montalto, Fernese, *the great duke of* Tuscany, *my gossip, with divers other princes."* [23]

The rarest secret of all resides within the soul of the maker. Only someone who possesses *"that, which is really and essentially in mee,"* the mountebank maintains, can hope to *"make of this oile."* The creative process, as Jonson envisions it here, foreshadows the modern, psychological concept of sublimation.[24] *Volpone* expresses base instincts that are "really and essentially in" Jonson, but it does so in a way that involves neither adverse consequences nor acute loss of pleasure. He accomplishes this feat by projecting his instinctual drives onto Volpone, his counterpart and foil within the text. Where Jonson has learned to channel his lust and aggressiveness into artistic creation, Volpone suffers from a childlike inability to defer gratification even for a moment.

When Volpone next appears without his disguise, he describes himself as a man who literally cannot find any outlet for his erotic desires:

> angry CUPID, bolting from her eyes,
> Hath shot himselfe into me, like a flame;
> Where, now, he flings about his burning heat,
> As in a fornace, an ambitious fire,
> Whose vent is stopt. The fight is all within me. (II.iv.3–7)

When Celia refuses to cuckold her husband upon Volpone's first entreaty, he immediately attempts to rape her and promptly falls into the hands of the law. Once again, Jonson's own experience offers an instructive coun-terexample. The author of *Volpone* prided himself on his self-control and told Drummond that he "lay diverse times with a woman, who shew him all that he wished except the last act, which she never would agree unto" (*Conv*, 292–294).

Volpone wins his acquittal by persuading the judges that he really is a dying old man, but this experience brings on a renewed sensation of phys-ical constriction: "'Fore god, my left legge 'gan to have the crampe; / And I apprehended, straight, some power had strooke me." Volpone responds to the hand of correction with an instinctive surge of aggression ("I shall conquer") and since he cannot conceive of how to sublimate this impulse, he acts it out: "Any device, now, of rare, ingenious knavery . . . / Would make me up, againe!" The sole purpose of Volpone's device is to inflict pain on his former clients, and it succeeds beyond his wildest dreams. As he publicly torments the legacy hunters with florid insults, Volpone's triumph is assured but so is his defeat. His distracted lawyer now reopens the trial that had previously been resolved in his favor, and this time the judges send him off to prison "till thou bee'st sicke, and lame indeed"— the very fate that Jonson had narrowly escaped just a few months previ-ously.[25]

Jonson could identify with his villain-hero because his own instinctual drives had taken him down the very path that leads Volpone to ruin. He too had been a "rider on mens wives" (IV.vi.24); he too was "a contemner and Scorner of others" (*Conv*, 680–681), to recall Drummond's appraisal, who used wit to inflict pain on others even when the cost of doing so was unacceptably high; he too had chosen patronage over family. The capacity to sublimate is the "*blessed* unguento" that preserves the mature artist from the maladies which beset his childish hero, and directs Jonson's de-structive energies toward profitable ends. The spectators undergo the same temptations that have bedeviled the author, but they neither engage in antisocial behavior nor experience any adverse results. By the end of the play an ideal theatergoer will have learned to anticipate the temptations that Volpone finds so irresistible, and to recognize the consequences of yielding to them.

Anyone who sets out to be a poet, Jonson maintained, has to have "the exact knowledge of all vertues, and their Contraries; with ability to render the one lov'd, the other hated, by his proper embattaling them" (*Disc*, 1039–41). Everyone can agree that it is advantageous to have an intimate awareness of "all vertues"; problems arise, however, with the identical claim about "their Contraries." Is it really desirable to have an exact knowledge of vice? Jonson had posed this question in the opening lines of the "Epode":

> Not to know vice at all, and keepe true state,
> > Is vertue, and not *Fate:*
> Next, to that vertue, is to know vice well,
> > And her blacke spight expell.   (*For,* 11.1–4)

The pun on "well" ("precisely," but also "intimately") plunges the reader into the struggle to combine awareness of vice with the rejection of it; the heavily stressed rhyme with "expell" decisively resolves the contest in favor of rejection. Jonson had struggled to maintain this precarious balance throughout the earlier part of his career. The illicit wishes that he could not afford to indulge in real life furnished him with a wellspring of creative energy, but he was initially reluctant to express those wishes in any direct or compelling way. Instead, he sequestered them within the "humors," those harmless buffoons who are always held at arm's length from the poet-hero. When Jonson discarded this defense mechanism, he became a great comic playwright. The violent eruptions of lust and aggressiveness that occur during the middle and final acts of *Volpone* derive from the humors, but they exude a brutal, seductive glamor that is wholly absent from Jonson's earlier comedies.

Volpone marks the arrival of Jonson's maturity in a psychological, as well as an artistic, sense. During the winter of 1605–6 he found that he was strong enough to confront and utilize impulses that he had hitherto kept at bay. Previously, he had prided himself on the fact that he pored over his plays for months at a time; in the Prologue to *Volpone* he boasts that "five weekes fully pen'd it" (16). What caused this sudden access of self-confidence?

During the latter half of 1605 Jonson had successfully resolved two major crises in his personal life. The first of these had to do with his marriage. He had abandoned his wife and family in the winter of 1602–3, just at the time when Volpone, who has pretended to be dead for "this three yeere," took up the trade of legacy hunting. After he left his wife, Jonson no longer had any lawful outlet for his sexual desires; he was obliged either to maintain an enforced celibacy or to regress to the philandering ways of his youth. Moreover, the death of his children absolved him of all parental responsibility just at the time when he was being offered lodging at the homes of Townshend (a wealthy gentleman), Cotton (an important civil servant), and Aubigny (a great peer). The temptation to exchange wedded love for adultery and family for patronage was very real for Jonson during this period, but in the end he did not succumb. Instead, he was reunited with his wife and, by December 1605, hard at work on the most erudite wedding masque that had ever been written.

Ben and Anne Jonson were reunited under the shadow of the same af-

fliction that had separated them three years previously. There was an outbreak of bubonic plague in the autumn of 1605 (the theaters were closed
from October 5 to December 15) and a serious epidemic in 1606. This
time Jonson remained at home. Sir John Roe "died in his armes of the
pest" early that winter and, since none of Roe's family were in town, Jonson paid for his funeral on January 17: "He furnished his charges 20 lb,
which was given him back." This incident reverses the pattern of Jonson's
experience in 1603. Instead of fleeing the plague, he confronted it and bore
the dying victim in his arms. In his epitaph "On Sir John Roe" he consoled
himself with the thought that his friend died "at home in his repaire."
Jonson himself was now prepared to meet the same fate: "Which if most
gracious heaven grant like thine, / Who wets my grave, can be no friend
of mine." [26]

The second crisis had to do with his imprisonment over *Eastward Ho*
and with the larger problem of his chronic rebelliousness. Prior to *Volpone,* Jonson had led a risky and violent life. Had he disappeared after
Eastward Ho, he would be remembered today as a shadowy outlaw poet
who squandered his chances. Recall the reckless passage at arms in Flanders, the scurrilous *Isle of Dogs,* the killing of Gabriel Spencer, the Poet's
Quarrel, the beating of Marston, the trouble with Chief Justice Popham
over *Poetaster* and with the Privy Council over *Sejanus,* the brawl with
Northampton's retainer, the run-in with Suffolk on Twelfth Night of 1604,
and finally, just when he was making a name for himself at court, the
egregious folly of *Eastward Ho.* This man appears to have spent the better
part of his adult life courting disaster. In the Fox, Jonson found a folk hero
who duplicated his own need for risk and excitement; the author's intention, however, was not to press the similarity but to establish differences.
He could afford to identify with his protagonist because he knew that they
were different in reality. Volpone's failure signifies Jonson's success.

After 1605 Jonson was never again in serious difficulty with the law.
Instead, he channeled his turbulent emotions into more constructive endeavors. The youth who had actively pursued other men's wives learned
to court them in verse during his thirties and forties. The sequel to Volpone's seductive love lyric, "*Come my* CELIA, *let us prove,* / *While we may,
the sports of love,*" is the mature poet's "Song: To Celia": "Drinke to me,
onely, with thine eyes." The disaffected intellectual of late Elizabethan England became a skillful infighter at the court of James I and a belligerent
defender of the King and commonwealth. The reckless individualist came
to value the "gather'd selfe" that creates its own refuge against the vagaries of fortune. [27]

Jonson's prudence was tested on the day before Easter Sunday, 1606,
when he appeared before the Consistory Court of London. Someone had

informed Edward Stanhope, the Bishop of London's Vicar-General, that the Jonsons had "absented themselves from the Communion [despite] beinge oftentimes admonished which hathe Continued as farr as we Can learne ever since the kinge Came in." Stanhope's informants also reported that Jonson "is by fame a seducer of youthe to the popishe Religion." The judges who questioned Jonson on April 26 would have wanted to know why he and his wife had not taken Communion on previous Easter Sundays and if they were prepared to do so tomorrow. Jonson replied that he and his wife regularly went to their parish church at St. Anne's on Sundays, "but for their receiving he sayethe he hathe refused to recive the Communion untill he shall be resolved either by the minister of the parish or some other in the scruple he maketh therin but his wife he sayethe for any thing he knowthe hathe gon to Churche and used alwayes to receive the Communion and is appointed to receive the Communion to morow." Jonson could not be certain whether or not Anne had taken Communion on previous Easters "since the kinge Came in" because the two of them had been separated from the spring of 1603 to the spring of 1605; the assertion that she had done so "for any thing he knowthe" enabled him to shield her without perjuring himself. He was equally equivocal on the question of his own compliance. He refused to receive Communion at this time, "having as he Confesseth heretofore bin of some othr opinion in Religion"; but, the clerk went on, "nowe uppon better advisement he is determined to alter," and to that end "desireth such learned men to be assigned unto him to confer withall he promising to Conforme him selfe according as they shall advise him and perswade him." Stanhope responded favorably to this suggestion and gave Jonson his choice of four divines, instructing him to meet with one of them twice every week and to report back to him on the "last Court day of the next terme" (HS, I, 220–223).

Jonson had resolved a potentially destructive conflict in a painless and responsible way. Had he defied the judges, he would have been liable to heavy fines, the confiscation of his property, and perhaps even another prison sentence. Had he simply yielded to their demands, he would have done severe damage to his self-esteem and jeopardized his soul for eternity. Instead of directly confronting this excruciating dilemma, Jonson intellectualized it; his compromise solution suppressed the emotionally charged conflict between the individual and the state, focused attention on the affectively bland "scruple," and allowed both parties to avoid taking any action on the matter. To the best of our knowledge, the issue never *was* resolved; it just faded away, as did the wave of anti-Catholic hysteria that ensued in the wake of the Gunpowder Plot.

Jonson had moved into the mainstream of Jacobean court life. The 1606 quarto of *Hymenaei* and the *Barriers* identified all of the participants, including the names of the courtiers who had jousted on behalf of "Truth" and "Opinion," and thus could be read as a public gesture of support for Salisbury and the Howards. On July 24, 1606, Salisbury paid him thirteen pounds six pence for an eight-line speech welcoming King James and his brother-in-law, King Christian IV of Denmark, to his estate at Theobalds. The size of this fee had nothing to do with either the quantity or the quality of Jonson's verses. It was rather a sign, first, that "the author thereof ... hath his place equall with the best in those Artes," to quote a contemporary observer, and second, that Salisbury wanted to include Jonson within his clientage network. More commissions were in the offing. When the Merchant Tailors' Company feasted the royal family a year later, they asked Sir John Swinnerton "to conferr with Mr Beniamin Johnson the Poet, aboute a speeche to be made to welcome his Majestie, and for musique and other inventions, which maye give liking and delight to his Majestie, by reason that the Company doubt that their Schoolemaster and Schollers be not acquainted with such kinde Entertainments." The company subsequently paid twenty pounds "to Mr Beniamin Johnson, the poett, for inventing the speech to his Majesty and for making the songs, and his direccions to others in that business." [28]

By the time *Volpone* went to press in 1607, the King's Men had performed the play before enthusiastic audiences at Oxford and Cambridge. The idea of a playhouse full of educated theatergoers struck a responsive chord in Jonson. Here, at last, were flesh-and-blood spectators whom he could address without scorn or condescension. Instead, he dedicated his play "AND HIMSELFE" to "THE TWO FAMOUS UNIVERSITIES FOR THEIR LOVE AND ACCEPTANCE SHEWN TO HIS POEME IN THE PRESENTATION," and set out to justify their goodwill in a public letter that appeared in the quarto of *Volpone* (HS, V, 17–21).

Jonson's public letter to the two universities is an apology for his own life written in the classical manner. He adopts the posture of the good man who speaks out of disinterested concern for poetry, and his self-defense thus becomes indistinguishable from his defense of poetry in general. The major premises of his apology had already been formulated in Horace's "Epistle to Augustus," in Sidney's *Apology for Poetry,* and in the "Apologetical Dialogue" that Jonson added to *Poetaster.* He once again draws a categorical distinction between the poet, "a teacher of things divine, no less then humane, a master in manners; and can alone (or with a few) effect the businesse of mankind," and the poetaster, who traffics in "ribaldry, profanation, blasphemy, all licence of offence to god, and man"

(28–30, 37–38). The distinction between them is a moral one: "For, if men will impartially, and not a-squint, looke toward the offices, and function of a Poet, they will easily conclude to themselves, the impossibility of any mans being the good Poet, without first being a good man" (20–23).

Although Jonson insists that his own work is diametrically opposed to that of the poetasters, the factual record of his career tells a rather different story. His epistle to the two universities does not simply recount his humanistic ideals; it also voices his continuing reaction against those aspects of his own life and work that did not conform to those ideals. Thus, he saves his most bitter denunciation for writers who "care not whose living faces they intrench, with their petulant stiles" (73–74)—the very offense that he himself had most frequently been accused of. Two of the passages in his epistle to the two universities echo the letter he had written to Salisbury during his imprisonment in 1605; *Eastward Ho* was still fresh in his memory. Although he could ask, with Erasmus, "what nation, societie, or generall order, or state I have provok'd?" he had to add parenthetically, "I speak of those [works] that are intirely mine" (51–52, 54–55) lest someone confront him with *The Isle of Dogs,* the original version of *Sejanus,* and *Eastward Ho.* At the end of the epistle he belligerently warns the enemies of poetry that "shee shall out of just rage incite her servants (who are *genus irritabile*) to spoute inke in their faces, that shall eate, farder than their marrow, into their fames" (138–141).

Jonson was playing a part, but it does not follow that he was being insincere. The framework of assumptions that he inherited from Horace, Erasmus, and Sidney provided him with a set of ideals to live up to and gave him a way of making his own life intelligible. The habit of self-consciously imitating classical authors, together with his employment as a maker of court entertainments, instilled a strong belief in the value of masks and roles. The same set of convictions bred a rooted dislike for the emerging Protestant cult of sincerity: from Jonson's standpoint, anyone who claimed to speak directly from the heart was bound to be a hypocrite.[29]

Turning to his "latest work," *Volpone,* he claims to have promulgated "the doctrine, which is the principall end of *poesie,* to inform men, in the best reason of living" (107–109) but he also cautions his readers not to confuse that doctrine with the gross mechanics of his plot. He punished Volpone in order "to put the snaffle in their mouths, that crie out, we never punish vice in our *enterludes*" (115–116)—that is, to silence the Puritan opponents of the stage. He could just as easily have "varied" the ending to suit the biases of "the learned, and charitable critick" who prefers the happy ending mandated by "the strict rigour of *comick* law" (111, 110). *Volpone,* like all of Jonson's satirical comedies, provides the reader with negative examples; it shows the audience how not to live. Volpone's instincts burn brightly—he is magnificently and seductively alive in that sense; but this man who has neither wife, parent, child, nor ally has no reason for living and his behavior is fundamentally suicidal.

Jonson, by contrast, had excellent reasons for living. Although he does not refer to his personal circumstances in the text of his letter, he does touch upon them in his closing words: "From my house in the Black-Friars this 11. of February. 1607." The impoverished playwright and court hanger-on was now a householder in a fashionable London neighborhood. He had been reunited with his wife for a year and a half or more, and they were on the verge of having children again. Anne became pregnant in the spring of 1607 and gave birth to their fourth child early in the following year (HS, XI, 575). It was a boy named Ben.

• CHAPTER EIGHT •

Man about Town

By his thirty-fifth year, Jonson had established a pattern of work that he would sustain for the next decade. He wrote celebratory masques for the court and satirical comedies for the playhouse; he addressed laudatory poems to eminent men and women, and defamatory ones to an equally select, if nameless, group of *bêtes noires*. He had divided his energies between praising and blaming since the beginning of his career, but between 1606 and 1616 he heeded Sidney's maxim that "the oblique must be known as well as the right," and brought these superficially disparate activities into a richly dialectical relationship.[1]

Here again, the winter of 1605–6, when he wrote *Hymenaei*, the *Barriers*, and *Volpone* within a space of two or three months, marks a watershed in his development. Although the two court entertainments and the stage comedy are radically different in form and tone, they take up a single set of questions (family versus the single life, lineage versus individual autonomy, concord versus aggressiveness) and arrive at a common understanding of them. The instability of the borderline that separated these opposed, but symmetrical, forms of discourse stimulated Jonson's imagination. He was committed to literary genres that held up exact models of virtue, but such claims were always liable to be contradicted by experience. It was anyone's guess, for example, whether the marriage between young Essex and Lady Frances Howard really would further the cause of unity, as Jonson prophesied in his entertainments of 1606, or would lead to new divisions and become, in its turn, an object of satire.

The classic solution to this dilemma was the humanist doctrine of *laudando praecipere* ("to teach by praising"), which held that when poets tell "kings and great persons . . . what they are, they represent to them what they should be." It is up to the kings and great men to make that ideal into a reality. In his epigram "To My Muse," which comes immediately after his last two epigrams to Salisbury in the published text of Jonson's *Epigrams,* he complains that his muse has committed "most fierce idolatrie" to a "worthlesse lord." In the throes of remorse, he imagines that he will revert to a more puristic stance: "Welcome povertie. / Shee shall instruct my after-thoughts to write / Things manly, and not smelling parasite." Yet he ultimately consoles himself with the thought that the worthless lord has only transformed a laudatory poem into a satiric one: "But I repent me: Stay. Who e're is rais'd, / For worth he has not, He is tax'd, not prais'd."[2]

But Jonson did not merely praise Salisbury and Suffolk. *Hymenaei* and the *Barriers* helped them, in however modest a way, to consolidate their political power, and thus implicated Jonson in political maneuvers that had real, rather than merely literary, consequences. He himself tacitly acknowledged the narrowly partisan aspect of these works when he published the names of the winning and losing tilters in the 1606 quarto of *Hymenaei.* In the preface to this quarto Jonson tries to recapture these hostages to fortune by asserting that the meaning of his masques transcends their particular historical moment: "Though their voice be taught to sound to present occasions, their *sense,* or doth, or should always lay hold on more remov'd *mysteries*" (HS, VII, 209). Yet this assertion—which is always cited as an example of Jonson's idealism—could just as easily be read as the defensive reaction of an author who now realized that praise and blame were politically charged rhetorical formulas that he could adapt to suit any occasion.

The contradictions between the serene vision of Jonson's masques and the harsh realities of court life became increasingly pointed during the next two years.

On a symbolic level, *The Masque of Beauty,* Jonson and Jones's Twelfth Night entertainment for 1608, was a rhapsodic tribute to the civilizing power of the female form. The Queen wanted Jonson to write a sequel to *The Masque of Blackness* and instructed him to keep "the same persons, the daughters of Niger, but their beauties varied, according to promise, and their time of absence excus'd, with foure more added to their number." When the sixteen daughters finally appeared in triumph, Inigo Jones's floating island, which replaced the coral-shell boat used in *Blackness,* supplied Queen Anne and her fifteen ladies with a complete and fully harmonious kingdom of their own. The person who has made the ladies' island into an earthly paradise was not James, who is scarcely mentioned, but Aethiopa, their Queen, who was played by Anne. In its midst, she has "raised them a *Throne,* that still is seene / To turne unto the motion of the World." Where *The Masque of Blackness* had acknowledged, however ambivalently, the sovereignty of male reason, *Beauty* sang of a Platonized sexuality powerful enough to persuade even a rooted misogynist that *"women were the soules of men."* Like *Hymenaei, The Masque of Beauty* invited the court to "enjoy that happinesse, ev'en to envy, 'as when / *Beautie,* at large, brake forth, and conquer'd men." [3]

BeF?

The subtext of the performance itself, to judge from the accounts of contemporary male observers, was feminine aggressiveness and masculine docility. La Boderie, the French Ambassador, estimated the cost of Anne's masque to be in excess of thirty thousand pounds and a source of great consternation to the King and the Privy Council. Chamberlain was astounded by the extravagance of the jewelry: "One Lady," he noted, "and that under a baronesse, is saide to be furnished for better then an hundred thousand pound, and the Lady Arbella goes beyond her, and the Q. must not come behinde." The Venetian Ambassador agreed: "What beggared all else and possibly exceeded the public expectations was the wealth of pearls and jewels that adorned the Queen and her ladies, so abundant and splendid that in everyone's opinion no other court could have displayed such pomp and riches. So well composed and ordered was it all that it is evident the mind of her Majesty, the authoress of the whole, is gifted no less highly than her person." Anne insisted that the Spanish Ambassador Le Taxis, whose company and religion she preferred, be invited even though James, who had to contend with a very disgruntled French Ambassador, vainly tried to prevent her from doing so. She also saw to it that many of the dancers, including four of the newcomers, were Catholics. La Boderie, who wondered if the King of England was master in his own house, was appalled: "One cannot believe the power that she always holds over him and the tricks that she employs." [4]

The discrepancy between the idealized figures of the masque and their counterparts in everyday life was even more pronounced in *The Haddington Masque,* which Jonson wrote for the wedding of Viscount Haddington and Lady Elizabeth Radcliffe on February 9, 1608. During the early years of the reign, the King actively promoted a number of marriages between Scottish courtiers and English heiresses in the hope that such matches would further the union of the two kingdoms. Jonson wrote *The Haddington Masque* for one of the most important of these occasions. Haddington, who had single-handedly saved James's life at the time of the Gowrie conspiracy, was among the most prominent of the King's Scottish favorites; his bride was the eldest daughter of the Earl of Sussex. Four of the Scots who danced in Haddington's masque (Sir John Kennedy, Lord

Hay, Lord Crichton of Sanquhar, and Jonson's patron Lord D'Aubigny) also married into English wealth.[5]

The Haddington Masque celebrated this union of English and Scottish blood with intricate classical precedents and visual puns. The action commenced in front of a high red cliff that alluded to the bride's name (Radcliffe), and symbolized the *"height, greatnesse, and antiquitie"* of her family. Inside the rock was Vulcan's workshop and the "strange, and curious peece" that he had wrought for the wedding of Haddington and Elizabeth Radcliffe. The twelve noble dancers hidden within the cliff wore the costumes of the twelve zodiacal signs "that are praesiding at all *nuptiall* howers"; the full ensemble represented the *"heaven of marriage."* Their intricately turned dance linked the English and Scottish courtiers into a lively image of the united kingdom that James was trying to forge. The scene also prompted associations with book VIII of the *Aeneid,* where Vulcan forges the armor of Aeneas. The famous picture he had embossed on Aeneas's shield foretold the unifying of Italy under the "royal line of the future" that would unite the Trojan and the Italian races; James, by the same token, believed that marriages like Haddington's would foster a new line of modern Britons in which English and Scottish blood would be inextricably mixed.[6]

As in 1606, Jonson was called upon to celebrate an arranged marriage that carried strong political overtones, and once again he made an elegant argument for a highly controversial position. The very fact that James frequently had to cajole, bully, and bribe the English parents, coupled with the anguished complaints that survive in the domestic state papers, amply testify to the unpopularity of these matches. To understand the parents' agitation, one need only look at the Scottish courtiers who danced at Haddington's wedding. Sir John Kennedy had been awarded Elizabeth Brydges, daughter and coheiress of Giles, Lord Chandos, back in 1603. Sir John, in Stone's succinct account, "was an unscrupulous ruffian who turned out to be a bigamist with another wife in Scotland, ran through Elizabeth's fortune, and ended by assaulting her house with a gang of Scottish friends and driving her half-naked into the night." Lord Crichton of Sanquhar, who married the daughter of Sir George Penmer a month after dancing in *The Haddington Masque,* was no bargain either. A few years later Sanquhar settled what he fancied to be an old score with an English fencing master by hiring two assassins to murder the man in cold blood— a crime for which he was duly hanged. Just a year before Haddington's marriage James had taken extraordinary measures to arrange the marriage of his crony Sir James Hay to Honora Denny, the only daughter and heiress of Sir Edward Denny. He granted a large manor to the couple and their future issue in 1604, conditional upon their marriage; he made Denny a baron; he made Hay a baron; and he withheld the patent on the manor until Denny at last gave in and the couple were married on January 6, 1607. A year after *The Haddington Masque* James used similar measures to extract Katherine Clifton, the only daughter and heiress of Lord Clifton, from her outraged parents and marry her to yet another of the Scottish dancers, Jonson's patron Aubigny.[7]

Nor was there any popular support for the union of the two kingdoms. The parliaments of 1606 and 1607 had already thwarted James's attempts to push through legislation that would have integrated the laws and governance of England and Scotland. Moreover, the continuing hostility between his English and Scottish courtiers was a grave scandal.[8] Both of Jonson's early wedding masques celebrated overarching unions that were founded on illusion. On the levels of speech and song, *Hymenaei* and *The Haddington Masque* sustained extraordinary images of concord, but Jonson's iconography could not allay the strong countercurrents of discord that persisted after the dancing was over.

By the following winter, when Queen Anne asked Jonson to prepare yet another of her "personall presentations," he had discovered a way of incorporating the opposed perspectives of celebration and satire into the text of the masque itself. Jonson divided *The Masque of Queens Celebrated from the House of Fame* into two symmetrical halves: first "a foile, or false-Masque" put on by professional actors and dancers, and then a main masque performed, as always, by courtiers. The twelve witches who came "fraught with spight, / To overthrow the glory of this night" were "faithfull Opposites" to the twelve queens who succeeded them on the dance floor. Their presence at these "bright Nights / Of Honor" implied that detraction and fame, subversion and celebration, depend on one another for their fullest expression; the creatures of the antimasque opposed, but also defined, the noble ladies who danced in the main masque.[9]

The main masque transforms female self-assertion—the dominant motif in all of the Queen's masques—into an all-encompassing virtue. *The Masque of Queens* portrays Anne and eleven of her ladies as warrior queens "sitting upon a Throne triumphall" in the upper story of the "*House of Fame*," where Jones's costumes reiterated the message conveyed by Jonson's verses: Anne and her ladies had transcended their gender and taken on the attributes and offices of their male counterparts. The eleven ladies-in-waiting, led by Lady Bedford, who was attired as "*Penthesilea, the brave Amazon*," took the roles of great national heroines, but Anne played herself and left Jonson to explain why she, a living woman, should occupy the central niche in a palace of memory. "Here," he admitted, "I discerne a possible Objection . . . As, *How I can bring* Persons, *of so different* Ages, *to appeare, properly, together? Or, Why (which is the more unnaturall) . . . I joine the living, with the dead?*" In response, he

Lucy, Countess of Bedford, as Penthesilea by Inigo Jones. From the drawings for Jonson's *Masque of Queens,* 1609. The battle helmet and sword transform Jonson's patroness into an androgynous warrior queen.

insists that poetry transcends history: "*For these all live; and together, in their Fame . . . if I would fly to the all-daring Power of Poetry, Where could I not take Sanctuary?*" But Queene Anne had caused this particular sanctuary to be erected at her own expense! Jonson sustains the pretense that the eleven queens of yesteryear have spontaneously chosen Anne to be sovereign over them ("These, without envy, 'on her / In life desir'd that honor to confer"); yet he also notes that Anne has "brought forth / *Their* Names to Memory" by commissioning *The Masque of Queens*. Jonson's attempt to explain away this lapse of historical memory has, as Loewenstein remarks, "the effect of an oddly bitter joke, for it hints that, under the occasional pressure of royal entertainment, antique authority is purely decorative." [10]

By the middle of 1609 Jonson had begun to explore the alternative of antifeminist satire. The first indication that he was thinking along these lines is his "Epigram on the Court Pucell," the only satirical poem he is known to have written about a living woman. Cecilia Bulstrode, Jonson's "pucell" (whore) was a Gentlewoman of the Bedchamber to Queen Anne, a cousin and close friend of Lady Bedford's, an intimate of Donne's, and the lover, apparently, of Jonson's friend Sir Thomas Roe. Jonson wrote the epigram because Cecilia had openly flouted him: "Do's the Court-Pucell then so censure me, / And thinkes I dare not her?" "On the Court Pucell" also hints that Cecilia has deliberately excluded Jonson from her circle of intimates. Many of his friends, including Donne, Sir Thomas Overbury, and Benjamin Rudyerd, gathered in her lodgings to play a verbal parlor game called "news," but Jonson himself, to judge from his epigram, was not included in the fun. [11]

Jonson responded with a savage attack on Cecilia's character. His epigram makes her out to be an oversexed bluestocking who writes her news "with Tribade lust" (lesbian desire) in an "epicoene fury." She rides "to Church, as others doe to Feasts and Playes, / To shew their Tires"; despite her array of cosmetics, "Her face there's none can like by Candle light"; she is subject to weekly fits of hysteria; she would be well advised to "steale away / From Court" while her "fame hath some small day." Now it was Cecilia's turn to take her revenge on Jonson. A gentleman of her acquaintance "drank him drousie," stole the poem "out of his pocket" and gave it to "Mistress Boulstraid, which brought him great displeasur": Lady Bedford, and perhaps Queen Anne, would want to know why Jonson was lashing out at a friend of theirs. [12]

Cecilia Bulstrode died in a state of morbid hysteria on August 4, 1609, and was buried at Lady Bedford's Twickenham estate two days later.

Shortly thereafter Donne's friend George Garrard sent Jonson a message asking him for a eulogy mourning her passing. With consummate professionalism he turned out a graceful epitaph ("Stay, view this stone") in praise of Cecilia while the messenger waited. His accompanying letter, which began, "See what the obedience of freindship is, and the hazard it runnes," pointedly notified Garrard that this "Virgin" Cecilia, who could have "taught Pallas language; Cynthia modesty," was a creation of pure artifice, concocted on short notice "to let you know your power in mee." Despite the haste with which he composed it Jonson predicted that his epigram would challenge comparison with the ones that "the greater Witts" (probably Donne and Sir Edward Herbert) had already written: "It hath somwhat in it *moris antiqui,* and suggesting the sodainesse [bearing in mind the speed of composition?] of it may passe." Almost as an afterthought, he mentioned that "the sad argument" of Garrard's letter "both strooke me and keepes me a heavy man." His principal regret, though, was that Cecilia, whose vexation with Jonson had caused him some embarrassment, should have died before he had a chance to meet with her and exonerate himself: "Would God, I had seene her before that some that live might have corrected some prejudices they have had injuriously of mee." [13]

This episode raises suspicions about Jonson's tributes to the Queen and her ladies. It indicates that he had come to resent his dependence on the favor of these powerful women. When one of the lesser members of Queen Anne's entourage criticized him, he unleashed his pent-up anger in the "Epigram on the Court Pucell," but to no avail: after the exchange of hostilities was over, and he had done his best to make amends, he was still worried that Cecilia's friends would hold him accountable for his attack on her.

There is also evidence to suggest that Jonson was growing disaffected with his own marriage. During the summer of 1609 one Londoner, or possibly two, named Ben Johnson sired children out of wedlock. On March 25, 1610, "Elisib. daughter of Ben Johnson" was baptized at St. Mary Matfellon, Whitechapel; two weeks later "Benjamin Johnson fil. Ben" was baptized at St. Martin in the Fields. Was Jonson the father of either, or both, of these children? Since no adult Johnson with the unusual given name of Ben or Benjamin appears on the Parish Registers of either St. Mary Matfellon or St. Martin in the Fields, it is reasonable to suppose that Jonson, whose family still resided in St. Anne's, Blackfriars, was the party in question. [14] The appearance of the familiar form "Ben" in the record of Elisabeth's baptism bears out this inference. Although the evidence for his philandering is circumstantial, its underlying logic is plausible enough: a man who feels threatened by strong, independent women resorts first to antifeminist diatribe and then to sexual philistinism, only to find that he is more entrapped than ever.

By the end of 1609 Jonson had completed a misogynist farce entitled *Epicoene; or, The Silent Woman* and delivered it to the Children of the Queen's Revels, who performed the play during the winter of 1609–10. He wrote *Epicoene* during a period of his life when he was preoccupied with masques that either celebrate weddings or praise women, and *Epicoene* is a satire on women and marriage. Its primary targets are the arranged match and the domineering female—the very subjects that the court poet was called upon to glorify. Whereas *Hymenaei* and *The Haddington Masque* celebrate the union of man and wife, the central acts of *Epicoene*, as Ian Donaldson has shown, celebrate a mock wedding in which the conventions of the masque become instruments of ridicule. Whereas *The Masque of Beauty* and *The Masque of Queens* pay tribute to powerful court ladies who are perfectly at home in a man's world, *Epicoene* is a lampoon on militant bluestockings who leave their husbands and take up residence in the newly fashionable neighborhoods that were springing up around the Strand.[15] *The Masque of Queens* eulogizes powerfully androgynous females who are strong enough to enact roles traditionally reserved for males; but to glorify women by turning them into men was, in that day and age, to rob them of their femininity, and *Queens* hovers perilously close to satire. *Epicoene*, like "On the Court Pucell," turns the androgynous woman into a figure of ridicule.

The mock wedding masque of Morose, the misanthrope, and Epicoene, the shrewish bride who has pretended to be a "silent woman," begins immediately after the exchange of vows. The moment Morose realizes that he has been duped, Epicoene's friend Truewit, who assumes the role of the "presenter," or master of ceremonies, blithely appears out of nowhere to ask, "Would you goe to bed so presently, sir, afore noone?" With consummate cheek, Truewit uses his intricate knowledge of festive protocols to mount a brutally aggressive attack on the old misanthrope's privacy. A "man of your head, and haire," he advises, "should owe more to that reverend ceremony, and not mount the marriage-bed, like a towne-bul, or a mountaine-goate; but stay the due season; and ascend it then with religion, and feare. Those delights are to be steep'd in the humor, and silence of the night; and give the day to other open pleasures, and jollities of feast, of musique, of revells, of discourse: wee'll have all, sir, that may make your *Hymen* high, and happy." In a moment of high irony Truewit's ultrasophisticated sense of decorum veers back to the primitive conventions of the masque. His appearance really does take the host by surprise; he brings guests that are neither invited nor expected; their sole reason for coming is to enjoy themselves. The notes published in the 1606 quarto of *Hymenaei* show that Jonson undertook a thorough study of ancient marriage customs before executing that commission, so he doubtless knew that the charivari, or mock wedding party, was a folk rite no less venerable than the epithalamion. Its target was the mismatch.[16] Jonson had been obliged to paper over the cracks in the wedding masques that he wrote for the court; now he seized the opportunity to expose them.

The sudden entrance of mysterious revelers, four <u>viragos</u> named Haughty, Centaur, Mavis, and Trusty, marks the beginning of the festivities. Instead of showering the couple with compliments as they should in a regular masque, these uninvited guests immediately break into complaints about the lack of a proper welcome: "Wee see no ensignes of a wedding, here; no character of a brideale: where be our skarfes, and our gloves?" (III.vi.70–72). The ladies who danced in *The Masque of Queens* during the winter of 1608–9 transcended the limits of gender and shouldered the heroic tasks of statesmanship and war; the "epicoene" females who cavorted at Morose's wedding party later that year had the opposed, but analogous, property of sexual indeterminacy. Their surprise visit with Morose, who is reduced to a state of childlike impotence in the course of the party, leads to his abject confession that "I am no man" (V.iv.44).

Hymenaei and *The Haddington Masque* repeatedly extol the idea of union: it is the great ordering power that underlies aesthetic harmony and domestic peace. The mock festivities of *Epicoene* evoke the contrary property of discord—the latent, unacknowledged theme of the two court bridals. The groom is at odds with the bride, the guests have come to vex their host, and the wedding party degenerates into petty quarrels and sadistic practical jokes. Both of Jonson's early wedding masques find a composite image of unity in music, the art that blends contraries into a pleasing whole. Conversely, the most expressive symbol of the failed marriage is noise, and Epicoene's friends bring the mock wedding party to its appropriately grating finale by ushering in an assortment of "noises" (a colloquial term for street musicians) to play the "rough music" of the charivari.[17]

Just as Jonson's wedding masques anticipated this, the first English comedy that ends in divorce, so *The Masque of Queens Celebrated from the House of Fame* found its ribald sequel in the defamation of bad women. By the time he turned to *Epicoene*, Jonson had become highly cynical about his own power to confer fame: the poet who creates reputations can just as easily destroy them. Fame conquers rumor in his masque of 1609, but in the less exalted medium of stage comedy, rumor could just as easily conquer fame. Within the play the trail of gossip and innuendo ultimately leads back to the elusive figure of the silent woman. At the climax of the divorce proceedings that take up the last act Epicoene's "friends" testify that she has a past, that she is sexually incontinent as well as bossy and talkative; but since the judges obstinately refuse to grant Morose a divorce, the scandal of his wife's promiscuity only reinforces the nightmare image of a weak male victimized and emasculated by a powerful female. The nightmare ends, however, with the removal of Epicoene's wig and the revelation that "she" is a boy actor in the employ of Morose's nephew Dauphine. The surprise ending turns the play's antifeminist rhetoric back upon itself. The male hidden in the falsely female body completes a closed circle of men who project their fantasies about women onto other men. To close the circle, as Jonson does at the end of *Epicoene,* is to expose the self-referential character of the sexist stereotypes that pervade the play. In this respect *Epicoene* counters <u>the unalloyed male chauvinism</u> of "On the Court Pucell." The author of the epigram is a prisoner of his own cliché antifeminism; the author of the comedy uses the same clichés to make his audience more critical of its preconceptions.

Jonson ill-advisedly chose to identify his fictive heroine with an important lady of the court. As a rule Jonson refrained from lampooning contemporary women on the stage; *Epicoene* is the sole exception to that rule. Late in December 1609 it was rumored that Arabella Stuart, a first cousin of the King's, a member of the Queen's household, and one of the dancers in *The Masque of Beauty,* was secretly planning to marry one Stephano Janiculo, an unscrupulous adventurer who pretended to be the Prince of Moldavia. Lady Arabella did her best to suppress this injurious piece of gossip, but in act V of *Epicoene* we hear of "the Prince of *Moldavia,* and of his mistris, mistris *Epicoene*" (V.i.24–25). On February 8, 1610, the Venetian Ambassador reported that "Lady Arabella is seldom seen outside her rooms and lives in greater dejection than ever. She complains that in a certain comedy the play-wright introduced an allusion to her person and the part played by the Prince of Moldavia. The play was suppressed. Her Excellency is very ill-pleased and shows a determination in this coming Parliament to secure the punishment of certain persons, we don't know who" (HS, V, 146). It is unclear whether or not *Epicoene* was ever "suppressed." John Browne entered Jonson's comedy in the Stationers' Register on September 20, 1610, but he never published it; Walter Burre acquired the rights to print the play in 1612, and Jonson's nineteenth-century editor Gifford makes a glancing reference to an edition dated that year, but there is no extant 1612 quarto of *The Silent Woman* (HS, V, 141–144). Did Arabella's friends block these early quartos? This episode recalls Jonson's quarrel with Cecilia <u>Bulstrode</u> during the previous year. He insults a prominent, but seemingly vulnerable, lady at court; she retaliates by seeking out powerful allies; he finds that he is on shaky ground.

The division of Jonson's work into mutually reinforcing spheres of courtly spectacle and sophisticated burlesque mirrored the geographical polarities of his daily life. His house in St. Anne's, Blackfriars, lay on the western edge of the City of London, while Westminster, the site of his court masques, stood a mile and a half to the west. The lifeline of the area between the London and Westminster was the Strand, and Jonson must have frequently walked along that thoroughfare while commuting between the city and the court. This neighborhood was filling up with townhouses and expensive shops during the years that followed the Spanish peace of 1604, and it had become a prime gathering place for affluent consumers. The Strand and Drury Lane were at once "the places where most of the *Gentry* lived" and bustling centers of trade. The institution that epitomized the conjunction of court and city was the New Exchange, a vast shopping center that Salisbury erected on the Strand. When the King and the royal family, together with "many great lords and ladies," attended the grand opening of the New Exchange in April 1609, they were greeted by Jonson and Jones's *Entertainment at Britain's Burse*. Although this work is not extant, it appears to have been something quite anomalous: a royal entertainment in praise of trade.[18]

Epicoene is set in this middle ground where the upstart bourgeois blends into his mirror image, the jaded courtier. Sir Amorous La Foole, the original host of the party that Truewit transfers to Morose's house, "has a lodging in the *Strand,*" where he "do's give playes, and suppers, and invites his guests to 'hem, aloud, out of his windore, as they ride by in coaches." The original hostess is Sir Amorous's kinswoman and "neighbour," the social-climbing Mistress Otter. Morose's house, in turn, is "but over the way" from his "neighbour" Mrs. Otter and her rowdy drunkard of a husband, Captain Tom Otter. The Otters' social life revolves around "a new foundation . . . here i' the towne, of ladies, that call themselves the Collegiates, an order betweene courtiers, and country-madames, that live from their husbands," and it is the college that supplies the main complement of uninvited guests to Morose's wedding party.[19] Although the word "town" denotes the specific geographical region in which *Epicoene* is set ("here i' the towne"), it also carries the now archaic, but then novel, meaning of "the fashionable society of London." The earliest citation for this usage in the *Oxford English Dictionary* is Francis Beaumont's "Letter to Ben Jonson" (ca. 1609–1612). Domiciled midway between the city and the court, and busily spending their way up the social ladder, these inhabitants of the emergent "town" are ideally suited to enact a burlesque of the court masque, for they are themselves a tribe of counterfeit courtiers.

Dauphine, Truewit, and Clerimont, the three gallants who stage Morose's charivari, affirm the values of intellectual superiority and male friendship, but they have no ongoing project or larger aim in life. Their raison d'être is to amuse one another. They are "men like Donne and others in Jonson's circle of friends," as Leo Salingar puts it, "enjoying a sophisticated idleness somewhere between the court and the City while they wait for the property that will establish them or the patronage that will direct their abilities or scholarship into a purposeful career."[20] For all their snobbery, the three gallants cannot conceive of any alternative to the vacuous comedy of the town. When Clerimont asks "Why, what should a man doe?" Truewit can only reply, "Why, nothing: or that, which when 'tis done, is as idle" (I.i.32–34). Their intellectual superiority affords them a measure of detachment from the town, but the town is the only medium in which their intellect can find any outlet.

Jonson had put himself into a similar predicament, for his satire on polite society was also his bid to capture the new genteel audience. In the Prologue he addressed to the spectators at the Whitefriars Theater, located on the western edge of the city, he concedes that he has written a play whose sole purpose is to entertain. "Truth sayes, of old," his Prologue begins, "the art of making plaies / Was to content the people." Using phrases that sum up his own position during the late Elizabethan era, Jonson takes note of "a sect of writers" that "onely, for particular likings care, / And will taste nothing that is populare," and then proceeds to renounce the elitist view ("With such we mingle neither braines, nor brests") in favor of a more genial one: "Our wishes, like to those (make publique feasts) / Are not to please the cookes tastes, but the guests."

"Yet," he assures the Whitefriars audience,

> if those cunning palates hether come,
> They shall find guests entreaty, and good roome;
> And though all relish not, sure, there will be some,
> That, when they leave their seates, shall make 'hem say,
> Who wrote that piece, could so have wrote a play:
> But that, he knew, this was the better way.

The "better way" is the Lucianic strategy of ironic affirmation: in celebrating the town, Jonson exposes its emptiness. Yet it is hard to distinguish between Truewit's witty self-justification and Jonson's own authorial stance—much harder than it was in the case of Volpone. The Fox is the protagonist of a Lucianic fable; Truewit has the wit, erudition, and de-

Francis Beaumont, artist unknown.

tachment of a Lucianic philosopher. When Dryden held the play up as a model for Restoration dramatists, he concluded, with no reservations, that Jonson had "describ'd the conversation of Gentlemen in the persons of *True-wit*, and his Friends, with more gaiety, aire and freedom, then in the rest of his Comedies." [21]

The larger import of Jonson's restless negotiation between panegyric and satire exceeds the sum of the parts. As the habit of looking at a single issue from opposed points of view becomes second nature, Jonson begins to sound like a thoroughgoing skeptic. Like Truewit, he can produce grave moral sentiments when the occasion calls for them, but unlike the younger Jonson, or the man who wrote the dedicatory epistle to *Volpone*, he relinquishes any claim to a superior moral vantage point. Within the play the stance adopted by the younger Jonson falls to Morose, who, in Barish's words, is a "later avatar of such contemners of the world as Asper and Crites," but "differs from them in having no world of transcendent virtue into which to retreat." [22] Without that moral shelter the high-minded outsider loses his reason for being and becomes yet another figure of fun.

In the meantime, Jonson himself was increasingly comfortable with the amenities of the town. The recipient of Beaumont's verse letter to Jonson from the country, whence Beaumont repaired at some point between 1609 and 1612, is well versed in the ways of tavern life and idle conversation. The Mermaid Tavern, as Beaumont describes it, was a place where men like Truewit, Clerimont, and Dauphine strove to excel one another in feats of cleverness. Having moved to the countryside, Beaumont discovers that "the litle witt I had is lost,"

> Since I saw you; for witt is like a Rest [spirited rally]
> Held upp at Tennis, which men doe the best
> with the best Gamsters. What things have wee seene
> Done at the Mermaide? heard words that have beene
> soe nimble, & soe full of subtill flame
> as if that every one from whom they came
> had meant to putt his whole witt in a Jeast
> and had resolv'd to live a foole the rest
> of his dull life; then, when there hath been throwne
> witt able [enough] to justifie the Towne.   (HS, XI, 375–376)

The feat of cleverness recalled in the last few lines aptly describes the achievement of Truewit and his friends: they too toss off enough wit "to justifie the Towne."

There are three men we can confidently number among Jonson's circle of friends during the years between *Volpone* and *Epicoene*, and all of them were regarded as wits. Beaumont, who contributed a commendatory

John Fletcher, artist unknown.

poem to the 1607 quarto of *Volpone,* is one. His collaborator John Fletcher, whose *Faithful Shepherdess* Jonson defended from "the wise, and many-headed *Bench,* that sits / Upon the Life, and Death of *Playes,* and *Wits*" in an epigram that dates from 1609, is another. Finally, there is Donne, who left his wife and children at Mitcham, took lodgings in the

John Donne, ca. 1595, artist unknown. Donne is attired as a melancholy lover.

Strand, and began to cultivate Jonson's patroness Lady Bedford in 1608. Jonson's epigram "To Lucy, Countess of Bedford, with Mr. Donne's Satires," probably accompanied a manuscript of Donne's satires that Jonson obtained for the Countess around this time. Donne's name also appears, along with Jonson's, in a list of drinking companions who congregated at the Mermaid a few years later. Despite the fanciful ruminations of nineteenth-century biographers, there is no reason to suppose that William Shakespeare, the glover's son from Stratford, who was ten years their senior, would have felt at home in this circle of younger sons and *déclassé* gentry, but Jonson clearly did. John Danby succinctly describes Beaumont's and Fletcher's strategy as a "twofold invasion": "On the one hand, they will capture the popular playhouse, on the other they will gatecrash court society."[23] Jonson was a much more complicated individual than Beaumont or Fletcher. He still thought of himself as a poet in the grand sense of the word as Sidney used it, rather than as a mere wit. But he could hardly sustain the posture of the aloof, uncompromising moralist when he himself had been absorbed into the casual comedy of the town.

• CHAPTER NINE •

Reluctant Patriot

James's eldest son, Prince Henry, had his sixteenth birthday, and began to commission court entertainments on his own behalf, in the winter of 1609–10. By this time it was clear that Henry intended to become a major literary patron. He had already taken Jonson's friend George Chapman and the translator Joshua Sylvester into his service; and he had recently acquired Lord Lumley's library, which was second only to Cotton's among the private collections in England, for the use of the scholars and writers attached to his household. At about the same time, Henry asked Jonson to write a learned commentary on *The Masque of Queens*. Jonson promptly did so, dedicating the 1609 quarto of that work to the Prince, and himself to Henry's future projects: "If my *Fate* (most excellent Prince, and *only Delicacy of mankind*) shall reserve mee to the Age of your Actions, whether in the Campe, or the Councell-Chamber, that I may write, at nights, the deedes of your dayes; I will then labor to bring forth some worke as worthy of your fame, as my ambition therin is of your pardon." Henry, in turn, commissioned Jonson to write *The Speeches at Prince Henry's Barriers*, which were performed on Twelfth Night 1610.[1]

Although he doubtless coveted this employment, it put him in an awkward position, for Henry was actively repudiating the Jacobean ideology that Jonson had embraced when James came to the throne. When he was still James VI of Scotland, the King had given his eldest son a name that recalled the nationalistic era of Queen Elizabeth's father, Henry VIII, and had invited Elizabeth to be Henry's godmother, in the belief that these associations would endear the boy to the Protestant Englishmen who would one day be his subjects. This program succeeded all too well, for as

Henry approached manhood, he eagerly seized upon the role that had been cut out for him. Whereas James, the ungainly and effeminate King, was peaceable, Henry, the athletic and virile Prince, was warlike. The father sought to prevent religious wars in Europe by promoting dynastic intermarriages; the son was eager to invade the Continent. James's court was sexually permissive and inclined to drink; Henry's was chaste and abstemious. The King leaned toward the Spanish faction; the Prince naturally inclined to the interests of France. James's government was dominated by the Howards and by Salisbury, whom Henry disliked intensely; Henry's favorite companions included the young Earl of Essex and Lady Bedford's brother, Sir John Harington. While the father was inaugurating a neo-Augustan era, his son began an Elizabethan revival. By 1608 Henry was in regular communication with Sir Walter Raleigh, who had been incarcerated, with the connivance of Salisbury and the Howards, shortly after James came to the throne. Between 1608 and 1610 Raleigh wrote a number of treatises on statesmanship and war for the Prince, and in 1610 another group of unofficial advisers presented him with a document entitled "Arguments for War"; in the same year, James commissioned Sir Robert Cotton to write "An Answer to the Propositions of War."[2]

Although Henry represented an important source of patronage, Jonson would have had several reservations about him. As a servant of the King and a member of the Catholic Church, Jonson could hardly be expected to endorse a call for war on Catholic Europe; as an orthodox Renaissance humanist, committed to a modern literature founded upon the systematic imitation of classical texts, he cannot have felt much enthusiasm for the chivalric legends that were the stuff of Henry's personal mythology. The same bias would have made him even more chary of Merlin the magician, who had once been King Arthur's and was now to be Prince Henry's tutelary genius. Like Daniel and Chapman, Jonson hedged his bets in the winter of 1609–10, deferring to the Prince's aggressive self-image but also involving him in alternative roles that stressed moderation and compromise.

The *Barriers* began with a long speech delivered by the Lady of the Lake, "whose actions, and whose name / Were so full fam'd in British ARTHURS court." The Lady delighted in the brilliance of James's court, but she also commented on the contrast between the splendor enthroned before her and the "cob-webd, and rusty" House of Chivalry in the background. King Arthur then appeared "discoverd as a starre above," and instructed the Lady to bring forth her knight, "that by the might / And magicke of his arme, he may restore / These ruin'd seates of vertue, and build more." When the painted flat slid back to reveal Prince Henry and his knights seated in St. George's Portico, the restored House of Chivalry, the sense of magic in the air must have been very strong indeed. Yet

BRITANNIAE / FRANCIAE / SCOTIAE / ET HYBERNIAE REX. ANNO MDCXIII

IACOBUS D.G. MAGNAE

HONI SOIT QUI MALI PENSE

Qui regis imperio divisos orbe Britannos,
Rex tot virorum fortium;
Qui terrore tui solius nominis hostes
Premis, quietis appetens;

A°. 16 13.

Crisp. Passæus figur. sculp. et exc.

Qui pace ecclesiam, jus litibus qui legibus ornas
Forum, scholas doctoribus;
Atq inter vates pangis pia carmina, sceptro
Jungis decenter lauream.

King James I, by Crispin van de Passe, 1613. The inscription below describes James as a peacemaker and man of learning.

the legend on Henry's shield, as Merlin expounds it, prophesies the advent of a world that is demythologized and rational. He expressly rules out "the deedes / Of antique knights" and declares that Henry's "arts must be to governe, and give lawes / To peace no lesse then armes." Although Merlin was the mightiest of magicians in Arthur's day, he flatly declares that those days are gone: "It is not since as then: / No giants, dwarfes, or monsters here, but men." In recounting the glories of Britain's past, Merlin counterbalances the glories of war and conquest with the bourgeois virtues of industry and thrift. The "first, and warlike Edward," he counsels the Prince, improved "trades and tillage." So with "the third *Heroe* of his name": "This was he erected first / The trade of clothing." [3]

The trade of clothing? This mixture of magic and common sense, of chivalric splendor and bourgeois prudence, creates an overall impression of ambivalence: was Jonson reinaugurating the Arthurian myth or debunking it? Was this a courtly tournament-at-arms or a Lord Mayor's pageant? Jonson was prepared to work within the literary traditions that the Prince and his followers had espoused, but he would not endorse their chivalric reveries and saber-rattling rhetoric.

Henry, Prince of Wales, miniature by Isaac Oliver, 1612. Henry's armor and the military tents in the background are emblems of war.

The Earl of Essex and Henry, Prince of Wales. From a painting attributed to Robert Peake, 1603. In the year of James's accession his nine-year-old son already appears as a powerfully masculine figure and a confident swordsman.

The commission to write Prince Henry's *Barriers* forced Jonson for the first time in his career to participate in a native tradition of popular patriotic literature. The Prologue to *The Alchemist*, which he wrote in the earlier part of 1610, sarcastically reaffirms his intention to celebrate the English national identity:

St. George's Portico, by Inigo Jones. From the drawings for Jonson's *Prince Henry's Barriers,* 1610. Henry aspired to revive both the classical and the medieval heritages of ancient Britain. The two rows of ruined buildings that lead to the back of the set are a jumble of motifs from Roman, romanesque, gothic, and Italian architecture. St. George's Portico (rear center) is a harmonious fusion of classical and medieval styles. Henry stood beneath its triumphal arch.

Our *Scene* is *London,* 'cause we would make knowne,
    No countries mirth is better then our owne.
No clime breeds better matter, for your whore,
    Bawd, squire, impostor, many persons more,
Whose manners, now call'd humors, feed the stage:
    And which have still beene subiect, for the rage
Or spleene of *comick*-writers.

Jonson's Prologue, like the play itself, belongs to the paradoxical genre of the mock encomium, or praise of "things without honor."[4] The mock encomiast displays the language of praise (in this case, praise of one's country) in a setting where nothing is praiseworthy; his performance simultaneously exposes the emptiness of conventional rhetoric and brings to light the blemishes that such rhetoric conceals. Flaws that are invisible from a distance become glaringly apparent when one focuses on a tiny cross-section of the same object. If the massive architectural forms and medievalized backdrop of *The Speeches at Prince Henry's Barriers* create the impression that England is a vast and timeless entity, the London setting of *The Alchemist* goes to the opposite extreme. Jonson's comedy of 1610 is a microscopic replica, warts and all, of the time and place at which it was first performed.

The year 1609 had seen the worst outbreak of the bubonic plague since 1603, and the epidemic persisted into 1610. Early that winter, when *The Alchemist* was in its formative stages, thirty to forty Londoners were dying of the plague every week. Whenever the weekly mortality rate reached this level, the authorities closed the playhouses; in the winter of 1610, they remained closed for at least a month and a half. The toll subsided during the spring, when Jonson would have been hard at work on *The Alchemist*, but by the last week of June it had climbed back to thirty, and the playhouses were again closed on July 14. By this time the King's Men had probably incorporated Jonson's new comedy into their repertory; around the last week of August, in which some ninety-nine Londoners died of the plague, they took *The Alchemist* to Oxford.[5]

Jonson wrote *The Alchemist* for an audience of city dwellers who remained in town during the plague, and the plot of his comedy mirrors the social conditions that prevailed in an actual epidemic. The opening lines of his Argument outline a scenario that was performed in every London neighborhood whenever the disease broke out:

> **T** *he sicknesses hot, a master quit, for feare,*
> **H** *is house in towne: and left one servant there.*
> **E** *ase him corrupted . . .*

The rest of the Argument describes a criminal syndicate whose existence coincides with the duration of the plague:

> *and gave meanes to know*
> **A** *cheater, and his punque; who, now brought low,*
> **L** *eaving their narrow practise, were become*
> **C** *os'ners at large: and, onely wanting some*
> **H** *ouse to set up, with him they here contract,*
> **E** *ach for a share, and all begin to act.*
> **M** *uch company they draw, and much abuse,*
> **I** *n casting figures, telling fortunes, newes,*
> **S** *elling of flyes, flat bawdry, with the stone:*
> **T** *ill it, and they, and all in* fume *are gone.*[6]

On the face of it, these lines describe a trio of sharpsters who set up shop in a vacant house and play a variety of confidence games on the various dupes whom they attract there. But the wordplay on "House," "contract," "share," and "act" turns the Argument into a metadramatic commentary on the play and its auspices of production. The swindlers are a company of players who have transformed the master's house into a theater; the populous "company they draw" is the audience in this metaphorical playhouse; the play they enact (as the reader discovers by scanning the vertical column of capital letters on the far left of the page) is *The Alchemist*.

Since Jonson situates the master's abandoned house on the exact site occupied by the Blackfriars Theater, the more attentive spectators could have seen that their situation was not just analogous, but identical, to that of their onstage counterparts. Despite the risk of disease, they too could not resist the allure of the crowded "House" in the Blackfriars. *The Alchemist* is the one play in the Elizabethan and Jacobean repertory that observes the three unities prescribed by neoclassical critics: the actors and the audience share a single time and place and they perform a single action.[7]

Jonson invited his audience to participate in a form of "deep" play, where, to use Clifford Geertz's formulation, "the stakes are so high that it is irrational, from [a] utilitarian standpoint, for men to engage in it at all." During performances the small, enclosed Blackfriars playhouse was notoriously congested, and contemporaries were certain that congestion was a primary cause of the disease. This belief helps account for the mounting concern over the size of the urban population (a royal proclamation of 1608 warned that "such an overflow of people" would lead to "infection of plague, and manifold disorders"); and it explains why the authorities closed the playhouses whenever the weekly mortality rate reached epidemic proportions.[8] Nevertheless, so long as the death rate hovered below forty a week, as it did in the spring of 1610, vast numbers of urban residents went to the theater anyway, in the full knowledge that they were endangering their own lives and those of their neighbors. The theatergoers who attended the original performances at the Blackfriars, like the fictive "company" of people who gather in the master's abandoned house, found themselves in precisely this position.

Jonson's relationship to this audience was deeply ambivalent. The Prologue's claim that the author "hopes to find no spirit so much diseas'd, / But will, with such faire correctives, be pleas'd" has a double edge. *The Alchemist* was a "faire corrective" to disease, yet it drew spectators to the theater, where they could expect to contract the plague. When the Prologue invokes the Horatian criterion of *dulce et utile* ("the wholsome remedies are sweet, / And, in their working, gaine, and profit meet"), there is a distinct undercurrent of sarcasm: does he refer to the audience's "gaine, and profit" or the actors'? Finally, would spectators who were foolish enough to attend a performance at the Blackfriars while the sickness was hot have the wit to see themselves in Jonson's mirror? "They are so natu-rall follies, but so showne, / As even the doers may see, and yet not owne." Yet the "doers" were the very people who stood to "gaine, and profit" from a play that showed them what they were doing when they went to the theater.[9]

The theatrical metaphor in *The Alchemist* restates a central theme of *Volpone,* but it has undergone a significant change. Whereas *Volpone* as-signs primary importance to various aspects of the actor's craft (makeup, posture, muscular control, facial expression), *The Alchemist* is largely concerned with the institution of theater and its place in the fantasy life of the popular audience. Jonson seeks not to perpetuate this institution but rather to mount an elaborate critique of the illusions that had sustained it during the remarkable century that culminated in Marlowe, Shakespeare, and himself.

In its broad outline *The Alchemist* resembles an old-fashioned morality play. As in Tudor moralities like *Mankind, Youth, Hickscorner, Nice Wan-ton, The Three Ladies of London,* and *A Looking Glass for London and England,* a confederacy of vice figures, whose abode is understood to be London, lures gullible mankind away from the path of righteousness and into the toils of sin. Face (the world), Dol Common (the flesh), and Subtle (the devil), the three scoundrels who take over the master's house, corre-spond to the "three temptations" of medieval homiletic tradition. The methods employed by the vice figures are, however, modern and sophisti-cated. Instead of a tavern (the usual den of iniquity in homiletic texts), their base of operations is a makeshift playhouse; instead of plying their victims with flesh and ale, they entice them with glorified versions of their everyday selves. The dandified clerk who "consorts with the small poets of the time" and "is the sole hope of his old grandmother" becomes the protagonist of a romantic comedy and has an audience with his aunt, the Fairy Queen. The ambitious young tradesman turns into the hero of a middle-class success story by Dekker or Deloney ("This summer, / He will be of the clothing of his companie: / And, next spring, call'd to the scar-let"). The country bumpkin joins the ranks of the roaring boys, is taught "to carry quarells, / As gallants doe," and learns the degrees of the lie. Sir Epicure Mammon, the sybaritic knight, becomes a Marlovian overreacher who "would ha' built / The citie new; and made a ditch about it / Of silver, should have runne with cream from *Hogsden.*" Ananias, the Anabaptist deacon, takes the part of the antitheatrical Puritan who goes to the play-house so that he may rail against it: "Please the prophane, to grieve the godly," says Ananias, "I may not"![10]

The hypnotic attraction of these fantasy selves was not confined to the theater. Jonson noted in his commonplace book that "our whole life is like a *Play:* wherein every man, forgetfull of himselfe, is in travaile with expression of another" (*Disc,* 1093–95). In the playhouse, where the spectators purchase the right to identify with roles designed expressly for their consumption, the opportunities for self-forgetfulness are vastly enhanced; but a playwright can also use the resources of the stage to sharpen the spectators' awareness of their extratheatrical selves. *The Alchemist* warned theatergoers of 1610 not to be taken in by the fictional roles that captivate their onstage counterparts. Since those roles were the legacy of Elizabethan England, Jonson's warning was immediately relevant to the wave of Tudor nostalgia that accompanied the rise of Prince Henry. *The Alchemist* reiterated the advice that Merlin had given to Henry the previous winter: "It is not since, as then."

Merlin is a reformed magician who urges Prince Henry to renounce a fictive role; Subtle, the analogous figure in *The Alchemist,* is a fraudulent magician who entraps his victims in fantasies of self-fashioning. Following an established Renaissance tradition, Jonson treats theater and magic as institutions that parallel and reinforce each other. Both the actor's "wooden O" and the wizard's circle of necromancy were the sites of magical transformations. Within these enclosures the most humble image ("what light through yonder window breaks?") could become the lightning rod for an influx of cosmic energy ("It is the east, and Juliet is the sun"). Jonson demystifies the analogy between theater and magic by relating it to shared patterns of wish fulfillment and illusion. His magician-hero is an actor whose performances have become a part of everyday social practice. Every theatrical role has a specific form of magic to bring it into being; every magical procedure is tailored to suit the individual customer's humor. Subtle tells the concupiscible Sir Epicure of a highly sexualized alchemy, with one element "supplying the place of male, / The other of the female, in all metalls"; he wins over the irascible Anabaptists by recounting "the vexations, and the martyrizations / Of metals, in the worke." [11]

The rise of Prince Henry had stimulated a revival of the Elizabethan alliance between magic and imperial Protestantism, and Frances Yates convincingly argues that Jonson wrote *The Alchemist* in conscious opposition to this trend. He enshrines the celebrated Elizabethan wizard John Dee in a sign above an apothecary's shop and mockingly alludes to Dee's associate Edward Kelley, the Munster Anabaptists Berndt Knipperdollinck and John of Leyden, the Familist Henric Nicholas, and the millenarian biblical historian Hugh Broughton. But a narrowly topical reading of *The Alchemist* misrepresents the scope of Jonson's project. Where the modern reader sees a curious amalgam of outmoded beliefs, Jonson confronted a thriving occupation that would not attain its full vigor until the Civil War and the Interregnum. At the close of the sixteenth century, as Keith Thomas reports, well-informed observers "thought the wizards roughly comparable in numbers to the parochial clergy"—an estimate confirmed by Robert Burton thirty years later. The complaints of contemporaries, distressed by the sheer volume of the traffic in wizardry (Thomas mentions one woman who saw upward of forty customers a week), indicate that the flood of customers in Subtle's establishment accurately mirrored the current level of demand for skilled magicians. Jonson told Drummond that he himself could "set Horoscopes" and had once "cousened a lady, with whom he had made ane apointment to meet ane old Astrologer in the suburbs, which she Keeped and it was himself disguised in a Longe Gowne & a white beard." [12]

Although he consistently associated magic with the idiot fringe of millenarian Protestantism, he also saw it as a national mania, a collective folly that required the corrective offices of the comic poet. In *The Alchemist* Jonson adopts for the first time the role of a public debunker, an ally of the classical authors who had discredited the supernatural explanations of prophetic dreams (Aristotle) and divination (Cicero) and of their modern counterparts Bacon and Selden. And *The Alchemist* was itself only the first, glorious battle in Jonson's lifelong quarrel with the wizards. The magicians whom he derides in his published works include Dee, Kelley, Simon Forman, Sir Christopher Heydon, Thomas Bretnor, Edward Gresham, Abraham Savory, and Robert Fludd. During the years ahead he would write comedies that lampoon witch-hunting magistrates and amateur demonologists, and masques that burlesque alchemy and Rosicrucianism. [13]

Merlin had already renounced the legacy of folklore and magic in *The Speeches at Prince Henry's Barriers;* the abrupt return of Master Lovewit, the rightful owner of the house that Face, Dol, and Subtle have expropriated, sets the stage for a similar renunciation in the final act of *The Alchemist*. Yet Lovewit notoriously refuses to take this step. Instead of wiping the slate clean, he forges an alliance with his servant, Face, appropriates the rogues' ill-gotten gains, and marries an attractive young widow whom they have lured into his house. Lovewit's eye for the main chance has provoked an extensive debate about his moral character. Is he a despicable cynic or an urbane man about town? Is Jonson a severe ironist who wants us to despise Lovewit's shabby opportunism, or a genial pragmatist who rejoices in the triumph of pure intelligence? Jonson could not provide a clear-cut answer to these questions because his own position was no less equivocal than Master Lovewit's. He was rejecting, but also appropriating, the legacy of Tudor drama; exposing, but also exploiting, its magico-theatrical heritage.

Even if Jonson had wished to bypass this heritage altogether, his employment as a writer of court masques left him with no choice but to participate in it. Later in 1610 Prince Henry employed him to prepare a masque entitled *Oberon, the Fairy Prince* for the coming holiday season. Since Oberon was a folk hero who had given his name both to the elfin Prince of *A Midsummer Night's Dream* and to the legendary British ruler who foreshadows Henry VIII in Spenser's *Faerie Queene*, this commission virtually compelled Jonson to write about popular English superstitions from a sympathetic point of view. Nevertheless, he suppressed these associations and once again declined the invitation to transform Henry into a symbol of England's storied past. The setting of his masque is Arcadian rather than British; the antimasquers who set the stage for Oberon's appearance are classical satyrs rather than homespun elves; and it is a Greek centaur who informs them that Oberon "is the height of all *our* race." Jonson glossed this line with a fine display of pseudolearning aimed at spectators who objected to his curiously Hellenic Oberon:

> And *Galen* observes out of *Hippocrat. Comment. 3. in 6. Epidemicor:* that both the *Athenians* and *Ionians,* call'd the *Satyres phēras,* or *phēreas;* which name the *Centaures* have with *Homer:* from whence, it were no unlikely conjecture, to thinke our word *Faeries* to come. *Viderint Critici.*

Let the critics decide for themselves! Had Jonson cared to consult them about his fanciful etymology, they could have informed him that Silenus was an aged satyr rather than a centaur and that the passage cited from Galen is the only text in all of Greek literature that refers to satyrs as *phēras* (animals). The Prince who led *"the nation of* Faies" across the dance floor at Whitehall wore the dress of a Roman emperor, resided in an Italianate palace, and would have been equally at home in Paris or Florence. No one would dream of confusing him with "the course, and countrey *Faery,* / That doth haunt the harth, or dairy." [14]

Earlier in 1610 an event had occurred that raised the issue of Jonson's patriotism in a more compelling way. On May 14 a religious fanatic named François Ravaillac had assassinated King Henri IV of France and opened the way for a Catholic dynasty across the Channel. The murder of King Henri, who was widely admired in England, aggravated James's fears about his own safety. King James concluded that Ravaillac belonged to an international ring of papist assassins and declared that "their aim was not at [Henri] alone but at other princes too, whereof I assure you I was one." On June 2 he issued a proclamation forbidding English Catholics "to repaire . . . to our court, or to the Court of our dearest wife the Queene, or of the Prince our Dear Son wheresoever." And he once again required his Catholic subjects to renounce the sovereignty of the Pope by swearing the Oath of Allegiance to the King of England.[15]

This extraordinary combination of circumstances probably explains Jonson's decision to rejoin the English Church in 1610. He had begun to drift away from Rome after the Gunpowder Plot in 1605. The Pope's refusal either to disavow Ravaillac or to permit English Catholics to take the Oath of Allegiance, coupled with the King's proclamation denying recusants access to his court, put Jonson in an exceedingly difficult position. And the increasing prominence of Prince Henry could only deepen the isolation of English Catholics. Jonson told Drummond that "at his first communion" after his return to the Anglican Church "in token of true Reconciliation, he drank out all the full cup of wine" (*Conv*, 315–316). Given Jonson's reputation as a drinker, he may have been speaking with his tongue in his cheek. In any case, this anecdote suggests that he regarded his reconversion as a symbolic act, or "token," that signified his reintegration into the body politic. His need for full membership in the Stuart establishment had superseded the pieties of his youth.

The tragedy of *Catiline His Conspiracy*, which he had completed by August 1611, reconfirmed his disaffection from the extremist wing of the Catholic community. Contemporary observers, beginning with King James, had already seized upon the analogy between Catiline's plan to assassinate Cicero and his fellow senators and the Gunpowder Plot of 1605. A number of passages in *Catiline* drew specific parallels between the two events. Like the participants in the Popish Plot, Catiline and his crew of down-at-heel gentlemen "take a solemne sacrament" to strengthen their resolve, and there are several subsequent references to this blasphemous "sacrament." When Cicero persuades the conspirator Curius to confess and turn informer, he pointedly reminds him that "no religion binds men to be traitors." Although the original Catilinarian conspirators drank blood and took an oath, the eucharistic "sacrament" and the religion that binds men to be traitors were, as Jonson surely realized, anachronisms that lent themselves to a modern topical allegory; and so were the many allusions suggestive of gunpowder and explosions. When Jonson's Cicero informs the senate that Catiline's intention "was, on the fifth (the kalends of *November*) / T'have slaughter'd this whole order," the ordinary spectator would have supposed that he meant the fifth of November—the date when the gunpowder plotters had planned to blow up the King and Parliament.[16]

The most vivid point of contact between the play and the plot is the lurid "sacrament" that binds Catiline to his co-conspirators:

> I have kill'd a slave,
> And of his bloud caus'd to be mixt with wine.
> Fill every man his bowle. There cannot be
> A fitter drinke, to make this *sanction* in.
> Here, I beginne the sacrament to all.
> . . . . .
> Be firme, my hand; not shed a drop: but powre
> Fiercenesse into me, with it, and fell thirst
> Of more, and more, till *Rome* be left as bloud-lesse,
> As ever her feares made her, or the sword. (I.483–487, 491–494)

Just a year previously, when Jonson rejoined the Anglican Communion, he "drank out the full cup" as a sign of "true Reconciliation"; Catiline's black mass is a blasphemous reversal of Jonson's Holy Eucharist, a mark of the conspirator's alienation from the community.

The savior of that community is Cicero, who (Jonson noted) was "said to be the only wit, that the people of *Rome* had equaled to their *Empire*." Since Cicero was the greatest of the Roman orators, and his defeat of Catiline the prototypical victory of commonwealth over faction, Jonson's audience would have expected his hero to deliver stirring orations on the theme of national honor. Jonson pointedly declined to satisfy such expectations. His hero is a remote and bookish figure who spends most of the play delivering long-winded orations lifted directly from the historical Cicero's own writings. He represents patriotism in the abstract, denuded of nationalistic fervor and emotional bonds. Indeed the consul is positively contemptuous of simpletons who take patriotic clichés at face value. When he exhorts the conspirator Curius to turn double agent along with the prostitute Fulvia (the one occasion on which he invokes the sentimental pieties of patriotism), he laces his appeal with sexual puns that deliberately undercut his own rhetoric: "*Stand / Firme* for your *count*rey," he pleads: "It were a noble life, / To be found *dead, embracing* her." [17]

A century earlier, Machiavelli had maintained that Cicero's humanistic ideals were largely irrelevant to his accomplishments as a practical politician: within the Florentine, and subsequently the Atlantic, Republican tradition, the legacy of Cicero was modified to suit the needs of a modern *realpolitik*. *Catiline* introduced English readers to this revisionist Cicero. The hero of Jonson's tragedy is an unrelenting pragmatist. He consistently uses spies and informants, those malodorous "lights in state" whom a younger Jonson had bitterly condemned; he dispenses bribes and ignores the misdeeds of anyone who can aid his cause. The emphasis upon pragmatic political involvement, as opposed to stoic renunciation, is one measure of the distance that separates the mature Jonson from the aloof satirist who wrote *Sejanus* in 1603. Jonson's earlier Roman play had focused on the plight of virtue when it became divorced from power under the Emperor Tiberius; his later one harks back to the last years of the republic and shows the ways in which a statesman can wield power effectively. Conversely, Cicero's inflexible ally Cato (who became the patron saint of the Germanicans) threatens to undermine the consul's statesmanship precisely because he is unwilling to make moral compromises. As Cicero complained in a famous letter written during his exile, "Cato means well, but he does hurt sometime to the *State;* for he talks as if he were in the republic of Plato and not in the dregs of Romulus." [18]

Jonson had positioned himself at the nexus of several conflicting political discourses. *Catiline* is both narrowly chauvinistic and broadly classical. Jonson appealed to the nationalistic prejudices of his seventeenth-century audience but also compelled them to endure an extended history lesson; he denounced the principle of sectarian violence but also avoided a head-on clash with the church to which he had belonged for the previous twelve years. The convert of 1610 had adopted the stance of a diehard centrist. Within a year of rejoining the Anglican Church he had written a comedy about millenarian Protestants and a tragedy about seditious cryptopapists. His own position presumably lay somewhere between these opposed extremes, but Jonson situates it beyond the reach of any recoverable meaning. Lovewit and Cicero, the freewheeling opportunist and the masterly politician who wield authority in *The Alchemist* and *Catiline,* respectively, are elusive figures: they show us what Jonson is reacting against but reveal nothing about his own beliefs and commitments.

The spectators who watched the King's Men perform *Catiline* in 1611 regarded Cicero as an unsatisfying, and indeed downright offensive, figure. The defiant epistle "To the Reader in Ordinairie" that accompanied the 1611 quarto of *Catiline* indicates that "the people" enjoyed the first two acts, which are largely devoted to Catiline and his crew, but deeply resented the insertion of Cicero's orations into the latter part of the play. Jonson had given them a villain whom they could hiss off the stage but not a hero with whom they could empathize. In response, he sarcastically promised to "finde the way to forgive you. Be anything you will be, at your owne charge." Anyone could have foreseen that *Catiline*, like its predecessor *Sejanus,* would fail to please the popular audience; the author's appeal to "the Reader extraordinary" who would vindicate his masterpiece was equally predictable, given Jonson's faith in the power of the printed word. In this case, however, his confidence was justified. Although *Catiline* never won a place in the popular repertory, the play was a re-

NB

sounding success with the reading audience in Stuart England. Bentley notes eighty-nine allusions to it prior to 1700—more than double the figure for *The Tempest,* the most frequently cited of Shakespeare's works—and concludes that it was "the most respected play of the century."[19]

Jonson's centrist politics enabled him to play a waiting game at a time when he did not have close ties to any of the dominant factions at court. His connection with Salisbury had not borne any visible fruit since 1609, the date of his last commission from the Earl; he later complained to Drummond that Salisbury "never cared for any man longer nor he could make use of him." He had kept his distance from the cult of Prince Henry. Northampton, the gray eminence of the Howard faction, remained "his mortall enemie." And the influence of his patroness Queen Anne had suffered a precipitous drop with the emergence of Sir Robert Carr, a handsome young Scot who had captured James's affections.[20] In *Love Freed from Ignorance and Folly* (February 13, 1611), the last of the Queen's masques, Jonson renounced the assertive femininity, extravagant spectacle, and weighty allegories that had characterized the earlier masques he had written for Anne. The Queen's love now had to be "freed" from these encumbrances so that it could flow directly to James.

At the same time, Jonson was vigorously cultivating patrons whose position at court (like his own) was relatively marginal. He dedicated the 1611 quarto of *Catiline* to Pembroke and stated in his prefatory letter to the Earl that *Catiline* was "the first (of this race) that ever I dedicated to any person." Jonson was residing at the Penshurst estate of Pembroke's uncle and ally Lord Lisle in November of 1611 when he composed an ode celebrating the twenty-first birthday of Lisle's eldest son, Sir Robert Sidney. The following year, he dedicated *The Alchemist* to Lisle's daughter and Pembroke's mistress, Lady Mary Wroth, and probably wrote "To Penshurst," his verse tribute to the Sidneys' country manor house. And finally, the most conspicuous family grouping in Jonson's *Epigrams,* which were registered for publication in the spring of 1612, are the Herberts, the Sidneys, and their allies.[21]

Jonson had already attached himself to Pembroke by 1605, when he wrote to him during the *Eastward Ho* crisis. Why did he decide to cement the connection in 1611–12? The obvious explanation lies, once again, in the rise of Prince Henry. Pembroke and Lisle were among the legatees of the militant Protestant faction that had originally been led by Sir Philip Sidney (Lisle's brother), and the Earl of Leicester; their group now had a strong leader for the first time since Essex a decade earlier. Moreover, Pembroke was in a position to strengthen Jonson's ties to the all-powerful

Salisbury, for he and his brother Montgomery were currently among Salisbury's most influential allies.[22]

But Jonson did not view Lisle and Pembroke merely as power brokers to be cultivated; to judge from his poems of 1611–12 and his *Epigrams* he valued them precisely because they represented an alternative to the fluid, anxiety-ridden world of court politics. Pembroke, "whose noblesse keeps one stature still, / And one true posture, though besieged with ill / Of what ambition, faction, pride can raise," compensates for his lack of power by setting a moral example. Lisle's country house at Penshurst is a self-sufficient agrarian paradise whose walls "are rear'd with no mans ruine, no mans grone." In his epistle "To Sir Robert Wroth," written prior to 1615, Jonson congratulates Lisle's son-in-law for avoiding London and Westminster altogether:

> How blest art thou, canst love the countrey, WROTH,
> Whether by choice, or fate, or both;
> And, though so neere the citie, and the court,
> Art tane with neithers vice, nor sport.

Jonson consistently portrays the Sidneys and the Herberts as members of a self-contained aristocratic community that is answerable only to its own ancestral traditions. Within this community Jonson discovers a code of values that he can endorse without reservation. Both the "Ode to Sir William Sidney on His Birthday" and "To Penshurst" stress the importance of lineage, nurture, and domestic life; and in both poems Jonson takes the part of the friend and retainer who articulates the family's ideal image of itself. He is physically present at Sir William Sidney's birthday feast but stands apart from the revelry to remind Sir William, "'Twill be exacted of your name, whose sonne, / Whose nephew, whose grand-child you are." At the end of "To Penshurst" he rejoices in the knowledge that Lisle's children can "reade, in their vertuous parents noble parts, / The mysteries of manners, armes, and arts."[23] The role of tutor or mentor was implicit in the figures of Merlin and Silenus; it becomes explicit in the birthday ode for Sir William Sidney; a year later Jonson would become the tutor of Sir Walter Raleigh's son Wat.

Jonson's own son Ben, the last of his legitimate offspring, died at the age of four and a half during, or shortly after, his father's visit to Penshurst, and was buried at St. Anne's, Blackfriars, on November 18, 1611. The death of Ben gave Jonson an additional motive for entering into the lives of his patrons' families and making their children his children: this had now become the outlet for his strong paternal instincts. Apart from "To Sir William Sidney" and "To Penshurst," the only poem by Jonson that can confidently be dated in the year 1611–12 is the "Epistle to Katherine, Lady Aubigny," which he wrote in the months following Ben's death, while his patron's wife was pregnant with her first child. His epistle to Lady Aubigny begins with a series of bleak complaints that express his sense of isolation and helplessness: "'Tis growne almost a danger to speak true / Of any good minde, now: There are so few." But when he contemplates the flowering of Lady Aubigny's family tree, he reverts to the prophetic manner of his early odes:

> Grow, grow, faire tree, and as thy branches shoote,
> Heare, what the *Muses* sing about thy roote,
> By me, their priest (if they can ought divine)
> Before the moones have fill'd their tripple trine,
> To crowne the burthen which you goe withall,
> It shall a ripe and timely issue fall,
> To expect the honors of great AUBIGNY
> And greater rites, yet writ in mysteries,
> But which the *Fates* forbid me to reveale.

Like the Sidney children, the "glad encrease" of Lady Aubigny's "blest womb" holds the promise of a regenerate social order centered in the noble household.[24] Jonson, her poet and client, is the custodian and interpreter of this promise. His patroness bears the child; he bears the vision of the future. In taking stock of this vision one should also bear in mind that Jonson may have recently sired one or two illegitimate children. When he idealized his patrons' noble lineage, was he tacitly disowning his own bastard offspring?

Jonson's idealized image of the noble household carries an implied reproach to the ladies and gentlemen who danced in his court masques. The masquers were conspicuous consumers of clothing and jewelry, and connoisseurs of imported finery; the occupants of the noble household upheld the homespun virtues of thrift, plainness, and artless affection. Sir Robert Wroth disdains

> to view the better cloth of state;
>   The richer hangings, or crowne-plate;
> Nor throng'st (when masquing is) to have a sight
>   Of the short braverie of the night;
> To view the jewells, stuffes, the paines, the wit
>   There wasted, some not paid for yet!   (*For,* 3.7–12)

Jonson was not criticizing the court per se; he was questioning practices that James and his courtiers had espoused during the first eight years of the reign. The court itself was a flexible institution and had the capacity to discard old values and adopt new ones. Given the climate of opinion at Whitehall in 1611–12, Jonson's rejection of "courtly" extravagance appears to be an adaptive, rather than a reactive, move: for by this time the King could no longer afford to pay for the "jewells, stuffes," and exquisite refinements that had hitherto been a staple ingredient of the Jacobean masque.

Jonson's earlier court entertainments, from *The Masque of Blackness* through *Oberon,* were calculated displays of regal munificence designed to enhance the prestige of the King and his court. But James had started running out of money by 1608; three years later he was plunging into the chronic insolvency that would vex him for the rest of his reign. His attempts to obtain either subsidies from Parliament or loans from the City of London had proved unsuccessful, and at the end of 1611 he had begun sending out letters requesting "loans" from prominent country gentlemen. By the holiday season of 1611–12, the early period of lavish and spectacular masques had come to an end: where the King and Prince had laid out nearly 1,500 pounds for *Oberon,* Jonson's Twelfth Night masque for the following year, *Love Restored,* cost only 280. Jonson prepared the latter work in circumstances which indicate that thrift had now become a paramount consideration within the royal household. Since spectacle was to be kept at a minimum, Inigo Jones's services were dispensed with. The printed text of *Love Restored* does not identify the participating courtiers but refers to them simply as "Gentlemen, the King's Servants." [25] The use of gentleman dancers, which continued for the next several years, represented yet another economy, for they did not need to be so expensively decked out as the Prince and the Queen, or the earls and their ladies, whose opulent display graced Jonson's earlier entertainments. The gentlemen had no rank of their own to maintain; it was enough simply to please the King.

This commission offered Jonson an unprecedented opportunity to "restore" the all but forgotten concepts of moderation, plain-speaking, and untutored love to the seasonal rite of the court masque. Yet he could scarcely afford to attack masquing as such lest he seem to ally himself with the Puritans who were criticizing James for subsidizing plays and entertainments. Hence, the villain of *Love Restored* is Plutus, the god of money, who wants to do away with masquing altogether. Plutus poses as Cupid, the god of love referred to in the title, but actually he is cupidity, the "reformed" (Puritanical) Cupid who substitutes money for affection. His real-life analogues were the Puritans, parliamentarians, and urban moneylenders who maintained that the King should reduce his expenses in order to pay his debts. Speaking on their behalf, the killjoy Plutus began the performance by informing his majesty that *Love Restored* would not be performed at all: "I tell thee, I will have no more masquing" (34).

The task of rescuing the evening's entertainment fell to "the honest plaine countery spirit, and harmlesse: ROBIN goodfellow, hee that sweeps the harth, and the house cleane, riddles for the countrey maides, and does all their other drudgerie, while they are at hot-cockles." Robin's eagerness to help the courtiers perform their masque reconfirmed the King's belief that the country, like the court (but unlike the Puritanical city), preserved a due regard for holiday festivities and would respond to his pleas for help. But Robin also reiterated, in a good-humored way, the case against opulence and spectacle. Under the current system, Jonson implies, the masque has grown so sophisticated and expensive that there is no place in it for a simple fellow from the country. The centerpiece of *Love Restored* was Robin's narrative of his attempts to get "into" the performance itself. His account of his inability to pass the "stiffe-necked porter" at Whitehall, and then of his futile endeavors to crash the gate by disguising himself as "the kind of persons the dore most open'd to," made a wry commentary on an institution that was groaning under the weight of its own superfluous appendages. First, Robin claimed that he "was an ingineer, and belong'd to the motions"; then he "tooke another figure, of an old tire-woman"; then he "pretended to be a musician"; then, "a feather-maker of *black-friers*." He toyed with the idea of becoming "a bombard man, that brought bouge for a countrey lady or two." And these were only the beginning: "Fortie other devices I had, of *Wire-men*, and the *Chandry*, and I know not what else: but all succeeded alike."[26]

Robin Goodfellow, the personification of homespun country cheer, simultaneously brought Jonson into the mainstream of the current patriotic revival and reaffirmed his loyalty to King James. Robin belongs to the native English landscape and its folk traditions, but not to fairyland. He would be perfectly comfortable either at Penshurst or Sir Robert Wroth's manor house at Durants. He feels out of place among the citizens who peddle their wares at Whitehall, but he can relax in the presence of the King. His blunt good sense exposes the hypocrisy of Plutus, the Puritanical god of money; and his instinctive affection for James unerringly leads him to the true Cupid whose triumphal entry paves the way for the noble dancers. Aubrey reports that "King James made [Jonson] write against the Puritans, who began to be troublesome in his time" (HS, I, 180). His majesty must have been delighted with *Love Restored*. In keeping with the King's own strategy Jonson had transformed a real quarrel between city and court into an imaginary one between city and country.

"To Penshurst" brings together the dominant themes that emerge in Jonson's writing during his fortieth year. Like the Sidney birthday ode and "To Katherine, Lady Aubigny," it celebrates the noble lineage and the bond of parent and child; like *Love Restored*, it exalts the homespun virtues of English country life.

Penshurst Place. Modern aerial view from the south. The Sidneys preserved the Gothic battlements that had protected Penshurst during the Middle Ages.

In Lisle's case, as in the King's, simplicity and thrift were more a matter of economic necessity than of personal preference. Like many of his fellow peers, Lisle was caught in a squeeze between inflation, which reduced the income he received from his rents, and the free-spending ways of his class. Jonson wrote "To Penshurst" at a time when Lisle was uncertain whether or not he would survive this "crisis of the aristocracy." The Viscount's letters to his wife, Barbara, reveal that throughout the earlier part of James's reign he believed himself to be on the edge of poverty and even ruin. In 1610 he contemplated enlarging his park in the hope that the King could be inveigled into hunting on his estate. But this scheme prompted his old servant Thomas Golding to remind him, in the autumn of 1611, of his "great and continual wants" and to observe that "this part of the countrey is not pleasant nor sportely, and therefore not likely to have it visited by such for whose sake you would inlardge it." "To Penshurst" was a tactful way of convincing Lisle to live within his means and of "persuading him that his inability to emulate the magnificence of greater courtiers, so far from being a cause for shame, is in fact a matter for congratulation." Jonson's preliminary dismissal of architectural ornament and novelty makes a virtue of Lisle's necessity:

> Thou are not, Penshurst, built to envious show,
> Of touch, or marble; nor canst boast a row
> Of polish'd pillars, or a roofe of gold:
> Thou hast no lantherne, whereof tales are told;
> Or staire, or courts; but standst an ancient pile.

Penshurst could not boast what its owner could not afford. Like Thomas Golding, Jonson urged Lisle to take satisfaction in what he had: "And though thy walls be of the countrey stone, / They'are rear'd with no mans ruine, no mans grone." [27]

By emphasizing the antiquity of Penshurst (the great hall was built in the fourteenth century) and the purity of its gothic style, Jonson associates Lisle's manor house with the chivalric past. Yet the Sidneys did not, in fact, belong to the "old" nobility. Lisle's father had bribed the heralds to fake a genealogy for them in 1568; they had acquired Penshurst from King Edward VI just sixty years before and they did not maintain an authentic medieval tradition. "Like the battlements, towers, and drawbridges of the 'sham castles' of the period," Don Wayne observes, "the crenelations at Penshurst are decorative and deliberately anachronistic. They were not built of the thickness required for real fortifications. And since they served no useful purpose, they could only have been meant to constitute a *sign*." The fake gothic walls signified an unbroken line of descent extending from the founders of the house down to its present owners. "To Penshurst" transforms the architectural signifier into a verbal one. Like the house itself, Jonson's representation of Penshurst blurs the historical divide that separates the Sidneys, a family of "new" men who acquired their property and status during the Reformation, from the "old" Catholic gentry, who erected Penshurst during the Middle Ages. [28]

Lisle erected his walls "of the countrey stone" in the spring of 1612 and probably received shortly thereafter the royal visit that he had been hoping for. Prior to this time the King's hunting excursions had taken him north to Royston or Newmarket; hence, Thomas Golding could feel certain that Lisle's hopes were ill-founded. In May 1612, however, James abruptly changed his habits and began to frequent his hunting lodge at Eltham, in Kent, which was just an hour or two's ride away from Penshurst. James spent much of that summer at Eltham and then, just as abruptly, stopped going there altogether. The climactic moment of "To Penshurst" is a chance appearance of the King and Prince that may well have occurred during this interval. As Jonson describes it, this mark of James's favor confirms the wisdom of Lisle's unostentatious manner of life. While wealthier peers were spending themselves into debt with lavish preparations for a royal visit, Lisle simply kept the home fires burning:

> That found King James, when hunting late, this way,
> With his brave sonne, the Prince, they saw thy fires
> Shine bright on every harth as the desires
> Of thy *Penates* had beene set on flame,
> To entertaine them . . .

With the arrival of the King and Prince, Lady Sidney reaps "the just reward of her high huswifery"; the domestic sphere widens to include the court; and the manor house where "the countrey came" becomes a microcosm of the entire commonwealth.[29]

"To Penshurst" refers to one other guest who dined at Lisle's estate: the poet. When Jonson recalls the welcome that he himself received, Lisle's board becomes the scene of a secular communion service

> Where the same beere, and bread, and selfe-same wine,
> That is his Lordships, shall be also mine.
> And I not faine to sit (as some, this day,
> At great mens tables) and yet dine away.   (*For,* 2.63–66)

At some point prior to 1612 Jonson had judged Salisbury's hospitality by the same criterion and found it wanting. While sitting "at the end of my Lord Salisburie's table with Inigo Jones," Drummond reports, Jonson was "demanded by my Lord, why he was not glad": "My Lord said he yow promised I should dine with yow, bot I doe not." Jonson was unhappy because "he had none of [Salisbury's] meate, he esteemed only that his meate which was of his owne dish" (*Conv,* 317–321). The contrast between Lisle's table manners and Salisbury's is emblematic of an important change in Jonson's status. When he was in Salisbury's employ, Jonson performed the functions of a skilled hireling, a well-paid rhymester who turned out verses for occasions like King Christian's visit to Theobalds or the opening of the Earl's new shopping center on the Strand. When he was residing at Penshurst, he filled the office of a trusted retainer, a custodian and interpreter of the Sidney family traditions.

Salisbury died on May 24, 1612, after a lingering illness had incapacitated him for nearly a year. The death of James's Secretary of State and Treasurer opened the way for a shift in the balance of power at court and a redistribution of offices and rewards. Did Jonson stand to benefit from such a rearrangement? On the face of it, he did not. The Earl's removal deprived Pembroke and his brother Montgomery, who had been Salisbury's agent in the Royal Bedchamber, of their most powerful ally; the eclipse of Pembroke's faction may be one reason why Jonson withheld his *Epigrams*, which had been entered on the Stationers' Register earlier that May, from publication. The obvious beneficiary of Salisbury's demise was Prince Henry, for whom Jonson had recently prepared the annotated quarto of *The Masque of Queens*, *The Speeches at Prince Henry's Barriers*, and *Oberon*. Although Jonson had yet to form a close attachment to Henry, he had laid the groundwork for such a connection. During that same spring Jonson became the tutor of Wat Raleigh, the son of Henry's chief mentor, and accompanied him to France (HS, XI, 581). But the host of clients who pinned their hopes on James's eldest son were in for a severe disappointment: at the end of the summer Henry contracted a mysterious ailment and died, quite unaccountably, on November 6, 1612.

At this time James created a commission to oversee the Treasury and became his own Secretary of State. While these measures secured the King some room in which to maneuver while he decided upon Salisbury's successor, they also made it impossible for office seekers like Jonson and Donne to take their bearings at court. No one could foresee who James's chief ministers would be in twelve months' time. Jonson could take some consolation from the knowledge that he was ideally situated to play a waiting game. Although his trip to the Continent would do nothing to enhance his prospects at court, at least it prevented him from hindering them.

· CHAPTER TEN ·

The Broken Compass

Jonson and Wat Raleigh journeyed to Paris at a time when the grand tour was still a new and controversial practice. Proponents of foreign travel viewed it as the final stage of an aristocratic education. Since a nobleman's ultimate goal was service at court, his training was not complete until he had acquired a firsthand knowledge of European languages, customs, and political systems. Where was such knowledge to be found, if not on the Continent? Critics of the grand tour complained that prolonged residence in Italy or France weakened the traveler's loyalty to his native land, exposed him to a giddy array of foreign vices, and (worst of all) threatened the constancy of his religious beliefs. Hence, "the golden rule for travel was never to be lured into discussion about religion." Such discussions could, and did, lead young English Protestants to convert to Catholicism; or, alternatively, to become freethinking skeptics like the English traveler in *Volpone,* who urges a young acquaintance to profess no religion whatsoever but rather to "wonder, at the diversitie of all." [1]

The tutor's job was to ensure that the grand tour did not degenerate into a moral holiday. The Elizabethan schoolmaster Roger Ascham summed up the conventional wisdom on this subject when he warned that foreign travel was "mervelous dangerous" for "a yonge jentleman, that doth not goe under the kepe and garde of such a man, as both, by wisedome can, and authoritie dare rewle him." Because the tutor had a vital and delicate task to perform, aristocratic families often recruited important statesmen or scholars (such as Thomas Hobbes) to fill this office. Nevertheless, "a gouvernor has not the power of a father," as one tutor complained; and

Sir Walter Raleigh and His Son, artist unknown, 1602. The son seems to have inherited his father's recklessly independent spirit. When he traveled to France as Wat Raleigh's tutor, Jonson discovered to his cost that his charge was "knavishly inclined."

when the young aristocrat was "knavishly inclined," like young Raleigh, his governor had no way of controlling him.[2] If, finally, the tutor proved to be a libertine in his own right, the possibilities for truancy were infinitely multiplied.

Jonson and his charge arrived in Paris during the spring of 1612. Later that summer Jonson joined a group of French and English auditors who had gathered to hear advocates of the Protestant and Catholic faiths dispute the doctrine of transubstantiation. The Protestant spokesman, Daniel Featley, had been Wat Raleigh's tutor at Oxford. Jonson's willingness to attend this event suggests that he was still ready, if only on an intellectual level, to consider the merits of the Roman Catholic view. In theory, a quasi-public debate on the real presence of Christ's body and blood in the Eucharist represented a test of Jonson's belief in the church to which he had recently reconverted; in actuality, this long-winded and acrimonious disputation probably reconfirmed his loathing for religious extremists of either persuasion and drew him closer to "those wiser Guides / Whom Faction had not drawne to studie sides."[3]

Six months later Jonson narrowly escaped being drawn into a much riskier form of religious controversy. By this time he and his charge had become drinking companions, and Raleigh caused him "to be Drunken and dead drunk, so that he knew not wher he was, therafter laid him on a Carr which he made to be Drawen by Pioners through the streets, at every corner showing his Governour streetched out & telling them that was a more Lively image of the Crucifix then any they had." Herford aptly comments that this exploit was "a dangerous insult to the Catholic religion which might well have cost the lives of both." Paris was, after all, the site of the St. Bartholomew massacre and the city in which Ravaillac had recently assassinated King Henri IV for the crime of being a lukewarm Catholic. Raleigh's prank would have been perfectly normal, however, during Mardi Gras, which fell on February 26, 1613. It is noteworthy, then, that Jonson and Raleigh departed from Paris as soon as the carnival was over. Just a few days after Mardi Gras, on March 3, Jean Beaulieu, the Secretary to the English Ambassador, notified a Brussels business agent named William Trumbull that Jonson "hath now taken a resolution to pass by Sedan into your parts"; on March 11 Beaulieu informed Trumbull that Jonson had requested a letter of introduction, "which I suppose he was desirous to have to prevent the rumour of some cross business wherein he hath been interested here."[4] Beaulieu did not say what the rumors were about, but Jonson had quite literally been involved in "some cross business" when Raleigh turned him into a "Lively image of the Crucifix" and carted him through the streets of Paris.

"What is good in him I was content to relate," Beaulieu concluded, adding that "he hath many worthy parts, for the rest you shall soon make a discovery thereof." By April 3, the pair had passed through Brussels and made their way up to Antwerp, where still another business agent, John Brownlowe, wrote to Trumbull enclosing a letter "for Mr. Rawlegh and Mr. Jonson's bills of exchange, who importuned me so earnestly for 10 l. more that I could not refuse" (HS, XI, 582).

At this stage of their journey, Jonson proceeded to Leiden where he paid a visit to the celebrated Dutch scholar Daniel Heinsius. The trip to Leiden took Jonson to the center of the international network of Protestant humanists and gave him an opportunity to do a favor for an English scholar named Thomas Farnaby. By 1613 Farnaby had nearly completed his monumental edition of Martial, but he had thus far relied on what Jonson called the "castrated" (expurgated) edition of Martial that had been prepared by the Jesuits. Farnaby badly wanted to consult the text of Martial "emended and edited by the famous Peter Scriverius" but was unable to obtain a copy of this unpublished manuscript "either through my own doings or the help of my friends" until Jonson supplied him "with emendations from the Martial of Scriverius, access to which was granted him at Leiden by Daniel Heinsius." Heinsius was currently trying to get King James's support for his own edition of Aristotle, and had been corresponding since 1611 with Isaac Casaubon, the great Huguenot scholar attached to the English court, about this matter; so he would have been eager to ingratiate himself with the leading poet in James's court. Jonson, in turn, gained an introduction to the preeminent classical scholar on the Continent.[5] Heinsius had completed important treatises on tragedy and satire, as well as definitive editions of Horace and of Aristotle's *Poetics*, within the previous four years. Jonson would subsequently translate long passages from these works into English and inscribe them in his commonplace book.

Jonson had returned to London by June 29, 1613, when he saw a discharge of artillery on stage set the Globe Theater on fire during a performance of Shakespeare's *Henry VIII*. But he apparently did not return to his home in St. Anne's, Blackfriars. When he mentioned his wife to Drummond in 1618, he stated that "5 yeers he had not bedded with her but remained with my Lord Aulbanie." Jonson was almost certainly referring to the previous five years of his life—the period that commenced with his return from France in the spring of 1613 and ended with his departure for Scotland in the summer of 1618. There is no other five-year interval during which his address is unknown.[6]

The Jonsons' second parting resembled their earlier separation of 1603–

1605. On both occasions Jonson's departure seems to have been preceded, and perhaps precipitated, by the death of a child. His eventual destination in 1604 and again in 1613 was the Blackfriars mansion of his patron Aubigny. If Jonson really were the father of one or more children born out of wedlock in 1610, their arrival would have placed an additional strain on his marriage. His oft-quoted remark that his wife "was a shrew, yet honest" (*Conv*, 254) should be taken with a large grain of salt: Anne had plenty to complain about.

Jonson had found camaraderie with a coterie of gentlemen about town. Most of the men who belonged to his circle of friends were lawyers, scholars, or courtiers (the three categories often overlapped), and most, like Jonson, were in their late thirties or early forties. The principal evidence for the existence of the coterie appears in two pamphlets by the travel writer Thomas Coryate. In 1610, Coryate had been unable to find a publisher for his *Crudities* (1611) until he hit upon the device of beginning the book with a collection of mock-commendatory poems written by gentlemen who prided themselves on their wit. Jonson's "Certaine Opening and Drawing Distiches" came first in the series of *Crudities* poems and was followed by the offerings of some fifty-five additional contributors, most of whom were either lawyers or courtiers. Several years later, while traveling in the Middle East, Coryate sent his *Greetings from the Court of the Great Mogul* to Laurence Whitaker, "the High Seneschall of the right Worshipfull Fraternitie of Sireniacal Gentlemen, that meet the first Friday of every Moneth, at the sign of the Mere-Maide in Bread streete in London," and specifically asked him to "remember the recommendations of my dutifull respect to al those whose names I have here expressed, being the lovers of vertue, and literature." [7]

The seventeen "Sireniacal Gentlemen" (so named because of the association between Sirens and mermaids) who held monthly meetings at the Mermaid were similar to, and in many cases identical with, the group that contributed poems to Coryate's *Crudities*. Three of them (Jonson, Jones, and John Williams, the King's goldsmith) were connected to the court. Three others (George Garrard, Richard Mocket, and Samuel Purchas) had taken holy orders, though Mocket also licensed books in the Stationers' Hall, and Purchas was the leading Jacobean travel writer. Hugh Holland was a minor poet and traveler; Richard Bing seems to have been "a mere good fellow, a man of no estate." The remainder of the Sireniacal Gentlemen (Whitaker, Donne, Cotton, Richard Martin, John Hoskins, Christopher Brooke, John Bond, and George Speake) were jurists and parliamentarians. [8]

Jonson's connections to the lawyers were particularly close during this period of his life. Between 1613 and 1616 he published commendatory poems for Brooke, John Stephens, and Selden, all of whom belonged to the Inns of Court; wrote an epigram for Chief Justice Coke; and dedicated the folio text of *Poetaster* to Richard Martin. Professional writers, like Shakespeare and Fletcher, are conspicuous by their absence from both of Coryate's rosters. The notion that they too congregated at the Mermaid or that "wit combats" between Jonson and Shakespeare took place there is a late tradition based on fancy rather than fact. The lawyers were not attending a writers' club; on the contrary, the writer Jonson was being included in a fraternity of lawyers and clerics who viewed literature as a gentlemanly avocation.[9]

At the time of his return from the Continent Jonson was also in regular contact with a number of eminent scholars. His periodic visits to Cotton's library kept him in touch with its owner and with the antiquarians who gathered there. Raleigh chose Jonson to be his son's tutor and employed him, along with the "best wits of England," in the writing of his *History of the World*. In the preface to his *Titles of Honor* (1614) Selden, who had been present at the banquet following Jonson's release from prison in 1605 and was now a prominent lawyer, linguist, and historian, mentions having consulted an edition of Euripides "in the well-furnisht Librarie of my beloved friend that singular Poet M. *Ben: Jonson*." Jonson in turn wrote verse tributes for the frontispiece of Raleigh's *History of the World* (1614), for the *Titles of Honor,* and for Farnaby's editions of Juvenal and Persius (1612) and of Seneca (1613). In the Latin preface to his edition of Martial (1615), Farnaby, the leading English classicist of his era, hails Jonson as "an excellent searcher-out of histories, habits, customs, and antiquities" who, as he knew from firsthand experience, was capable of extracting "the deepest meanings by reason, reading, and genius." Farnaby added that his colleague was worthy "of a better theater than that by which he feeds the envy of ill-wishers."[10] Jonson's contemporaries had always regarded him as the scholarly playwright *par excellence;* now he was acquiring the reputation of a scholar in his own right.

By the summer of 1613, Jonson had completed at least one scene of a new comedy called *Bartholomew Fair* and had read it aloud to certain of his friends in the legal and scholarly communities. Selden, who heard the original version of this scene, recalled that in it "Ben Johnson Satyrically express'd the vain Disputes of Divines by *Inigo Lanthorne,* disputing with his puppet." The sobriquet "Inigo Lanthorne" did not, however, survive the original draft. Hugh Holland believed that this character was a lampoon of Inigo Jones and said as much to Donne's friend Sir Henry Goodyear; Goodyear, in turn, asked Donne to lay the matter before Jonson. On July 17 Donne replied, "I did your commandment with Mr. Johnson; both our interests in him needed not to have been employed in it. There was

John Selden, studio of Sir Peter Lely(?), before 1650. An advocate of plainness and moderation, Selden wears a simple black scholar's gown and a flat linen collar.

nothing obnoxious but the very name, and he hath changed that. If upon having read it before to divers, it should be spoken that the person was concerned in it, he sees not how Mr. Holland will be excused in it, for he protests that no hearer but Mr. Holland apprehended it so." Jonson's disclaimer sounds a little disingenuous. Lantern Leatherhead, as he came to be called, does in fact exhibit the very prejudices that Jonson would later attribute to his collaborator. Just as Jones staged and decorated the masques, Lantern is "the Master o' the Motion" who attends to the scenic and visual aspects of the puppet show that concludes *Bartholomew Fair*. Like Jones, who viewed masques as "nothing else but pictures with Light and Motion," Lantern has a marked antiliterary bias. He instructs the author of the puppet show "to reduce it to a more familiar straine for our people" and complains that "they put too much learning i' their things now o' dayes." [11]

The butt of the scene that "Satyrically express'd the vain Disputes of Divines" is not Inigo Lanthorne but a sectarian preacher named Zeal-of-the-Land-Busy. Busy objects to the puppets on religious grounds and threatens to "remove *Dagon* there, I say, that *Idoll*, that heathenish *Idoll*, that remains . . . a beame in the eye, in the eye of the brethren." Here again, Jonson had a personal as well as a professional animus toward the object of his satire. In a sermon preached at Paul's Cross and published the previous year, a particularly vehement opponent of the stage named Robert Milles castigated Londoners for preferring "the idle and scurrile invention of an illiterate bricklayer to the holy, pure, and powerful word of God." [12] Although Jonson did not reply directly to these slurs, he used the puppets as a stalking horse in his quarrel with the divines.

Puppet Dionysus defeats Busy by inveigling the Puritan "hypocrite" onto the (for him) unfamiliar terrain of an academic disputation, similar to the one Jonson had recently witnessed in Paris. Like the Parisian disputants, the sectarian and the puppet argue about the correct interpretation of a specific biblical text: does the scriptural taboo on transvestism (Deuteronomy 22:5) apply to male puppets who wear female attire? This passage was repeatedly cited by Puritan preachers who demanded that the playhouses be closed because the boy actors wore female clothing. But the logic-chopping Puppet Dionysus is "well studied in these controversies, betweene the hypocrites and us," and he knows where Busy's weakness lies. The word "hypocrite" denotes a conscious fraud in modern English, but it had a different meaning for Jonson and his contemporaries. In his *Discoveries*, he rigorously distinguishes between impostors, who "beleeve not themselves, what they would perswade others," and the "Puritan hypocrite, whose opinion of his own perspicacity (in that he thinks he has detected certain errors in a few church dogmas) disturbs his sanity: thence

A Sermon at Paul's Cross, artist unknown, ca. 1616. Paul's Cross is the octagonal structure on the lower left. Dignitaries from the royal family, Privy Council, and the municipal government sat in the galleries on the side of the cathedral. A sermon preached there around 1612 chastised theatergoers for preferring "the idle and scurrile invention of an illiterate bricklayer" to the word of God.

struck with a sacred madness he fights frantically against the magistrate, thus thinking to show his obedience before God." When Busy declares, "my maine argument against you, is, that you are an *abomination:* for the Male, among you, putteth on the apparell of the *Female,* and the *Female* of the *Male,*" he speaks with the wild assurance of a man who believes his own nonsense. The Puritan thereby becomes an easy mark for the sexless puppet, who rejoins that *"we have neither* MALE *nor* FEMALE *amongst us"*—a telling allusion to Galatians 3:28 ("there is neither male nor female, for ye are all one in Christ Jesus")—and clinches the argument by pulling up his garment. Unlike the "impostor," the hypocrite has no defense against a superior display of casuistry; so it is shocking, but entirely appropriate, that Busy should now be "converted" to the cause of play: "Let it goe on. For I am changed, and will become a beholder with you!" [13]

The central themes of this scene mirror the preoccupations of the lawyers and scholars who heard Jonson read it aloud in 1613. Selden saw Busy as a foil that threw his own viewpoint into sharp relief. Whereas the sectarian preacher's approach to Scripture is rabidly partisan, the hero of Jonson's "Epistle to Master John Selden" personifies the ideal of disinterested scholarly inquiry; whereas the one "derides all *Antiquity; defies any other *Learning* then *Inspiration,*" the other harks back to the remote frontiers of human knowledge in his search for truth:

> What fables have you vext! what truth redeem'd!
> Antiquities search'd! Opinions dis-esteem'd!
> Impostures branded! and Authorities urg'd!
> What blots and errours, have you watch'd and purg'd
> Records, and Authors of! how rectified
> Times, manners, customes! Innovations spide!
> Sought out the Fountaines, Sources, Creekes, paths, wayes,
> And noted the beginnings and decayes!

These lines sum up the humanistic ideals that Jonson shared with Selden and Bacon, and with their European counterparts—whom he repeatedly cites in his *Discoveries*—J. C. Scaliger, Casaubon, and Heinsius. (Following the death of Casaubon in 1614, Selden became Heinsius's principal contact in England.) As Jonson indicates, Selden, whom he regarded as "the bravest man in all Languages," scorned second-hand accounts and made extraordinary efforts to ascertain the primary sources of historical traditions. In the very phrases that supply the imagery of Jonson's tribute, Selden assured readers of *The Duello* that "I vent to you nothing quoted at second hand, but ever lov'd the Fountain, and, when I could come at it, used that Medium only, which would not at all, or least, deceive by Refraction." [14]

Selden was especially critical of sweeping appeals to biblical precept. "The [biblical] text serves only to guess by," he insisted, "we must satisfy ourselves fully out of the Authors that lived about those times." The claim that Deuteronomy 22:5 prohibited transvestite performances in modern London epitomized the kind of self-serving exegesis that Selden objected to. Shortly after *Bartholomew Fair* was completed, he sent Jonson his "notes touching the literal sense and historical of the holy text usually brought against the counterfeiting of sexes by apparell." Selden included a literal translation of the apposite passage in the Hebrew Bible—"the text itself is thus out of the original word for word: *A man's armour shall not be upon a woman, and a man shall not put on a woman's garment*"—and explained that it had originally been written to prohibit magical rites in which men and women exchanged apparel.[15] Selden's commentary completes the work of Jonson's satire by removing the holy text from the sphere of political debate altogether and locating it in a specific practice in the ancient world.

The supposedly disinterested introduction of comparative philology into biblical interpretation served political ends that were less obvious, but no less urgent, than Busy's. Scaliger, Casaubon, and Heinsius, like their allies in the English Church, belonged to the mainstream of liberal Protestantism in Northern Europe. Finding themselves assailed by Rome on one side and Geneva on the other, they regarded the twin ideals of historical research and critical inquiry as antidotes to religious extremism. By exposing superstition and false traditions they were simultaneously liberating human knowledge from the shackles of religious dogma and justifying their own position in the middle of the road. Scaliger brought the history of the Jews—hitherto regarded as the province of theologians—within the compass of modern historical scholarship. Selden's *De Diis Syriis* was a pioneering study of Near Eastern mythology in the biblical era, and his most famous work, *The History of Tithes*, demonstrated that the practice of collecting tithes did not have any basis in Scripture.

This kind of research lent support to the Erastian doctrine of state supremacy in religious affairs. Like Cotton and Donne, Selden was a lawyer as well as a scholar, and his insistence that divines were subject to secular authorities reflects a strong professional commitment to the autonomy of the law. The "lawyers of the Renaissance," writes William Bouwsma, "were the first theorists since the Sophists to argue that legal systems should not be required to reflect the will of God in any direct way or to mediate between eternal reason and the practical needs of men." The specter of Church-sponsored terrorism reinforced the Erastian position. Bacon began the 1612 edition of his *Essays* with "Of Religion," an antisectarian polemic which argues that the national interest supersedes the claims of any individual creed. While acknowledging that "the true God . . . is the jealous God," he insists that "the bonds of religious unity, are so to be strengthened, as the bonds of humane society be not dissolved." It is a "blasphemy greater than Satan's" when men "make the cause of *Religion* descend, to the execrable accions of murthering of Princes, butchery of people, and firing of States." Selden too insisted that "divines ought to do no more than the state permits," advocated a strong national church, and vigorously opposed religious persecution. His discourse on religion takes Bacon's line of reasoning to its logical conclusion: "*Question.* Whether is the Church or the Scripture Judge of Religion? *Answer.* In truth neither, but the State . . . the Protestants say they will be judged by the Scriptures; the Papists say so too; but that cannot speak. A Judge is no Judge, except he can both speak and command Execution; but the truth is they never intend to agree." Such disputes can never be resolved "because there wants Measure by which the Business can be decided." By way of illustration Selden refers his reader to "Inigo Lanthorne, disputing with his Puppet in a *Bartholomew* Fair: It is so; It is not so; It is so; It is not so, crying thus to one another a quarter of an Hour together." [16]

Jonson's reasons for adopting the Erastian viewpoint have already been mentioned: the Gunpowder Plot, the killing of Henri IV, his reconversion to the English Church, and his experiences in Paris, all would have led him to embrace Selden's position; indeed, that position is already implicit in his scathing lampoons of Deacon Ananias, the power-hungry separatist, and Catiline, the crypto-Catholic adventurer. But his choice of this theme at this particular moment was uncannily apt, for in the summer of 1613 King James was about to assert his own supremacy over the divines in a bold and unambiguous way.

The months that Jonson spent on the Continent were a period of transition at court. At the time of his return neither of the leading factions had yet been able to capitalize on the opportunities created by the death of Salisbury and Prince Henry. It had been clear for some time that Robert Carr, the King's favorite, would have the principal say in the reallocation of offices; but Carr at first could not make up his mind whether to align himself with the former Essexians or the Howards. In the spring of 1613 he finally decided on the latter and proposed to cement the alliance by marrying Suffolk's daughter, Lady Frances Howard. Only one obstacle stood in his way: the bride of his choice was still married to the third Earl of Essex.

The marriage of Lady Frances and Essex, which Jonson had celebrated in *Hymenaei* and the *Barriers* of 1606, had gradually turned into a disas-

Robert Carr, Earl of Somerset, after J. Hoskins. James's favorite at the height of his career at court.

ter. Far from promoting union between the two families, it became a fresh source of discord. In 1607, shortly after the wedding, Essex went abroad. Lady Frances remained at court, where she "ran at random," in the words of Sir Simonds D'Ewes, "and played her pranks as the toy took her in the head, sometimes publicly, sometimes privately, whereby she both disparaged her reputation and brought herself into the contempt of the world."

Lady Frances Howard, Countess of Somerset, artist unknown, ca. 1615. The anonymous painter evokes Lady Somerset's unabashed sexuality and menacing gaze.

By 1612 Frances had become Carr's lover and badly wanted to marry him. Her family promoted the match because it offered them an irresistible opportunity to strengthen their hand at court. James, who was now actively backing the Howard faction, lent his assistance. When Sir Thomas Overbury, Carr's mentor and the main foe of the alliance, refused to be made

Special Ambassador to France, Holland, or Russia—transparent pretexts for getting him out of the way—the King imprisoned him in the Tower of London.[17]

By this time Essex had come around to the idea of an annulment, provided that his honor could remain intact. It could not. After the King had appointed commissioners to hear the case, Lady Essex filed a complaint alleging that although she had sought to have sexual intercourse with her husband on numerous occasions, and although he had "purposely endeavored and attempted to consummate marriage with me," he "never had carnal copulation with me." George Abbot, Archbishop of Canterbury and the head of James's commission, determined that a verdict of annulment under these circumstances would make a mockery of the sacrament of marriage and could have profound consequences: "If the gap be open, who will not run in? And the judge must dispense indifferently to all, if the proofs be accordingly; for we may not say, that it is for noble personages, and great peers in state, and not for others of inferior rank. Whatsoever couple therefore have no children, and live discontented, come presently to take part of this general jubilee." Chamberlain was of the same opinion: "If such a gap be once let open, it will not be so easilie stopt but that infinite inconveniencies will follow."[18] Public opinion swung behind the Archbishop. James finally had to pack the commission with two additional, and corruptible, bishops in order to get a verdict of annulment; but Abbot had made a fair assessment. In the meantime, Overbury died in suspicious circumstances while imprisoned in the Tower.

The wedding of Lady Frances and Robert Carr, now Earl of Somerset, was a moment of high cynicism. The triumph of a new favorite invariably meant that fresh opportunities for gain and preferment were in the air, and the death of Prince Henry and Salisbury had left Somerset with a clear field. The excitement was compounded by the knowledge that a primary moral constraint had been compromised as well. Frankie and Robin, as James affectionately dubbed the pair, enjoyed such power over the King that it would have been folly to cross them. The Earl and his bride-to-be must have seemed all the more powerful for their brazen disregard of public opinion. The wedding presents were lavish and the literary offerings were equally sumptuous. The latter included verse tributes from Donne, Chapman, and Jonson; masques by Bacon, Campion, and Jonson; and the *Challenge at Tilt* that Jonson wrote for the tournament which followed the wedding on December 26.

The most common way of praising this marriage was to portray it as the triumph of fertility over barrenness, with poor Essex tacitly bearing the odium of the man who had failed to perform. Jonson's tournament conformed to this pattern. For his *Challenge at Tilt* he resuscitated the device of two opposed Cupids, which he had used in *Love Restored,* but instead of a good and a bad Cupid he depicts two Cupids who are equally, and outrageously, preoccupied with sex. Until now, Jonson had refrained from using smutty language in his entertainments at court. These, however, are bawdy Cupids. First Cupid, who speaks on behalf of Somerset, warns his mate that he is "too rude . . . in this presence" (line 9), but to no avail. "That cannot put modestie into me," he replies, "to make me come behind you though, I will stand for mine inches with you" (10–11). Bawdry always suffers in translation, but an alert spectator would have noticed, and maybe even enjoyed, the train of wordplay that runs through *come* (have an orgasm), *stand* (have an erection), and *mine inches* (the length of my erection).

The boys press the rival claims of their master and mistress, the Earl and his Lady, by portraying them as a pair of sexual athletes vying for supremacy. First Cupid speaks for the groom energetically enough ("His very undressing was it not loves arming?"), but his effort pales beside that of Lady Frances's champion. When Second Cupid appears arrayed for the tilt, he invites the ladies to behold him "as I use to reigne and revell in your fancies": "Laying little strawes about your hearts, to kindle bone-fires, shall flame out at your eies; playing in your blouds, like fishes in a streame, or diving like the *boyes* i' the *Bath,* and then rising on end, like a *Monarch,* and treading humour like water, bending those stiffe pickardills of yours, under this yoke, my bow." Once again a train of innuendo runs through *bone-fires* (the pain of venereal disease), *rising* (having an erection), and *treading* (copulation), to say nothing of the commonplace analogy between fishing and sexual intercourse. Further commentary would be supererogatory, though Second Cupid's riposte just before the tilting began—"O, most *stiffely* spoken! and fit for the sexe you *stand* for"— reminded the spectators, if any reminder were needed, of the latent sexual imagery of the tilt itself.[19] In sharp contrast to the austere and philosophical *Barriers* that Jonson had written for Lady Frances's marriage to Essex, this wedding tilt was gamey; but then, so were the bride and groom. Presumably the Somersets, the poor man's Nero and Poppea, wanted to be portrayed in this way. Public misbehavior was, after all, a way of putting themselves beyond the law, and thus was a sign of their power.

Jonson's epigram in praise of Somerset was "delivered to the Earle" on the same day. In the opening lines of this poem he distinguishes between the throng of flatterers who "are present with their face, / And clothes, and guifts," and sincere well-wishers like himself "whose heart, and thought / Do waite upon thee: and their Love not bought." Jonson had good reason to be concerned about this issue. He had recently been cultivating the rival faction headed by Pembroke, and it is hard (though just possible) to believe that he felt much enthusiasm for the burgeoning alliance of Somerset and the Howards. Naturally, Jonson assures the Earl that he himself is one of those who "weare true wedding robes, and are true freindes, / That bid, God give thee joy, and have no endes." Yet the epigram hints at reservations about this pair. Although he hopes that their marriage will compensate for Essex's "fault," in the closing lines we encounter a couplet that echoes the prayer with which he had concluded *Hymenaei* seven years previously: "And when your yeares rise more, then would be told, / Yet neither of you seeme to th'other old." [20]

The parallelism between the Essex-Howard match and Jonson's own marital history is equally striking. In 1606 he had left the household of his patron Aubigny, returned to his wife, Anne, and written a masque and tournament for Lady Frances Howard's first wedding; in 1613, he left Anne, returned to Aubigny, and wrote a masque and tournament for Lady Frances's second wedding. Her first marriage coincided with his reconciliation to Anne; her divorce coincided with his separation from Anne. Both marriages were dissolved on the grounds of personal preference, and in both cases the patronage system took precedence over familial ties. As Bishop Abbot had foreseen, "if the gap be open, who will not run in?"

In his epistle to Selden, which was published in 1614, Jonson voices grave misgivings about his client status. Like the epigram delivered to Somerset on his wedding day, this poem dwells on the distinction between sincere praise and flattery. In the case of Selden, however, a long-established friendship precluded the need for any protestations. "I know to whom I write," he begins, "Here, I am sure, / Though I am short, I cannot be obscure" (*Und*, 14.1–2). About half of this epistle deals with the politics of epideictic poetry. Praising his friend's book is a rare pleasure, Jonson explains, because it really *is* excellent: he can be laudatory and truthful at the same time. For the first time in his career, he confesses that he has not always been so circumspect:

> I have too oft preferr'd
> Men past their termes, and prais'd some names too much,
> But 'twas with purpose to have made them such
> Since, being deceiv'd, I turne a sharper eye
> Upon my selfe, and aske to whom? and why?
> And what I write? and vexe it many dayes
> Before men get a verse: much lesse a Praise;
> So that my Reader is assur'd, I now
> Meane what I speake: and still will keepe that Vow. (20–28)

Although he invokes the classical doctrine which holds that the praiser merely tells people what they ought to be like and therefore cannot be held responsible for their failings, Jonson does not fall back on this line of defense. Instead, he admits that he has been "deceiv'd" and promises to "turne a sharper eye / Upon my selfe" hereafter. By way of conclusion, he congratulates Selden for dedicating his *Titles of Honor* "to no greate Name, / That would, perhaps, have prais'd, and thank'd the same" (69–70), but rather to his "learned Chamber-fellow," John Hayward. Jonson, by contrast, had recently been singing the praises of the Somersets and was, in all likelihood, carefully weighing the strategic value of the many individual dedications and verse tributes that he would shortly publish in the 1616 folio of his works. Despite his vow to refrain from praising unworthy subjects in the future, he could not alter the fact that while Selden was relatively independent from the patronage system, he was not.

The central metaphor of this poem conveys the essential difference between Selden's professional life and Jonson's. Selden resembles a "Compasse" who "keeping one foot still / Upon your Center, doe your circle fill / Of generall knowledge." The compass was a venerable fixture of Renaissance iconography. Its moving leg signified the mind's journey along the outer periphery of knowledge; its fixed leg, the mind's capacity to weigh and evaluate the materials gathered in the course of that journey. Selden's research takes him out to the hinterlands of learning (he was the first English Orientalist; his account of *Titles of Honor* goes back to the period before the Flood), yet the "Center" of his intellectual being provides a stable point of reference for the enduring self that renders judgment. Five years later, Jonson told Drummond that his own "Impressa was a Compass with one foot in Center, the other Broken, the word. Deest quod duceret orbem" (that which should guide the circle is missing). The "missing" section of the outer leg enables the user of the compass to steer an even course in his journey across the periphery of experience.[21] Its absence implies Jonson's lack of full control over the nature and scope of his own work; however stridently he asserts his independence, his writing is bound to reflect the preferences of his patrons.

Selden, more than any of Jonson's contemporaries, exemplified the ideal of unbiased scholarship. Parliamentary historians remember him for championing the rights of the Lower House, but the Lords also consulted Selden about their privileges when the need arose. His biographer concludes that his basic principles—typified by maxims like "All is as the state pleases," or "Every law is a contract between the king and the people, and therefore to be kept"—were "destructive of the claims to *jus divinum* alike of kings, bishops, and presbyters."[22] Jonson, of course, did not enjoy anything like this kind of independence. The conventions of the masque, like those of every courtly ritual, stipulated that "all is as the king pleases," and a court entertainer always had to honor that principle.

Entreprendre par deſſus ſa force.

★Celluy qui ſon eſprit efforce
Et veult plus qu'il ne peult cõprendre,
C'eſt comme qui veult entreprendre
Oultre ſon pouoir & ſa force.

Emblem of a broken compass. From Giles Corrozet, *Hecatongraphie,* 2d ed., Paris, 1543. An example of Jonson's *imprese.* The inscriptions above and below the compass indicate that it represents the danger of venturing beyond one's capacities, of undertaking enterprises that are beyond one's control.

Jonson's escapade with Wat Raleigh in Paris raised a further question about his lack of autonomy: how could he impose order on the world around him when he could not even control his own drinking and eating? At the age of twenty-nine, according to Dekker and Marston, Jonson was a "leane . . . hollow-cheek't Scrag," like his alter ego Maci-lente ("emaciated"), the "lanke raw-bon'd anatomie," who "walkes up and downe like a charg'd musket" in *Every Man out of His Humour.* Ten years later, the poet John Davies of Hereford complimented him on being "sound in Body"; but by his late forties, he had grown exceedingly fat.[23]

He was apparently becoming corpulent, then, during the years when he traveled to France and wrote *Bartholomew Fair*—a play in which the model transgressions are eating and drinking.

His drunken spree in Paris continued to weigh on his mind after his return from the Continent. In *Bartholomew Fair,* which he had completed by the autumn of 1614, an irascible tutor named Humphrey Wasp reluctantly accompanies his nineteen-year-old charge to the fair, drinks to excess, loses control of himself and his pupil, and becomes a public spectacle. At the end of the day, when his tutee confronts him with his follies, Wasp concedes that "my government is at an end. He that will correct another, must want fault in himselfe" (V.iv.98–100).

When Jonson reimagined his folly in Paris, he situated it within a carnival. Although he had read Rabelais by the time he wrote *Bartholomew Fair,* Jonson did not need to consult books to discover what happened at French carnivals. He had witnessed the pre-Lenten festival of 1613 and had become involved in a carnivalesque pattern of experience—and perhaps in the carnival itself. In the course of his "cross business," he had surrendered the perquisites of his rank and office, merged with the life of the streets, offered his body as an object of celebration and vilification, and enacted a burlesque of the *via dolorosa.*

The carnival setting of *Bartholomew Fair* made it possible for him to redeem this drunken caprice. The play locates his personal folly within an elaborate network of inversionary jokes about the dethronement of false authorities. The same carnival that exposes the frailties of his alter ego, Humphrey Wasp, also unmasks the pretensions of Zeal-of-the-Land-Busy and the pretentious magistrate Adam Overdo. The overthrow of Busy and Adam and the pervasive interrogation of authoritarian religious dogma recall, in turn, the anticlerical bias of Selden and his circle. Jonson's carnivalesque mockery of Busy and Adam is the vulgar analogue of Selden's critical inquiries into the scope of biblical precept.

Jonson sold *Bartholomew Fair* to Lady Elizabeth's Men, a marginal company of adult actors whom Henslowe had recently amalgamated with the Children of the Queen's Revels. The presence of numerous children and teenagers on stage reinforced Jonson's portrayal of adult behavior as inherently childish, but he also had a personal connection with Lady Elizabeth's Men. The star of the new company was Jonson's "scholar" Nathan Field, who was actively involved in the acquisition of scripts for Lady Elizabeth's Men and, doubtless, helped them obtain *Bartholomew Fair.* Field's participation in this venture was particularly apt because his father, John Field, a fanatical Puritan preacher and a leading opponent of the stage, was one of the prototypes for Zeal-of-the-Land-Busy. Nathan Field himself had unwillingly entered the acting profession at the age of thirteen,

Nathan Field, artist unknown. By the time he acted in *Bartholomew Fair,* Jonson's "scholar" had become one of the most celebrated players of the age.

when he was forcibly abducted by the patentees of the Queen's Revels. After joining the company he found a surrogate father in Jonson, who "read to him the Satyres of Horace and some Epigrames of Martiall." Now, at the height of his career on the stage (a character in *Bartholomew Fair* refers to him as "your best *Actor*"), Field took a leading role in Jonson's lampoon of his father's antitheatrical prejudices.[24]

Jonson's endorsement of carnival also reinforced an important tenet of Jacobean ideology. Despite the protests of Puritan preachers like Zeal-of-the-Land-Busy, and of municipal magistrates like Adam Overdo, James maintained that his subjects' right to disport themselves at wakes, fairs, and carnivals fell within the scope of the royal prerogative. The Prologue to the court performance of *Bartholomew Fair* emphasizes this issue, deferentially warning James that he must expect "such place, such men, such language, and such ware" as a fair affords, but also promising him a lampoon of "your lands *Faction*"—the militant Puritans—"whereof the petulant wayes / Your selfe have knowne, and have bin vext with long." [25]

Yet Jonson maintains a discreet distance from the world of carnival. When he wrote *Bartholomew Fair,* he wanted to assert his mastery over the festive impulses that had mastered him during the previous year. The Induction to his new comedy explicitly and repeatedly insists on the author's autonomy vis-à-vis the flesh-and-blood Bartholomew Fair that took place every summer in Smithfield. The first character to appear onstage is an old Stage-keeper who complains that Jonson has remained aloof from the life of the "real" Bartholomew Fair. He has neither "convers'd with the *Bartholomew*-birds" nor reproduced the sights, sounds, and physical sensations of an authentic carnival: "And some writer (that I know) had had but the penning o' this matter, hee would ha' made you such a *Jig-a-jogge* i' the boothes, you should ha' thought an earthquake had beene i' the *Faire*" (13, 23–26). The Stage-keeper offered to share his firsthand knowledge of the Fair with Jonson, but this gesture was not appreciated: "Hee has (*sirreverence*) kick'd me three, or foure times about the Tiring-House, I thanke him, for but offering to putt in, with my experience" (28–30).

A moment later, a Book-holder (that is, a prompter) and a Scrivener enter and drive the Stage-keeper away. As Jonathan Haynes points out, this moment is emblematic of the opposition between an older, festive dramaturgy and the new coterie theater that Jonson, more than any other individual, had helped bring into being: "The Stage-keeper with his memories of an improvisational popular theater" is expelled by "the Book-holder and Scrivener, men of the master-poet's written text"; "the communal possession of, and participation in, a tradition that was always extra-official, 'with the people'" is superseded by "legal relations expressed in the formal articles the Scrivener reads out." The "Articles of Agreement, indented, between the *Spectators* or *Hearers*" and "the *Author of Bartholomew Faire*" prohibit the spectators from either uniting into a group or participating in the performance in any way. Instead, Jonson requires them "to remaine in the places, their money or friends have put them in, with patience, for the space of two houres and a halfe"; to form independent judgments "and not censure by *Contagion,* or upon *trust*"; and to notify the author if anyone attempts to draw parallels between the characters in the play and particular members of the community. In other words, if they agree to compose themselves into an audience of passive, isolated individuals, Jonson will give them "a new sufficient Play called *BARTHOLOMEW FAIR,* merry, and as full of noise, as sport." [26]

Once Jonson has renounced carnival as a social practice, he is free to reaffirm it as a form of literary expression. Although his version of carnival (like its Smithfield namesake) is belated, English, and commercial, he fills it with reminiscences of the medieval folk festivals that persisted, in an attenuated form, in France and the Low Countries. Ursula, the "she-bear" who plies the fairgoers with pork, ale, tobacco, and flesh, descends from the mothers-of-misrule who presided at European carnivals: the French "Mère Folle," for example, and the Flemish "Dame Oiseuse." To enter Ursula's booth—and by extension, to visit the fair—is to commence the journey through the underworld that recurs in carnival narratives of every color. On an anatomical level, the visitors wend their way through what Mikhail Bakhtin calls "the lower bodily stratum." Ursula's booth is "the very *wombe,* and *bedde* of enormitie," and its proprietress is characterized as a great vaginal orifice: "Hee that would venture for't, I assure him, might sinke into her, and be drown'd a weeke, ere any friend hee had, could find where he were." Just nine months previously Jonson had alluded to this intrauterine itinerary in *A Challenge at Tilt.* Sixteen thirteen is also the likeliest date for "The Famous Voyage," his mock epic account of two gallants who row a wherry up the Fleet ditch. In the course of "The Famous Voyage," the ditch, a vast open sewer flowing through London down to the Thames, becomes an allegorical image of the rectal canal within the human body. The voyagers enter through the anus, proceed through the lower intestines, and seek out "Madame Caesar," who, like Ursula, is a procuress. [27]

From a religious standpoint, Ursula, the "Mother o' the *Furies*" who sits "tormented, within, i' the fire," presides over a comic version of hell. Zeal-of-the-Land-Busy solemnly warns his flock that Ursula "is above all to be avoided, having the marks upon her, of the three enemies of Man, the World, as being in the *Faire;* the Devill, as being in the fire; and the Flesh, as being her selfe." The killjoy Puritan, intent upon spiritualizing the corporeal world, likens the cookhouse to hell. Ursula, however, likens hell to a cookhouse—nay, she insists that hell is actually an improvement on her fiery kitchen, "a kind of cold cellar to't, a very fine vault o'my conscience!" By affirming the triumph of the corporeal over the spiritual, Ursula achieves the victory of laughter over fear that Bakhtin attributes to all carnivalesque representations of hell. Her pig booth momentarily defeats the specter of eternal damnation, and so reinforces the festive exemption from moral judgments: "Judge not that ye be not judged."[28]

As Jonson knew from firsthand experience, carnival was a time for mock liturgies, travesties of saints' lives, and parodic reenactments of scriptural events. These customs were already on the wane in France and had never taken hold across the Channel. When Jonson imported them, he empowered himself to blur, question, and invert the central doctrines of the Christian Church. Although *Bartholomew Fair* participates in a folk tradition of spontaneous, festive blasphemy, its aims are infinitely more complex than its rough-and-tumble antecedents would suggest. Taken in its entirety, the play offers a fully parodic reworking of the story of salvation.

The stage plan of *Bartholomew Fair* calls for two fixed booths—one for Ursula's "bower," the other for Leatherhead's puppet show—and these recall the "mansions" in which the medieval mystery cycles were performed.[29] The mystery cycles, which persisted until Elizabeth's Protestant government suppressed them in the late sixteenth century, depicted the

Mère Folle and her children, ca. 1610. From M. du Tilliot, *Histoires de la fête des foux,* 1771. Jonson could have seen this precursor of Ursula, the pig woman in *Bartholomew Fair,* while traveling in France. The caption advises readers that "the world is full of fools, and anyone who doesn't want to acknowledge this should hold himself entirely aloof and break his mirror."

entire history of existence from the Creation to the Second Coming. Jonson parodies this older tradition of biblical narrative throughout *Bartholomew Fair*, but he does so most insistently in the emblematic figure of Adam Overdo, Chief Justice of the court of pie powders (from French *pieds poudrés*, "dusty feet"), which had jurisdiction over Bartholomew Fair. As his name implies, Adam combines vast pretensions (besides God and Christ, his avatars include Hercules, Cicero, Columbus, Drake, and Magellan) with feet of clay. Throughout the play, he enacts a parody of Christ, the "second" Adam, who descends from on high, adopts the form of a lowly man, preaches a sermon to the multitudes, and is persecuted and physically beaten. Adam's beating prompts him to reflect on the paradox of his dual identity and "to thinke, that by a spice of collateral Justice, *Adam Overdoo* deserv'd this beating." Adam has undergone a fortunate fall, and he already foresees the comic denouement that will ensue "when, sitting at the upper end o' my Table," he will "deliver to 'hem, it was I, that was cudgell'd, and shew 'hem the marks" of his stigmata. As the end draws near, Adam adopts the idiom of the risen Christ, who will appear at the Second Coming "wherin cloud-like, I will breake out in raine, and haile, lightning, and thunder, upon the head of enormity." But a "new," merciful Adam is finally prevailed upon to "drowne the memory of all enormity in your bigg'st bowle" at the nuptial feast that follows the play.[30]

Although the fall of Adam is an occasion for communal rejoicing, just as it would be in a real carnival, *Bartholomew Fair* also looks ahead to a post-festive order in which the saved will be segregated from the damned. On the level of Jonson's allegory the question of salvation is posed by the madman Trouble'all, who has been driven insane by the "old," legalistic Adam, "so that ever since, hee will doe nothing, but by Justice *Overdoo's* warrant." When Adam becomes aware of Trouble'all's ailment, the magistrate obligingly writes him up a blank warrant and congratulates himself with yet another inane recollection of St. Paul: "*Adam* hath offer'd satisfaction! The sting is removed from hence." But Adam mistakenly confers the gift of grace on Tom Quarlous, a professional gambler, Oxford alumnus, and former law student, who lurks on the margins of the scriptural allegory. Quarlous grasps the formal structure of this allegory even though he does not believe in it himself; he embodies what Greenblatt calls "the subversive perception of another's truth as an ideological construct," and this insight enables him to exploit medieval forms of culture that are fundamentally alien to him. After he obtains the "new" Adam's warrant, which is good for anything "that thou want'st now, or at any time hereafter," Quarlous decides that he wants Grace—which is precisely what poor Trouble'all needs.[31] Quarlous refers, however, not to the scriptural gift of grace, but to Adam Overdo's ward, Grace Wellborn, a wealthy heiress whom he sells to his friend Ned Winwife.

Quarlous's detached, exploitative attitude to the fair mirrors Jonson's stance in the Induction scene. Like his protagonist, Jonson treats the biblical narrative of the mystery cycles as a manipulable fiction that he can always twist to his own advantage. He would eventually feel remorse about having taken God's word in vain. Aubrey reports that during the last years of his life Jonson was "much aflickted, that hee had profain'd the scripture, in his playes" (HS, I, 181). At the time he wrote *Bartholomew Fair,* however, Jonson was evolving a more relativistic view of religious belief. Four years earlier, he had drunk the full cup in token of "true Reconciliation" to the Anglican Church; four years later, Drummond found that Jonson was "for any religion as being versed in both" (*Conv,* 315, 690). By then, he had come around to the position of Selden: "All is as the state pleases."

Although Jonson does not invoke the superior authority of the state within *Bartholomew Fair,* he raises this issue in an Epilogue addressed to the King at the close of the court performance on November 1, 1614. The Epilogue asks James to resolve the question that subsequently came back to haunt Jonson: Is his play "prophane"?

> You know the scope of *Writers,* and what store
> of *leave* is given them, if they take not more,
> And turne it into *licence:* you can tell
> if we have us'd that *leave* you gave us, well:
> Or whether wee to rage, or *licence* breake,
> or be *prophane,* or make *prophane* men speake?
> This is your power to judge (great Sir) and not
> the envy of a few. (Epilogue, 3–10)

King James steps into the place vacated by Busy and Overdo; their fantasy of absolute and incontestable authority is his reality. On October 30 Jonson required the spectators who saw the play at the Hope Theater to agree in advance not "to challenge the *Author* of scurrilitie" because his language occasionally savors of "prophanenesse" (Induction, 149–150, 152). A day later, he asked the King to render a definitive judgment on this very question. Moreover, the King's verdict was to be final: Jonson kept *Bartholomew Fair* out of print until 1631, when the pressure of penury compelled him to publish it, and there is no record of any subsequent performance prior to the Restoration.

Jonson knew that James was unlikely to return a verdict of guilty. The most offensive features of *Bartholomew Fair*—its preoccupation with brute sexuality, its cynical traffic in wardships, and its manipulation of divine ordinances to suit crass human ends—were merely the vulgar analogues of practices that had recently been condoned by the King himself. To have condemned the fair would have been to condemn his own court: "He that will correct another, must want fault in himselfe." Indeed, James, as will shortly be clear, had been a great deal more tolerant than he should have been.

◆ CHAPTER ELEVEN ◆

The Making of a Jacobean Poet

"All rising to great place," according to Bacon's famous adage, "is by a winding stair; and if there be factions, it is good to side a man's self whilst he is in the rising." Jonson's masques for the holiday seasons of 1614–15 and 1615–16 indicate that he actively sided with the Earl of Pembroke during the period when his patron finally seized the initiative at court. Prior to 1614 Pembroke did not lead a faction that was powerful enough to count for anything in the view of contemporary observers. He was "rather regarded and esteemed of King James than loved and favored," the Earl of Clarendon recalled, "attracting the support of all who were displeased and unsatisfied in the court or with the court." Jonson makes the same assessment in his epigram "To William, Earl of Pembroke." He portrays the Earl as a man whose exclusion from faction confirms his good qualities and attracts followers to his side. Unlike the time-servers who "follow vertue, for reward, to day; / To morrow vice, if shee give better pay," Pembroke is the man who "must draw more." [1] Pembroke started to "draw more" in 1614 when he and his circle vigorously began to oppose the Earl of Somerset. *The Golden Age Restored,* Jonson's Twelfth Night masque for 1614–15, was tailor-made for their purposes.

Earlier that year Pembroke is said to have convened a meeting at Baynard's Castle, the Herberts' London residence. The participants included Archbishop Abbot, various legatees of the old Essex faction, and other persons opposed to Somerset, and to the Howards and their pro-Spanish policies. Their objective was to break Somerset's hold on the King, and they decided to accomplish this end by furnishing James with a young man capable of dislodging Somerset from his affections. The strategy had been used before. Somerset's original backer, Lord Hay, had promoted him in the hope that he would weaken the Howard influence. Pembroke's faction chose George Villiers, the personable son of an obscure Leicestershire squire, and they promptly got down to work. After Pembroke and his ally Sir Thomas Lake presented Villiers to the King at Apthorp, Lady Bedford ushered him into the Presence Chamber; later in 1614 Pembroke got him the office of Cupbearer, his first regular post in the royal household. In the meantime Queen Anne pressed James to make Villiers a Gentleman of the Bedchamber; since only one Englishman (Pembroke's brother Montgomery) belonged to the elite group that attended James in his private apartments, Villiers was now on the verge of becoming a significant factor in the balance of power at court.[2]

In the winter of 1614–15 he was a man on the way up, though it was still unclear how far he would go. On December 1 Chamberlain wrote to Carleton that "for al this penurious world we speak of a maske this christmas towards which the K. geves 1500 pounds, the principall motive wherof is thought to be the gracing of younge villers and to bring him on the stage" (HS, X, 553). The incumbent favorite did what he could to mar the occasion. Sir John Finnett, the Master of Ceremonies, wrote a long account of the diplomatic wrangling that preceded *The Golden Age Restored* and put the blame on "the Earl of Sommerset (then Lord *Chamberlain*)," who "gave me directions to invite the Spanish and the Venetian [ambassadors] (not usually coupled . . .)" (HS, X, 554). Somerset's deliberate affront to the ambassadors almost caused the masque to be postponed, but a compromise over seating arrangements was eventually worked out, and Villiers got his chance to perform.

The script that Jonson wrote for Villiers's debut cast him as the harbinger of a new era. At the outset of the performance Pallas, goddess of Athens and of Wisdom, announces that Jove (King James)

> meanes to settle
> ASTRAEA in her seat againe;
> And let downe in his golden chaine
> The age of better mettle.

Briskly dispensing with Iron Age and his cohort, Pallas summons Astrea (Justice) and Golden Age, who, after assuring themselves that they are indeed welcome, complain that they have no followers in James's court: "But how without a traine / Shall we our state sustaine?" "Leave that to JOVE," Pallas replies. Off in the distance, "set far within the shade, / And

---

Opposite: *George Villiers, Duke of Buckingham, as a Young Man*, artist unknown. Villiers displays the dancer's legs that James found so appealing.

in *Elysian* bowres," were the choice spirits "that for their living good, now semigods are made"—an apt description of what was happening to George Villiers, the most conspicuous of the masquers sitting in the Elysian bower.[3]

Where Somerset had been depicted in images of frank sexuality the year before, the emerging favorite, who was still new to this game, exuded the freshness of unfallen nature. In the incipient "age of better mettle," spiritual values (mettle) would replace the materialistic worship of gold (metal):

> Then earth unplough'd shall yeeld her crop,
> Pure honey from the oake shall drop,
>   The fountaine shall runne milke:
> The thistle shall the lilly beare,
> And every bramble roses weare,
>   And every worme make silke.

Jonson's vision of an agrarian earthly paradise associated Villiers with James's recent efforts to remake the image of his own court. On October 24, 1614, the King had issued a proclamation ordering "all Our Lieutenants and Noblemen" to "repaire unto their severall Countreys to attend their service there, and to keepe House and Hospitalitie." Ten weeks later the gentlemen dancers of *The Golden Age Restored* ushered in a new age of pastoral plenty. Jonson's fiction allowed Villiers to represent the new rural gentry that James was so avidly promoting; yet the masque also, paradoxically, helped to ensure that he would never actually have to *be* a part of the reconstructed countryside, for James's proclamation specifically exempted individuals who bore "any Office about the Person, or Court, of Our selves," and Villiers was seeking admission to that select group. *The Golden Age Restored* took him a step closer to his goal. "The only matter I can advertise since I wrote the last weeke," Chamberlain reported, "is the successe of the maske on twelfe night, which was so well liked and aplauded that the king had it represented again the sonday night after, in the very same manner."[4] The aspiring favorite attained his objective early in the following spring, when Queen Anne and Bishop Abbot finally prevailed over the frantic protests of Somerset, and Villiers was sworn into the Bedchamber and the Privy Council, with an annual pension of a thousand pounds a year.

Even so, Pembroke's faction had not yet broken Somerset's hold on the King, and they could easily have faltered at this point. But they enjoyed a remarkable stroke of luck the next autumn, when James discovered that agents of Somerset's Countess had murdered Sir Thomas Overbury while he was incarcerated in the Tower because of his opposition to the Somerset-Howard match. The crime was unconscionable. By placing Overbury in the Tower (his own prison) James had taken him under royal protection. The King had no choice but to punish the malefactors.

Lady Somerset's underlings went before the bar in October and November of 1615. These trials made public a cornucopia of sordid details, not least the exceedingly foul device that finished Overbury off, a poisoned enema. As the prosecutor, Sir Edward Coke, relentlessly hammered away at the defendants, a seamy network of pimps, apothecaries, assassins-for-hire, quack physicians, and corruptible officers gradually came to light. Back in 1610, when Lady Frances was trying to win the heart of Robert Carr, she had turned for help to Frances Turner, a dressmaker whom Inigo Jones employed to design costumes for court masques. Mrs. Turner offered a variety of services. She was a procuress; she dabbled in aphrodisiacs and cosmetics; she catered parties for Sir Thomas Monson, a Howard client who was implicated in the Overbury murder; she performed abortions. Mrs. Turner had introduced Lady Frances to "Doctor" Simon Forman, who, before his death in 1611, supplied her with sexual depressants (for Essex) and aphrodisiacs (for Carr). Forman too had many strings to his bow, combining the trades of alchemist, ladies' physician, fortuneteller, and astrologer.[5]

None of this testimony was strictly relevant to the question of what had occurred at the time of Overbury's death, but it had an electrifying effect on public opinion. James placed Somerset and Lady Frances under house arrest before the trials got underway, and shortly thereafter he forced the Earl to step down from the office of Lord Chamberlain, his most important post. Somerset would not stand trial until the following spring, but a new era was in the offing. Northampton, the political genius of the Howard family, had died in 1614. The Earl of Suffolk had become an object of suspicion on account of his daughter's scandalous behavior and would never again be as powerful as he had been. The King, a large part of his court, and the general public were appalled by the extent of the corruption that came to light in the Overbury murder trials. In December of 1615 the Lord Chamberlain's office fell to Pembroke; George Villiers, his ally in the Bedchamber, became the new royal favorite.

Mercury Vindicated from the Alchemists at Court, Jonson's Twelfth Night masque for 1615–16, celebrates this transformation of the royal household. The antimasque of "alchemists at court" mockingly alludes to the sinister, brutally manipulative experiments that had recently been conducted at, or perilously near, the court by Lady Somerset's confederates. The most sensational moment during the trials of the previous autumn had occurred when the prosecution, in the course of exhibiting various oddments from Dr. Forman's shop, produced "certain pictures of a man and woman in copulation, made in lead, as also the mould of brass, wherein they were cast." While these obscene mannequins were on display, "there was heard a crack from the scaffolds, which caused great fear, tumult and confusion among the spectators, and throughout the hall, everyone fearing hurt, as if the devil had been present, and grown angry to have his workmanship shewed." Like Dr. Forman, the "alchemists at court" who dance the first antimasque specialize in the manufacture of artificial human beings. As the antimasque reaches its climax, Mercury warns that "in yonder vessels, which you see in their laboratorie, they have inclos'd *Materials,* to produce men." These "men" subsequently appeared on the dance floor and performed a *"second* Antimasque *of imperfect creatures, with helmes of lymbecks on their heads."* [6]

The alchemists who fabricated these revolting humanoids made an apt foil to King James. He too was creating "new men," and the twelve courtiers who now came forward and danced the masque were the fruits of his handiwork. The masquers appear in the company of their mother, Nature, who symbolizes the superiority of nature to art; but her twelve sons have been "made" by James, the sovereign artist who inspires Nature herself to sing

> How yong and fresh am I to night,
> To see't kept day, by so much light,
> And twelve my sonnes stand in their Makers sight?　(202–204)

Where the alchemists had manufactured synthetic creatures without substance or form, James, the godlike giver of honors, was creating a new nobility to serve him in the years ahead.

Jonson's own prospects of entering the King's service had never been better. His patron Pembroke had become James's new Lord Chamberlain just three weeks previously; Pembroke's ally Villiers had already joined Aubigny, Jonson's other long-time patron, and Montgomery in the Bedchamber. Jonson did not merely belong to the ascendant Pembroke-Villiers faction; he had abetted and celebrated its rise, and could expect to share in the fruits of its victory. On February 6 James decided that Jonson too deserved to be rewarded and granted him a royal pension of one hundred marks (sixty-six pounds, thirteen shillings, four pence) per year, payable for life. The patent for Jonson's pension does not indicate who or what persuaded James to award it but merely mentions "divers good consideracions us att this present especially moving"; it specifies no *quid pro quo* but simply refers to the unspecified "service" that Jonson had performed in the past and would continue to perform in the future. [7]

The climactic moment of Jonson's career at court coincided with the publication of his collected *Works.* The printing of the 1616 folio apparently began late in 1615 and was completed early the following summer.[8] Both the pension and the folio were the end result of a prolonged effort on Jonson's part. The royal annuity officially reinstated him in the status that his courtier grandfather had once enjoyed; the folio *Works* transformed him into the major literary celebrity of his age. The two events were closely bound up with each other. The imminent publication of the 1616 folio helped to justify, perhaps even to motivate, James's decision to make him his unofficial poet laureate. The *Works* offered a retrospective survey of the career that had brought Jonson to this eminence. The pension, in turn, validated the pretensions of the author of the *Works*.

The precise timing of Jonson's decision to assemble and publish the 1616 folio remains unclear. The first hint that he was thinking along these lines occurs in the winter of 1609–10, when he stopped bringing out quartos of his masques. He completed *Catiline*, the last of the plays to be included in the folio, in 1611. He had decided to publish his poems by May 15, 1612, when Stepneth registered Jonson's *Epigrams* for publication; virtually none of the contemporary events referred to in the folio poems falls after 1612. He had undoubtedly committed himself to publishing his *Works* by January 20, 1615, when William Stansby, who printed the folio, took out the copyright for Jonson's unpublished masques and entertainments (HS, IX, 13). Jonson must have begun to prepare the copy for his *Works* well before then, however, for the book is over a thousand pages long, and he painstakingly revised all the plays that he included in it. Yet he was still introducing new material into the folio in the winter of 1615–16, when he gave Stansby the text of *The Golden Age Restored*.

The publication of *The Works of Benjamin Jonson* later that year was the decisive event in Jonson's lifelong struggle to establish control over his own writing. The printing press, as Elizabeth Eisenstein has shown, invested the literary enterprise with a new aura of permanence. It did away with the vagaries of gloss, commentary, and idiosyncratic scribes, all of which were hallmarks of the manuscript tradition, and made possible a standardized, uniform *book*. The discrepancy between handwritten copy and printed text was particularly telling in the case of plays, since the author's manuscript became the property of the actors, who freely altered it to suit their own preferences. By collecting and editing his work, and seeing it through the press, Jonson created an "authorized" text that could be shared again and again with an educated readership. The earliest continental editions of classical authors had long since established a widely recognized canon of ancient texts, and Jonson appropriated the format of these editions for his own *Works*. In revising his early quartos, he adopted the systems of scene division and lineation employed in the earliest editions of Plautus, Terence, and Aristophanes. Individual scenes are unnumbered; entrances and exits are unmarked; dialogue is printed in continuous pentameter lines, even when two or more characters share an

A Renaissance printing house. *Impressio Librorum,* by Jan van der Straet in *Nova Reperta,* ca. 1600. The compositor in the foreground is taking type from the composing case and putting it in his composing stick. Immediately behind him a man wearing glasses reads proof. The figure to the right is inking a set form with inking balls.

individual line of verse. Although these modifications created a text unsuitable for actors, they notified the reader that Jonson was himself a "classic" author. The motto from Horace that he inscribed immediately below the title of his *Works* conveyed the same message: "*Neque, me ut miretur turba, laboro: / Contentus paucis lectoribus*" ("I do not work so that the crowd may admire me: I am contented with a few readers").[9]

In selecting and revising the folio texts, Jonson smoothed over the ragged edges of his artistic development and created a strong, internally con-

Opposite: Title page of Jonson's *Works,* 1616. The Latin motto on the frieze above the title is from Horace's *Ars Poetica*: "Let each variety hold the place [*Locum teneant*] properly allotted to it." "Tragoedia" and "Comoedia" stand to the left and the right of the title with representatives of the lesser genres above. "Satyr" sits astride the left side of the upper arch; "Pastor," the shepherd, is on the right; and "Tragi-comoedia" stands in the topmost niche. *Plaustrum,* the wagon to the lower left, is the one that supposedly bore Thespis and the earliest Greek tragedians, while *Visorium,* the Roman auditorium on the lower right, signifies the apex of the evolutionary cycle that carried ancient drama from Greece to Rome.

sistent authorial persona. The decision to include only nine of his plays meant that the folio texts would henceforth constitute a set canon of Jonsonian drama. Since only two of the plays excluded from the folio have survived (*The Case Is Altered* and *Bartholomew Fair*), it is impossible to speak about the remainder with any assurance, but Jonson did tell Drummond "that the half of his comedies were not in Print" (*Conv*, 393), so there must have been a sizable body of plays outside the canon.

Jonson's revisions minimized the discrepancies among the canonical works and created the impression that he had foreseen the course of his career from its very outset. He transferred the locale of *Every Man in His Humour*, the first of the folio plays, from Florence to London and added a Prologue that holds the play up as an example of what "other playes should be" (14). The revised text makes it appear as though Jonson already knew in 1598 that London was to be the setting for the masterpieces he would write over a decade later. His masterly, self-assured Prologue, with its deprecating remarks about the native dramatic tradition, has led legions of critics to suppose (wrongly) that *Every Man in His Humour* was widely acclaimed at the time of its debut. In retrospect, the novice playwright who joined the Bricklayers' Guild shortly after completing *Every Man in His Humour* became the arbiter of literary fashion who took Shakespeare to task for writing plays that "fight over *Yorke*, and *Lancasters* long jarres: / And in the tiring-house bring wounds, to scarres" (11–12).

In revising *Cynthia's Revels; or, The Fountain of Self Love*, Jonson reversed the alternative titles (the court entertainment now took precedence over the satirical comedy), transliterated the hero's name from Latin into Greek, and stressed the importance of Crites's promotion to the office of masque writer. Unlike his counterpart in the quarto, Crites participates in a rudimentary antimasque that Jonson inserted in the middle of act V, immediately before the scenes in which Crites's masque is commissioned and performed. The new version of act V "is part of a larger pattern in the play, a pattern of generic rivalry between masque (*Cynthia's Revels*) and satire (*The Fountaine of Selfe-Love*)." The revised text of *Poetaster* includes a long dialogue between Horace and the lawyer Trebatius that Jonson took directly from Horace's *Satires*. This dialogue is the last and the most strident of Horace's *apologia* for the satirist's vocation. Previously he had maintained that his satires were merely quiet conversation pieces touching upon generalized social vices, and intended for a small circle of friends (*Satires*, I.iv). In the dialogue that Jonson inserted into the folio *Poetaster*, Horace, who in the meantime had secured the patronage of Maecenas, adopts the posture of a public reformer: for the first time he claims the right to attack living individuals, provided they strike the first blow.[10] Jonson had not been prepared to make this claim in 1601; but in 1607 he had published an equally self-assertive dedicatory epistle to *Volpone*, and by 1616 he too had found his Maecenas.

Jonson was not content merely to revise his early quartos: by dating the folio texts from the time of their original performances, he also fostered the illusion that he had *not* revised them. At the conclusion of the folio version of *Every Man in His Humour* he inserted this statement: "This Comoedie was first Acted, in the yeere 1598. *By the then* L. Chamberlaine *his Servants.*" Jonson's pretense of total accuracy is exceedingly disingenuous. "This" comedy had been extensively rewritten at some point between 1604 and 1612, and it is not clear when (if ever) the original acting company went to the bother of committing the new script to memory. Statements of this kind appear either on the title pages or at the end of all nine folio plays. They invariably mislead the reader, for Jonson revised all of these texts, if only to eliminate blasphemies and obscenities. He also expunged various clues about his own changing circumstances. The early spellings of his name no longer have the medial "h"; "Sall" Pavy becomes "Child" in the folio text of *Cynthia's Revels;* the dated reference to his house in the Blackfriars no longer appears at the end of the dedicatory epistle to *Volpone*. The 1616 folio, in Richard Newton's words, is "a study not of Jonson's development, but of the unfolding in time of his timeless and unchanging talent." [11]

By placing *Catiline* last in the folio ordering and keeping *Bartholomew Fair* out of print, Jonson superimposed a definitive and logical shape on his artistic development. The final transition from *The Alchemist* to *Catiline* takes him out of the native and into the classical tradition and marks his passage from the lesser genre of comedy to the greater one of tragedy; his career as a dramatic poet is now complete. But Jonson's *gradus ad Parnassam* goes awry when one takes account of his unpublished plays. Between 1610 and the middle of 1616 Jonson published *The Alchemist* and *Catiline,* but he also wrote *Bartholomew Fair,* and began *The Devil Is an Ass,* another London comedy. The best modern editor of *Every Man in His Humour* conjectures that the folio text of that play, with its English setting, was actually completed in 1612.[12] In 1616, then, Jonson was following a course diametrically opposed to the one he charts in his *Works.* His investment in comedy, and in native literary traditions, had actually increased since the completion of *Catiline* in 1611.

Jonson rewrote yet another chapter of his personal success story by printing *Mercury Vindicated* before *The Golden Age Restored,* even though, in the chronological order that obtains for the rest of the folio masques, it should have come last. The printed texts of the two works, like the quarto of *Blackness* and *Beauty,* thus reflected the overarching structural pattern of the form that Jonson had wrought over the previous twelve years. The dominant tonality of *Mercury Vindicated* is satirical and prosaic: it is essentially one long antimasque. *The Golden Age Restored* waxes lyrical from the outset: it is almost all masque. On the political level the transformation of disorder into order that occurs between the two works corresponds to the fall of Somerset and the rise of Pembroke, the new Lord Chamberlain, and of Villiers, who had danced in *The Golden Age Restored* and probably in *Mercury Vindicated* as well.

The ascendancy of Pembroke and his circle is an important motif in the folio as a whole. Jonson carefully expunged all of the pro-Howard material in the 1606 quarto of *Hymenaei* and the *Barriers* from the folio text. The followers of Truth and Opinion are no longer identified by name. Pembroke, however, is the only person to have two works in the folio dedicated to him, and he also garners the last two dedications. In 1611 *Catiline* had been "the first (of this race) that ever I dedicated to any person"; in 1616 the dedication to *Epigrams* accords Jonson's patron "the honor of leading forth so many good, and great names (as my verses mention on the better part) to their remembrance with posteritie." Both dedications refer to the Earl as "Lord Chamberlain," an office that he did not attain until December 1615, after James had finally discharged Somerset from that post.[13] Jonson was tinkering with the folio text until the very last minute.

After finishing *Catiline,* the last of the author's published plays, the reader of the folio proceeded to two collections of unpublished verse, *Epigrams* and *The Forest.* The simultaneous publication of these volumes significantly altered Jonson's public image. Apart from the *Panegyre* of 1604 and a scattered assortment of anthology pieces and poems praising books by his friends, he had published no verse to speak of prior to 1616. Now he proclaimed that the culminating achievement of his literary career lay neither in his plays nor in his masques but in his poetry. In dedicating *Epigrams* to Pembroke, Jonson describes it as "the ripest of my studies," the mature fruit of a long and patient endeavor (HS, VIII, 25). Within the pages of Jonson's *Works* the journey to Parnassus leads him away from the stage and into the study.

He must have recognized that these volumes would greatly enhance the attractions of his *Works* and may have withheld them from publication in 1612 for that reason. Jonson was the first English dramatist to publish his plays in folio, and many contemporaries doubtless agreed with the wag who asked *"the reason why he call'd his playes works"*:

William, Third Earl of Pembroke, by Abraham van Blyenberch, ca. 1618. The white staff of office indicates that Jonson's patron was now Lord Chamberlain of the King's household.

Pray tell me *Ben,* where doth the mystery lurke,
What others call a play you call a worke.   (HS, IX, 13)

The publication of *Epigrams* and *The Forest* deflected such criticisms by establishing Jonson's credentials as a lyric poet.

At the same time, and perhaps with some reluctance, Jonson thereby forfeited his status as an amateur poet. His favorite genres—epigram, epistle, and song—were forms of occasional verse. Anyone who thought of himself as a poet knew how to ridicule an enemy, praise a great man, counsel a friend, or court a mistress, in verse. Jonson had risen to such occasions many times, but we cannot assume that he did so with publication in mind. Gentlemen still regarded poetry as a form of elegant recreation. They wrote for themselves, or circulated their poems in manuscript among their friends, but shunned the medium of print. Almost all the verse of Wyatt, Surrey, Sidney, Raleigh, Greville, and Donne, for example, was published posthumously. Until the appearance of the folio virtually all of Jonson's poetry remained within the tradition of the gentlemanly amateur. Upon the publication of *Epigrams* and *The Forest* he joined ranks with Spenser, Chapman, Daniel, and Drayton, the leading professional poets of his era. In the course of collecting and arranging his poetry Jonson successfully bridged the gap that separated the amateur from the professional. *Epigrams* preserves the spontaneity of the occasional poem, yet it is also a finished book that surveys the career of a Jacobean poet. *The Forest* retains the loose, unplanned format of a poetical miscellany, yet it also depicts Jonson's ongoing search for his "owne true fire." [14]

The one hundred and thirty-three poems included in *Epigrams* fall, for the most part, into two categories. Fifty-six of them are addressed to contemporary men, women, and children—Jonson mentions some forty-one persons by name; most of the remainder are short, pointed satires (like "Spies" or "Playwright") excoriating generalized types. Jonson himself assumes the role of a man situated midway between a sinister underclass of cheats and posers and a resplendent aristocracy of birth and accomplishment. He serves the commonwealth by castigating the former and praising the latter. His motives are broadly political. The poet's task, as Jonson describes it in his *Discoveries,* is to "faine a *Commonwealth,*" a project that requires "the exact knowledge of all vertues, and their Contraries, with the ability to render the one lov'd, the other hated, by his proper embattaling them" (*Disc,* 1035, 1039–41). In his epistle to Lady D'Aubigny, written in the year that his *Epigrams* were registered for publication, Jonson uses the same imagery to describe himself:

I, therefore, who professe myselfe in love
   With every vertue, wheresoere it move,

And howsoever; as I am at fewd
  With sinne and vice, though with a throne endew'd.   (*For,* 13.7–10)

In the course of conducting his feud with vice and his love affair with virtue, Jonson retells the story of his own career.

By putting the epigrams to Camden and to Mary Jonson, the daughter of his "youth," near the beginning of the collection, Jonson intimates that the numbered sequence of poems addressed to specific men and women will form a biographical narrative. The first half of this sequence offers a portrait of the artist as a young man. The nameless greatly outnumber the named in this part of Jonson's book, and many of the latter (Mary and Ben Jonson, Margaret Radcliffe, Sir John Roe) die at an early age. Apart from James, Jonson mentions only four living contemporaries (Camden, Donne, Beaumont, and Salisbury) prior to Epigram 60, and only one of these (Salisbury) was a potential patron. The tone of his early poems of praise is studiously diffident. Jonson portrays himself as a youthful apprentice who still has a great deal to learn about his craft. He salutes Camden as the "reverend head" to whom he owes "all that I am in arts, all that I know, / (How nothing's that?)," and concludes by apologizing for his own poem: "Many of thine this better could, then I, / But for their powers, accept my pietie." He is equally abashed by Donne, whom "I meant to praise, and, yet, I would; / But leave, because I cannot as I should." He informs Salisbury that he has no hope "of adding to thy fame; thine may to me." Even Francis Beaumont, a man who (Jonson subsequently remarked) "loved too much himself and his own verses," puts this neophyte on the defensive: "How I doe fear my selfe, that am not worth / The least indulgent thought thy pen drops forth!" [15]

Jonson begins to take the initiative in "To William, Lord Mounteagle," the first poem in which he claims the vatic power of conferring fame:

Loe, what my countrey should have done (have rais'd
  An obeliske, or columne to thy name,
Or, if shee would but modestly have prais'd
  Thy fact, in brasse or marble writ the same)
I, that am glad of thy great chance, here doo!   (*Ep,* 60.1–5)

Jonson's epigram on the hero of the Gunpowder Plot marks a turning point both in the sequence as a whole and in the Jonsonian career pattern. Until now he has found much to blame and little to commend; from this point onward the proportions are reversed: forty-two of the final seventy-three epigrams, and thirty-one of the last forty, are poems of praise. The addressees of these poems include a Secretary of State, two Lord Treasurers, a Lord Chamberlain, a Lord Chancellor, a Provost of Eton College, a

Lord Lieutenant of Cornwall, and a Gentleman of the Royal Bedchamber. There are three earls and two barons. The families named in these epigrams include many of the most important houses in early modern England: Cecil, Howard, Russell, Manners, Vere, Herbert, Sidney, Neville, and Stuart. Anyone perusing the 1616 folio would have immediately registered the aura of power and prestige that surrounded these names and would have sensed that the poet's fortunes were on the rise.

The first identifiable group of noble addressees consists of five individuals who came to the fore during the first few years of James's reign: Mounteagle (60), Salisbury (63–64), Sir Henry Cary (66), Suffolk (67), and Egerton (74). Most, perhaps all, of these poems refer to events that occurred between 1603 and 1607. They correspond to the period of Jonson's life when he made his first approaches to James's ministers of government, sought the good offices of Suffolk and Salisbury after being imprisoned for his share of *Eastward Ho,* and received his first commissions from the royal household.

The epigrams to Lucy, Countess of Bedford (76), and Elizabeth, Countess of Rutland (79), mark Jonson's entry into a new and more closely knit patronage network. Apart from Sir John and William Roe, none of the living contemporaries mentioned prior to Epigram 76 are related by ties of blood or marriage, or by the analogous bond of client and patron. Beginning with the first epigram to Lady Bedford (76), the poet makes his way into an extended circle of blood relations and family retainers that revolves around the Herberts and the Sidneys. The central figure in this network is Pembroke (102). His brother Montgomery was married to Susan Vere (104), a cousin of Sir Horace Vere (91); his uncle Lord Lisle was the father of Elizabeth, Countess of Rutland (79), Mary, Lady Wroth (103 and 105), and Mistress Philip Sidney (118); and his cousin Sir Edward Herbert (106) was a friend of Jonson's and Donne's (94, 96). Donne's patroness Lady Bedford (76, 84, and 94) was the granddaughter of her namesake Lucy Sidney, and hence related, more distantly, to the Sidney-Herbert clan.

"Inviting a Friend to Supper" (101) offers a tentative assessment of Jonson's improved, yet still precarious, position in society. The speaker in this poem is a man of independent albeit modest means who entreats a "grave sir" to visit his "poore house" for supper. If the invitation refers to a specific supper party, Jonson probably issued it between 1605 and 1612 while living at his house in St. Anne's, Blackfriars. Although he portrays himself as a dispenser, rather than a recipient, of bounty, he is still dependent on the favor of the grave sir, "whose grace may make that seeme / Something, which else, could hope for no esteeme." His bill of fare, as Loewenstein observes, is tantalizingly equivocal:

> a coney
> Is not to be despair'd of, for our money;
> And, though fowle, now, be scarce, yet there are clarkes,
> The skie not falling, thinke we may have larkes.
> Ile tell you of more, and lie, so you will come:
> Of partrich, pheasant, wood-cock, of which some
> May yet be there; and godwit, if we can:
> Knat, raile, and ruffe too.

Does Jonson describe a meal that he intends to serve or one that he wishes he could afford to serve? Although he assures the grave sir that "wee'll speake our minds," the "libertie" of the feast is contingent on Jonson's promise that no informers will be present ("we will have no *Pooly'* or *Parrot* by") and his pledge that the revelers will drink "but moderately." Robert Poley and Henry Parrot were professional spies and quite possibly the "two damn'd villains" who tried to entrap Jonson during his imprisonment over *The Isle of Dogs*. Even though they are excluded from the feast, the very mention of their names reminds the reader that Jonson's "libertie" is imperiled by state-supported surveillance and repression. The possibility that he was—even here—indemnifying himself against a charge of libel by alluding to spies whose names could also refer to animals (poll, parrot) only heightens the feeling of insecurity.[16]

A younger Jonson had suffered repeatedly at the hands of spies and informers; had been accused of libel over *The Isle of Dogs, Poetaster, Sejanus,* and *Eastward Ho;* had attended one of Robert Catesby's supper parties; and had himself offered to furnish Salisbury with information about the recusant community in 1605. A decade later Jonson's own faction was in the ascendant, and he was in a position to voice his views more openly than at any period in his life. Within the pages of his *Epigrams* the private and guarded milieu of "Inviting a Friend to Supper" (101) sets the stage for "To William, Earl of Pembroke" (102), a public expression of support for the leading figure in the emergent regime.

"I doe but name thee PEMBROKE, and I find, / It is an *Epigramme,* on all man-kind." Names, as Harris Friedberg has suggested, "provide the poet with a paradigm of unambiguous reference, a model of contact with the world outside the poems." In contrast to the Sir Politic Would-be's who "talke reserv'd, lock'd up, and full of feare, / Nay, aske you, how the day goes, in your eare," or the great peers, scarcely one of whom "knowes, / To which, yet, of the sides himselfe he owes," Jonson makes an open, unequivocal choice—and chooses wisely. Epigrams 102 through 106 reiterate that choice by praising four members of the Sidney and Herbert families. All five of these poems work variations on the theme of "what's in a name?" Like the Elizabethan "miniature," or the modern campaign button, they reinforce assumptions that do not need to be justified or explained. Jonson and his addressees belong to a political world that still adheres to the ethic of the feudal contract. Pembroke's faction does not subscribe to any common ideology or creed; it is united by the personal ties that bind the Earl to his followers. Instead of telling his readers what to think, Jonson instructs them to follow Pembroke, for "they, that hope to see / The common-wealth still safe, must studie thee."[17]

Many of the "good, and great names" that Pembroke leads forth to their remembrance with posterity had already heeded this advice and were looking to the Earl for leadership at the time that *Epigrams* went to press. Egerton (74), Lady Bedford (76, 84, 94), and Pembroke had been working together against the pro-Spanish Somerset-Howard faction since 1614. Sir Horace Vere (91), commander of the English army in the Netherlands and a firm supporter of the Protestant cause, lined up on Pembroke's side, as did the parliamentarian Sir Henry Neville (109), who in 1613 got the Earl's support in his bid to succeed Salisbury as James's Secretary of State. Benjamin Rudyerd (121–123) had a long-standing bond to Pembroke that went back to their student days at Oxford. Joshua Sylvester (132), the last person to be praised in the *Epigrams,* had joined Pembroke's circle by 1614.[18] And finally, Sir Thomas Overbury (113) was the man who, more than anyone else, symbolized the widespread antagonism toward Somerset that erupted near the end of 1614. By the close of the sequence, then, Jonson has firmly ensconced himself in a patronage network of rising power.

By this time he has exchanged the suspect role of the biting satirist for the happier office of a genial commenter on human follies. Many of the satirical epigrams that appear in the latter part of the collection—"The New Cry" (92), "On the New Motion" (97), "To Captain Hungry" (107), "To a Weak Gamester in Poetry" (112), "On the Town's Honest Man" (115), and "To Mime" (129)—are longer and more leisurely than their counterparts in the earlier half of the book. The speaker in these poems has the assurance of a clubman; he sounds like the intimate of Selden, and of the Sireniacal gentlemen who congregated at the Mermaid. He is now less inclined to straitjacket his victims in a single, reiterated motif ("*Item* ... *Item* ...") and more likely to appeal to a community of educated readers who share his views and endorse his judgments.

The placement of "The Famous Voyage" at the conclusion of *Epigrams* calls into question the upward trajectory of the sequence as a whole. The Oxford editors call it a "bad joke"; Wilson regards it as a symptom of Jonson's anal-erotic compulsions.[19] Since the famous voyagers are themselves an example of failed transcendence—a final, hallucinatory image of two gallants who remain mired in the London underworld—the poem raises the issue of Jonson's ability to complete his personal odyssey.

In his parting tribute to William Roe, the last of his heroic exemplars, Jonson invokes the classic example of a successful descent-and-return:

> This is that good AENEAS, past through fire,
> Through seas, stormes, tempests: and imbarqu'd for hell,
> Came back untouch'd. This man hath travail'd well.

Aeneas's safe passage through the underworld was a familiar image of the good man's ability to glean something of value from the basest regions of experience while keeping his virtue intact. Where Roe possesses this capacity to travel (or "travail") well, the protagonists of "The Famous Voyage" perform a burlesque of the Virgilian ideal as

> they unfrighted passe, though many a privie
> Spake to 'hem louder, then the oxe in LIVIE;
> And many a sinke pour'd out her rage anenst 'hem;
> But still their valour, and their vertue fenc't 'hem.

Jonson's personal enactment of the journey into the depths hovers somewhere between the mythic ideal and its scurrilous antitype. His conviction that comedy and satire should encompass the grossest aspects of everyday life led him into the nether regions of the city streets and the human anatomy. The record of his drinking bouts, his wenching, his quarrels, and his "cross business" in Paris, indicates that he did not always maintain the posture of the detached observer during his own excursions into the underworld. Yet Jonson believed (or wanted to believe) that he came back unscathed and transformed his vagrant moments into art; that he, like Roe, had the requisite inner stability "to know vice well, / And her blacke spight expell." In the words of the passage in Seneca from which he took his motto ("*tanquam explorator*"), Jonson "was wont to cross over even into the enemy's camp—not as a deserter, but as a scout."[20] Whereas the protagonists of "The Famous Voyage" merely commute between the tavern and the brothel, the poet-narrator of *Epigrams* has gradually disengaged himself from this milieu.

In the last line of "The Famous Voyage" Jonson wishes that "my *Muse* had plough'd with his, that sung A-JAX." Readers with long memories might have recalled that his muse *had* ploughed with his that sang a jakes. Just a year after Harington's *Metamorphosis of Ajax* (a jakes) appeared in 1596, the coprophiliac Jaques de Prie had launched Jonson's career as a comic playwright. The allusion also conjures up associations with the sewage ditch that ran down Hartshorn Lane and with the bricklayer stepfather who had (figuratively if not literally) ploughed it during Jonson's childhood. The jakes is a last vestige of the life that he was putting behind him in 1616. Jaques does not appear in the pages of his folio, and he himself now moved inexorably away from the world of his childhood.

Although Jonson aptly characterized *Epigrams* as "the ripest of my studies," he had also written a number of epistles, odes, and songs prior to 1616. Any or all of these could easily have found their way into his *Works*, but he availed himself of yet another opportunity to mold his public self-image and only included a quarter of them in *The Forest*.

He discarded the commendatory epigrams and epistles he had written for Thomas Palmer, Nicholas Breton, Thomas Wright, Christopher Brooke, Thomas Farnaby, John Selden, and Sir Walter Raleigh, but published his verse letters to the Countesses of Rutland and Aubigny, Sir Robert Wroth, and Penshurst, and his epistolary "Ode: To Sir William Sidney on His Birthday," none of which had previously appeared in print. He also included the "Epode" that he had written for Sir John Salusbury in 1601, together with "And Must I Sing," a new version of the "Proludium" that had originally preceded the "Epode" in *The Passionate Pilgrim*. Of the eighteen songs in his plays and masques Jonson chose only two: "Come My Celia" from *Volpone* and its fragmentary sequel "That the Curious May Not Know."

In winnowing out this group of poems Jonson suppressed any hint that he had ever written for a living or had friends who toiled in the professions. As a result, the transition from *Epigrams* to *The Forest* reinforces the motif of social advancement that pervades the folio as a whole. Many of Jonson's *Epigrams* and the vast majority of the poems that he discarded in 1616 are addressed to men employed in the law, the army, the civil service, the theater, the schools and universities, and the arts. The author of *The Forest*, by contrast, writes for an audience of aristocrats and landowners, and adopts the stance of an amateur poet attached to a noble household. The speaker in the odes and epistles is a philosopher-poet and transmitter of ancestral values who has forged intimate ties with the Sidney family; the singer of the songs is an idle libertine who lives for the "stolne delights" of his love affairs.

The Forest, quietly but insistently, addresses tensions and ambiguities in Jonson's self-conception as a courtly amateur. The most glaring disjunction in *The Forest* is that between the praiser of virtue and the cynical amorist. When he rounded out the collection, either with new work or with poems that he had at hand when he prepared the folio for publica-

tion, Jonson reinforced this dichotomy by adding four more love songs to
the two he had borrowed from *Volpone*. The crassest of these poems was
written at the express request of a patroness. Jonson told Drummond that
when Pembroke and his Lady were "discoursing the Earl said the Woemen
were mens shadowes, and she maintained them, both appealing to Johnson, he affirmed it true, for which my Lady gave a pennance to prove it in
Verse." Jonson's penance, "That Women Are But Men's Shadows," offers
a fleeting glimpse into the idle hours of a courtier poet. Its frank acceptance of sexual gamesmanship and its crudely misogynistic premises ("So
men at weakest, they are strongest, / But grant us perfect, they're not
knowne") doubtless appealed to Jonson's womanizing patron.[21] But the
singer in *The Forest* refuses to be defined by the Earl's code of values. In
the last of his love lyrics, the third "Song: To Celia," he renounces the need
to dominate and possess the object of his desire.

The first two songs to Celia (as anyone who had read or seen *Volpone*
would recall) express the singer's lust for another man's wife; but the last
of the lyrics addressed to the poet's mistress sings of a desire that is de-
ferred and Platonized:

Drinke to me, onely, with thine eyes,
    And I will pledge with mine;
Or leave a kisse but in the cup,
    And Ile not looke for wine.
The thirst, that from the soule doth rise,
    Doth aske a drinke divine:
But might I of JOVE's *Nectar* sup,
    I would not change for thine.

The opening line of this famous song is an exemplary display of sublimated desire. One immediately hears the voice of the idealist who places
Celia beyond the reach of carnal desire ("I do not ask for your body, your
gaze is enough"). But the voice of the sensualist who says, "Drink to *me
only* with thine eyes, and not to anyone else," is audible here as well. He
wants her to have eyes only for him and knows that she may betray him
for another. In choosing the idealized image of Celia, the hearer discards
the sensualist's view of her and thereby completes the work of sublimation. William Empson long ago called attention to a similar ambiguity in
the last two lines. By rights, the poet should be saying, "but even if I could
sup Jove's nectar, I would not exchange thine for it." Yet the literal sense
of the passage goes in the opposite direction: "but if I *could* sup Jove's
nectar, I would not exchange it for thine." Alternatively, there is the gloss
proposed by Yvor Winters: "Apart from this one exception, I would not

exchange it for thine." Whatever the "correct" choice may be—Jove's nectar or Celia's—readers who work their way through these various possibilities will make that decision in a spirit of rational self-awareness. "In reading to reject unacceptable meanings," Newton concludes, "we experience a certainty of definition beyond the realm of most lyrics"; Jonson "teaches us to say 'no' so that what we affirm can be clear and perspicacious."[22]

The discrepancy between Jonson's role as a eulogist of aristocratic families and his corrosive pessimism about the human condition is yet another source of tension in *The Forest*. He hints at his skepticism about the Sidney mystique in his deliberately understated "Ode: To Sir William Sidney on His Birthday." In the midst of the feast Jonson stands apart from the "noise / Of these forc'd joyes" and warns Sir William that "they that swell / With dust of ancestors, in graves but dwell." Jonson inscribed a more vivid sign of his disillusionment with the aristocracy at the conclusion of his verse letter to Sir William's cousin Elizabeth, Countess of Rutland. The manuscript version of *The Forest*, 12, concludes with an affectionate vignette of the absent Rutland, "wheresoere he be, on what dear coast, / Now thincking on you, though to England lost," and expresses the poet's hope that before the year's "swift and circled race be run, / My best of wishes, may you beare a sonne." But Rutland turned out to be impotent and came to resent his wife's friendship with Jonson, who, in turn, altered the ending of his epistle. The final lines of the folio version read as follows:

> And your brave friend, and mine so well did love.
> Who wheresoere he be. . . . . . .
> *The rest is lost.*

The "hopefulness of the poem is maimed by its deliberate incompleteness," notes Jonathan Kamholtz: "Jonson has chosen to let the scar show."[23] The same impulse to undercut or qualify his praise is also evident in the organization of the sequence as a whole. Jonson inserted a virtuous young gentlewoman's farewell "To the World" after his first two eulogies; his final four poems of praise are followed by "To Heaven," an expression of Jonson's own scorn for the world.

The persistence of Jonson's scorn, both in *The Forest* and in the poems and plays that precede it, might suggest that Jonson is himself a chronic malcontent. Does he reject the world because he despairs of ever feeling at home in it? Or does he yearn for something better?

Jonson confronts these questions in "To Heaven." The crux of the matter, as he presents it in the opening lines, lies in the distinction between melancholy and piety:

Good, and great GOD, can I not thinke of thee,
  But it must, straight, my melancholy bee?
Is it interpreted in me disease,
  That, laden with my sinnes, I seeke for ease?

The confusion about Jonson's motives arises because in his case the "disease" of melancholy (turning away from the world) has become indistinguishable from the "ease" of piety (turning toward God). Only God could make this distinction, and in this, the last poem in the folio, Jonson lays his case before Him:

I know my state, both full of shame, and scorne,
  Conceiv'd in sinne, and unto labour borne,
Standing with feare, and must with horror fall,
  And destin'd unto judgement, after all.
I feele my griefes too, and there scarce is ground,
  Upon my flesh t'inflict another wound.

Jonson's state bristles with contradictions, with both "shame, and scorne," humility and anger. He does not merely confess that he harbors feelings of resentment; he also expresses those feelings. Why should he be "destin'd unto judgement, after all" that he has been through? Or continue to "feele my griefes *too*" when there "scarce is ground" (in both a legal and a spatial sense) to inflict another wound?[24]

The gravest of Jonson's wounds was the loss of his four children. In 1603, around the time of his first daughter's death, Manningham had characterized Jonson as a man who "scornes the world." The death of his first son, Ben, later that year took him to the vanishing point where pious self-abnegation blends into suicidal despair: "For why / Will man lament the state he should envie?" The same question arises, albeit less obtrusively, in the seven other epitaphs for dead children that Jonson published in *Epigrams,* and it resurfaces in the closing lines of "To Heaven." Although he feels the attractiveness of death,

Yet dare I not complaine, or wish for death
  With holy PAUL, lest it be thought the breath
Of discontent; or that these prayers bee
  For wearinesse of life, not love of thee.

Unlike holy Paul, who wanted to die so that he could be united with Christ, Jonson can never be certain that God will acknowledge the sanctity of his death wish. To hint, as Jonson does, that God might actually misconstrue his motives can only remind the reader that those motives indeed are suspect. Even when disavowing the breath of discontent, Jonson is unable to silence it. What are the final words of this poem: "not love of thee" or "love of thee"?[25]

In his description of the ideal poet Jonson dwells upon the importance of "Study": "Indeed, things, wrote with labour, deserve to be so read, and will last their Age." His *Works* give every appearance of having been written with labor, and the literati of his own age, reading them in that spirit, admired his exacting craftsmanship. The wag who asked why Ben called his plays "works" was *thus answer'd by a friend in Mr. Johnson's defence*:

> The authors friend thus for the author sayes,
> *Bens* plays are works, when others works are plaies.

Posterity has not been so generous. The potential hazards of Jonson's self-consciously classical persona are already apparent in Dryden's well-known comparison of Jonson and Shakespeare: "If I would compare him with *Shakespeare*, I must acknowledge him the more correct Poet, but *Shakespeare* the greater wit. *Shakespeare* was the *Homer*, or Father of our Dramatick Poets; *Johnson* was the *Virgil*, the pattern of elaborate writing; I admire him, but I love *Shakespeare*."[26] Dryden contrives to seem even-handed in his assessment of the two, but no one can miss his preference. Who would not rather be loved than admired?

The worst was yet to come. Samuel Taylor Coleridge, writing in the early nineteenth century, patronized the neoclassical Jonson in grand style. For Coleridge, Jonson is "like the mammoth and megatherion, fitted and destined to live only during a given period, and then to exist a skeleton, hard, dry, uncouth perhaps, yet massive and not to be contemplated without mixture of wonder and admiration." The opening words of T. S. Eliot's 1922 essay "Ben Jonson" summed up the damage that the poet had sustained during a century and a half dominated by romantic ideas of poetic excellence: "The reputation of Jonson has been of the most deadly kind that can be compelled upon the memory of a great poet. To be universally accepted; to be damned by the praise that quenches all desire to read the book; to be afflicted by the imputation of the virtues which excite the least pleasure; and to be read only by historians and antiquaries—this is the most perfect conspiracy of approval."

Now that the romantic prejudice against the classical genres has ceased to carry any real conviction, perhaps the boldness and originality of Jonson's achievement may again reflect to his credit. Jonson freely acknowledged that the first requisite of a poet is "goodnes of naturall wit," and Shakespeare's preeminence in that regard is hardly open to question. Jonson probably recognized as much by the time he wrote the fine verse tribute "To the Memory of My Beloved, the AUTHOR Mr. William Shakespeare, and What He Hath Left Us" that he contributed to the Shakespeare first folio.[27] It was Jonson, however, who set the example of professional artistry that paved the way for that great book.

• CHAPTER TWELVE •

"Our Wel Beloved Servant"

By the summer of 1616, around the time when his *Works* appeared on Stansby's bookstall, Jonson had begun work on a new comedy called *The Devil Is an Ass*. The play was finished by mid-autumn, when the King's Men performed it at the Blackfriars Theater.

At first glance, his decision to write this play is perplexing. The author of the folio is moving away from the stage and into the study, the manor house, and the court; the author of *The Devil Is an Ass* remains preoccupied with the genre of stage comedy. He is keenly, almost obsessively aware of his own contributions to that genre. As critics have pointed out, an "extraordinary amount of *The Devil Is an Ass* is familiar from Jonson's earlier plays." [1] Although he prided himself on his originality and derided his rivals for recycling old material, on this occasion Jonson self-consciously recapitulated plot formulas that he had already used in *Volpone, Epicoene, The Alchemist,* and *Bartholomew Fair.*

In trying to unravel this puzzle, one should first of all bear in mind that the authorial persona immured between the covers of Jonson's *Works* is an artifact rather than an actual human being. When the folio went to press, the man who fashioned it had spent much of the previous two or three years poring over his earlier comedies. In the spring of 1616 his mind was filled with echoes of the plays he had recently been revising, editing, and proofreading. And these supplied the nucleus for *The Devil Is an Ass.* Moreover, Jonson takes a highly innovative approach to the material that he borrows from his own work. Indeed, the whole question of what it

means for a playwright like Jonson to repeat himself is sufficiently complicated to warrant our attention for a moment.

Any critic of Jonson knows that between 1598 and 1614 he relies upon
a limited repertory of character types and structural devices. The two gallants, the confidence man, the shaming of the cuckold, and the quarrel
that escalates out of control recur again and again in the folio comedies
and *Bartholomew Fair*. In this sense a good deal of any canonical Jonsonian comedy is familiar from his earlier work. When Jonson revised his
plays for the folio, he made a thorough survey of his own oeuvre; for
perhaps the first time he was in a position to appreciate both its novelty
and its repetitiveness. The results of this prolonged self-scrutiny are everywhere apparent in *The Devil Is an Ass*. Although Jonson borrows extensively from his own plays, he also alters his artistic practice in two crucial
respects. In the first place, the reminiscences of his earlier comedies that
crop up in *The Devil Is an Ass* recall specific moments in individual plays
rather than a generalized nexus of stock characters and plot formulas.
Instead of unconsciously repeating the mechanics of Jonsonian comedy, he
self-consciously cites particular comedies by Ben Jonson. To a reader familiar with his work, the overall effect is very close to self-parody. As
Barton comments, this play could have been subtitled "The Further Adventures of Face and Subtle."[2]

In the second place, Jonson inscribes his borrowings within a historical
framework that reveals both the novelty and the limitations of the comic
form he had devised. The initial term in Jonson's evolutionary scheme is
the Tudor morality play—the principal dramatic form of the previous ep-
och. *The Devil Is an Ass* begins in Hell with a dialogue between two super-
annuated representatives of that genre. When Pug, the asinine fiend who
gives the play its name, asks for permission to spend a day in Jacobean
London, Satan advises him that old-fashioned evil has gone out of style:
"They have their *Vices,* there, most like to *Vertues,*" he explains, "You
cannot know 'hem, apart, by any difference" (I.i.121–122). Satan does not
simply allude to modern London; he also refers to the comedy of its truest
interpreter, Ben Jonson, for the great achievement of Jonson's mature comedies had been to create an urban environment where vice is indistinguishable from virtue. As Satan foresees, Pug cannot possibly hope to compete
with the sharp operators whom he will encounter there. From the fiend's
point of view, *The Devil Is an Ass* is a parable about the obsolescence of
evil in the world of Jonsonian comedy.

When Pug meets Frances Fitzdotterel, his earthly master's wife, he immediately decides that his first act "shall be, to make this Master of mine
cuckold: / The primitive worke of darknesse, I will practise!" But Pug's

motives are too transparent ("I'll ha' my share. Most delicate damn'd flesh!") and his entreaties are too crude—"Deare delicate Mistresse, I am your slave, Your little *worme,* that loves you: your fine *Monkey;* Your *Dogge,* your *Jacke,* your *Pug . . ."*—for him to have any hope of success. He is roundly beaten for his pains. Afterward, he is understandably bewildered by the unfairness of it all: "*Hell!* why is shee so brave?"[3] The answer to Pug's question takes us into the familiar terrain of Jonsonian comedy. Frances looks so brave because she is in the midst of arranging an assignation with another would-be paramour, the gallant Wittipol. The ensuing encounter between Wittipol, Frances, and her suspicious lout of a husband is a paradigmatic moment from Jonson's earlier comedy. Five of the seven folio comedies and *Bartholomew Fair* depict triangular love affairs involving a maladroit husband, a cynical gallant, and an unattached wife. With the exception of *Epicoene* all of these plays include an interrupted seduction scene in which the aggrieved spouse apprehends his wife and her gallant in compromising circumstances.

Recall also that Jonson had a personal stake in this plot formula. His own adulterous liaisons reportedly occurred during his "youth," but two of the occasions on which he had himself been taken *in flagrante delicto* by an aggrieved husband were still a vivid memory when he visited Drummond two years after completing *The Devil Is an Ass.* In 1616 Jonson was separated from his wife and living with Aubigny. Once again, his only alternatives were celibacy and adultery. Moreover, at some point in his mid- to late forties Jonson specifically identified his own case with that of Wittipol. *A Celebration of Charis in Ten Lyric Pieces* (1623), his late sequence of love poems, recounts a love affair between Charis and a middle-aged poet named "Ben." In the course of this liaison Ben reappropriates the love song that Wittipol addresses to Frances and sings it to his own mistress.[4]

Wittipol represents the most advanced species of adulterer that can be imagined within a society that still honors the ideal of wedded love. Whereas Pug has a direct and uncomplicated relationship to his lust, Wittipol uses altruism (he wants to rescue his mistress from the clutches of her clownish husband) and sublimation (he celebrates her beauty in lyric stanzas) to legitimate his desire. He is a far more appealing and benevolent figure than his predecessors in Jonson's earlier works, a man who resembles the author himself. Like all the protagonists of Jonson's middle comedies, Wittipol entwines vice and virtue so deftly that "you cannot know 'hem, apart, by any difference." Given the buffoonery of her spouse and the impossibility of obtaining a divorce, Frances might have been well advised to take him for her lover.

Nevertheless, Wittipol, like his primitive forerunner Pug, still itches to perform the primitive act of darkness. Shortly before he asks, "*Have you seene but a bright Lilly grow, / Before rude hands have touch'd it*" (IV.vi.104–105), a marginal stage direction states that "*he playes with her paps, kisseth her hands, etc.*" On an allegorical level, this residue of unsublimated libido takes the form of Pug. Wittipol's demonic alter ego appears onstage behind Frances at the outset of this scene, fetches her husband while Wittipol is fondling her breasts, and brings the wooing to a halt just when the gallant is at the height of his passion. Although Wittipol succeeds in blurring the distinction between vice and virtue, he cannot transcend it. So long as he lusts after Frances's body, his finely sublimated passion will be betrayed by its origins.

Jonson resolves this dilemma during Wittipol's last rendezvous with Frances. In this final seduction scene the skein of resemblances between Wittipol and the protagonists of Jonson's middle comedies becomes remarkably dense and vivid. Like the boy actor who plays the part of Epicoene, Wittipol disguises himself as a woman and infiltrates an assembly of bluestockings; like Surly and Lovewit, he wears a Spanish cloak as he spirits his mistress off to the bedchamber; like Quarlous, he obtains a "deed of *Feoffment*" that gives him control over the lady's estate. At this climactic moment the gallant has Jonson's entire bag of tricks at his disposal, but he puts them to a new use. Wittipol chooses to be Frances's "true friend" (IV.vi.4) rather than her lover. Instead of seducing her he assures his mistress that "I can love *goodnes* in you, more / Then I did *Beauty*" (IV.vi.37–38). Instead of appropriating the deed of Feoffment he conveys it to his friend Manly, who prevents it from falling into the hands of the projector Merecraft. As the two gallants finally and decisively sever their ties with the underclass, their aspirations merge with those of their creator, Ben Jonson.

In this scene Jonson renounces the moral ambivalence of his greatest comedies. His intention in those plays, as he himself defines it, is to "sport with humane follies." Manly, however, solemnly declares that "it is not manly to take joy, or pride / In humane errours." At the same time Jonson tacitly abandons the claim that the comedies published in his 1616 *Works* constitute a timeless model of what "other plays should bee."[5] From his current perspective those works could be seen as part of an evolutionary process that led from the Tudor morality play, through his own cynical farces about urban life, and on to the high-minded sentimental comedy of Wittipol's renunciation scene. Although he did not choose to explore it in 1616, Jonson gave his audience a tantalizing glimpse of a new dramatic convention.

In the final act Jonson raises the further question of whether or not a trio of virtuous individuals can survive for long in a society as fundamen-

tally corrupt as this one. When Merecraft learns that he has been outma-
neuvered, he goes before the magistrate and accuses Wittipol, Manly, and
Frances of bewitching the hapless Fitzdotterel. Pug sees these fraudulent
proceedings as a golden opportunity to show his *"divels* nature" and offers
to teach the rogues the tricks of his trade; but Merecraft's methods have
already been tested in act V of *Volpone,* and he has no need of real demons. For a skilled professional like Merecraft, witchcraft is "no hard
thing to out doe the *Devill* in: / A Boy o'thirteene yeere old made him an
Asse / But t'other day." Jonson was referring to a well-known case of sham
possession that occurred just a couple of months before *The Devil* was on
the boards. In July 1616 a thirteen-year-old boy named John Smith accused fifteen elderly Leicestershire women of bewitching him; nine of these
were promptly hanged on the orders of Sir Humphrey Winch and Sergeant
Randal Crewe. A month later, when the King's summer progress took him
through Leicestershire, he examined young Smith and discovered that the
boy was an impostor, thus sparing the lives of six innocent women.[6] But
no higher authority overrules the foolish magistrate who arraigns Wittipol, Manly, and Frances. It is rather Satan, the *deus ex machina* who reappears in act V to fetch Pug back to Hell, who awakens Justice Eitherside's
sense of right and wrong. And even so, Merecraft and his accomplices go
scot-free at the end of the play.

In the final analysis, the playwright acknowledges that the world of
Jonsonian comedy, like the urban society it mirrors, is irremediably corrupt. Only the King could restore order to it. Just as James had successfully intervened in the Leicestershire witchcraft trials, he (and he alone)
has the power to introduce lasting reforms into Jacobean London. But was
there any likelihood that James would exercise this power? Merecraft's
chief project, an elaborate scheme "for recovery of drown'd land, /
Whereof the *Crowne's* to have his moiety," raised the issue of James's responsibility in a very direct way. Although the King officially repudiated
the practice of granting monopolies, he had recently awarded the right to
reclaim the fens to Sir Robert Car, a Scot ("neere about the prince," Chamberlain noted) who had danced in *The Golden Age Restored.* Thanks to
James's openhandedness, Merecraft's confidence game was Car's legitimate business venture. Interestingly, Jonson's Prologue does not include
the customary assurances that he has refrained from attacking specific individuals. His temerity came to the King's attention. Jonson told Drummond that he had been "accused" over *The Devil Is an Ass.* Although he
did not identify his accusers, he did say that "the King desired him to
conceal" his satire on the Duke of Drowned Land. Was James annoyed
because one of his own actions had fallen within the poet's line of fire? Or
was he, as the word "desired" implies, shielding Jonson from someone

(Car?) who complained that the playwright had gone too far?[7] In any event, this episode was a pointed reminder that Jonson's sinecure did not entitle him to lampoon the King's servants in the public playhouse.

Jonson found it easy to heed this reminder. *The Devil Is an Ass* is the palinode to his career on the Elizabethan and Jacobean stage; it extends and ratifies the process of self-definition he had gone through while preparing his folio for the press. The opening lines of his epilogue echo the couplet that Shakespeare's magician-hero Prospero had uttered in similar circumstances just five years earlier. Shakespeare's "Now my charms are all o'erthrown, / And what strength I have's mine own" turns into Jonson's "Thus, the *Projector,* here, is over-throwne. / But I have now a *Project* of mine own."[8] Did Jonson surmise, as countless readers have done, that Prospero's epilogue foreshadowed Shakespeare's retirement from the stage? Jonson had reached a point in his own career when such an interpretation could easily have occurred to him. Like his great competitor, who had died in Stratford-upon-Avon the previous spring, Jonson was now severing his connection with the playhouse. For the remaining decade of James's reign, Jonson's project would consist entirely of court masques, occasional poems, and scholarly works.

Jonson's abrupt withdrawal from the theater at the moment when he was the leading comic playwright of his age poses the central paradox of his life's work. On the strength of his plays, he was fully entitled to the "classic" status that the folio claims for him: *Volpone, The Silent Woman, The Alchemist,* and *Bartholomew Fair* challenge comparison with the best comedies that anyone had ever written. But Jonson had a low regard for this line of endeavor and ceased to write for the stage when a better opportunity came his way. Like Racine, who left the stage and became historiographer to the court of Louis XIV, he regarded the theater as a stepping stone to something better. Posterity may look askance at his choice, but Jonson probably thought he was entering the promised land. His ambivalence about the theater went all the way back to his stormy debut in the late 1590s; now that ambivalence had been resolved to his liking.

The King awarded the pension, in the words of the Patent Roll, in consideration of services "done and to be done unto us by our welbeloved Servaunt Benjamin Johnson." These services may have included many minor commissions. On June 14, 1616, just a few months after the pension was granted, George Gerrard attended a feast where "dyers, cloth dressers with their shuttles, and Hamburgians were presented to the King, and spake such language as Ben Jonson putt in their mouthes."[9] But the most conspicuous of the services to be done was, of course, the continuing provision of Twelfth Night masques and holiday entertainments for the court. Jonson was now in a position to devote all of his energies to that task. For the first time in his career he enjoyed the status of an established master whose fees were paid in advance. The royal consort of James, Prince Charles, and George Villiers turned out to be remarkably stable, and Jonson thus came to enjoy the luxury of writing for the same patrons over an extended period of time. He was now more free to pursue a motif or idea through a series of works, and he now had a better idea of what his patrons wanted to hear.

Jonson entered the King's service at a time when the celebration of Christmas holidays was rapidly becoming an important political issue in its own right. After noting with displeasure that many of the rural gentry came to London "during the Christmas time," a royal proclamation of 1614 ordered the newly urbanized gentlemen to "repaire unto their severall Countreys . . . and to keepe House and Hospitalitie." The following December saw another proclamation requiring "all Noblemen, and Gentlemen whatsoever, to live in the steps and examples of their worthy Ancestours, by keeping and entertaining Hospitalitie." In his *Speech in the Star Chamber,* which he delivered on June 20, 1616, and published in the closing pages of his folio *Works* (1616), James again instructed the migrant gentry to "get them into the Countrey . . . especially at Festivall times, as Christmas and Easter." [10] The annual Christmas feast in manor houses like Penshurst epitomized James's vision of a renascent countryside. During "Festivall times" the lord of the manor bestowed food and drink on his tenants, exchanged gifts with them, relieved the poor, and participated in an ancient ritual that reaffirmed the integrity of the manorial community.

The future of this institution, as James recognized, was precarious. To begin with, the number of country gentlemen who chose to spend Christmas in London, rather than on their estates, was increasing at an alarming rate. At the conclusion of his *Speech in the Star Chamber* James likens the growth of the city to a humoral disease in the body politic and complains that "all the countrey is gotten into *London.*" In addition, the King had to contend with "Puritanes and Novelists," [11] who contended that feast days were pagan relics that had been imposed on English culture by the Church of Rome. From their standpoint, holidays were "holy days" that should be devoted to prayer and meditation rather than feasting and merriment. Since the antifestive position was especially prevalent in London, where Puritanism was a potent political force, the Sabbatarian controversy deepened the divisions between court and city.

Jonson articulated his royal master's view in *Christmas His Masque*

(1617), his first entertainment since entering the King's service. This work is both a nostalgic recreation of the old-fashioned Christmas customs that James sought to revive and an acerbic caricature of modern Londoners, who have lost touch with their own past. Captain Christmas of London, who has the leading role, begins the performance with assurances that he shares his majesty's reverence for holiday traditions. "Why, I am no dangerous person," he protests, "I am old *Gregorie Christmas* still, and though I come out of *Popes-head-alley,* as good a Protestant, as any i' my Parish." The captain styles himself Gregory Christmas because it was Pope Gregory the Great who instructed missionaries to England that pagan festivals should be adapted to the usages of the English Church, and who thus became, in the fullness of time, an arch-villain in the Puritan version of English ecclesiastical history. Old Gregory Christmas will have none of this guilt by association: his Popish origin makes him no worse a Protestant. The Londoners of medieval England had performed mummers' plays at court during the Christmas holidays; the ten mummers whom Cupid leads in to dance before the King (Misrule, Caroll, Minc'd-Pie, Gamboll, Post and Paire, New-Yeare's-Gift, Mumming, Wassail, Offering, and Babie-Cake) attempt to revive this custom and keep *"a right* Christmas *as of old it was."* [12]

Jonson also reminded James that these were not citizen amateurs at all, but rather a company of players whom the court has hired in order to maintain the *pretense* of an old-fashioned Christmas. Midway through the performance Cupid's mother, Venus, barges in and brags about her son's future on the stage: "I could ha' had money enough for him, an I would ha' beene tempted, and ha' let him out by the weeke, to the Kings Players: Master *Burbadge* has beene about and about with me; and so has old Mr. *Hemings* too." These allusions notified the courtiers that they were watching a group of paid professionals, including, in all likelihood, the very players whom Venus mentions by name. Jonson underscores this message by having the hireling actors grope nervously for their "traditional" accoutrements:

> *Caroll* Why? here be halfe of the properties
> forgotten, Father.
> *Offering* Post and Paire wants his pur-chops, and his
> pur-dogs.
> *Caroll* Ha' you nere a Son at the Groom-Porters to
> beg, or borrow a paire of Cards quickly?

The farce reaches a climax when Cupid, who represents "the Love o' the Citie" (for James), forgets his lines. As he stands there mindlessly repeating the only three words that he can remember (*"And which* Cupid—*And which* Cupid, &c.") the audience sees him as just an actor, and a bad actor at that. Meanwhile Venus, in a stunning outburst of crass opportunism, tries to wheedle a pension out of the King: "How does his Majestie like him, I pray? will he give eight pence a day, thinke you?"[13]

When Gerrard observed that dyers, cloth dressers, and Hamburgians were presented to the King and spoke such language as Jonson put into their mouths, he implicitly likened the visitors at court to a troupe of actors. *Christmas His Masque* uses the same analogy to criticize Londoners who are out of touch with their traditional roles in society. Actors who forget their lines and citizens who forget their heritage both signify a larger failure of cultural memory. The holiday customs commemorated in *Christmas His Masque* owe their survival neither to the citizenry nor to the players. The true celebrant of Christmas is Jonson, the King's poet, who simultaneously preserves the festive traditions of yesteryear and chastises James's subjects for failing to do so themselves. This entertainment flaunts Jonson's superiority to the citizens and players who come before the King and recite the words that Jonson has written for them. He is a poet who belongs to the royal household; they are pretenders who blunder into the feast.

Christmas His Masque is a truncated mummers' play, or an extended antimasque, rather than a regular masque. It offers a comic image of failed mirth but no corresponding scene of exalted revelry. Jonson made amends on Twelfth Night in *The Vision of Delight,* his most extravagant tribute to the civilizing power of mirth.

The Vision of Delight leads the spectator through a hierarchy of lesser and greater pleasures that recalls the closing pages of James's 1616 *Works.* The King complained that the gentry lived in the city after "the fashion of *Italy*" and dressed like Frenchmen; Jonson set his first antimasque before the facade of a Serlian city street and peopled it with grotesque puppets from the Italian *commedia dell'arte* who perform a French ballet. In his second antimasque a group of figures taken from *Les songes drolatiques de Pantagruel,* dance an Italian ballet. James ordered the rural landowners to "get them into the Countrey" during festival times; the Twelfth Night masquers of 1617 issued forth from a verdant pastoral bower.[14]

At the same time, *The Vision of Delight* celebrates the ascendancy within the court of James's new entourage. It was rumored that the King intended to make Villiers an earl "before the end of Christmas," and he did so on January 5. A night later, moments before "the newmade earle . . . dawnced with the queene" in *The Vision of Delight,* Jonson exhorted the court to

> Behold a King
> Whose presence maketh this perpetuall *Spring,*

The glories of which Spring grow in that Bower,
And are the marks and beauties of his power.

The line of vision that ran from the throne to the bower which held the newly created Earl of Buckingham directed James's gaze to the object of his delight; at this climactic moment the operation of the royal will became fully visible to everyone in the Banqueting Hall.[15] This rhymed analogy between the rural enclosure and the revivified court—between "bower" and "power"—puts Jonson's celebration of country life under an enormous strain. On one level, *The Vision of Delight* exhorts the citified gentry to return to their happy rural seats; but this masque also celebrates a paradise within the court reserved for men like Buckingham and now, in a more modest way, Jonson himself, who basked in the sunshine of James's favor.

The complex of images linking the purified court with the renascent country, the King's eye with the nurturing sun, and the masquers with growing organisms, first appears in the works that Jonson wrote for various "Gentlemen, the King's Servants" beginning in 1612; it coincides with the rise of Somerset and Buckingham. Within the context of a live performance the nurturing warmth of the King's gaze signifies the flow of royal favor from sovereign to subject:

It is but standing in his eye,
    You'll feele your selves chang'd by and by,
Few live, that know, how quick a spring
    Workes in the presence of a king.

Jonson portrays the gentlemen dancers not as heroic leaders, or as the scions of noble houses, but rather as passive recipients of James's bounty, "new" men who have been raised to eminence by the King's favor. The printed texts of these masques do not identify any of the gentlemen by name, but we know from other sources that their ranks included men like one Abercrombie, a "Scottish dancing Courtier," who received the "making of two Irish Barons" in the spring of 1617; John Auchmouty, another Scottish dancer, who held a pension worth two hundred pounds per annum and served as a groom in James's bedchamber; and of course the astounding George Villiers, a dancer *par excellence,* who, as one contemporary put it, "jumpt *higher* than ever *Englishman* did in so short a time."[16] The pairing of *Christmas His Masque* and *The Vision of Delight* suggests an invidious distinction between the citizen hirelings who put on their mummers' play in exchange for a night's wages and the genteel amateurs who danced for the King out of sheer "delight." But the gentleman dancers were simply professionals of a more subtle sort.

Jonson's close affiliation with James's glamorous favorites is one of the great ironies of his career. He aspired to serve the King by offering him counsel in the form of poetry and masques, but in order to secure his place at court he put his services at the disposal of men whose only asset was their personal charm. In his earliest work for the Jacobean court, the *Althorpe Entertainment* of 1603, Jonson repudiates the example set by Sir Christopher Hatton, who had danced his way into the heart of the Queen. Buckingham and his cronies were Hatton's successors. And the court paid Jonson handsomely for his services. Not long after Buckingham received his earldom, Jonson delivered at the King's dinner table "A Grace Extempore," blessing "Buckingham the fortunate"; the King promptly rewarded him, according to Aubrey, with a gift of one hundred pounds.[17]

Yet Jonson refused to lapse into utter sycophancy, or to become a pliable instrument in the hands of James's glamorous favorites. Within months of receiving his pension he had ridiculed Sir Robert Car, the Scottish dancer turned monopolist. And in the winter of 1617 he made an initial effort to improve the morals of the masquers themselves. Lord Hay—another Scottish dancer—commissioned Jonson's *Lovers Made Men* for a private, and very lavish, reception in honor of the Special Ambassador from France, Charles Cachon, Baron du Tour. Because the King was absent, Jonson was able to devise a pattern of aesthetic and moral change that made perfect sense without reference to any external agency. His lovesick courtiers are "made men" through the redemptive offices of art rather than the omnipotent gaze of the sovereign. The noble dancers in *Lovers Made Men* took the parts both of the fools in the antimasque and of the exemplary figures in the masque proper, an innovation that reinforced Jonson's claim about the educative powers of his art: for the first time, the courtiers appear in the guise of imperfect beings who are raised to a higher state of moral awareness, not by the King, but by the poet.

The following winter, Jonson made a much bolder attempt to reform the morals of the court. *Pleasure Reconciled to Virtue* (1617–18), the first Prince's masque since *Oberon*, commemorated Charles's investiture as Prince of Wales. Since Charles was an austere, and rather priggish, young man, his investiture furnished an ideal opportunity to remind the courtiers that life did not entirely consist of cakes and ale. Whereas the previous year's masque had dealt with the relatively innocuous matter of delight, *Pleasure Reconciled to Virtue* takes up the more touchy subjects of eating and drinking. And whereas *The Vision of Delight* made the court out to be an earthly paradise, the courtiers who performed in *Pleasure Reconciled to Virtue* danced to the accompaniment of grave moral admonitions. Jonson's Twelfth Night masque for 1618 was a test case, a salutary occasion on which the masque writer tried to put his high ideals into practice.

His antimasque is an imaginary episode from the life of Hercules, the legendary chooser of virtue over pleasure. In the opening scenes, Hercules subdues first the drunken Comus, who has stolen the hero's great drinking bowl, and second, a crew of drunken pygmies who attack him while he is asleep. These encounters are allegorical images of Hercules' victory over his own concupiscence (the Belly-god Comus) and irascibility (the Anger-worshipping pygmies). The god becomes the hero of a Jonsonian comedy of humors. He does not value pleasure as an end in itself, but welcomes it as the just recompense for his labors. Having slain Antaeus, he claims the reward of sleep, as Achilles does at the end of the *Iliad:* repose follows work, just as pleasure complements virtue.

The completion of Hercules' labors coincides with the appearance of Prince Charles and his fellow masquers, who have been immured behind the rugged face of Mount Atlas:

Ope, aged Atlas, open then thy lap
and from thy beamy bosom, strike a light,
that men may read in thy mysterious map
    all lines
      and signes
of roial education.

As the spectators lifted their gaze from the comic stage where the anti-masque had just been performed and peered into the "hill / of skill" that contained the mysterious talismans of royal education, they surveyed the path of Jonson's own aspirations. The tutelary singer who leads Charles down from the hill and into the court is Daedalus, the poet-priest who combines the roles of artist, educator, and bard. In contrast to the lush, painterly images of *The Vision of Delight,* Jonson repeatedly uses word-play to keep the fundamental interconnection of pleasure and virtue in the foreground. He evidently hoped, against formidable odds, that the court would listen closely to what he was saying. The singer puns most insistently on the word "lines," which can refer to lines of verse, to a noble lineage, to lines of choreography, or to all of these at once. The dance floor becomes a "laborinth"—both a delightful maze and a set of obstacles to be worked through. Although the masque offers Charles and his companions a respite from their studies, the singer reminds the revelers that

Dauncing is an exercise
  not only shews the movers wit,
but maketh the beholder wise,
  as he hath powre to rise to it.

The courtier who rises intellectually to the occasion will, of course, understand that the dancers must in turn rise from it and "returne unto the Hill."[18]

Pleasure Reconciled to Virtue notoriously failed to create such an understanding among the courtiers who beheld it on January 6, 1618. According to Orazio Busino, Chaplain to the Venetian Ambassador, the King himself was the first to complain. "Why don't they dance?" James shouted, "What did they make me come here for? Devil take you all, dance." Busino's report indicates that it was tepid dancing, rather than didactic verses, that irritated the King. But these elements are always intertwined in a live performance, and Busino makes it clear that James preferred dancing over poetry—a preference that goes entirely against the grain of Jonson's text. Nor was James alone: *Pleasure Reconciled to Virtue* is the only Jonsonian masque to incur widespread disapproval at court. "The masque it selfe in generall not well liked," Sir Edward Harwood concluded, "the Conceite good, the poetry not so." When Edward Sherburn sent a copy of the text to Dudley Carleton, he warned him that "it came far short of the expectation." Chamberlain declared that "there was nothing in it extraordinary, but rather the invention proved dull." The unkindest cut of all was Nathaniel Brent's: "The maske on 12th night is not commended of any. the poet is growen so dul that his devise is not worthy the relating, much lesse the copying out. divers thinke fit he should retourne to his ould trade of bricke laying againe." [19] Commentators have inferred that the court lacked the sophistication to appreciate Jonson and Jones's handiwork, and they are doubtless right. But the sneer that Brent was hearing in diverse quarters suggests that the courtiers understood Jonson's message all too well. If the King's servant proposed to set himself up as arbiter of the court's morals, he was welcome to return to his old trade of bricklaying.

Pleasure Reconciled to Virtue, a great success in the estimation of modern critics, fared so poorly with its original audience because Jonson's admonitions were totally at odds with the code of behavior that regulated the dancers' everyday lives. The men who attended King James were expected to spend lavish sums on food, drink, and gambling. Moderation was fine in theory, but a courtier's prestige was directly proportional to the size of his outlay. When Lord Hay returned from his embassy to Paris in 1616, he raised the level of culinary opulence to unprecedented heights. Hay spent more than 2,200 pounds and engaged "the workemanship and inventions of thirtie master cookes for twelve dayes" for the feast at which *Lovers Made Men* was performed. Comus's Bowl-Bearer praises the belly as the "giver of wit"; Hay's *pièce de résistance,* the notorious ante-supper, set standards of spendthrift ingenuity that Comus himself would have envied. The meal began with a lavish feast that was set on the table, uncovered, and then abruptly removed, before a single bite had been eaten. His guests' appetite having been aroused, the host then set a second feast, even more lavish than the first, before them. Hay was not one to reconcile pleasure and virtue; he only wanted to enhance pleasure. [20]

Hay's vanities were not as pointless as they appear. He was, as Clarendon saw, a representative figure for his age. Lacking any real accomplishments in the arts of war or peace, and surrounded by rival courtiers whose birth and capacities were basically identical to his own, Hay used such performances to keep himself in the limelight. James, for his part, encouraged Hay's behavior by covering his debts repeatedly, marrying him off to a wealthy heiress, financing his escapades, and creating him Viscount Doncaster in 1618. Despite his sober exhortations to follow the mean in matters of personal conduct, James did not practice what he preached. Although he publicly admonished his son to avoid excessive drinking, his own physician, Theodore Mayerne, noted that his Majesty "errs as to quality, quantity, frequency, time, and order. He promiscuously drinks beer, ale, Spanish wine, sweet French wine, white wine (his normal drink), Muscatelle, and sometimes Alicant wine. He does not care whether the wine be strong or not, so it is sweet." In a lesser person such behavior would signify the weakness of the flesh; in a king it set a high example. "The end of all," wrote the French Ambassador Tillières, "is ever the bottle." [21]

Queen Anne had been too ill to attend the Twelfth Night production of *Pleasure Reconciled to Virtue,* so a second performance for her benefit was put on six weeks later. Jonson rewrote the masque for this occasion, substituting a new antimasque of Welsh rustics for the original byplay between Hercules, Comus, and the pygmies, and retitling the work *For the Honour of Wales.* In the 1640 folio of Jonson's *Works* a self-congratulatory note stating that "this pleas'd the King so well, as he would see it againe, when it was presented with these additions" (HS, X, 576) appears between the texts of the two masques. But the "additions" look more like the author's attempt to placate philistine critics of his original version.

The first words of the revised text are spoken by a comic Welshman cautioning his mates not to be "too byssie and forward." After some more banter about the dangers of "rassnesse" and a preliminary salute to the King, they complain to James about *Pleasure Reconciled to Virtue:* "'is a great huge deale of anger upon yow, from aull Wales and the Nation; that your ursippe would suffer our yong Master *Sarles,* your 'ursips Sonne and Heire, and Prince of *Wales,* the first time he ever play Dance, to be pit up in a Mountaine (got knowes where) by a palterly *Poet.*" The Welsh patriots object to Jonson's use of classical sites when there are Welsh mountains "of as good standing, and as good discent, as the prowdest *Adlas* christned." So they proceed to recast Jones's scenery as Welsh landscape, to invent mock-Welsh pedigrees for the noble dancers, and to cast aspersions at the antimasque performed on January 6: "Is not better this now then *Pigmies?*" [22]

The courtiers of 1617–18 undoubtedly thought that it was. *Pleasure Reconciled to Virtue,* the first of the masques that Jonson wrote for Prince Charles, had failed to please. It reflected the heir apparent's liking for high-minded moral sentiments but was grossly at odds with the mood of James's court. Jonson, ever the professional, provided a new antimasque that was thoroughly, indeed ludicrously, deferential.

Shortly thereafter he departed on a walking tour to Scotland, where he remained during the winter of 1618–19. His decision to absent himself from court for an entire year may have stemmed from his disappointment over the reception of *Pleasure Reconciled to Virtue.* Or he may have been frustrated by his inability to follow his own advice, for Jonson was deeply implicated in the vices that he pilloried. The following winter Drummond concluded that his guest was a quarrelsome drunkard, "jealous of every word and action of those about him (especially after drink) which is one of the Elements in which he liveth." Jonson admonished Prince Charles to avoid the vice of petty animosity, but he himself struck Drummond as "a contemner and Scorner of others." Jonson turns his anti-hero Comus into a grossly corpulent *"Belly-god"* (he is a slender youth in the classical sources) so as to show the unhappy consequences of gourmandizing; by his mid-forties, however, Jonson had become just such a figure. At the age of twenty-nine, according to Dekker and Marston, Jonson was slender and wiry; by 1619 he had acquired what he referred to a year later as "my mountaine belly." And it was mountainous: the middle-aged poet informed Lady Covell that his weight fluctuated between 250 and 270 pounds.[23] The author of *Pleasure Reconciled to Virtue* had put himself in the unwise position of chastising vices that he himself embodied in a public and visible way. He praised Hercules, but he emulated Antaeus. His walking trip to Scotland removed him from the court, where the pressure to conform to his public image was most intense. The mere fact that he was James's pensioner and Aubigny's client ensured his welcome in noble houses north of the Tweed.

Jonson also had a professional reason for making the journey north. In the course of the trip he gathered topographical lore and regional antiquities, just as his master Camden had in his summer-long treks across the length and breadth of Britain some forty years earlier; afterward, he planned to write a descriptive poem about Scotland, entitled *Discovery* (*Conv,* 406–408). He hoped that this project would catch the eye of the King, who had made his first progress to Scotland during the previous summer, and James did in fact take some notice of it (HS, I, 207).

His resolve to go the whole way on foot gave the expedition a mildly absurd appearance. Prior to his departure, Bacon told him that he "loved not to sie poesy go on other feet than poetical dactylus and spondaeus" (*Conv*, 333–335). John Taylor, a former Thames waterman who published his verses under the sobriquet "Water Poet," began his own walk to Scotland shortly after Jonson's departure, and the parallel between the two "poets" created the impression that they were a pair of wayfaring buffoons. Jonson thought that "Taylor was sent along here to scorn him" (*Conv*, 607), and Taylor's subsequent denunciation of "many shallow-brain'd Critickes" who "doe lay an aspersion on me, that I was set on by others, or that I did undergo this project, either in malice, or mockage of Maister *Benjamin Jonson*" (HS, XI, 382) cannot have done much to dispel this impression.

Nevertheless, Jonson received a triumphant reception when he arrived in Edinburgh that summer. His 1616 *Works* had magnified his reputation to the point where he could justly claim to be the leading poet in England, and King James had tacitly endorsed that claim by his award of the royal pension. His five-year residence with Aubigny doubtless furnished him with many contacts among the Scottish gentry. Taylor mentioned seeing his "long approved and assured good friend Master *Benjamin Johnson,* at one Master *John Stuarts* house" in Leith on September 18. The meeting must have been amiable, for Jonson gave the Water Poet "a piece of golde of two and twentie shillings to drinke his health in *England,*" after which Taylor bade him "a friendly farewell," leaving him "amongst Noble-men and Gentlemen that knowes his true worth" (HS, XI, 382–383). Two days later the Edinburgh Town Council authorized the dean of their guild to make "Benjamin Jonsoun inglisman" an honorary burgess and guild brother. The dean paid thirteen pounds, six shillings, and eight pence "to Alexander patersone for writting and gilting of Benjamine Johnestounes burges ticket." In October the council laid out the handsome sum of two hundred and twenty-one pounds for a dinner in Jonson's honor (HS, I, 233–234).

That winter the English visitor spent about three weeks with Drummond at his estate in Hawthornden, just south of Edinburgh. Although Jonson had been lionized throughout the previous summer and autumn, in his conversations with Drummond he sounds quite disenchanted with his lofty station in life. Instead of the self-assured master who had assembled the folio and won the esteem of King James, the Laird encountered a restless and jaded poet of forty-seven who was frustrated by his dependent status at court. "He heth a mind to be a Churchman," Drummond learned, "and so he might have favour to make one Sermon to the King, he careth not what thereafter s[h]ould befall him, for he would not

Gloria Reddit

Hos Honores

Guilielmus
de Havthorn-

Drummond
den

R Gaywood fecit 1654

William Drummond, Laird of Hawthornden, artist unknown. From early editions of his *Works*.

flatter though he saw Death" (*Conv*, 330–332). The likelihood that many people did regard him as a flatterer weighed on Jonson's mind. His host discovered that "of all stiles he loved most to be named honest, and hath of that ane hundred letters so naming him" (*Conv*, 631–632); a man who has a hundred letters vouching for his honesty clearly anticipates that people are going to call him a liar or a hypocrite.

Jonson repeatedly questioned the worth of his own vocation: "He dissuaded me from Poetrie, for that she had beggered him, when he might have been a rich lawer, Physitian or Marchant." Jonson did not merely say this for Drummond's benefit; he records the same opinion in the privacy of his commonplace book: "*Poetry*, in this latter Age, hath prov'd but a meane *Mistresse*, to such as have wholly addicted themselves to her." His reflections on the lives of contemporary poets ran in the same vein: Spenser "died for lake of bread in King street"; "Southwell was hanged"; and "Done himself for not being understood would perish." "The King," he noted, "said Sir P. Sidney was no poet neither did he see ever any verse in England to the Scullors" (namely, the Water Poet). Once again, the identical sentiment crops up in the *Discoveries*: "*Nothing* in our Age, I have observ'd, is more preposterous, then the *running Judgements* upon *Poetry*, and *Poets* . . . *Heath's Epigrams*, and the *Skullers Poems* have their applause . . . Nay, if it were put to the question of the Water-rimers workes, against *Spencers*; I doubt not but they would find more *Suffrages*." Jonson summed up a career mainly devoted to writing for the stage with the observation that "of all his Playes he never Gained 2 hundreth pounds." Having lived through an efflorescence of drama rivaled only by Athens in its prime, he had almost nothing to say about contemporary playwrights, and what he did say about them (apart from Beaumont and Fletcher) was curt and dismissive. "Shaksperr wanted Arte"; "Sharpham, Day, Dicker were all Rogues." [24]

Jonson had a number of ideas about how he wanted to employ his own talent, but all of his projects were still in the planning stages. The ones that he mentioned to Drummond create an overall impression of discontinuity: they do not have much in common either with Jonson's earlier work, or with one another. Tragicomedy and pastoral, the two dramatic genres that were not represented in the 1616 folio, evidently held some fascination for him. He had temporarily given up on the former, since he could not find two actors who resembled one another closely enough to sustain a plot based on mistaken identity; but he frequently recurs to the subject of pastoral, saying that those of Sidney and Guarini are too literary, that he has already written one called *The May Lord*, and that "he heth intention to writt a fisher or Pastorall play & sett the stage of it in the Lowmond Lake." "The most common place of his repetition," Drummond noted, "was a dialogue Pastoral between a shepherd & shipherdesse about singing."[25]

Other projects smack of grander aspirations. He told Drummond that he intended "to perfect ane Epick Poeme intitled Heroologia of the Worthies of his Country, rowsed by fame, and was to dedicate it to his Country" (*Conv*, 1–4). He also spoke of *Discovery*, the topographical poem about Scotland that he hoped would take the King's fancy. Drummond thought his metaphor for Edinburgh, "the hart of Scotland Britaines other eye," worth recording, and he promised Jonson "to send him descriptions of Edinbrough Borrow lawes" and "of the Lowmond" (407–408, 644–645). But nothing remains of either the *Heroologia* or the *Discovery:* they survive only as conversation pieces. The fire that ravaged Jonson's library five years later makes it difficult to speak with much assurance about what he actually was writing between 1616 and 1623. His inventory of the works lost in that unlucky accident includes "my journey into *Scotland* song" (*Und*, 43.94), but makes no mention of the *Heroologia*.

Some of the work mentioned in the *Conversations* does survive, however. The dialogue between a shepherd and a shepherdess would eventually appear in *The Underwood* (a collection of Jonson's verse published after his death) bearing the title "The Musical Strife, in a Pastoral Dialogue" (*Und*, 3). Allusions to eight other poems subsequently published in *The Underwood* also crop up in the *Conversations*. Four of these are early, or at any rate trivial, efforts. But "The Musical Strife," the lyric excerpted from *Charis* (*Und*, 2, sec. vii), and "The Hour Glass" (*Und*, 8), look like new work—there was no reason to omit them from the folio if they were completed before 1616—and "My Picture Left in Scotland" (*Und*, 9) clearly was written in 1619. These poems afford a valuable clue about the kind of poetry that Jonson would write in the future. Their themes—song, seduction, the transience of the flesh—reflect the preoccupations of the courtier class to which he had recently become closely allied. Their reason for existence, put simply, was to while away the hours with persons like Drummond. Within the folio, the closest analogue to these nine poems are the five love lyrics in *The Forest*. Like almost all of the poems collected in *The Underwood*, these were still in manuscript at the time of Jonson's death. The success that came his way upon the publication of the folio and the grant of the pension had raised Jonson to such an eminence that he ceased, ironically enough, to write for publication, and reverted to the ways of the gentlemanly amateur.

Shortly after his departure from Hawthornden in January 1619, Jonson sent Drummond manuscripts of a "Madrigal on a lovers dust, made sand for ane Houre Glasse" and of "this which is (as he said) a picture of himselfe":

> I doubt that love is rather deafe than blinde
>   for else it could not bee
>   that shee,
>   whom I adore so much should so slight mee,
> and cast my sute behinde.
>   I'am sure my Language to her is as sweet
>   and all my closes meet
>   in numbers of as subtile feete,
>   as makes the youngest hee
>   that sits in shadow of Apollos tree.
>
> O, but my conscious feares
>   that flye my thoughts betweene,
> prompt mee, that shee hath seene
>   my hundred of Gray haires,
>   told Six and forty yeares,
> read so much Waste as she cannot embrace
>   my Mountaine belly and my rockye face.
> and all these through her eies, have stop'd her eares.

In his forty-seventh year Jonson borrowed still another mask from Horace. The likeliest inspiration for this vignette of the aging poet-in-love is the ode in which his Roman precursor implores Venus not "to bend a man, now at his fiftieth yeare." He also recalled Anacreon's lyric "On Himself": "Whether there are hairs or whether they are gone, I know not; but this I know, that it becomes more for an old man to play at what is pleasant, by how much nearer is the period of his fate."[26] His own initial meditation on this theme—there will be others—focuses on the discrepancy between his sprightly verses, which remain oblivious to the passage of time, and his slovenly body, which plainly shows the ravages of age.

When Jonson tries to conceive of himself as an amorous swain, his personal history betrays him. In openly displaying his bulk, though, the poet affirms and boasts of his own integrity, his wish "to be named honest." Unlike the youth who lurks in the shadow of Apollo's tree, Jonson puts his corpulent body in the foreground. Although his mountain belly and rocky face are gross, they are also massive and craggy; like Atlas, the animated mountain in *Pleasure Reconciled to Virtue*, his enormous body contains a hidden reservoir of stoic wisdom.

Early that spring, around the time of Jonson's return to London, the death of master Vincent Corbet occasioned another meditation on the disabilities of age. Corbet's son Richard was a friend of Jonson's, chaplain to King James, and a celebrated wit and *bon vivant*. The father's manner of life was diametrically opposed to that of his son. Although he owned property in London, old Vincent Corbet lived in the village of Whitton, in

Surrey, where he worked as a gardener under an assumed name. In contrast to the incontinent Jonson, the seventy-nine-year-old Corbet had vigorously resisted the wear and tear of time, and so arduously

> wrestled with Diseases strong,
> That though they did possesse each limbe,
> Yet he broke them, e're they could him,
> With the just Canon of his life.

Old Corbet set an example that Jonson could admire but not emulate. "Much from him I professe I wonne," he continued, "and more, and more, I should have done."[27] When read in conjunction with "My Picture Left in Scotland," the "Epitaph on Master Vincent Corbet" recapitulates the choice that Jonson had posed to the court some fifteen months previously. Where Corbet had taken the road of virtue, Jonson was dallying with pleasure.

• CHAPTER THIRTEEN •

Celebrity and Decline

Hoping to interest James in his *Discovery*, Jonson wrote to Drummond asking for various pieces of information about Scotland. On January 17, while Jonson was still on his way south, the Laird sent him "that Epigram which you desired, with another of the like Argument" (HS, I, 204). On April 30 Drummond explained that the "uncertaintie where to directe letters hath made mee this tyme past not to write" and enclosed "the oth of our knights, as it was given mee by Harald Drysdale," adding that "if I can serve you in any other matter, yee shall find mee most willing" (HS, I, 206). In a letter from London, dated May 10 and requesting more Scottish arcana, Jonson wrote that his "reports" were "not unacceptable to His Majesty," and that James "professed (I thank God) some Joy to see me, and is pleased to hear the Purpose of my Book" (HS, I, 207). By July 1 Drummond had already discharged Jonson's latest requests and was sending along "the *Impressaes* and Emblemes on a Bed of State wrought and embroidered all with gold and silk by the late Queen *Mary* mother to our sacred Soveraign" (HS, I, 208). If James really was interested in hearing reports about the *Discovery*, Drummond's description of the twenty-nine mottoes embroidered on Queen Mary's bed-of-state undoubtedly helped Jonson to flesh them out.

The King's pensioner now had a considerable reputation to uphold. Jonson returned from Scotland a Burgess and Guild Brother of the City of Edinburgh, and more honors were in the offing. In 1617 his friend Edmund Bolton began petitioning James to found a royal academy or "College of Honor" composed of the leading scholars, artists, and authors in the realm; Jonson's name appeared on the earliest roster of eighty-four prospective members. His patron Pembroke became Chancellor of Oxford University in 1617 and on May 17, 1619, wrote to the Delegates of the University asking that they grant Jonson an honorary Master of Arts degree. The delegates complied, noting that Jonson was "happily versed in all humane literature," that he had been "honored by our most serene King with an annual pension," and that he was "also recommended by our most illustrious Chancellor." Two years earlier Jonson told Drummond that Pembroke provided his scholarly client with a stipend of twenty pounds per annum for the purchase of books. Jonson secured lodgings at "Gresham College in London" at some point between his return from Scotland in 1619 and the autumn of 1623, when he told the Court of Chancery that he was residing there; he may have held the post of Deputy Professor of Rhetoric there.[1]

Jonson also wielded influence at court. When Selden's *History of Tithes* (1618) prompted an irate King James to summon him to Theobalds in December 1619, Selden turned to Jonson for help. "We went there together in a carriage," Selden recalled, "where, since I had heard that the King was much enraged on account of that writing about the tithes, Jonson enlisted the aid of George, Earl of Buckingham, then the highest Admiral in England (afterwards Duke), a famous hero, very distinguished in the King's favor, so that he might present me in court before the King in a friendly manner, and placate him in my case. And indeed that was accomplished by the Earl, although those Bishops were resisting" (trans. from HS, XI, 384–385). For a mere poet to intervene, and prevail, in a matter of such consequence was an extraordinary coup.

The Dutch artist Abraham van Blyenberch, who painted portraits of Pembroke, Bacon, and Prince Charles between 1617 and 1620, probably executed his portrait of Jonson during the same period. Although the original of this painting has been lost, an anonymous artist made a fine copy of it prior to 1650. Since the copyist appears to have been a meticulous craftsman, we can assume that his work closely approximates van Blyenberch's original likeness.[2] The portrait shows that the middle-aged Jonson (notwithstanding his "Picture Left in Scotland") was a handsome man: he has a full head of dark brown hair, an aquiline nose, and a finely modeled, full-lipped mouth. But the artist faithfully reproduces the irregular features of his countenance as well. Jonson's face is marked with warts; his round cheeks and heavy jowls indicate that he is overweight; and, as Aubrey noted, one eye is lower and bigger than the other. The pale eyebrows, deep eye-sockets, and crease over the nose accentuate the sitter's heavy, pendulous brow. He has not been assimilated into the world of elegant gentlemen and ladies who ordinarily sat for artists like van Blyenberch. He wears none of the lace, embroidery, pleats, buttons, and jewels that

Ben Jonson, artist unknown, after Abraham van Blyenberch. Copy of a portrait probably painted while Jonson was in his late forties.

one expects to see in a formal portrait from this period—just a black woolen doublet and a flat linen collar. His eyes refuse to meet those of the artist, but instead look down and away in a furtive glance, as if to forego any easy intimacies with the viewer. He seems reluctant either to enter the painter's medium or to accept the fact of his own eminence.

Although Jonson now enjoyed more wealth and prestige than at any time in his life, he was heading into an eclipse. The note of disillusionment is already audible in the conversations with Drummond and in his savagely satirical "Epistle to a Friend, to Persuade Him to the Wars" (*Und*, 15; 1619?). By 1623, when he penned his "Epistle Answering to One That Asked to Be Sealed of the Tribe of Ben" (*Und*, 47), Jonson had become thoroughly disaffected from the court, where he gained his livelihood, and sensed his place there slipping away from him.

In sorting out the reasons for Jonson's decline one must begin by questioning the wisdom of his decision to abandon the stage. Despite his derogatory view of the playwright's profession, his best-known works were plays; despite his contempt for the common spectators, when he communicated with them in their own language he wrote comedies that have pleased many and pleased long. After 1616 Jonson was a preacher without a pulpit, and when he finally did return to the stage he was never able to reestablish a satisfactory rapport with the audience that he had relinquished a decade previously.

The King and his court were a more elite but equally fickle source of patronage, and their reception of *Pleasure Reconciled to Virtue* made it clear that they would not countenance a masque writer who lectured to them about their own morals. True, the playhouse audience preferred bombast to classical oratory; but James, if Jonson is to be believed, esteemed John Taylor, the Water Poet, more highly than Sir Philip Sidney. True, the groundlings preferred patriotic chronicle histories to grave Roman tragedies; but the King's bias in favor of Scottish themes and authors was equally chauvinistic. During the years when he depended on James for his livelihood, Jonson's major projects were his *Discovery* and his translation of Alexander Barclay's *Argenis,* a long, neo-Latin romance by a Scottish poet whom James admired. He began the first of these works in the hope of pleasing James; Chamberlain noted in 1622 that the King "hath geven order to Ben Johnson" to undertake the second.[3] Since neither work has survived, it is impossible to say whether or not they justified the effort that Jonson put into them. On the face of it, they were a waste of his talent.

More important, the course of Jonson's career was now inextricably tied to the King's fortunes. At the time of Jonson's return from Scotland, James's affairs were taking a permanent turn for the worse. The last six years of the reign saw the death of the Queen, the King's near-fatal illness of 1619, the loss of his daughter and son-in-law's kingdom in the Palatinate, the collapse of his treasury amidst accusations of graft, blistering parliamentary attacks on his most trusted ministers, and widespread public opposition to the proposed match between Prince Charles and the Spanish Infanta. By 1621 the treasury had begun suspending payments on crown pensions.⁴ After his return from Scotland, Jonson was the court poet for a court that had lost its way, an important man writing unimportant literature.

Masques celebrated the auspicious moments of court life. When the auspices were bad, as they consistently were during the twilight of James's monarchy, the commissions became more difficult to execute. The court had previously furnished Jonson with many optimistic themes and occasions. The union of England and Scotland, the investiture of Prince Henry, the realignment of the court in 1615–16, and the investiture of Prince Charles, all opened up hopeful prospects, even if the hopes they engendered turned out to be ill-founded. When Jonson celebrated these moments, he could at least maintain the pretense that he was expressing a national consensus.

By the winter of 1619–20 that pretense had worn exceedingly thin. During the previous summer James's son-in-law, Frederick, the Elector Palatine, had laid claim to the kingdom of Bohemia. When this act brought him into conflict with Spain, Frederick, who was very popular with English Protestants, turned to James for help. Even though the survival of his son-in-law's kingdom was at stake, James refused to become involved in a religious war in Europe. His seeming indifference to Frederick's plight met with widespread public opposition. "It is a strange thing," wrote the French Ambassador, "the hatred in which this King is held, in free speaking, cartoons, defamatory libels—the ordinary precursors of civil war." By 1620 London printers had begun making translations of Dutch newsletters, which were usually slanted toward the Protestant side, available to the reading public. As the crisis in the Palatinate unfolded, James not only faced political dissent in parliament; he also had to deal with an emergent opposition press and its increasingly outspoken readership. In his "Proclamation against Excess of Lavish and Licentious Speech of Matters of State" (December 24, 1620), the King warned his subjects that government policies were "no Theames, or subjects fit for vulgar persons" and commanded them to "take heede, how they intermeddle by Penne, or Speech, with causes of State, and secrets of Empire, either at home, or abroad."⁵ Jonson reiterated these admonitions in his later Twelfth Night masques. As Sara Pearl has shown, these works consistently take the position that "comment on matters of state was beyond the capacities of ordinary people, that such matters involved a concept of higher truth available only to James."⁶

In *News from the New World Discovered in the Moon* (1619–20), his first Twelfth Night masque since returning from Scotland, Jonson portrays himself as a minor celebrity ("one of our greatest Poets"), a man who attracts the attention of a Printer, a Chronicler, and a Factor of News.

This trio exhibits the intrusive curiosity and aggressive marketing techniques that provoked James's proclamation of 1620. The Printer will pay "anything for a good Copie now, be it true or false, so't be newes"; the Chronicler seeks "matter of State . . . to fill up my great booke"; the Factor is well supplied with "my Puritan newes, my Protestant newes, and my Pontificiall newes." Jonson, however, refuses to cooperate with them. As the Printer remarks, "he has been restive, they say . . . for we have had nothing from him; he has set out nothing, I am sure." [7]

The Printer's informants were not entirely accurate—Jonson had in fact been writing, but he had been avoiding the printers and had withheld all of the masques he had written since the 1616 folio from the reading public. The Printer's complaint would not appear in print until 1640, three years after Jonson's death. Jonson's "news" of 1619–20 was intended exclusively for the ears of the King and his court. As James retreated into the seclusion of his inner circle, Jonson withdrew from the literary marketplace.

He assures the courtiers attending the first performance of *News from the New World Discovered in the Moon* that there is "no newes," that nothing has changed. He banishes the specter of novelty by invoking James, the unmoved mover who imparts change yet never undergoes it. In the presence of this infinite source the noble dancers could just as well go on forever:

> for he
> That did this motion give,
> And made it so long live,
> Could likewise give it perpetuitie.

The astronomical imagery of *News from the New World* likens the King "to a physical principle," Orgel comments, "pure potential, through whom the ultimate scientific mysteries of perpetual motion and infinite power are finally explained." [8] Jonson expands the scope of James's sovereignty by sealing it off from history; he situates James in a kingdom that has neither past nor future but remains continuously subservient to the operations of his sovereign will.

Jonson no longer conceived of the court as embodying a particular ideological or ethical stance; instead, his late masques seek to remove James and his entourage from the sphere of political discourse and heroic action altogether. *Pan's Anniversary,* which he composed for James's fifty-fourth birthday on June 19, 1620, transforms the court into the site of pastoral leisure: "All Envious, and Prophane, away, / This is the Shepherds Holyday." The genre of pastoral (a recurrent theme in the conversations with Drummond) gave Jonson access to a literary tradition that was both antiheroic and self-contained. In James's birthday masque, Jonson adopts the mask of the pastoral singer who forsakes representational realism and self-consciously echoes the songs of his predecessors. James becomes Pan, the good shepherd who teaches his Arcadian courtiers "the rites of true socie-tie": "*Pan* is our All, by him we breath, wee live, / Wee move, we are."[9]

Jonson addressed these affectionate tributes to a lonely old man who desperately needed to be loved by his son and by Buck-ingham. The most important political event in the late Jacobean court was the love affair between James and his youthful favorite; but the story of "Dad's" affection for his "humble slave and dogge" did not lend itself to a public, ceremonial presentation.[10] Jonson's sense of probity, to say noth-ing of the King's, would have restrained him from writing a Twelfth Night masque about the qualities that had made Buckingham into a great man (his looks, his gaiety, his luck). But on one occasion, and one occasion only, Jonson cast discretion to the winds and celebrated the relationship that was rapidly turning into a nationwide scandal.

The Gypsies Metamorphosed was privately commissioned by Buck-ingham in the summer of 1621. It likens the Earl, his family, and his re-tainers to a band of gypsies who are "metamorphosed" into great court-iers by the magic of the King's favor. The analogy is inescapable, for Buckingham and his followers played the parts of gypsies in the anti-masque—parts that would have gone to professional actors in an ordinary masque. Since gypsies were regarded as pariahs, the comparison appears to be an unflattering one; one modern scholar has even argued that Jonson was deliberately satirizing Buckingham. But why would the Earl, to say nothing of his relatives and retainers, commission and perform in a masque that put him in a bad light? Gypsies were paradoxical figures in Stuart England. Despite a long tradition of moralizing commentary berat-ing them for their indolent ways, they held a deep fascination for Jonson and his contemporaries. If gypsies were scapegoats, they were also folk heroes. Because it was their fate to be idle, they came to be seen as a race of merrymen who voiced a truth that the moralists could not fathom: better to be lucky than diligent, better to play than to work. Dekker's enormously popular pamphlet *Lanthorn and Candlelight* (1608; revised as *With Canting Songs,* 1620) already had transformed the gypsy into a likable comic hero; Jonson's courtier gypsies carried the process of assim-ilation a stage further. The *"Kings Gypsies"* exemplify the Stuart ethic of "sport" in its radical form. Theirs is the merriest England of all, a true land of Cockaigne where appetite reigns supreme and self-indulgent play takes the place of work.[11]

Above: A chalk drawing of Buckingham, by Peter Paul Rubens, ca. 1625.

Opposite: *James I,* by Daniel Mytens, ca. 1621. The King's face shows the effects of age and care. James's happiness now depended on the affection of his favorite and lover, Buckingham.

The gypsy's widespread appeal raises a further question: why would Jonson have wanted to celebrate the risqué charms of James's favorite? By the summer of 1621 Buckingham had discarded his former backer Pembroke and was rapidly becoming one of the most hated men in England. Bear in mind, however, that Buckingham had done Jonson a handsome favor just a year and a half earlier, when the Earl interceded with the King on behalf of Selden. Moreover, Buckingham commissioned *The Gypsies Metamorphosed* at a time when Jonson was badly in need of money. On June 1, 1621, Jonson had assigned the next two payments of his pension to a creditor named John Hull (HS, I, 236); just three weeks later Buckingham paid him an advance of a hundred pounds (more than twice his usual fee) to prepare the masque (HS, X, 613). Jonson needed to repay these favors.

He wrote *The Gypsies Metamorphosed,* which was not published until after his death, for a private occasion in a remote corner of England. Buckingham had recently acquired Lady Bedford's stately home at Burley-on-the-Hill, in Rutland; the purpose of the masque was to welcome King James when he visited him there in August of 1621. The intimate setting of this entertainment permitted a degree of frankness that would have been out of place at Whitehall. Many of the spectators at Burley must have known that Buckingham was the King's lover. Just four months previously Sir Henry Yelverton had stunned the House of Lords by comparing him to Hugh Spencer, the homosexual favorite of Edward II. Buckingham himself alludes to this side of their relationship in letters like the one asking James if he still remembered "the time which I shall never forget at Farnham, wher the bed's head could not be found between the master and his dog." Members of their inner circle must have admired the cheek of Jonson's "Porter" when he declared to James, at the entryway to Buckingham's new abode, "The *Master* is your Creature, as the *Place,*" and invited the King to take possession of his own: "please you enter / *Him,* and his house, and searche him to the Center." [12] Public references to this love affair (Yelverton's, for example) were of course likely to incur the wrath of the law; but in the privacy of Buckingham's new home, the same innuendo could be a source of delight, and a mark of the favorite's freedom from ordinary moral constraints.

Once James entered the house, he assumed the place of its lord and master, and Buckingham took the role of a Gypsy Captain who pays him a surprise visit. The host's disguise made an apt commentary on his actual relationship to the King. Like the real-life court favorite, the Gypsy Captain has no place in the social hierarchy. Both gypsies and court favorites are marginal beings, but their very marginality gives them an empowering and attractive freedom. When a clown asks one of the courtier gypsies,

"How Came your Captaines place firste to be Called the *Devills arse?*" (1034–36), the captain replies by singing a ballad explaining how their ancestral "place" got its curious name. Here, as in the Porter's speech, Jonson is punning on the multiple senses of the word "place," which can signify either a residence, a position in the social hierarchy, or a particular spot on the body.

The gypsy ballad is a story about Cock Lorel, the captain's forebear and the early Tudor prototype of the rogue hero. It describes what happened when Cock had the devil to dinner at the Devil's Arse, a famous cave in the Derbyshire hills, and a site that Jonson probably visited in the course of his wanderings. The framework of the ballad evokes and parodies the event commemorated by *The Gypsies Metamorphosed:* the great vassal (Cock Lorel, Buckingham) has his liege lord (the devil, King James) to supper at his stately hilltop home in the north of England. In the primordial version of this revel Cock becomes Cook Lorel and serves the devil a banquet consisting of (among other things) poached Puritan, promoter in plum broth, usurer stewed in his own marrow, Justice of the Peace trussed with two clerks, lawyer's head in green sauce, two roasted sheriffs, and Lord Mayor stuffed with pudding of maintenance. Cock's feast is a carnivalesque version of the journey into Hell Mouth. His infernal guest gaily devours the urban middle classes and transforms them into excrement: "All which he blewe away with a fart, / From whence it was called the *Devills arse.*" [13] The Ballad of Cock Lorel reaffirms the innocence of the King and his entourage: no one in the court will be eaten by the devil. But it also acknowledges—and gratifies—their own wish to devour Puritans, promoters, usurers, and overfed Lord Mayors.

The Gypsies Metamorphosed enjoyed a stunning success. It had a repeat performance at Belvoir, the Earl of Rutland's nearby estate, on August 5. Later that year, there was still a third performance at Windsor, and Jonson revised the text so that the gypsies could read the fortunes of the courtiers who attended James while he was there. Seventeenth-century readers would transcribe the Ballad of Cock Lorel more often than any other poem by Jonson. On September 15 the Reverend Joseph Mead wrote to Sir Martin Stutevile that Jonson was to be "knighted, but scaped it narrowly, for that his majestie would have done it, had there not been means made (himself not unwilling) to avoid it." Shortly thereafter, Jonson was granted a patent for the reversion of the Mastership of the Revels in the event that Sir George Buc, the incumbent, and Sir John Astley, who was next in line, died before he did. Chamberlain heard that Jonson's pension had been increased "from a 100 marks to 200 pounds" per year.[14]

The glow of success pales, however, on closer scrutiny. Jonson did not want the knighthood, he never obtained the Mastership of the Revels, and

The Devil's Arse. From an eighteenth-century map by Charles Rice. A central locale in *The Gypsies Metamorphosed,* Jonson's masque about the relationship of James and Buckingham. Jonson had probably visited the Devil's Arse by 1621.

the rumor that his pension had been increased turned out to be inaccurate. Moreover, his masterpiece of 1621 was, to all appearances, a cynical poem written at the behest of a cynical man for an exorbitant fee: Jonson's success came at the expense of the high moral posture he had adopted in the 1616 folio. *The Gypsies Metamorphosed,* the most brilliant of Jonson's later works, has the allure of forbidden fruit: it was irresistible, but it was not intended for public consumption. It caused a sensation, but Jonson did not attempt to repeat the experiment.

By the autumn of 1621 James was finding it difficult to remunerate his own pensioners. The gypsy who read the palm of Lord Treasurer Cranfield during the Windsor performance of *The Gypsies Metamorphosed* optimistically predicted that Cranfield would "putt all that have pensions soone out of their paine, / By bringing th'Exchequer in Creditt againe"; but the best way to restore the credit of the Exchequer was to suspend payments on royal pensions—a policy that could only aggravate the pensioners' pain.[15]

The depleted state of James's treasury may explain why Jonson began writing versified begging letters during the waning years of the reign. Two of these poems are addressed to the very officials who dispensed funds within the royal household. His "Epistle to Mr. Arthur Squib," a teller in the Exchequer, is both a request for five pounds and a promissory note for that sum: "Take this letter / For your securitie. I can no better" (*Und,* 54.19–20). The ink that John Burgess, another clerk in the Exchequer, gave to Jonson represented a more modest outlay, but it too could only be repaid in kind. Jonson apologizes that "since the Wine hath steep'd my braine, / I only can the Paper staine." Yet in the poet's hands even mere ink becomes "a Dye, that feares no Moth, / But Scarlet-like out-lasts the Cloth" (*Und,* 55.5–6, 7–8).

The Masque of Augurs (1621–22) openly alludes to the anemic state of the King's finances and raises the question of whether Jonson's creativity is not "drawne drie" as well. The antimasque begins in the Court Butteryhatch, where a bargeman warns a brewer's clerk not to go too near the King "least you chance to have a Tally made of your pate, and bee clawed with a cudgell." A moment later, the clerk accuses a groom of pilfering the players' bread and beer and of stealing torches from the chandlery: "Come, this is not the first time you have carried coales to your owne house." To make matters worse, the clerk has heard that "neither the Kings Poet, nor his Architect had wherewithall left to entertaine so much as a Baboone of quality." His friend Vangoose, a "Projector of Masques," confirms that Jonson and Jones have run out of inspiration: "Dat is all true, exceeding true . . . dey have no ting, no ting van deir owne, but vat dey take vrom de eard, or de zea, or de heaven, or de hell, or de rest van de veir Elementen." But Vangoose's substitute antimasque, a bizarre display of "all de brave error in de world," illustrates the futility of ignoring nature and introducing costly monstrosities in her place.[16]

Jonson proceeded to show the court that he retained the capacity to interpret the language of nature. Augurs had the gift of divining the meanings that lay hidden in the seemingly random movements of natural phenomena. After Vangoose vainly attempts to confect symbolic meanings by hoisting monsters and machines onto the floor of the Banqueting Hall,

Apollo exhorts the courtly masquers to imitate the mysterious tracery of the lightning and the birds:

> Which way, and whence the lightning flew,
> Or how it burned, bright, and blew,
> Designe, and figure by your lights:
> Then forth, and shew the severall flights
> Your Birds have made, or what the wing,
> Or voice in Augurie doth bring.   (346–351)

The court cannot improve its self-image by importing exotic symbols; but for those who have eyes to see and ears to hear, meaning is everywhere and the auspices are favorable. The dancers enact a visual riddle, or *imprese*, like Jonson's broken compass. At the heart of the riddle lies the dual emblem of Jove and Apollo, who are also King James and Prince Charles, the past and the future: "Still, still the Auspice is so good, / We wish it were but understood" (394–395). For those who can read them aright, riddles are good luck charms. Jonson's antimasque pokes fun at the naysayers of 1621–22, while gently suggesting that the court would fare more jovially if its beer and torches were distributed more equitably; the main masque declares that the omens are good for those who have the gift of augury.

Many of King James's subjects continued to see the future in a radically different light, and they were increasingly bold about stating their views in public. James's plan to marry Prince Charles to the Spanish Infanta was anathema to everyone at all sympathetic to the Puritan side, and the opposition took its case to the stage and the printing presses. The King's edict "Against Excess of Lavish and Licentious Speech of Matters of State" had little effect. A second proclamation, issued a year and a half later, stated that "notwithstanding the strictnesse of Our commandement, the inordinate libertie of unreverent speech, touching matters of high nature, unfit for vulgar discourse, doth daily more and more increase." [17] Nevertheless, pro-Puritan newsletters continued to appear on a weekly basis. In *Time Vindicated to Himself and to His Honors,* the Twelfth Night masque for 1622–23, Jonson returns to the subject of bad art and singles out lavish and licentious speech as his principal target.

The thrust of Jonson's attack falls upon "Chronomastix," a "gentleman-like *Satyre*" who is modeled upon the contemporary poet George Wither. Wither had popularized a new concept of the satirist's vocation, and Jonson did not like it. The satyr who snarls and bites his way through the pages of Marston and Hall, and of *Every Man out of His Humour,* is a malcontent intellectual addressing a relatively narrow audience of people who share, or are concerned about, his plight. Wither retained the pose of moral superiority, but cast aside the unwieldy baggage of bad manners and self-irony. Compared to his predecessors, he sounds positively genteel. By making the satirist into a "gentleman," Wither also turned him into a popular figure. He boasted that *Wither's Motto* sold thirty thousand copies during the first few months after it was published. Whereas Marston, Hall, and Jonson had renounced satire and moved into the establishment, Wither became a folk hero to the newly literate urban readership. He also gave the satirist's diatribe a doctrinaire cast. Wither belonged to the reformist wing of the Anglican Church (he later became a militant Puritan), and openly contested James's pro-Spanish policies. A few months after the publication of *Wither's Motto* he was called before the House of Lords, and subsequently imprisoned, on the grounds that his satire had violated the King's proclamation "Against Excess of Lavish and Licentious Speech of Matters of State." [18]

Wither's antigovernment stance was threatening because of his popularity, and popularity is the trait that Jonson singles out in his lampoon of him. Chronomastix's base of operations is St. Paul's Cathedral, the ecclesiastical center of the city and the favored haunt of booksellers and gossips. His works are published by a subterranean "printer in disguise" who "keepes / His presse in a hollow tree" and "workes by glow-worme light"—early editions of *Wither's Motto* had no title page. He gets a veneer of legitimacy from a schoolmaster (in reality, Alexander Gill of St. Paul's) who "is turning all his workes . . . into *Latine*" and "calls him the times *Juvenal*." When Fame, the legitimate arbitress of literary worth, spurns Chronomastix ("Away, I know thee not, wretched Impostor"), he appeals to the popular audience to vouch for his greatness: "The Sempster hath sate still as I pass'd by, / And dropt her needle! Fish-wives staid their cry!" The "pudding-wife, that would despise the Times" takes her cue from the gentleman satyr, and passes the word "into the Chamber-maid, / And she unto her Lady," who exacerbates the problem by sending him pensions.[19]

Wither epitomized everything that Jonson despised. He appealed to a popular, rather than an elite, audience; he was literate but not learned; his geographical base lay in St. Paul's and the city rather than Westminster and the country manor house; he was reform-minded and sympathetic to the Puritan cause. Hitherto, Jonson had refrained from satirizing individuals in his court masques, but Wither was too inviting a target to pass up. Jonson's audacity led him, ironically enough, to commit the very offense for which he castigated Chronomastix. Five weeks after the performance on January 19, 1623, Chamberlain wrote to Carleton that Jonson was "like to heare of it on both sides of the head for personating George withers a poet or poetaster as he termes him, as hunting after fame by beeing a cronomastix or whipper of the time, which is become so tender an argument that it must not be touched either in jest or earnest" (HS, X, 648). The terms of Jonson's employment left him little room in which to maneuver. His natural instinct was to vindicate the times by satirizing the voices of dissent; but the court had become so sensitive about its own unpopularity that the issue could "not be touched either in jest or earnest."

In the midst of his tedious quarrel with Wither, the publication of *Mr. William Shakespeare's Comedies, Histories, and Tragedies* in 1623 reopened the central rivalry of Jonson's career. Although he had previously sneered at Shakespeare's artistry, the publication of the 1623 folio made it possible for him to view Shakespeare as a figure rather like himself. Since his own *Works* of 1616 had set the precedent for a book of this kind, the publication of Shakespeare's first folio represented a triumph of sorts for Jonson. The realization that Shakespeare's plays transcended the medium of performance, and belonged in print, bore out Jonson's lifelong contention that plays are (or should be) a serious form of literature. Moreover, the men who prepared the folio for the press (and Jonson may well have been one of them) remade Shakespeare in Jonson's image. Heminge's and Condell's prefatory letter "To the Great Variety of Readers" echoes Jonson's Induction to *Bartholomew Fair*, his preface to *The Alchemist*, his epigram "To My Bookseller," and his *Discoveries*. The prefatory poems by Jonson, Hugh Holland, James Mabbe, and Leonard Digges transform Shakespeare into a specifically literary figure whose works have achieved the status of modern classics; the closest analogue to these tributes are the poems prefixed to Jonson's 1616 folio.[20]

The scribes who prepared the copy for the Shakespeare folio abandoned the "light pointing" or "playhouse punctuation" of the Shakespeare quartos and adopted the so-called logical pointing that Jonson had employed in his *Works*. The extensive use of parentheses, semicolons, and end-stopped lines in the 1623 folio owes more to Jonson's example than to Shakespeare's habits of composition. The Shakespearean line that Jonson singled out as particularly ridiculous ("Caesar never did wrong, but with just cause") does not appear, interestingly enough, in the folio; it has been replaced by the unexceptionably logical "*Caesar* doth not wrong, nor without cause / Will he be satisfied."[21]

Jonson's tribute "To the Memory of My Beloved, the AUTHOR Mr. William Shakespeare and What He Hath Left Us" announces that the time has come to treat Shakespeare as an object of literary criticism. Anyone, he declares, can sing Shakespeare's praises; but uninformed praise could just as well be the result of "seeliest Ignorance" or "blinde Affection" or even "crafty Malice." Instead, he offers a critique of Shakespeare's dramatic poetry. He refrains from comparing him to the great English narrative poets ("I will not lodge thee by / *Chaucer,* or *Spenser,*") but rather sets him alongside his "peers," the leading playwrights of the mid-Elizabethan era, noting "how farre thou didst our *Lily* out-shine / Or sporting *Kid,* or *Marlowes* mighty line." Ranging farther afield, Jonson argues that although Shakespare himself "hadst small *Latine* and lesse *Greeke,*" he nonetheless challenges comparison with the great playwrights of Greece and Rome. His eulogist need not seek

> For names; but call forth thund'ring *Aeschilus,*
>   *Euripides,* and *Sophocles* to us,
> *Paccuvius, Accius,* him of *Cordova* dead,
>   To life againe, to heare thy Buskin tread,
> And shake a Stage: Or, when thy Sockes were on,
>   Leave thee alone, for the comparison
> Of all, that insolent *Greece,* or haughtie *Rome*
>   Sent forth, or since did from their ashes come.

Jonson reminds the reader that Shakespeare was an actor as well as a playwright. He "makes performance a metaphor for the creation of literature," Sara Van den Berg observes, and summons the Greek playwrights to be Shakespeare's audience. The paradox of the native genius who rivals the best that insolent Greece or haughty Rome has to offer leads, in turn, to Jonson's central assertion. Recalling the familiar antithesis of nature (or original genius) versus art (or study), he attributes Shakespeare's greatness to his unrivaled grasp of nature: she herself "was proud of his designes, / And joy'd to weare the dressing of his lines." Yet he also insists that his "Art / . . . must enjoy a part," and maintains that Shakespeare was a careful reviser of his own work. The concluding apotheosis transforms him into the "Starre of *Poets,*" whom Jonson implores to "influence, chide, or cheere the drooping Stage." [22]

Much of what Jonson has to say in this poem is strikingly at odds with his previous references to Shakespeare, to the earlier Elizabethan dramatists, to actor-playwrights, and to *"presumers on their owne Naturalls."* Heretofore, he had always championed the cause of art and had repeatedly chastised the popular playwrights of his day for relying on their own raw talent; now Jonson turned the tables and praised Shakespeare for the very qualities he had derided in the past. Since Plato, Aristotle, Cicero, and Seneca had all ascribed primary importance to "nature," in the sense of "talent" or "genius," Jonson's reappraisal remained within the broad tradition of classical criticism. But his willingness to grant that Shakespeare actually satisfied this criterion comes as a surprise and has even prompted critics to question his sincerity. Readers invariably seize upon the phrase "small *Latine* and lesse *Greeke,*" which sounds dismissive and patronizing when taken out of context; Dryden even characterizes Jonson's eulogy as an "insolent, sparing, and invidious panegyric." [23]

Such misreadings betray a deep-rooted reluctance, which is shared by many of Jonson's warmest admirers, to grant that he could ever change his mind. In this case, however, there is reason to believe that he did so. A younger Jonson had every incentive to underestimate his rival's achievement. By 1623, however, seven years had passed since Shakespeare's death and Jonson's own withdrawal from the stage; moreover, he had now had an opportunity to read the texts of eighteen plays by Shakespeare that had not appeared in print prior to the folio. Jonson "lov'd the man" (*Disc,* 654); he had enough sagacity to love the plays as well, once the full body of work was set before him. By 1623 Jonson was in an excellent position to appreciate the ironies of his own career pattern. Unlike Shakespeare, he had used the stage as a stepping-stone to a position at court, and the court had diverted his energy into projects that were largely trivial. During his formative years in the 1590s Jonson had scorned Lyly, Kyd, Marlowe, and Spenser. From his current standpoint he could see that they, like Shakespeare, had come forward at the moment when "all the *Muses* still were in their prime" (*UV,* 26.44) and created a national literature. And so had he: in celebrating the greatness of Shakespeare and his era, Jonson was reaffirming the reputation of Shakespeare's only serious rival.

It is an irony of literary history that future readers not only accepted Jonson's claim about Shakespeare's "natural" genius, but also turned it into an indictment of Jonson, the plodding and laborious exponent of "art." In the eyes of posterity Jonson's "principal function," as Harry Levin says, "has been to serve as a stalking horse for Shakespeare. Others abide our question, Shakespeare transcends it; and if you would understand, point for point, the limitations he transcends, go read Jonson." [24]

The terms of this comparison are foreshadowed in the earliest engravings of the two men. Consider first the famous portrait that Martin Droeshout engraved for the 1623 folio of Shakespeare's works. Nothing in this engraving would lead one to suppose that Shakespeare was a poet. He appears simply to be a prosperous, confident Jacobean gentleman. The fancy pleated collar (it was called a "whisk") leaps to the viewer's attention; one also notices the shoulder crescents, the intricate embroidery on the shiny taffeta doublet, and the row of fancy gold buttons down the bodice. Apart from the hint of a smile, the smooth, unmarked face is quite nondescript. Robert Vaughan's likeness of Jonson, which was done between 1622 and 1627, goes to the opposite extreme. The format of Vaughan's engraving derives from the engraved portraits of monarchs and "worthies" that were collected in Henry Holland's *Baziliologia* (1617) and *Heroologia* (1620).[25] The Latin motto inscribed in the oval border informs the viewer that this is "the true likeness of the most learned of English poets, Ben Jonson." The rectangular frame, the ornamental enclosure, the laurel wreath, the books at the lower corners of the oval, and the words on the pedestal effectively confine Jonson within the context of that description.

The face enclosed within the oval is the one that van Blyenberch had painted in the recent past. Vaughan seems to have based his work either on the lost van Blyenberch portrait or a copy of it; when the engraving was printed the features were reversed, so that the head is now tilted toward the left. In adapting his predecessor's work, Vaughan altered Jonson's countenance so as to make it appear somewhat older: the lines by the nose and mouth are more heavily accented, the cleft in the chin is more pronounced, the head is balder, and the hair is flecked with gray. As befits his august station, Jonson is now attired in a taffeta doublet with shoulder crescents and a row of buttons down the bodice; his cape is draped over his arm, and he is holding a pair of gloves. Vaughan has raised the sitter's eyes so that they look directly at us; they are morose and ponderous. In contrast to Shakespeare's piercing, self-contented gaze, Jonson has the look of a man who is resigned to his fate.

By his fiftieth birthday Jonson had begun work on a sequel to *The Forest.* "A Satirical Shrub," which Jonson wrote when he was "at fifty yeares, almost," and its companion piece "A Little Shrub Growing By," indicate by their titles that as of 1622 he had decided to entitle his new verse miscellany *The Underwood.* During the next two years, he wrote, or completed, at least four of the most ambitious poems in this anthology: *A Celebration of Charis in Ten Lyric Pieces,* "An Epistle Answering to One That Asked to Be Sealed of the Tribe of Ben," "An Execration upon Vulcan," and "An Elegy" ("Let me be what I am").[26]

What prompted this outburst of creative energy? The passing of his fiftieth birthday apparently stimulated Jonson's imagination, for the subject of his age or, more broadly, of his longevity and capacity for survival is an important theme in all these poems. Jonson had now reached a stage of life where personal relationships were more important to him than professional ones. Unlike its predecessors, *Epigrams* and *The Forest, The Underwood* focuses on Jonson's private life—on his amours (real or imagined), his friendships, and his personal misfortunes. "Ben," the new persona whom he invented for this miscellany, is much more forthcoming about his idiosyncrasies and emotional needs than is his counterpart in the

Mr. WILLIAM

SHAKESPEARES

COMEDIES,
HISTORIES, &
TRAGEDIES.

Publiſhed according to the True Originall Copies.

LONDON
Printed by Iſaac Iaggard, and Ed. Blount. 1623.

William Shakespeare, by Martin Droeshout. From *Mr. William Shakespeare's Comedies, Histories, and Tragedies*, 1623. Jonson's old rival became increasingly famous after the publication of the 1623 folio.

BEN. IOHNSONII. ✳ VERA EFFIGIES DOCTISSIMI POETARVM ANGLORVM

Ro: Vaughan fecit.

Johnſoni typus, ecce!qui furoris,   Defuncta Pater Eruditionis,
Antiſtes ſacer, Enthei, Camenis,   Et Scenæ veteris novator audax.
Vindex Jngenij recens Sepulti,   Nec fœlix minus,aut minus politus
Antiquæ reparator vnus artis,   Cui solus similis, Figura,viv et.
     O could there be an art found out that might
     Produce his ſhape ſoe lively as to Write. Ab:Holl:

Are to be ſould in Popes head alley at the white horſe by Geo: Humble.

Ben Jonson, by Robert Vaughan, 1622–1627. The earliest datable likeness of Jonson. The inscription styles him the most learned of English poets.

1616 folio. In the poems of 1623, Ben pursues a love affair with a beautiful lady who attends the Queen, and he inducts his "sons" into the Tribe of Ben. Like almost all of the verse in *The Underwood,* these poems were not intended for the reading public but for a select circle of intimates who could respond to Ben on a personal level without being swayed by the vagaries of court life or the literary marketplace. The flora in *The Underwood* did not advance Jonson's career; they provided him with a respite from it.

Ben's "Excuse for Loving," the first lyric in the *Charis* sequence, acknowledges that he is now "fiftie yeares" old, but argues that

> it is not always face,
> Clothes, or Fortune gives the grace;
> Or the feature, or the youth:
> But the Language, and the Truth,
> With the Ardor, and the Passion,
> Gives the Lover weight, and fashion.

The claim that Ben's poetic "Language" can compensate for his physical unattractiveness figures in several of the poems in *The Underwood.* If the lady in "My Picture Left in Scotland" had listened rather than looked, she would have heard verses that are as mellifluous "as hath the youngest Hee, / That sits in shadow of *Apollo's* tree." After warning Lady Covell that her new "servant" is fat and old, "laden with Bellie, and doth hardly approach / His friends, but to breake Chaires, or cracke a Coach," he assures her that his "muse is one, can tread the Aire, / And stroke the water, nimble, chast, and faire." "I am not so voluminous, and vast," he writes to Burlase, "But there are lines, wherewith I might be embrac'd." [27]

Charis tells the story of Ben's attempt to put this theory into practice. When Ben first encounters Charis, in a medievalized *reverdie,* she reduces him to the level of a foolish old man ("*Cupids* Statue with a Beard"). But he transcends the liabilities of age by deifying his mistress in the masque-like lyric stanzas that form the centerpiece of the sequence:

> Have you seene but a bright Lillie grow,
> Before rude hands have touch'd it?
> Have you mark'd but the fall o'the Snow
> Before the soyle hath smutch'd it?

Although Charis will find it persuasive, Ben's celebration of her is cast in a register of loss and disillusionment. As soon as he touches, marks, smudges the object of his desire, she will lose the maidenly perfection that excites his ardor. This scenario is even clearer in the manuscript variant of the last two lines: "Have you tasted virginitie? / O so yong, o so streight, O so chast, so chast is shee!" When Charis does grant Ben sexual favors, nostalgia recedes before the banality of everyday life. The ornate verse forms of the earlier sections are replaced by *vers de société;* the goddess becomes a coquette; Ben and Charis turn into Alceste and Célimène.[28]

The sequel to *Charis,* and the prototype of the Platonized love poetry that he would write in the last decade of his life, is "An Elegy," written about a year after *Charis* was completed. The speaker in "An Elegy" renounces sexual love and claims his place among the disinterested lovers of beauty. "Let me be what I am," he begins,

> as *Virgil* cold;
> As *Horace* fat; or as *Anacreon* old;
> No Poets verses yet did ever move,
> Whose Readers did not thinke he was in love.
> Who shall forbid me then in Rithme to bee
> As light, and active as the youngest hee.

Despite the disapproval of "Fathers, and Husbands," he claims "a right / In all that is call'd lovely," while still insisting that he does not lust after their daughters and wives. After spending "twentie yeare" at court, he can assess its finery with equanimity: "I have leave to span."[29]

If the middle-aged Jonson regarded his love affairs as a game, a masquerade that involved him in a world of pretense and artifice, he was altogether serious about his friendships with other men. The word "friend" hardly ever appears in *Epigrams* and *The Forest,* and apart from "Inviting a Friend to Supper" (*Ep,* 101), it does not occur in the title of any poem published in the 1616 folio; but twelve of the poems printed in *The Underwood* are verse letters from Jonson to his friends, and two more, "An Ode" (26) and the epigram "To a Friend and Son" (69), closely resemble them. These poems focus on questions of reciprocity and indebtedness: what do he and his friends owe one another? In the case of Sir Edward Sackville (13), Mr. Arthur Squib (45) and the anonymous recipient of *Underwood* 17, the friend has lent or given Jonson money; since the poet lacks the wherewithal to repay his friend in cash, he sends a verse epistle as a kind of substitute. Jonson recognized the hazards of such transactions; as a playwright and satirist, he had written often about the corrosive effects of purchased friendship. In these epistles he seeks out an alternative to the base exchange of flattery for cash: instead of complimenting his benefactors, Jonson sends them excerpts from ancient texts on friendship. He repays Sackville with a lengthy verse paraphrase of Seneca's *Of Benefits,* the seminal treatise on gift giving; borrowing a leaf from Plutarch, he shows Mr. Squib *How to Tell Flatterers;* he excuses his failure to reimburse the "friend" of *Underwood* 17 by appealing to the authority of Aristotle's *Nicomachean Ethics.*[30]

In stressing the distinction between flattery and friendship, expediency and benevolence, Jonson made yet another attempt to disengage himself from the patronage system on which he depended. The very word "friend" was equivocal in this regard. Contemporaries ordinarily used it to designate a confederate, a backer, or a person who could be counted on for assistance. The eighteenth-century (and modern) sense of "friend" as "one who comforts you and supports you while others do not" or one "with whom to compare minds and cherish private virtues" (Dr. Johnson) was largely absent in early modern England. This was a society where, in Stone's estimation, most individuals "found it very difficult to establish close emotional ties to any other person."[31]

Jonson does not simply anticipate the more intimate usage of the word "friend"; he also writes about the obstacles that made it difficult for men like himself to form affective ties with other individuals. Two particularly lucid meditations on this theme, "An Ode" (*Und*, 26) and "Epistle to a Friend" (*Und*, 37), reveal the ways in which the man who bragged to Drummond that "he would not flatter though he saw death" attempted to criticize his friends without estranging them. He acknowledges that

> It is an Act of tyrannie, not love,
>   In practiz'd friendship wholly to reprove,
>   As flatt'ry with friends humours still to move. (37.25–27)

He therefore strives for a form of utterance that strikes a midpoint between compliment and criticism. "I send nor Balmes, nor Cor'sives to your wound," he explains to the "high-spirited friend" (1) of *Underwood* 26: "Yet doth some wholsome Physick for the mind, / Wrapt in this paper lie" (9–10). Like the Sidney birthday ode, "High-Spirited Friend" combines the stanzaic form of a Pindaric ode with the content of a moralizing verse letter. Jonson commemorates his friend's victory in a duel by advising him to show more restraint in the future.

By the early 1620s Jonson was presiding over a club of friends that met in the Apollo Room of the Devil and St. Dunstan Tavern near Temple Bar. Borrowing from the verse epistles of Horace and Martial, he devised for the benefit of the group a set of *Leges Convivales*, translated by Alexander Brome as *Ben Jonson's Sociable Rules for the Apollo*. Jonson also provided a poem of welcome inscribed next to the terra-cotta bust of Apollo that stood over the door. The Apollo Room was a sanctuary dedicated to the ritualized reenactment of antique ceremonies and sealed off from the alien popular culture represented by the likes of George Wither and Alexander Gill. Drayton's ode "The Sacrifice to Apollo" depicts the room as the modern descendant of the temple at Delphi: "This for the *Delphian* Prophets is prepar'd: / The prophane Vulgar are from hence debar'd." The lines that Jonson wrote to go over the doorway draw the same comparison: "Wel-

Bust of Apollo, attributed to Edward Marshall, early seventeenth century. This bust stood above the door of the Apollo Room in the Devil Tavern, where the Tribe of Ben congregated during the 1620s.

come all, who lead or follow, / To the Oracle of Apollo." The role of high priest would have come naturally to Jonson by his early fifties. He had called upon Apollo for inspiration in many poems; just a year previously the "sons" of Apollo had danced before their father in Jonson's *Masque of Augurs*. Thomas Randolph's "Gratulatory to Mr. Ben Johnson for His Adopting of Him to Be His Son" shows that Jonson did indeed preside over rites initiating his adoptive "sons" into the ancient fraternity of poets. "Thou hast given me pow'r to call / *Phoebus* himselfe my grandsire," Randolph proudly writes, "by this graunt / Each Sister of the nine is made my Aunt."[32]

"An Epistle Answering to One That Asked to Be Sealed of the Tribe of Ben" conducts an initiate into the Jonson cult on a journey to the center of Ben's inmost self. In the main, satirical section of the poem Ben leads the novice through the vestiges of false selfhood that he must now renounce. Here they encounter the tavern companions who assemble to boast about their drinking and whoring, and "jeast / On all Soules that are absent; even the dead," and the time-servers who preoccupy themselves with the latest news. Ben's attitude toward the clamorous debate over James's foreign policy is identical to the position he adopts in his masques of 1620–1623. He unquestioningly follows "my Kings desire" and refuses to venture any opinion whatever about the great issues of the day. "What is't to me," he asks, "Whether the Dispensation yet be sent, / Or that the Match from *Spaine* was ever meant?" Nevertheless, "if, for honour, we must draw the Sword," Ben will fight "without inquirie." Despite his disdain for news, Ben weaves in enough factual information to provide a fairly precise idea of when the poem was written. The year is 1623, Prince Charles will shortly return from Spain, and Ben has been excluded from the "mysterie of reception" that will welcome him home, even though he is no less deserving than his rival Inigo, who "guides the Motions, and directs the beares."[33] Ben too must submit to rites of purification, voicing his vexation with the ins and outs of court politics so that he may put them behind him.

In the concluding section of "The Tribe of Ben," Ben grows laconic as he unveils his inmost self:

> Well, with mine owne fraile Pitcher, what to doe
> I have decreed; keepe it from waves, and presse;
>   Lest it be justled, crack'd, made nought, or lesse:
> Live to that point I will, for which I am man,
>   And dwell as in my Center, as I can.   (56–60)

The spareness of Ben's language masks a remarkably rich range of connotations. Moving away from the "waves, and presse," his body becomes a fragile vessel, bearing its invisible cargo across the hazardous seas of life. The frail pitcher seeks out calm, uncrowded waters, just as Ben withdraws into his center, out of an instinctive will to survive. There is more to this pitcher than meets the eye. As in "My Picture Left in Scotland," the "Epistle to My Lady Covell," the "Answer" to Sir William Burlase ("The Poet to the Painter"), and *Charis,* Ben's rotund exterior conceals an inner richness.

But only for those who have ears to hear. As Ben discloses his "center," the man who described himself to Burlase as a great "tun" fades into a timeless realm of poetic allusions. The classical images of the watertight jar (Lucretius), the drinking vessel turned ship (Seneca), the floating earthen pot that stays out of the brass pot's way (Aesop), and the light craft that rides out the storm (Horace), are so deeply embedded in the sensibility of the tribe as to require only the briefest mention to trigger the appropriate associations. Brevity is not only a stylistic ideal for Jonson; it is also the infallible sign of friendship. Shared understandings minimize the need for excess talk. "Here, I am sure," he writes to Selden, "though I am short, I cannot be obscure." Members of the tribe need not explain themselves to one another; they already know.

> So short you read my Character, and theirs
>   I would call mine, to which not many Staires
> Are asked to climbe. First give me faith, who know
>   My selfe a little. I will take you so,
> As you have writ your selfe. Now stand, and then,
>   Sir, you are Sealed of the Tribe of *Ben.*

The initiate of 1623 would have recognized the allusions to the stairs leading up to the Apollo Room and to the famous inscription on the Delphic oracle, "Know thyself." The Apollonian code of reticence provided Ben and his friends with their surest defense against the pressures of life at court. The courtier, and above all the masquer, fashioned his self-image by putting himself on public display; conversely, members of the tribe discovered their identities by withdrawing into the privacy of the self. "The Tribe of Ben" ventures to resolve the question that Stanley Fish places at the center of Jonson's career: "How can a poet operating in the world of patronage assert and maintain a claim of independence?" Jonson's "response to this challenge," Fish continues, was to create "a poetry which declares unreal the network of dependencies and obligations that to all appearances directs and regulates his every action."[34]

Jonson's only hope of securing his independence in a more strictly professional sense lay in his longer poems and his scholarly works. By the autumn of 1623 he had written part (perhaps all) of his *Discovery,* and on

October 2, 1623, his translation of Barclay's *Argenis* was entered on the Stationers' Register (HS, XI, 78). But these works, together with his entire scholarly career, literally went up in smoke when a fire in his study destroyed the bulk of his unpublished writings shortly thereafter.

He mourned their passing in "An Execration upon Vulcan." Jonson's mock-serious complaint depicts his study as yet another private place of creative activity, a domestic analogue to the Apollo Room. Besides his "journey into *Scotland* song," and three books of his translation of the *Argenis,* the fire consumed "parcels of a play" (probably *The Staple of News*); his translation of Horace's *Ars Poetica* annotated from Aristotle's *Poetics;* his English Grammar; his history of the reign of Henry V, "eight of his nine yeare"; and "twice-twelve-yeares stor'd up humanitie, / With humble Gleanings in Divinitie." Vulcan, the fiery intruder who destroys this precious repository, personifies everything that is antagonistic to the writer and his work. The "lame Lord of fire" is a fatherless vagrant, a shiftless patron of industry and trade who persecutes artists and intellectuals because he was forbidden to marry Minerva, the bride of his choice. He sneaks into Jonson's study like a government spy searching for "treason . . . or heresie," but his real target is the written word. As a dedicated foe of the liberal arts Vulcan instinctively seeks out sites of cultural production. Having already destroyed the Temple of Diana at Ephesus, the library at Alexandria, the archives at Chancery, the Globe and Fortune theaters, and the Banqueting House at Whitehall, he now lays waste to Jonson's study.[35]

The witty tone of "An Execration upon Vulcan" masks a keen sense of victimage. The body of work consumed by the fire might have convincingly ratified the honors bestowed upon Jonson by the King and by Oxford University. Jonson himself links the master's degree of 1619 to the lost works of 1623, stating that the latter were "of search, and mastry in the Arts." Now he was in the awkward position of having to account for his own lack of productivity. At least one contemporary claimed that Jonson had fabricated the whole story of his "lost" works in order to placate King James. In the manuscript "Invective of Mr. George Chapman against Mr. Ben Johnson," his old, and now former, friend flatly accused him of fraud:

> Thow dost thinges backwardes, are men thought to knowe
> Mastries in th'artes with saying they doe soe
> and criing fire out In a dreame to kinges,
> Burne thinges unborne, and that way generate thinges?

In a marginal note, Chapman further complains that Pembroke "made [Jonson] Master of Arts with his letter." Chapman's own career had gone badly, and his "Invective" reeks of envy. Moreover, Jonson's translation of Horace, his *English Grammar,* and his "twice-twelve yeares stored-up humanitie" (*Discoveries*) were eventually rewritten and published; and the clerk at the Stationers' Office would have wanted to peruse Jonson's *Argenis* before entering it on their register. Nevertheless, Chapman's harsh attack, which his editor surmises was written in 1624, doubtless reflects the kind of thing that Jonson's enemies were saying at this dreary juncture of his life.[36]

During the waning months of 1624, Jonson's status in the King's household looked more precarious than ever. A year earlier he had been reprimanded for satirizing George Wither, an opponent of James's policies, in *Time Vindicated;* by the next year's holiday season, a dramatic change in the climate of opinion at court virtually compelled him to write a masque that celebrated the collapse of James's favorite project, the Spanish Match. Jonson thus found himself in a situation where it would be impossible (he feared) "to satisfie *Expectation*"; regardless of what he wrote, someone would take offense.[37]

Earlier that spring, Buckingham and Charles had undertaken a secret and ill-advised journey to Madrid where the Prince made a last, desperate effort to secure favorable terms from the Infanta and her brother King Philip IV. When Philip refused to make any concessions, the Spanish Match became more unpopular than ever; when he made a concerted effort to convert the Prince to Catholicism and toyed with the idea of detaining him in Madrid indefinitely, the expedition hovered on the brink of disaster. In the summer of 1623 the likelihood of a peaceful succession was suddenly in doubt, and the prospect of a future civil war hung in the balance. There was great jubilation when Prince Charles finally landed at Plymouth on October 5. The sentiments of high and low, of jaded courtiers and Puritan pamphleteers, converged on a single event that transcended politics yet had enormous political reverberations. "I have not heard of more demonstrations of public joy than were here and every where from the highest to the lowest," Chamberlain wrote. "The people were so mad with excess of joy that if they met with any cart loaden with woode they wold take out the horses and set cart and all on fire."[38] Many of these who made merry in October were just the sort of people whom Jonson had satirized in *Time Vindicated* nine months earlier; they were openly delighted over the failure of the Prince's mission and the likelihood that James's plans had come to nothing.

During the months that followed, Charles and Buckingham reverted to the belligerently anti-Spanish position that Leicester, Sidney, and Essex

had adopted under Elizabeth. When the King, who still hoped that negotiations for the match could be successfully completed, instructed Buckingham to feast the Spanish Ambassadors, the Duke contrived to insult his
guests of honor. "There was a maske of Young Maynard's invention,"
Chamberlain learned, "whereof I heare litle or no commendation, but
rather that the Spaniards tooke offence at it: the maine argument of it was
a congratulation for the Princes returne." A month later Buckingham and
Charles took a keen interest in the preparations for *Neptune's Triumph for
the Return of Albion,* Jonson's Twelfth Night masque for 1623–24. Secretary of State Conway noted that "the Prince and the Duke . . . practise
the maske diligently every day." Chamberlain observed "much practising
against a maske on Twelfth Night and many meetings at noblemens houses
in the afternoones." The King wanted to avoid another embarrassing incident with the Spanish Ambassadors, and he too became involved in the
preparations for Jonson's masque. Early in January the Venetian Ambassador reported that "the usual verses written for the masque containing
some rather free remarks against the Spaniards, they were altered by his
[James's] command."[39]

Jonson voiced his misgivings about his commission in the Induction to
Neptune's Triumph. When the Poet (alias the "Author") complains that it
is "a heavy and hard taske, to satisfie *Expectation,*" his colleague, the
Cook, reminds him that she "must be satisfied: So must her sister, Madam
Curiosity, who hath as daintie palate as she." Mistress Expectation and
Madame Curiosity personify the grossly inquisitive spectator whom Jonson loathes and fears. They hunger after scraps of scandalous "news" and
reduce the poet's meaning to a crude, edible commodity. What was he to
give them? The Cook, who represents the purely sensuous dimension
of Jonson's art, resolves the Poet's quandary by preparing "a *metaphori-
call* dish" consisting of the very persons who "doe relish nothing, but *di
stato.*" Archy Armstrong, the loudmouthed court fool who fouls the air
with gossip, furnishes the garlic; Master Ambler, the newsmaster of St.
Paul's, provides the capon; and Captain Buz, his emissary, underwrites for
Turkey. The spreaders of gossip supply food for the "palate of the Understanding"; the rumormongers who "know all things the wrong way" become the foil for the "more remov'd *mysteries*" of *Neptune's Triumph.*[40]

The pageantry of the main masque corrects the "popular" response to
the Prince's return by identifying the renewed sense of national unity with
the magic of the royal presence. In the original script Prince Charles, Buckingham, and the rest of the noble dancers were to enter on a floating island
that moved across the floor of the Banqueting Hall and "joined it selfe
with the shore," where James sat in state. The iconography of this spectacle faithfully replicates the absolutist notion that the King "is" the state.

Jonson portrays the Prince (Albion) as a physical extension of England, a part of the King's mystical body politic that had been separated from, and was now rejoining, the whole (King James) who sat enthroned before him. The movable islands were direct descendants of the Tudor pageant wagons, and they provided an opportunity for Jonson to evoke the maritime glories of Elizabethan England:

> See, yond', his fleete, ready to goe, or come,
> Or fetch the riches of the *Ocean* home,
> So to secure him both in peace, and warres,
> Till not one ship alone, but all be starres.

The Poet re-presents Charles's disastrous expedition to Spain as a triumph of intrepid diplomacy. The purpose of the voyage, Jonson intimates, was not to wed the Infanta, but to discover Spain's true intentions; instead of failing in the marriage negotiations, the Prince had successfully resisted the wiles of the Infanta.[41] But these covert meanings were caviar to the general; they could only be grasped by spectators who were sophisticated enough to decode Jonson's allegory. Although the message of *Neptune's Triumph* was broadly anti-Spanish, its medium was unrelentingly elitist.

Jonson's compromise solution was to no avail. The Twelfth Night performance of *Neptune's Triumph* was "put of," Chamberlain learned, "by reason of the King's indisposition, as was pretended." Chamberlain heard that the King's sickness was a ruse: "The true cause is thought to be the competition of the French and Spanish ambasadors, which could not be accommodated in presence."[42] Alternatively, James may have feared that even the censored version of *Neptune's Triumph* would offend the Spanish Ambassador. In any event, the performance was not postponed until a later date—the usual procedure in such cases; it was canceled, and the court never saw this, the most brilliant of Jonson's later Twelfth Night masques.

The abrupt cancellation of *Neptune's Triumph* bore out Jonson's fear that he had become "a kind of *Christmas* Ingine"[43] whose sole function was to provide the court with innocuous amusements. He seems to have responded to this rebuff with wry acceptance. During the year that followed, he harked back to three predecessors who had formerly entertained royalty with innocent buffoonery and made them the central figures in the last of his Jacobean masques.

When Prince Charles visited Kenilworth on August 19, 1624, Jonson greeted him with the Ghost of Captain Cox, who had entertained Queen Elizabeth there forty-nine years previously. Where the flesh-and-blood Captain Cox had diverted the Queen by staging a neo-medieval Hock Tuesday play, Jonson amused Prince Charles with *The Masque of Owls*, a burlesque of his Elizabethan predecessor's work. Five months later, Jonson's *Fortunate Isles and Their Union* diverted the holiday revelers with the ghosts of Henry Scogan, "a fine gentleman, and a *Master of Arts, / Of Henry* the fourth's times, that made disguises / For the Kings sonnes" (284–286), and "*Domine Skelton, /* The worshipfull *Poet* Laureat to K. *Harry*" (306–307). Like Captain Cox's hobby horse and six owls, Scogan and Skelton's gallimaufry of Tudor jestbook figures (Howleglas, Elinor Rumming, Ruffian Fitzale, Maire Ambree, Long Meg of Westminster, Tom Thumbe, and Doctor Rat) evokes mingled feelings of condescension and nostalgia. Their vapid fooleries offer the spectator a yardstick by which to measure the superior complexity and sophistication of Jonson's later court entertainments, but they also recall the carefree mirth of an era when the masque was not expected to be morally serious or politically engaged. Like the Cook in *Neptune's Triumph*, they are not despised rivals but fellow artists who actively participate in the making of the poet's fable.

Jonson's decision to invoke them in a spirit of creative anachronism is yet another sign of his continuing adaptivity. As his circumstances worsened during the 1620s, he invariably found new uses for adversity. The disheveled physique, the empty purse, the moribund court, the disreputable patron, and the destruction of his unpublished works furnished themes for new poems and masques. In the last year of James's reign, when Jonson was on the verge of losing his sinecure at court (it would be six years before he prepared another masque), he summoned the shades of Captain Cox, Henry Scogan, and John Skelton to vouch for the longevity of his calling and the modernity of his work. Jonson had mastered the art of capitalizing on misfortune—a skill that would stand him in good stead during the remaining fourteen years of his life.

PART
THREE

Growing Old

under

Charles I

• CHAPTER FOURTEEN •

Return to the Playhouse

King James died on March 27, 1625. His son Charles I immediately imposed a more austere standard of behavior on the royal household. Within days of Charles's succession the Venetian Ambassador reported, "The King observes a rule of great decorum . . . and he has declared that he desires the rules and maxims of the late Queen Elizabeth"; by April 9, Chamberlain had already noticed that "the court is kept more strait and privat than in the former time." Decades later, the widow of a colonel in Cromwell's army would agree with this assessment. "The face of the court was much changed in the change of the king," Lucy Hutchinson recalled, "for King Charles was temperate, chaste, and serious; so that the fools and bawds, mimics and catamites, of the former court, grew out of fashion." The new emphasis on gravity and decorum was accompanied by a systematic program of financial retrenchment. During the first year of Charles's monarchy the Exchequer virtually ceased paying wages to officers of the King's household and attempted to reduce expenses throughout the court. In the midst of these economies Charles decided to dispense with the Twelfth Night masque.[1]

The King's decision seriously altered the course of Jonson's professional life. Although he remained Charles's servant, he no longer had any duties within the royal household. In theory he was still entitled to his pension of one hundred marks a year, but he could hardly feel confident about collecting it now that he no longer performed any services for the King. Jonson thus found himself in a situation the reverse of that he had faced a decade previously. When he was taken into the King's service in 1616, he left the stage; when he ceased to find employment at court in 1626, he returned to the playhouse and offered *The Staple of News,* his first comedy in over a decade, to Caroline audiences.

Jonson was not forsaking the Banqueting House for the Blackfriars Theater; on the contrary, the stage was now his only entrée into the "strait and privat" milieu of the Caroline court. Although Charles did not subsidize any masques during the first year of his reign, the King's Men did make several appearances at court in 1625 and 1626, and they probably performed *The Staple of News* before Charles "at the Coronation" in February 1626.[2] This performance gave Jonson an opportunity to advise the new monarch about the condition of the realm and to offer his own services as Charles's counselor. He cast his advice in the form of a morality play. *The Staple of News* tells the story of a prodigal heir named Penniboy, Jr., who ignores the advice of "Frank" Penniboy, his father-in-disguise, and squanders his newly inherited wealth on the fledgling newspaper industry. Jonson modeled his plot on the Tudor "morality of state." Penniboy, Jr., is an allegorical image of the Prince who is confronted with a choice between good and evil counselors. Jonson even hints that Young Penniboy can be directly identified with Charles I, though he does not press this analogy. The topical allegory in *The Staple of News* mainly concerns the *psychomachia* between Frank Penniboy, the good counselor who is "*a kin to the* Poet" (4th Int., 4–5), and the newspapermen.

Jonson had previously lampooned newsmongers, gossips, and professional journalists in *News from the New World, Time Vindicated,* and *Neptune's Triumph,* all of which voiced the courtier's contempt for the anti-Spanish popular press. By the winter of 1625, however, the political situation had changed: Charles had recently declared war on Spain and was currently attempting to raise money for an army of invasion. Hence, the King's views momentarily converged with those of the popular newswriters. *The Staple of News* advised Charles not to listen to them. When Penniboy, Jr., visits the staple ("depot" or "storehouse") of news he is barraged with a farrago of sensationalist stories from the Continent:

> They write the *King of Spaine* is chosen *Pope.*

> And *Spinola* is made *Generall* of the *Jesuits.*

> All the pretence to the fifth *Monarchy,*
> Was held but vaine, untill the *ecclesiastique,*
> And *secular* powers, were united, thus,
> Both in one person.

These spurious news reports are, as Pearl says, a parody of "the horror stories of encroaching Catholic hegemony over Europe." Jonson's comedy is not a straightforward political satire, like Middleton's popular *Game at*

Chess, but rather a "critique of political satire."[3] The play expresses the author's fear that popular journalists and playwrights would seize the initiative during the early months of Charles's monarchy while true poets (such as himself) sank into oblivion.

His spokesman within the play is Frank Penniboy, the aging balladeer who assumes the role of the hero's paternal mentor. The other characters refer to him as the Chanter, a sobriquet which indicates that he is a lyric poet by vocation. The Chanter uses the very same verbal strategies as the middle-aged poet who created him. His given name, "Frank," bespeaks his honesty, and his speech is laced with ironic affirmations, sententious maxims, and extended satirical set pieces. After he accompanies his adoptive son to the Apollo Room at the Devil Tavern, the gossipy chorus of spectators begins to suspect, with good reason, that Jonson has written himself into the part of the Chanter:

> *Mirth* A beggerly *Jacke* it is, I warrant him, and a kin to the *Poet.*
> *Tattle* Like enough, for hee had the chiefest part in his play, if you
>   marke it.
> *Expectation* Absurdity on him, for a huge overgrowne *Playmaker!*

As the gossips suggest, the topical allegory applies to the author's personal situation. The Chanter, alias Ben Jonson, who "was wont to name himself the Poet," contends with the new journalists—the poetasters of the 1620s—for the soul of the Prince. The Chanter uses the poet's venerable weapons of irony, wit, and satire in a desperate effort to keep his charge from siding with the newspapermen; but as the play unfolds, it becomes clear that this weaponry will not suffice. In order for the Chanter to prevail, he must reincarnate himself as Old Penniboy, the protagonist's dead father come back to life. Needless to say, this was a fantasy solution and the chorus of spectators refuses to accept it: "Why should he make him live againe, when they, and we all thought him dead?"[4]

Mirth, Tattle, Expectation, Gossip, and Censure, the five gossips who have come to jeer the poet and his play, convey Jonson's fears that his counsel will not be heard, that he himself faces the prospect of failure and supersession. Mirth has been backstage with the actors, and has seen the author "rowling himselfe up and downe like a tun, i' the midst of 'hem, and spurges, never did vessel of wort, or wine worke so!" Expectation anticipates that Jonson's play will prove "an excellent dull thing." Censure finds it appallingly bad: "duller and duller! intolerable! scurvy!" The author, they conclude, is a "decay'd wit . . . broken . . . Non-solvent . . . And for ever forfet . . . *To scorne.*"[5]

Jonson tried to ward off the hostility of the spectators of 1626 by anticipating their responses and incorporating them into his text; but the original Blackfriars audience proved all too similar to the one depicted in the play. The letter "To the *Readers*" that Jonson inserted before act III in the printed text of his comedy bitterly complained that the spectators had misconstrued "the *Prodigall,* and his *Princesse Pecunia,* wherein the *allegory,* and purpose of the *Author* hath hitherto beene wholly mistaken, and so sinister an interpretation beene made, as if the soules of most of the *Spectators* had liv'd in the eyes and eares of these ridiculous Gossips that tattle betweene the *Acts.*" "Such complaints," Bentley notes, "do not accompany successful plays." Although Jonson scolded his audience for "misinterpreting" his comedy, he had put them in a position where they could hardly do otherwise. Consider, for example, the allegory of "the *Prodigall* and his *Princesse*" that Jonson mentions in his letter. When Penniboy, Jr., the young heir, pays an unexpected visit to a young heiress named Princess Aurelia Clara Pecunia, Infanta of the Mines, whose "setting forth . . . / Will cost as much as furnishing a Fleete," anyone in the audience might have surmised that Jonson was alluding to Prince Charles's recent interlude with the Spanish Infanta. Speaking through the choric figure of Mirth, Jonson warns such spectators to "take heed, it lie not in the vice of your interpretation . . . is there nothing to be call'd *Infanta,* but what is subject to exception?"[6] This combination of sly innuendo and hectoring self-justification evidently strained the patience of the play's original audience. The spectators who made "so sinister an interpretation" of Jonson's allegory were advising him to avoid political satire altogether; and despite his vexation with them, he would follow their advice in the future.

"Disease, the Enemie, and his Ingineeres / *Want,* with the rest of his conceal'd compeeres," began to "cast a trench" around Jonson during the second year of the new reign. Subsequent references to his failing health suggest that he suffered a mild stroke—a predictable consequence of his age, weight, and drinking habits—during the year 1626. At the same time, his creditors, the emissaries of "want," began to seek legal redress. On January 11, 1626, a man named Robert Clarke filed a petition with the Lord Chamberlain alleging that Jonson had failed to repay a debt of ten pounds and five shillings; a year later one Nathanaell Field (no relation to the actor) sought repayment of sixteen pounds from Jonson. Nevertheless, the King's pensioner continued to live in comfortable circumstances. At some point between 1623, when he was domiciled at Gresham College, and 1628, when a law clerk referred to him as "Benjamin Johnson of Westminster," he moved into a private residence situated between St. Margaret's Church and Henry VII's Chapel, in the heart of Westminster. Aubrey describes the last of Jonson's dwelling places as the house "under which you passe, as you goe out of the Church yard into the old Palace"; contemporaries called it the Talbot.[7]

The onset of disease may account for the lull in Jonson's productivity that commences around this time; it would be three years before he completed another play. But the King's bedridden servant also faced obstacles of a less visceral nature. As Charles's *de facto* court poet, he was nominally obliged to support the King; but Jonson cannot have felt much enthusiasm for Charles's futile attempt to make war simultaneously on France and Spain. Although he prided himself on his own military service, and always maintained that soldiership was an honorable calling, he had never shown any sympathy whatever for international Protestantism.

"A Speech According to Horace," the most ambitious of the poems that dates from this period, voices his continuing concern that the urban middle classes would seize the initiative during the current hostilities with Spain. The poem is a mock encomium in praise of the Artillery Company, an amateur London militia that had become increasingly powerful during the previous decade:

> Well, I say, thrive, thrive brave Artillerie yard,
> > Thou Seed-plot of the warre, that hast not spar'd
> Powder, or paper, to bring up the youth
> > Of *London,* in the Militarie truth.

Although Jonson is being ironic—the company conducts its mock battles "without the hazard of a drop of blood"—he acknowledges that the citizens have taken over a function traditionally performed by the gentry. His principal target is not the Artillery Company, but the idle gentry who fail to uphold their responsibilities as military leaders. "Go on," he exhorts the citizens,

> In the stead of bold
> *Beauchamps,* and *Nevills, Cliffords, Audleys* old;
> Insert thy *Hodges,* and those newer men,
> > As *Stiles, Dike, Ditchfield, Millar, Crips,* and *Fen*
> That keepe the warre, though now't be growne more tame,
> > Alive yet, in the noise; and still the same;
> And could (if our great men would let their Sonnes
> > Come to their Schooles,) show 'hem the use of Guns;
> And there instruct the noble English heires
> > In Politique, and Militar Affaires.

The root of the problem lies not with the citizens, but with the "Tempestuous Grandlings" who "neither love the Troubles nor the harmes" of military training. "What love you then?" Jonson asks, "your whore. What study? gate, / Carriage, and dressing."[8]

Between 1604 and 1625 Jonson served and supported a pacifist king who successfully prevented England from becoming involved in any foreign wars. But these twenty years of peace also meant that the nobility, in Stone's words, "were now almost entirely absorbed in private and civilian pursuits, and no longer looked to war as a natural outlet for their energies." By the autumn of 1626, when Charles was in the midst of a series of humiliating defeats on the Continent, Jonson had come to regard the erosion of military service among the gentry as a crucial symptom of national degeneracy; the image of an earlier England, where Beauchamps, Nevilles, Cliffords, and Audleys had instructed their sons in the arts of chivalry, took on a new attractiveness for him. When Michael Drayton published his heroic poem *The Battle of Agincourt* in 1627, Jonson sent him a prefatory tribute which is so fulsome that editors have often questioned its sincerity. Prior to this time Jonson had shown no enthusiasm for bellicose patriotic oratory and had told Drummond that Drayton's "long verses pleased him not." In "The Vision of Ben Jonson on the Muses of His Friend M. Drayton," he became Drayton's warmest admirer, praising his new-found friend for urging "our *English* Youth" to "cry / An *Agincourt*, an *Agincourt* or die."[9]

The most glaring example of the military ineptitude of the English aristocracy was Charles's chief counselor Buckingham. The Duke was widely blamed both for the failure of the English expedition to Cadiz in 1625 and for the defeat of the German adventurer Mansfield, whom Charles unwisely sent to the Continent with an English army in 1626. Buckingham's own defeat at La Ré in the autumn of that year dealt a devastating blow to English national pride. On April 22, 1628, his disastrous military career was brought to an abrupt end by a disgruntled junior officer named John Felton, who stabbed him in the chest. Shortly thereafter Cotton obtained a copy of an anonymous eulogy of Buckingham's assassin entitled "To His Confined Friend Mr. Felton." When Jonson subsequently visited Cotton's house he "was asked concerning thos verses, as if himself had beene the auther thereof." Jonson, by his own testimony, "redd them, and condemned them and with deep protestations affirmed that they were not made by him." Although we have no reason to doubt Jonson's disavowal of "To His Confined Friend Mr. Felton," it is easy to see why members of Cotton's circle attributed the poem to him. The eulogist's diction and phrasing resemble Jonson's at several points and he shares Jonson's concern about the failings of England's military leaders. By killing Buckingham, the eulogist maintained, Felton had exacted retribution for the shocking defeats that had occurred during the previous three years: "Farewell: For thy brave sake wee shall not send / Henceforth Commaunders Enemies to defend." [10]

Clearly by the summer of 1628 some of Jonson's most intimate associates saw him as a bitter opponent of Buckingham. That perception may help to explain how Jonson came to be appointed Chronologer to the City of London on September 2. The chronologer drew an annual pension of one hundred nobles (a little over thirty-three pounds), so the post was an attractive sinecure; the municipal authorities who awarded it to Jonson presumably concluded that his political views were compatible with their own. In return for his stipend, Jonson was expected to "collect and set down all memorable acts of this City and occurences thereof," and to undertake "such other employments as this Court shall have occasion to use him in" (HS, I, 240–241).

In the meanwhile, someone informed Attorney General Edward Heath that Jonson was the author of "To His Confined Friend Mr. Felton." When Heath questioned him on October 26, Jonson repudiated the eulogy of Felton but indicated that he was a friend of its alleged author, a young preacher named Zouch Townlye who had fled to Holland. When "asked whether he gave a dagger to the said Mr. Townlye," Jonson admitted that he had done so, although he noted that this transaction took place "before he sawe thes verses, or had herd of them" (HS, I, 242–243). While Jonson kept on the windy side of the law, he intimated that he sympathized with Townlye.

The contemporary figure who best exemplified the chivalric ideals of "A Speech According to Horace" and *The Vision of Ben Jonson* was William Cavendish, Jonson's most important patron during the Caroline period. Throughout his long and eventful career Cavendish upheld an ethic of knightly service that had gone out of fashion with the passing of Elizabeth I. After a brief stay at Cambridge, where he took "more delight in sports than in learning," Cavendish bypassed the Inns of Court and completed his education at the Royal Mews. During his late teens he studied horsemanship with Prince Henry on the Royal Tiltyard and became adept at the equestrian exercises that were the foundation of a knight's training. Shortly after coming to the throne, Charles made him Lord Lieutenant of Nottinghamshire. As the King's representative in the county, the thirty-two-year-old Cavendish was responsible for mustering, arming, and training the local militia, a force that had grown dangerously weak during the twenty years' peace under James. He performed these duties with zeal and dispatch. In August 1627 Cavendish informed Charles that the Nottinghamshire militia had been "mustered and found completely furnished in every way after the modern fashion" and sent a levy of a hundred recruits to Charles's uncle, King Christian of Denmark. A year later James made Cavendish Earl of Newcastle.[11]

By this time Jonson had written many verses for the Cavendish family, including the epitaph engraved on the tombstone of Cavendish's father in 1617; *An Entertainment at Blackfriars* for the christening of his son in 1620 (Charles was the godfather); an epitaph for his wealthy aunt, Lady Jane Ogle, in 1625; and "An Epigram to William, Earl of Newcastle." The last of these poems, which celebrates Newcastle's equestrian skills, casts the poet in the role of a guest at Newcastle's Bolsover estate. Jonson here conceives of his host explicitly as a neo-Elizabethan figure. In praising Newcastle's horsemanship, he echoes first Pamela's praise of Mucedorus's horsemanship in Sidney's *Arcadia,* and then Sidney's commendation of his Italian riding master, John Pietro Pugliano, in the opening sentences of *An Apology for Poetry.*[12]

By the autumn of 1628 Jonson had begun work on a comedy called *The New Inn.* He evidently had Newcastle in mind when he conceived of Lovel, the hero of the play, for during the fourth act Lovel delivers an oration on fencing that echoes and closely resembles *Underwood* 59, Jonson's epigram in praise of Newcastle's swordsmanship. Like Newcastle, Lovel is a throwback to the feudal military class that had flourished during the reign of Elizabeth. His fondest memories go back to the period when he, like many Elizabethan gentlemen, served in the religious wars in France. Lovel followed one Lord Beaufort ("I was his page / And ere he dy'd, his friend!") and "waited on his studies: which were right." Under Beaufort's tutelage he studied the "examples / Of the *Heroick* virtue" that Sidney recommends in the *Apology for Poetry.* Although he ruefully concedes that times have changed, his allegiance to the noble household, that "Academy of honour" where the well-bred youth learned "to vault, to ride, to fence, / To move his body gracefuller," has never wavered. And Lovel's nostalgia for the Elizabethan era is characteristic of the entire play. Barton comments that in writing *The New Inn* "Jonson found himself harking back to the vanished age of Elizabeth and celebrating things in it which, as a young man, he had slighted or not appreciated at all." In addition to his affectionate tribute to "these nourceries of nobility" where men like Lovel were schooled, the play contains reminiscences of Sidney, Spenser, Lyly, Kyd, and Shakespeare.[13]

At the same time, Jonson deftly reshaped the legacy of Elizabeth in the image of the new Queen. After the death of Buckingham, Charles and Henrietta Maria became deeply devoted to each other; for the first time since the reign of Henry VII, England had a King and Queen who were happily married. Where James's attitude toward women was unabashedly

William Cavendish, Earl of Newcastle, schooling one of his horses at Bolsover, by Abraham van Diepenbenke. From Cavendish's *La méthode nouvelle de dresser les cheveaux,* 1657. In his epigram "To William, Earl of Newcastle," Jonson says that when he saw his patron on horseback he "began to wish my selfe a horse" (*Und,* 53). Newcastle's estate at Bolsover, which Jonson visited in the 1620s, appears in the background.

misogynous, his son, as the comic opera of his quest for the Infanta would suggest, took the high road of chivalry and sentiment. Henrietta had grown up in the years when the Marquise de Rambouillet established her famous salon in protest against the coarseness and crudity of the court of Henri IV. The salon devised a new code of manners, called *préciosité,* for the purpose of refining the courtiers' speech and their relations with the opposite sex; this system of etiquette was tailor-made for Charles, who seems to have been similarly repelled by the grossness of his father's household. Henrietta imported it into the English court, where the etiolated emotions, feminized etiquette, and Platonic ideals of the *précieuses* rapidly assumed the status of a genteel fad. The advent of *préciosité* stimulated an interest in literary forms that had gone into eclipse during the previous reign. The new code of behavior had arisen in reaction to the vulgarity of an urban, sybaritic court, and it showed to best advantage in distant, sylvan landscapes; the literary model for the salon was Honore D'Urfé's enormously popular pastoral romance, *L'astrée*. The life of the salon revolved around the great lady and her admirers, and it readily assumed the form of a medievalized court of love where *la belle dame* presided over male "servants" who penned Petrarchan sonnets in praise of her beauty. Since the pastoral romance and the love sonnet were the legacy of Sidney and Spenser, Charles's court soon became the scene of a full-scale Elizabethan revival. Under James, the heritage of Elizabeth had been associated with patriotism, with the city, and with international Protestantism. That form of nostalgia persisted under Charles, but alongside it there arose a neo-Elizabethan style that was perfectly compatible with continental art and literature, with the court, and with the Roman Catholic queen who presided over it.[14]

The New Inn is one of the first plays to reflect Henrietta's preferences; Jonson, who wrote a separate Epilogue for a court performance, doubtless hoped that she would see it. During the central acts of his new comedy, Lovel, the nostalgic Elizabethan gentleman, pays court to Lady Frances Frampul, the emergent Caroline *précieuse*. Lady Frances "thinks nought a happinesse, but to have / A multitude of servants." When she decides to establish a Court of Love at the Light Heart Inn, Lovel, who is one of her "servants," takes the part of the high-minded wooer. He edifies the court with philosophical discourses on love and valor; Lady Frances duly compliments him on his eloquence: "Who hath read *Plato, Heliodore,* or *Tatius,* / *Sydney, D'Urfé,* or all Loves *Fathers,* like him?" "Most *Socratick* Lady!" her maid appreciatively exclaims, "Or, if you will, *Ironick!* gi' you joy / O' your *Platonick* love here, Mr. *Lovel.*" Yet in the end, the idealizing rhetoric of the salon inhibits the expression of genuine feeling—is Lady Frances being Platonic or ironic? By the beginning of the last act, Lovel despairs of ever touching the lady's heart. The Host of the inn, who had hoped "like a noble Poet, to have had / My last act best" finds that "all failes i' the plot."[15]

The Host, who goes by the name of Goodstock, is a fictionalized image of the actual author meditating upon his own relationship to the new world he has created. The opening lines of his Prologue remind the audience that inns, which were the original Tudor playhouses, are like theaters: "*You are welcome, welcome all, to the new* Inne; / *Though the old house*"—the Blackfriars Theater—where "the same Cooke, / Still, and the fat," plies his venerable trade. As the action gets underway, the curiously articulate Host compares his own inn, the Light Heart, to the comic stage, "Where, I imagine all the world's a Play." When Lovel characterizes the Host as "some round-growne thing! a Jug, / Fac'd, with a beard," he describes the older Ben Jonson. When he observes that the Host is remarkably well-bred and learned for a man who works in a public house, he characterizes Jonson's own relationship to the public playhouses—and the Host agrees that he "was borne to somewhat, Sir, above it." Lovel obliquely raises the question of Jonson's vexed relations with the popular audience by asking why "a man / Of your sagacity, and cleare nostrill" would choose

> a place
> So sordid, as the keeping of an Inne:
> Where every *Jovial* Tinker, for his chinke,
> May cry, *Mine host, to crambe, give us drinke;*
> *And do not slinke, but skinke, or else you stinke.*

At the time that the Host became the proprietor of the Light Heart its sole occupant was Fly, "the Parasite o' the house," who was assigned to the Host "over, in the Inventory, / As an old implement, a peice of household-stuffe." [16] Fly is the tricky servant—the indispensable handyman in Jonson's comedy of humors—and for the duration of *The New Inn* this relic of the "old" inn plies his venerable trade in the cellar of the house. There he presides over a below-stairs farce that attracts the shopworn remnants of Jonson's earlier comedies: a braggart warrior, a citizen who makes his overdressed wife available to the gallants, a gamester, a roaring boy. By relegating these humors to the cellar, by associating them with the Host's past, and by keeping them as gross and threadbare as he can Jonson contrives to notify his audience that they no longer hold any appeal for him.

Nevertheless, this noble poet concedes that he is unable to bring the above-stairs romance of the "new" inn to a satisfactory conclusion. Despite his uncanny grasp of human behavior, the Host still does not know how to make a man and a woman fall in love: "All failes i' the plot." Jonson's way of rescuing his plot is to turn it into a Hellenistic romance about separated parents and missing children. In the last act he reveals that three of his principal characters (the Host, his adoptive son Frank, and the nurse who cares for Frank) are long-lost members of the Frampul family. The Blackfriars audience found this plot impossible to follow. Within the play, however, these revelations remove, as if by magic, all impediments to a happy outcome.

The central figure in this complex series of disclosures is the Host. At the climactic moment in act V the Host reveals that he is really Lady Frances's father Lord Frampul (his name literally means "troublesome") and confesses that he is "the cause of all this trouble." The trouble began when the Host abandoned his wife after the birth of their second daughter and went "to turne Puppet-master," to "travell with *Yong Goose,* the Motion-man," and to "lie, and live with the *Gipsies* halfe a yeare / Together," from his wife. Later, he became host of the Light Heart Inn, where he found

> A seat, to sit at ease here, i'mine Inne,
> To see the *Comedy;* and laugh, and chuck
> At the variety, and throng of humours,
> And dispositions, that come justling in,
> And out still, as they one drove hence another.

There he tutors his adoptive son, Frank, who "prates Latine / And 'twere a parrat, or a play-boy," just as Jonson had instructed his "Schollar," the child actor Nathan Field. In reality, Frank is his lost daughter. When Lord Frampul finally unmasks, he attributes his desertion of his family to excessive intellectual curiosity:

> I am he
> Have measur'd all the Shires of *England* over:
> *Wales,* and her mountaines, seene those wilder nations,
> Of people in the *Peake,* and *Lancashire;*
> Their Pipers, Fidlers, Rushers, Puppet-masters,
> Juglers, and Gipseys, all the sorts of Canters,
> And Colonies of beggars, Tumblers, Ape-carriers,
> For to these savages I was addicted,
> To search their natures, and make odde discoveries!

The analogy between the Host and the author now takes on an added poignancy. Jonson left his own wife during his stint as a strolling player in the 1590s; he was separated from her in 1619, when he told Drummond that he had not slept with her for five years. He too had been an antiquarian and searcher-out of "odde discoveries" who walked across the shires of England; he too was versed in the ways of "Puppet-masters" (*Bartholomew Fair*), "Gypsies" (*The Gypsies Metamorphosed*), and "all the sorts of Canters" (*The Staple of News*); he too had visited "the *Peake.*"[17] At the end of *The New Inn,* Jonson relinquishes these compulsions. Lord Frampul's pursuit of knowledge was not a noble ideal but a debilitating obsession. It has deprived him of female companionship for the better part of his life and has cost him his family.

How did the playwright arrive at this new self-assessment? In his fifty-seventh year Jonson, now an elderly man by Jacobean standards, found himself excluded from the court, afflicted by disease, and worried about money. He lived apart from his wife, had long since lost the last of his legitimate children, and now faced the prospect of a lonely old age. During the previous three years, after a hiatus of at least a decade, he had written three epitaphs for the young (*Und*, 16, 35, 60). The image of the lost child, which had been such a powerful stimulus to his imagination during his early thirties, took on a renewed interest for him during his mid-fifties. The Host's drawn-out tale of parental neglect appears, then, to be an act of atonement for Jonson's abandonment of his own wife and children. After decades of speaking through the mask of the detached observer, Jonson finally acknowledges that he is "the cause of all this trouble." Within the make-believe world of *The New Inn* this self-disclosure magically resolves all of the speaker's difficulties. The Host no sooner utters it than he recovers his wife and children, bequeaths the inn to Fly, and becomes Lord Frampul, a member of the aristocracy.

While Jonson was erecting this castle in the air, he suffered a second stroke, which rendered him a paralytic invalid for the remainder of his life. He subsequently informed Newcastle that this stroke occurred "in the Yeare 1628," but we can date it more precisely than that. Since Jonson was using old-style dating in this letter, the year 1628 extended until March 25, 1629. Although Jonson had been afflicted with "Disease" since 1626 (*Und*, 71), he must have been in reasonably good health on October 26, 1628, when he informed Attorney General Heath that he was a frequent visitor at Cotton's house and had recently gone to hear Zouch Townlye preach a sermon. So the stroke occurred between the end of October and January 19, 1629, when Bishop Williams, the Dean of Westminster Abbey, sent a grant of five pounds to "Mr. Benjamin Johnson in his sickness and want" (HS, I, 213, 242–244).

The Epilogue to *The New Inn* explicitly refers to the author's recent affliction and begs the spectators' indulgence because of it:

> The maker is sick, and sad. But doe him right,
> He meant to please you: for he sent things fit,
>   In all the numbers, both of sense, and wit,
> If they ha' not miscarried! if they have,
>   All that his faint, and faltring tongue doth crave,
> Is, that you not impute it to his braine.
>   That's yet unhurt, although set round with paine.
> It cannot long hold out. All strength must yeeld.   (4–11)

At the conclusion of his Epilogue Jonson chides King Charles and Queen Henrietta for not ministering to his needs: "*Had he liv'd the care of King, and Queene, / His Art in somthing more yet had beene seene*" (21–22).

The spectators at the Blackfriars turned a deaf ear to these entreaties.

Despite Jonson's extraordinary efforts to accommodate the Caroline audience, *The New Inn* was reportedly "cry'd down the first Day." On the title page of the printed text of his play, Jonson complains that "it was never acted, but most negligently play'd, by some, the King's Servants. And more squeamishly beheld, and censured by others, the Kings Subjects." His dedicatory epistle mentions "a hundred fastidious *impertinents,* who were there present the first day, yet never made piece of their prospect the right way." The spectators of 1629 had valid reasons for disliking his comedy. The essayist Owen Felltham's complaint about the subplot scores a palpable hit:

> *Jug, Pierce, Peck, Fly,* and all
>   Your Jests so nominal,
> Are things so far beneath an able Brain,
>   As they do throw a stain
> Through all th' unlikely plot.[18]

Jonson's parody of his own comic style wears very thin and no one, including modern critics who admire the play, has ever claimed that it is funny. He also worked a number of long, discursive orations into his script, just as he had done in *Sejanus* and *Catiline,* and these would have tried the patience of the Blackfriars audience.

The new year brought Jonson cold comfort. His return to the stage had turned into a disaster; his comic genius had, to all appearances, deserted him; he had not prepared a court masque for the previous five years and had no prospect of doing so in the foreseeable future. He had undergone a severe stroke and would remain confined to his house for the rest of his life. And on January 15 a creditor named Peter Johnson dunned him for a debt of twenty-five pounds (HS, XI, 585). Nevertheless, his mood was defiant.

• CHAPTER FIFTEEN •

"Come Leave the Lothed Stage"

The failure of *The New Inn* reinvigorated Jonson's strong antitheatrical prejudice. In the defiant "Ode to Himself" that he wrote in 1629, he vowed once again to "leave the lothed stage, / And the more lothsome age." Instead, he would "take the *Alcaick* Lute; / Or thine owne *Horace,* or *Anacreons* Lyre; / Warme thee, by *Pindares* fire," and serve the King, "tuning forth the acts of his sweet raigne: / And raising *Charles* his chariot, 'bove his *Waine*" (HS, VI, 492–494).

Contemporaries greeted this manifesto with varying degrees of scorn and regret. His detractors accused him of staging a temper tantrum to attract attention, and they suggested that his mind had begun to deteriorate as well as his body. "Come leave this saucy way," countered Owen Felltham, "of baiting those that pay / Dear for the sight of your declining wit." He told the bedridden poet what people were saying about him: "If men vouch not things Apocryphal, / You bellow, rave and spatter round your gall." "What dismale fate is this, thus on thee seaseth?" asked the anonymous author of "The Country's Censure on Ben Jonson's New Inn." "Thy worth doth faile; thy Arrogance Increaseth." Jonson's admirer Thomas Carew frankly informed him that "thy comique Muse from the exalted line / Toucht by thy Alchymist, doth since decline," and advised him to show more restraint in replying to his critics: "Why should the follies then, of this dull Age / Drawe from thy penn such an immodest rage"? R. Goodwin, another admirer, likewise urged Jonson "use not that pen, / that could affright the world, 'gainst such poore Men" as the "Silken fooles" who had jeered *The New Inn*. Thomas Randolph concurred: "This only in my *Ben* I faulty find / He's angry, they'le not see him that are blind." Jonson's friends counseled him to ignore his critics and continue to write for the stage: "Why should the Scene be Mute / Cause thou canst touch a Lute"?[1]

Why indeed? One J. C. was the only contemporary who wholeheartedly endorsed Jonson's decision. In his "Ode to Ben Jonson upon His Ode to Himself," J. C. encouraged the defiant poet to fulfill his pledge:

> Whilst thou tak'st that high spirit,
> Well purchas'd by thy merit,
> Great Prince of Poets, though thy head be gray,
>   Crowne it with *Delphick* Bay.   (HS, XI, 338)

J. C. offered a timely reminder that Jonson had frequently characterized the act of writing as a quasi-religious experience, a rhapsodic rather than a purely rational process. Recall, for example, Young Lorenzo's oration at the conclusion of *Every Man in His Humour*, or the "Apologetical Dialogue" appended to the folio text of *Poetaster*, or the ceremonies at the Apollo Club. Jonson's resolve to crown his gray head with the Delphic bay was not a mere fit of pique, but a final attempt to realize ambitions that he had harbored throughout his career. In the months that followed the disastrous debut of *The New Inn* he lacked nothing but a subject to inspire him. Later that summer, the death of an obscure English soldier on the coast of Wales provided the theme for his Pindaric ode.

Sir Henry Morison (b. 1608) and Sir Lucius Cary (b. 1610) had served together in Ireland; at the time they met Jonson they were looking forward to military careers. The two young friends both wrote poetry and became acquainted with Jonson through the medium of his folio *Works*. According to Cary, Morison had been studying Virgil, Ovid, and Lucan, when he discovered Jonson, "Our *Metropolitane* in *Poetry*," during his late teens (HS, XI, 401). In his "Epistle to His Noble Father Mr. Jonson," Cary describes the mixed feelings of admiration ("I knew / so long as English liv'd, so long would you") and trepidation ("I thought you proud, for I did surely knowe, / had I Ben: Jonson, bene, I had beene soe") that preceded their initiation into Jonson's circle of friends (HS, XI, 403). Morison, who "had often heard [Jonson's] Songs, was often fir'd / With their inchanting power," became a devoted follower of the older poet (HS, XI, 431).

Morison died of smallpox while on his way back to Ireland in the summer of 1629. His friend Cary reacted to this news with untoward recklessness. When the King recalled Cary's father from Ireland that August, he also transferred Sir Lucius's command to Sir Charles Willoughby. Cary responded by challenging Willoughby, who was entitled to the post, to a duel. Though Willoughby patiently tried to dissuade him, Cary renewed

Lucius Cary, Viscount Falkland, artist unknown. While Cary's face retains its youthful impetuosity, the dark robes and loose hair convey a feeling of poetic melancholy.

the challenge. The King finally incarcerated this "Sir What Care I," as he was labeled by a bemused contemporary, in the Fleet prison. After his father, Lord Falkland, secured his release, Cary, who had recently inherited his aunt's estates at Great Tew and Burford Priory, impetuously married Morison's dowerless sister, Lettice. This act destroyed his father's chances of repairing his own ruined fortunes by negotiating a lucrative marriage for his son; Falkland remained estranged from Cary for the rest of his life. Sir Lucius then went abroad, intending to take up military service in Holland, but the Dutch would not have him.[2]

Cary voiced his feelings of suicidal despair in the "Elegy on the Death of My Dearest (and Almost Only) Friend Sir Henry Morison," which he wrote during the troubled months that followed Morison's death. In writing his elegy, Cary faced the same problem that Milton would confront in "Lycidas": What can be said of a poet who never had a chance to write, or of a soldier whose battles were all unfought? The dilemma was compounded by the fact that Cary, unlike Milton, was too thoroughgoing a humanist to find any consolation in the prospect of Morison's going to his eternal reward. Now, as later, when he spent the 1630s trying to discover the rational bases for Christian belief, Cary's god was reason; and "reason," he wrote, "findes such reason to deplore / My losse, she grieves that I canne grieve noe more." Cary tried to fill the void by making Morison out to be one of the master spirits of the age. Had the momentary flashes of wit "that from him with out heeded did drop and fall / Into a volume but collected beene," he would have bested Homer. Closer to home, "Dun [Donne] did feare (more then feare, for he did know it) / That he was like to arise the maister poet." In Cary's fantasies, Morison the soldier was readying himself to free the Dutch provinces from Spain, and no less a person than Prince Henry of Orange "feard, though he the States long serv'd, / That his reward was for this youth reserv'd." But hyperbole could only deepen Cary's grief, since he now had to reckon with a world bereft of wit and soldiership alike. At the close, he turns unsteadily toward Lettice Morrison, vowing "that you, his aunt and sister, he beinge gonn, / Shall be to mee my Harrie Morrison."[3]

Cary's fumbling efforts to cope with his despair provide the background for Jonson's tribute "To the Immortal Memory and Friendship of the Noble Pair, Sir Lucius Cary and Sir Henry Morison" (*Und,* 70), the first sustained imitation of the Pindaric ode in English. Jonson adopted the same strategy that he had used in his "Ode: To Sir William Sidney on His Birthday" (*For,* 14) and "High Spirited Friend" (*Und,* 26). His paean to Cary and Morison combines the stanzaic form of a Pindaric ode with extended passages of moral advice borrowed from Seneca's ninety-third epistle. By drawing on the very different resources available from these two models, Jonson contrives to extol the beauty of Morison's life even as he concedes the modesty of his accomplishments. The ornate diction and musical properties of the choral ode give his poem the tonality of a victory song for Morison, the heroic man who ran the good race; the numerous borrowings from Seneca's epistle "On the Brevity, as Contrasted with the Length of Life," supply the burden of wholesome counsel, quietly insisting that the victory garland is not contingent on the length of the race or the size of the arena, but only on the quality of the performance.[4]

Jonson begins with the most extreme instance of a short life that could be imagined. According to Pliny's *Natural History,* the "Infant of Saguntum" was born just as Hannibal was razing that town, and returned to the womb at once, completing the circuit of his life at the point of its inception. Jonson's apparent readiness to hold the child up for admiration ("Brave Infant of *Saguntum,* cleare / Thy comming forth in that great yeare") has earned the Cary-Morison ode a good deal of notoriety. Does Jonson endorse suicide, or retreat in the face of adversity? The brave infant epitomizes an attitude toward life that is common to many of the epitaphs preserved in the Greek anthology and to many of Jonson's best poems. "On My First Son," "Epitaph on Elizabeth L. H.," "To the World: A Farewell for a Gentlewoman Virtuous and Noble," "To Heaven," and "An Epistle to a Friend to Persuade Him to the Wars," all ask the reader to ponder the idea that the best life is the shortest one. In its starkest form this proposition is irreconcilable with any form of humanism available to Jonson, yet it held a deep attraction for him. The child's enigmatic act carries this stoic view of existence to its logical, if absurd, conclusion: "How summ'd a circle didst thou leave man-kind / Of deepest lore, could we the Center find!"[5] The center of the circle lies beyond the threshold of human understanding, but its circumference prefigures the wider arc of Morison's brief but paradigmatic life.

The infant of Saguntum offers a provocative illustration of Seneca's thesis that one should measure lives "by their performance, not by their duration": "For, what is life, if measur'd by the space, / Not by the act?" Jonson brings this question closer to home by citing the antithetical case of the "stirrer." The stirrer made a great beginning, but gave up on life as he entered manhood: "How well at twentie had he falne, or stood! / For three of his foure-score, he did no good." The imagery of falling and standing, of passivity and action, leads, in turn, to a fresh perspective on the hero of the poem: "Alas, but *Morison* fell young: / Hee never fell, thou fall'st, my tongue." The puns on the physical and moral senses of "stand" and "fall" reformulate the question of Morison's unfulfilled promise—the barely concealed source of anxiety in Cary's elegy. What matters is not how much Morison accomplished, but rather the exemplary quality of his life. There is no need to invoke the Prince Henry of Orange or the John Donne that Sir Henry Morison might have become. Soldiership consists not in mounting great campaigns but in standing "to the last right end." If Morison left no verses behind him, his life was nevertheless a poem in its own right:

> All Offices were done
> By him, so ample, full, and round,
> In weight, in measure, number, sound,
> As though his age imperfect might appeare,
> His life was of Humanitie the Spheare.

An exemplary life is always complete. Conversely, the problem with living for a long time is the difficulty of maintaining one's "stand" through the wear and tear of many years. Jonson, who had recently gone through the debacle of *The New Inn* and was now confined to his bed, had little reason to be enamored of great age in the autumn of his fifty-eighth year. At the time of his first son's death he had consoled himself with the thought that young Ben had "so soone scap'd worlds, and fleshes rage, / And, if no other miserie, yet age"; now he was experiencing the vexations that his son had avoided. "Goe now, and tell out dayes summ'd up with feares," he chides himself; "Produce thy masse of miseries on the Stage / To swell thine age." "Life" remains indifferent to the sheer bulk of Jonson's achievements: "Her measures are, how well / Each syllab'e answer'd, and was form'd, how faire; / These make the lines of life, and that's her aire."[6]

The famous central stanza comparing the oak and the lily at once proclaims the value of Morison's fleeting existence and alleviates Jonson's dejection:

> It is not growing like a tree
> In bulke, doth make man better be;
> Or standing long an Oake, three hundred yeare,
> To fall a logge at last, dry, bald, and seare;
> A Lillie of a Day,
> Is fairer farre, in May,
> Although it fall, and die that night;
> It was the Plant, and flowre of light.
> In small proportions, we just beautie see:
> And in short measures, life may perfect bee.

The comparison honors Morison, the insignificant man who died in trivial circumstances, by claiming that beauty and perfection inhere in such lives. It also pertains to Cary, who as it happens was unusually short ("Just as one of small stature can be a perfect man," Seneca observes, "so in a life of small compass can be a perfect life").[7] In a more general way, the passage reaffirms Jonson's lifelong commitment to brief poems about mundane facts and his philosophical belief that a worthy life resides rather in a forceful response to circumstance than in actions of great magnitude. Although he draws his premises from Seneca and Aristotle, his admonition to consider the lilies of the field also recalls the biblical parable about the beauty of brief and uncomplicated lives.

As the ode moves from Senecan advice to Pindaric celebration, the singer assures Cary that Morison has already been resurrected in memory and song:

> Call, noble *Lucius,* then for Wine,
> And let thy lookes with gladnesse shine:
> Accept this garland, plant it on thy head,
> And thinke, nay know, thy *Morison's* not dead.

Jonson invites his readers to recreate the scene of Morison's resurrection within their own imaginations. Seated beneath the bust of Apollo, Ben, the poet-priest, tells his grief-stricken "son" Lucius, whom he has been consoling, to call for wine. The garland of verse that passes from father to son is the immutable Henry Morison that Ben has restored in the lines of the poem. Morison's continuing existence will henceforth depend on the capacity of readers to reimagine this scene years, and even centuries, later. Cary's dead friend now lives in

> that bright eternall Day:
> Of which we *Priests* and *Poets* say
> Such truths, as we expect for happy men,
> And there he lives with memorie; and *Ben*

> The Stand

> *Jonson,* who sung this of him, e're he went
> Himselfe to rest . . .

The abrupt enjambment between the two stanzas makes us linger for a moment over the word "*Ben.*" A contemporary reader who paused at this point might have surmised that the poet was referring to his first son Ben, who now lived in memory with Jonson's adoptive son Morison. The paternal "*Jonson,* who sung this of him" only emerges at the beginning of the next stanza. Jonson had previously used this form of chiasmus in his epitaph "On My First Son," where he instructs young Ben to "rest in soft peace, and, ask'd, say here doth lie / BEN. JONSON [the son] his [the father's] best piece of *poetrie.*"[8] The grieving father of 1603 identified with a buried child in order to fortify himself against the misery of age; the paternal mentor of 1629 was looking forward to the time when he would join all his sons in a bright eternal day of his own imagining.

A decade earlier, Jonson had intended "to perfect ane Epick Poeme in-titled Heroologia of the Worthies of his Country," but he never made any headway on this project and seems to have abandoned it before the fire of 1623. It is hard to imagine what Jonson, who had never shown much enthusiasm for the worthies of his country, would have found to say about the Knights of the Round Table, or the exploits of Hawkins and Drake; but the modesty of Morison's accomplishments struck a responsive chord in him. The Cary-Morison ode is the one poem by Jonson that fulfills the intention he had voiced in 1619. Among the genres of lyric poetry, the Pindaric ode is the closest approximation to "Heroicall," or epic, poetry. Sidney concedes that "a man may say that Pindar many times praiseth highly victories of small moment," but goes on to claim that the Pindaric ode "is that kind most capable and most fit to awake the thoughts from the sleep of idleness, to embrace honorable enterprises."[9] Jonson's ode had the same end in view; its purpose was to bring Cary out of his dejection and arouse him to "honorable enterprises."

Whether or not Jonson's ode accomplished this end it does seem to have helped Cary shake off his despondency. A year or two later Sir Lucius began his "Third Anniversary" on Morison's death (the second has dis-appeared) with a warm tribute to Jonson. The "Third Anniversary" is far more self-possessed and well written than Cary's eulogy of 1629, and Jon-son's influence comes through in several places. While conceding that Morison "lov'd, yet made no verse," Cary praises his friend for having been "a living *Epick Poeme*." He omits any mention of Morison's soldier-ship, but compliments him on his even-tempered disposition under trying circumstances. Following Jonson's lead, he depicts him as an exemplary case of the *puer senex:* "Hee had an Infant's innocence, and truth, / the judgment of Gray-Haires, the witt of Youth" (HS, XI, 400–402). The "Third Anniversary" is hardly a memorable poem, but it does indicate that Jonson had helped Cary come to terms with the trauma of Morison's death.

Cary, in turn, felt deeply grateful to his friend and mentor. His "Epistle to His Noble Father Mr. Jonson" speaks admiringly of Jonson's ability to confer fame and asks if there can be any bliss comparable to his "whom this your *Quill* (not differing from your hart) / hath often mencioned, on the better part?" Cary, who became a wealthy man after inheriting his grandmother's estates, had the wherewithal to repay Jonson for his solic-itude. The future Earl of Clarendon, who moved in the same circles as Jonson and Cary, recalled that Sir Lucius "seemed to have his Estate in Trust, for all worthy Persons, who stood in want of Supplies and Encour-agement, as Ben. Johnson, and many others of that Time, whose Fortunes required, and whose Spirits made them superior to, ordinary Obligations." [10] In Jonson's case the patron had already received a handsome return on his investment; the poet surely earned whatever stipend he received from Sir Lucius Cary.

Jonson's pledge to "sing / The glories of thy *King*" ("Ode to Himself," 51–52) may have been prompted by Charles's gift of a hundred pounds early in 1629 (*Und,* 63). In any case, it marks the beginning of a concerted effort on Jonson's part to reestablish his ties to the court. *The Underwood* does not include any verse addressed to Charles or Henrietta Maria before the spring of 1629; but seven of the ten poems that Jonson wrote for them fall in 1629–30, and in the winter of 1630–31 he would prepare his first court masque since the death of King James.

Jonson kept his promise to sing Charles's glory, but he refused to play the part of a sycophant. Although the poems that he addressed to the King and Queen between 1629 and 1631 eulogize their majesties, Jonson frequently refers to the nagging reality of their unpopularity. He portrays himself as one prepared to sing their praises when no one else will, and makes it clear that he expects some consideration in return. This combination of criticism and compliment ran the risk of offending Charles, who did not share his father's love of raillery and wit. But Jonson may have felt that he had little to lose at this stage of his career: better to impress the King strongly, if not altogether favorably, than to wither in obscurity. Moreover, Jonson's criticisms were timely and well taken. He began writing poems in praise of Charles and his family at a moment when the monarch was rapidly becoming a very unpopular figure. Relations between the King and parliament had steadily deteriorated during 1628–29. On March 2, 1629, Charles dissolved that body—he would not summon another parliament for eleven years—and inaugurated the era of Personal Rule. As a frequent visitor at the house of Cotton, who had opposed the King in parliament, and an intimate friend of Selden, whom the King had imprisoned after the dissolution of that body, Jonson must have appreciated the views of the King's critics.

"An Epigram to Our Great and Good King Charles on His Anniversary Day, 1629" (March 27), perhaps the earliest of the poems to the King, acknowledges that Charles (unlike his father) has set a good example for his subjects by leading a morally circumspect life:

Indeed, when had great *Britaine* greater cause
    Then now, to love the Soveraigne, and the Lawes?
When you that raigne, are her Example growne,
    And what are bounds to her, you make your owne?

Sir Robert Cotton, by Cornelius Johnson, 1629. Cotton's house, with its famous library, stood just a few hundred yards from Jonson's residence in Westminster.

Yet the poem ends on a note of frustration: "None will know / How much to heaven for thee, great CHARLES, they owe!" This epigram succinctly formulates what historians have come to recognize as a crucial, unresolved problem of Charles's monarchy. Although the King, in accordance with orthodox political theory, set an impeccable standard of circumspection and piety for his subjects, the power of his example never reached beyond the court. The birth of Charles's first son on May 29, 1630, was more notable for the dismay it occasioned among the Puritans, who viewed the perpetuation of the Stuart line as a bad omen, than for any displays of public rejoicing. Although Jonson's "Epigram on the Prince's Birth" duly proffers his congratulations, he concludes with a tag from Martial ("He deserves not to displease you, Caesar, who hastes to please you"), which indicates that he expects to be rewarded for his loyalty.[11]

"The Humble Petition of Poor Ben, to the Best of Monarchs, Masters, Men, King Charles" (written prior to March 26, 1630) openly refers to the indignities Jonson has borne as a result of being in the King's pay. He bluntly informs Charles that his annual pension of a hundred marks

> Hath drawne on me, from the times,
> All the envie of the *Rymes,*
> And the ratling pit-pat-noise,
> Of the lesse-*Poetique* boyes;   (*Und,* 76.17–20)

Such loyalty, he continues, is worth more than a hundred marks a year; he therefore requests that his pension be increased by one-third, to one hundred pounds *per annum.* Charles apparently agreed with him, for on March 26, 1630, he granted the increase and added an annual allotment of one tierce (forty-two gallons) of canary wine for good measure (HS, I, 245–248).

Nevertheless, Jonson still had ample cause to be concerned about his financial situation. The death of his old patron Pembroke in April 1630 deprived him of a dependable source of income and of a powerful ally at a time when he badly needed both. On May 17 one Richard Milward filed a petition with the Lord Chamberlain stating that Jonson owed him twenty-five pounds. Worse yet, Jonson found it difficult to collect his new emoluments from the royal household. Richard Weston, who became Lord Treasurer in 1628, had learned his trade under the parsimonious Lionel Cranfield, and one of his first moves upon taking office was to order a stay of all royal annuities. Weston's biographer estimates that he reduced payments to royal pensioners from 125,000 to 80,000 pounds per year between 1630 and 1635. Moreover, the effects of this retrenchment "were felt by the humbler, and more deserving, pensioners, rather than by the court grandees." Weston's servants predictably refused to honor the terms of Charles's grant to Jonson. "An Epigram to the Household, 1630" asks,

"What can the cause be, when the *King* hath given / His *Poet* Sack, the *House-hold* will not pay?" and declares that "'T were better spare a Butt, then spill his *Muse*. / For in the *Genius* of a *Poets* Verse, / The Kings fame lives." In his verse epistle "To Master John Burgess," a clerk in the Exchequer, Jonson further complains that Sir Robert Pye, Remembrancer of the Exchequer, refuses

> To take Apprehension
> Of a yeares Pension,
> And more is behind:
> Put him in mind
> Christmas is neere;
> And neither good Cheare,
> Mirth, fooling, nor wit,
> Nor any least fit
> Of gambol, or sport
> Will come at the Court,
> if there be no money.[12]

Since the King had decided to commission a masque for the coming holiday season, Jonson's threat to withhold his services "if there be no money" was not merely a rhetorical gesture. His bargaining position at court was now stronger than it had been at any time since 1625.

Meanwhile, Charles's and Henrietta's popularity continued to decline. Jonson's "Ode, or Song, by All the Muses, in Celebration of Her Majesty's Birthday, 1630" (November 26) begins by reminding the Queen that since the church bells and the guns in the Tower of London are not pealing in her honor, the poet has to compensate for the absence of any public rejoicing:

> 1. Clio.   And though the Parish-steeple
>   Be silent, to the people
>   Ring thou it Holy-day.
> 2. Mel.   What, though the thriftie Tower
>   And Gunnes there, spare to poure
>   Their noises forth in Thunder:
>   As fearfull to awake
>   This Citie, or to shake
>   Their guarded gates asunder?
> 3. Thal.   Yet, let our Trumpets sound.   (*Und*, 67.4–13)

These allusions set Jonson's loyalty to Henrietta in the foreground. They notify the royal readers that the poet has taken it upon himself to uphold an unpopular position, and that he retains the capacity and the willingness to celebrate Charles's monarchy.

"Come Leave the Lothed Stage"

Although Jonson did receive the commission to write *Love's Triumph through Callipolis* for the holiday revels in January, his contribution was relatively modest in comparison to that of Jones. Jonson's later Jacobean masques typically contain several hundred lines of speech and song; the performers in this, his first entertainment for the Caroline court, delivered a mere hundred and eighty lines. The antimasque, which had blossomed into a miniaturized comic drama during the 1620s, became an elaborate dumbshow in 1631. The printed text of *Love's Triumph* is largely given over to elaborate descriptions of Jones's scenery, costumes, and choreography; the function of the script, in many places, is simply to gloss the visual imagery.

The new emphasis on seeing, as opposed to hearing, reflected Jones's belief that visual images, in the words of Orgel and Strong, "had meaning and moral force; that seeing was believing, and that art could give us a vision of the good and the true; that the illusion represented, in short, a Platonic reality." In 1632 Jones would write that he had devised Henrietta's costume "so that corporeal beauty, consisting in symmetry, colour, and certain unexpressable graces, shining in the Queen's majesty, may draw us to the contemplation of the beauty of the soul, unto which it hath analogy." Her husband Charles, "being the only prototype to all the kingdoms under his monarchy of religion, justice, and all the virtues joined together" likewise incorporated the ideal image of "Heroic Virtue." Jones was simply articulating Charles's and Henrietta's conceptions of themselves. Contemporary political theorists held that "a king's behaviour sways his subjects lives / As the first mover all the first stars drives." The King took this maxim quite literally. Earlier that year Charles informed Henrietta's mother, Marie de Medici, that their union had attained a state of perfect harmony: "I have no need to use other authority than that of love," he wrote. "The only dispute that now exists between us is that of conquering each other by affection, both of us esteeming ourselves victorious in following the will of the other." He now believed that he and Henrietta embodied the Platonic forms of Beauty and Heroic Virtue, and that the two of them would, in the words of his 1630 orders for the regulation of the royal household, "establish government and order in our court which from thence may spread with more order through all parts of our kingdoms." [13]

The text of *Love's Triumph through Callipolis* tells an ingeniously allegorical story about the union of Heroic Love (Charles) with Beauty (Henrietta Maria) in Callipolis—Plato's "City of Heavenly Beauty." But the appearance of the King and Queen on the dance floor was bound to focus attention on the purely visual dimension of the masque. They were the fable; their presence transcended any text that the poet could weave

Charles I with His Wife, Queen Henrietta Maria, and Two of Their Children, by Anthony
van Dyck, 1632. Widely imitated portrayal of the early Stuart dynasty. The Queen's affectionate glance softens the rigidity of the King's formal pose and stately regalia. At Charles's
knee, the two-year-old Prince of Wales points toward the infant Princess.

around them. Jonson had long ago insisted that he was not a mere deviser of picture captions, "one to write, *This is a Dog;* or *This is a Hare*" (HS, VII, 91); moreover, he did not have much faith in the efficacy of Charles's and Henrietta's Platonized self-images. Nevertheless, he successfully collaborated with Jones on *Love's Triumph through Callipolis* and on its sequel *Chloridia* (February 22). Both works beautifully articulated Charles's Platonic politics. As a result, Jonson now found himself, ironically enough, in a subordinate position to his collaborator. Jonson's texts had been the *sine qua non* of the court masque throughout the previous reign; now it was just as likely that other poets could provide the kind of scaled-down script that Jones required.

In January 1631 Jonson offered the reading public a quarto text of *Love's Triumph through Callipolis.* The title page named "The Inventors. *Ben Jonson. Inigo Jones,*" and notified prospective purchasers that these copies had been printed "for *Thomas Walkley,* and are to be sold at his shop at the signe of the *Eagle* and *Child* in *Brittains-burse.*" The publication of this work was an unusual move for Jonson. Although souvenir copies of his late Jacobean masques had been privately printed for members of the court, he had not sold an entertainment to a London bookseller for over twenty years. Why did he choose to do so now? If nothing else, the 1631 quarto of *Love's Triumph through Callipolis* publicly reasserted Jonson's status as the King's masque writer at a time when he may well have suspected that he was in danger of losing his post. The appearance of Jones's name alongside his own is tantalizingly ambiguous. Since Jonson had never before put his collaborator's name on the title page, his readiness to acknowledge Jones's coauthorship of *Love's Triumph* can be read as a conciliatory gesture. Nevertheless, Jonson put his own name first and Jones's second—a nicety that did not escape Inigo's attention. When Jonson sold *Chloridia* to Walkley a month later, he did not put either of their names on the title page; but this expedient was unlikely to placate a man who believed, as Jones did, that "these shows are nothing else but pictures with light and motion."[14]

Later that spring, the shade of a court lady who had danced in *Chloridia* revived Jonson's recurrent death wish.

> What gentle Ghost, besprent with *April* deaw,
>   Hailes me, so solemnly, to yonder Yewgh?
> And beckning wooes me, from the fatall tree
>   To pluck a Garland, for her selfe, or mee?
> I doe obey you, Beautie! for in death,
>   You seeme a faire one!

The spirit who hailed the poet was Lady Jane Paulet, a young noblewoman who died, "big with child," on April 15, at the age of twenty-three. Unlike

Inigo Jones, by Anthony van Dyck. Van Dyck drew this picture of Jonson's old enemy for a series of engravings of famous men of arts.

Jonson's earlier funereal verse, his elegy on Lady Paulet conceives of death in explicitly Christian terms. When the young lady's doctors (or "torturers") came to "burne, lance, or cut" her physical wounds, she replied, "'Tis but a body which you can torment / And I, into the world, all Soule, was sent"; when the angels carried away the soul of this pregnant young woman, "her mortalitie / Became her Birth-day to Eternitie!" Lady Paulet tacitly encourages the palsy-ridden poet to rejoice in the infirmities of the mortal body whose decay he has chronicled during the previous twelve years; she urges him to take solace neither in his nimble muse nor in his still-healthy brain, but rather in his immortal soul. In his closing lines Jonson envisions a celestial masque performed by the redeemed soul who bruises "the Serpents head: Gets above Death, and Sinne, / And, sure of Heaven, rides triumphing in." [15]

Jonson still had one unutilized source of income and prestige at his disposal: the four comedies he had written between 1614 and 1629 remained unpublished. Despite his unprecedentedly low standing in the eyes of the playhouse audience, he could still appeal, as he had in the past, to the sensibilities of educated readers. Besides the quartos of *Love's Triumph through Callipolis* and *Chloridia,* the year 1631 saw an octavo edition of *The New Inn* and individual folios of *Bartholomew Fair, The Devil Is an Ass,* and *The Staple of News;* the last three texts were meant to be bound together in a single volume (HS, IX, 85). The Horatian tag on the title page of *The New Inn* concisely stated the author's motive for publishing his plays: "*Me lectori credere mallem: / Quam spectatoris fastidia ferre superbi*" ("I prefer entrusting myself to a reader to bearing the disdain of a scornful spectator"). In his "Dedication, to the Reader," he solicited the good will of anyone who "canst but spell, and joine my sense" (HS, VI, 395, 397).

The folio editions were intended to be sent out as presentation copies to a more elite circle of patrons and admirers. But there were delays in the printing house. In a letter to Newcastle, Jonson explained that it was "the Lewd Printers fault that I can send your Lordship, no more of my Booke done" than *Bartholomew Fair* and *The Devil Is an Ass* (HS, I, 211). Jonson's strained relations with John Beale, the "Lewd Printer," may explain why he was unable to supply his patron with a single folio containing all three comedies. The project was abandoned and the publisher's widow eventually inherited the unbound sheets of Jonson's abortive second folio (HS, IX, 85–86). If he had hoped to reduplicate some measure of the success achieved by his 1616 *Works,* he must have been sadly disappointed.

The downward spiral of Jonson's fortunes continued into the following winter. As the holiday season drew near, he learned that the King had commissioned an obscure courtier named Aurelian Townsend to collaborate with Jones on *Tempe Restored,* the second of Charles's Twelfth Night masques. John Pory subsequently wrote to a friend that Jonson had been "for this time, discarded by reason of the predominant power of his antagonist, Inigo Jones, who, this time twelve month, was angry with him for putting his own name before his in the title-page." More bad news was in the offing. On December 10 the Court of Aldermen decided to "forbeare to pay any more fee or wages unto Benjamine Johnson the Citties Cronologer untill he shall have presented unto this Court some fruits of his labours in that his place." They conveyed these unwelcome tidings to Jonson nine days later, during "the weeke Ushering Christmas." [16]

The following day, Jonson wrote to Newcastle about a dream he had experienced in the early morning hours of the twentieth. He prefaced his account of the dream with a description of the circumstances that led up to it. Several months previously, Sir Thomas Badger, Master of the King's Harriers, had given the bedridden poet a pet fox, "which Creature," Jonson explained, "by handling, I endeavored to make tame, aswell for the abateing of my disease, as the delight I tooke in speculation of his Nature." He mentions two motives for trying to domesticate the fox. First, foxes were thought to cure the palsy: as Jonson stroked it, the fox was supposed to infuse its vital spirits into the handler's paralytic limbs. Second, Jonson liked to speculate about the fox's nature. In the course of these meditations it must have occurred to him that the hero of his greatest comedy had been a foxlike man who pretends to be an aging, paralytic invalid. At the end of *Volpone* the poet condemns the fox to remain immobile "till thou bee'st sicke, and lame indeed"—the very fate that had now overtaken the poet. [17]

In Jonson's dream, his pet turns into a manlike fox, "cynically expressing his owne lott, to be condemn'd to the house of a Poett, where nothing was to bee seene but the bare walls, and not any thing heard but the noise of a Sawe, dividing billatts all the weeke long, more to keepe the family in exercise, then to comfort any person there with fire, save the Paralytick master; and went on in this way as the Foxe seem'd the better Fabler, of the two." The strangely articulate beast expresses the impoverished poet's mute feelings of deprivation and want. When the poet "call'd him stinking Vermine," the fox instructed him to "looke into your Cellar, which is your Larder too, You'le find a worse vermin there." When the cellar turned out to be infested with "a Colony of Moles," the dreaming poet—continuing to take the fox's fable on a strictly literal level—"sent presently into Tuttle-street, for the Kings most Excellent Mole-Chatcher to releive mee, and hunt them." But the mole catcher informed him that "the King or some good Man of a Noble Nature must helpe you," for these were metaphorical beasts: "This kind of Mole is call'd a *Want,* which will destroy you, and your family, if you prevent not the workeing of it in time" (HS, I, 213–214). "Want" is an archaic word for mole. The "interpretation both of the Fable, and Dreame," Jonson concluded, is "that I wakeing doe find Want the worst, and most workeing Vermine in a house." The talking fox, far from being a vermin, had enabled the poet to seek relief for his wants.

Lest Newcastle fail to grasp this point, Jonson concluded his letter with a request for whatever "your bounty can give mee, in the name of good Letters, and the bond of an ever-gratefull and acknowledging servant." He indicated the precise extent of his want in a postscript stating that "yesterday the barbarous Court of Aldermen have withdrawne their Chander-ly Pension, for Verjuice, and Mustard. 33l—6s—8d.—" (HS, I, 213–214).

The same quibble on "want" and "mole" crops up in Jonson's versified begging letter "To the Right Honourable, the Lord High Treasurer of England. An Epistle Mendicant, 1631" (written before March 25, 1632). Jonson penned his appeal to Lord Treasurer Weston in circumstances that plainly called for deference, yet the "Epistle Mendicant," like the December 20 letter to Newcastle, is remarkable mainly for its wit and self-assurance. Likening himself to the ruler of a besieged city, Jonson addresses the Lord Treasurer—who was known for his pride—as if he were one of his peers:

> My Lord;
> Poore wretched states, prest by extremities,
> Are faine to seeke for succours, and supplies
> Of *Princes* aides, or *good mens* Charities.

"*Disease*" and "Want," he continues, have besieged him so relentlessly that "the *Muse* not peepes out, one of hundred dayes." The central metaphor of Jonson's petition expresses his feelings of constriction and impotence, but also invests him with the status of a civic presence, an authority. From the inmost recesses of his sickroom, where his muse lies "fix'd to the bed, and boords, unlike to win / Health, or scarce breath, as she had never bin," he asks whether the Crown "dare thinke it, to relieve, no lesse renowne, / A *Bed-rid* Wit, then a *besieged* Towne." [18]

On February 4 Jonson appealed to Newcastle yet again, sending the Earl "a packet of mine owne praises, which I should not have done, if I had any stock of modestie in store." The packet included verse letters to Jonson from Cary, from an Oxford undergraduate named Nicholas Oldisworth, and from R. Goodwin. Jonson excused his lack of humility on the grounds that Newcastle "commanded it" and ruefully added that he was "now like an old bankerupt in witt, that am driven to pay debts, on my freinds creditts, and for want of satisfieing letters, to subscribe bills of Exchange" (HS, I, 210). A final, undated letter to Newcastle beseeches the Earl "to succour my present necessities this good time of Easter, and it shall conclude all begging requests hereafter" (HS, I, 212).

Did Jonson continue to languish in poverty? Notwithstanding Herford's grimly pathetic, and highly influential, portrait of an "old poet, struggling with disease and want, wringing plays and entertainments from a jaded

and reluctant brain," Jonson appears to have obtained the funds that were required to maintain his household at the Talbot. He wrote several poems in praise of Lord Treasurer Weston and his son Jerome between 1632 and 1634; he would hardly have done so if Weston had stopped payments on his crown pension. Weston also gave Jonson forty pounds by way of thanks for his epigram "To the Right Honourable, the Lord Treasurer of England" (*Und*, 77). When writing to Newcastle two or three years later, Jonson saluted him as "my best Patron" and rejoiced in being among "so sure a Clientele," phrases which suggest that the Earl had responded favorably to his pleas of 1631–32. If he needed to, Jonson could also call on Pembroke's brother, the Earl of Montgomery, on Lucius Cary (now Lord Falkland), and on his friend and patron Sir Kenelm Digby. At the request of King Charles, the city resumed payments on Jonson's pension in 1634.[19] During the 1630s Jonson was a celebrity with many enemies, living in a society that regarded penury as legitimate grounds for ridicule, yet not one of the various poems holding him up to scorn makes any reference to poverty.

Jonson's own poems from this period do not voice any complaints about miserly patrons; they do, however, express his resentment toward the architects and artists who were currently seizing the initiative in the competition for patronage at court. The arch-villain, of course, was Jones, whom Jonson (as Pory noted) "made the subject of a bitter satire or two." His "Expostulation with Inigo Jones" (1631) concedes defeat while sarcastically celebrating the triumph of matter over mind: "Oh, to make Boardes to speake! There is a taske / Painting & Carpentry are the Soule of Masque." The same animus informs his epigram "To the Right Honourable, the Lord Treasurer of England." This epigram—it is the one that prompted Weston to give Jonson forty pounds—begins by ironically apologizing for the fact that Jonson cannot afford to send Weston paintings by "*Romano, Tintoret,* / *Titian,* or *Raphael, Michael Angelo,*" and concludes by claiming that

> though I cannot as an Architect
> In glorious Piles, or Pyramids erect
> Unto your honour; I can tune in song
>   Aloud; and (happ'ly) it may last as long.

Opposite: *Sir Richard Weston, Earl of Portland,* by Anthony van Dyck. Jonson's patron invested large sums in painting and sculpture. In his epigram "To Richard, Earl of Portland" Jonson argues that poetry is more true to life, and a better investment, than painting.

As Jonson recognized, both Weston and King Charles I were expressing a strong preference in favor of painting and architecture at precisely this historical moment. The conferring of knighthood on Rubens, the first artist to be so honored, in 1630, and on Van Dyck, who in 1632 was given the title of Painter-in-Residence and an annual pension of two hundred pounds, is a clear sign of the painters' newly enhanced prestige.[20]

Although Jonson could not hope to live at such a noble rate as Jones, Rubens, or Van Dyck, he continued to reside in the fashionable neighborhood of Westminster. The "family" of servants that he mentions in his letter of December 1631 to Newcastle may have diminished, but it did not vanish altogether. True, he continued to run up debts; true, his possessions were valued at eight pounds, eight shillings, and handed over to a creditor named William Scandret, at the time of his death (HS, XI, 585; I, 249). But these facts merely show that Jonson, like many of the men with whom he passed his time, lived beyond his means. The claim that poverty and disease compelled him to keep on writing even though his heart was not in it cannot be substantiated, and indeed does Jonson a certain injustice. His last plays are the most sentimental works that he ever wrote, and he appears to have undertaken them not for money, but precisely for reasons of the heart.

• CHAPTER SIXTEEN •

Endings

When Nicholas Oldisworth visited Jonson in the early 1630s the elderly master behaved more like a divine than a comic playwright. Oldisworth and a friend went to Jonson's house in Westminster hoping "to heare / From him some flashes and fantastique Guere [gear]," but their host preached a sermon to them instead:

> His whole Discourse
> Was how Mankinde grew daily worse and worse,
> How God was disregarded, how Men went
> Downe even to Hell, and never did repent,
> With many such sadd Tales . . .

Afterward, the chastened but frustrated young visitor jestingly voiced his concern lest "future Times will, by a grosse Mistake, / *Johnson* a Bishop, not a Poët make" (HS, I, 113 n.). Oldisworth had little to fear, for Jonson would continue to write poems and plays for the remainder of his life. But the great comedian was now a crippled invalid who had no commerce with the outside world, who spent much of his time in solitude, and who was approaching the end of his days. In September 1632, Pory referred to him as "Ben Jonson, who I thought had been dead" (HS, I, 92).

These are circumstances that make for a meditative frame of mind. During the last five years of his life Jonson often reflected upon the course of his career and, sensing that the end was at hand, attempted to bring it to an orderly conclusion. The Induction to *The Magnetic Lady; or, The Humours Reconciled,* a new comedy that he was writing around the time of his sixtieth birthday, informed interested spectators that "The *Author,* beginning his studies of this kind, with *every man in his Humour;* and after, *every man out of his Humour:* and since, continuing in all his *Playes,* whereof the *New-Inne* was the last, some recent humours still, or manners of men, that went along with the times, finding himselfe now neare the close, or shutting up of his Circle, hath phant'sied to himselfe, in *Idea,* this *Magnetick Mistris"* (99–106). The figure of the circle, like that of Jonson's *imprese,* the broken compass, intimated that the end of his career would take him back to its beginnings, just as a circle closes when it returns to its point of origin.

The Magnetic Lady brought the arc of Jonson's development back to the form he had devised at the turn of the century. Compass, the scholar, and Ironside, the swordsman, correspond to the original two gallants, Lorenzo, Jr., and Prospero, while Mistress Plesance, who is young, "ripe for a man and marriageable" (Induction, 108), assumes the role played by Hesperida in *Every Man in His Humour.* Like her forebear, this *"Magnetic Mistris"* dwells in a comfortable bourgeois household in the city, and she too elopes to a nearby church with the scholar-hero as soon as the opportunity presents itself.

The new element in Jonson's reconstructed comedy of humors is the thread of romantic narrative that leads from the preservation of an infant who is about to be abandoned, through the discovery of another lost child, to the making of three marriages in the final scene. *The Magnetic Lady* was evidently meant to be a grand final synthesis that united the disparate genres of satirical farce and Hellenistic romance. Jonson's recent attempt to construct a romantic narrative had turned into a fiasco when the playgoers of 1629 found the plot of *The New Inn* impossible to follow. Hoping to avoid a repetition of this experience, he revived the chorus of spectators that he had employed in *Every Man out of His Humour* and delegated the job he had formerly assigned to his "friend" Cordatus to John Try-gust, the "Poet's servant," who (like Jonson) "learn'd *Terence,* i' the third forme at *Westminster"* (Induction, 47). Cordatus, his spokesman of 1599, had endeavored to create an ideal audience by explaining fine points of comic theory to the slow-witted Mitis; thirty-three years later, John Try-gust merely sought to guide Mr. Damplay ("damn play"), the prototype of the hostile, intrusive spectator who had cried down *The New Inn,* through the complex plot of *The Magnetic Lady.*

Within the play itself, the task of completing Jonson's circle falls to the aptly named Compass. The name alludes to Jonson's *imprese,* and he strongly hints that his scholar-hero is a surrogate for the author of the play. After hearing one of Compass's satirical portraits, his friend Ironside pointedly asks, "Who made this EPIGRAMME, you?" "No," Compass replies, "a great Clarke / As any'is of his bulke, (*Ben: Jonson*) made it."[1] But

Compass—unlike his predecessor Lorenzo, Jr.—has more urgent business at hand than the composition of epigrams. In order to achieve a happy outcome, Compass must rescue an innocent baby from the clutches of a predatory grandmother, an irresponsible nurse, and a murderous midwife, and then discover the true identity of another lost child, his bride-to-be, Plesance.

Although these developments cause the obtuse Mr. Damplay to complain that the thread of the plot is "pucker'd, and pull'd into that knot, by your Poet, which I cannot easily, with all the strength of my imagination, untie" (IV, Chorus, 2–4), they lead the author back to yet another theme with which he had been preoccupied in the years when he wrote his early comedies. During his late twenties Jonson had returned again and again to the plight of children who perish. At the end of his life, when he ventured to graft a romance plot onto the old comedy of humors, he went back to this motif and put it at the center of his comic fiction. From time immemorial, romantic comedies have been resolved by the discovery of lost children; Jonson, who had found this kind of resolution excessively facile, endowed it with a new measure of realism by dramatizing the interval in which a child who is about to be "lost" comes to term, is delivered, and stands on the verge of abandonment. The attentive spectator, who can "follow the right thred, or find it" (IV, Chorus, 20), will discover that the fortunes of this unwanted offspring are inextricably linked with those of Compass's bride, Plesance, the child who lost her identity fourteen years previously.

Three years earlier, when Jonson wrote *The New Inn,* the pressure of his family history compelled him to jettison the comedy of manners that takes up the first four acts and to replace it with a wildly improbable story about lost children and parental abandonment. Although the autobiographical material in *The Magnetic Lady* is less explicit, the same compulsions appear to be at work in his comedy of 1632. Lord Frampul, the protagonist of *The New Inn,* embodies Jonson's perception of himself as a parent who has abandoned his children and needs to atone for that act. Compass, his alter ego of 1633, vicariously fulfills Jonson's wish to be a discoverer of lost children, the savior of a child threatened with infanticide; in closing his circle, he became the hero of his own family romance.

Whatever therapeutic value *The Magnetic Lady* may have possessed for its author, this medley of satire, romance, and sentimental melodrama failed to please those who saw the King's Men perform it at the Blackfriars. Spectators who went to the play hoping to be diverted by the kind of "fantastique Guere" for which Jonson was famous must have gone away disappointed. Young Alexander Gill, who came to jeer, advised the poet that his "Ladie" might have entertained the apprentices and apple-vendors who frequented the Fortune Theater, but she could not pass muster at the Blackfriars, where "silkes and plush and all the wittes / Are Calde to see, and Censure as befittes" (HS, XI, 347). Gill also noted that the play was only performed three times and warned the author not to compound his folly by publishing it.

Jonson bore the censures of the Blackfriars audience with unaccustomed magnanimity. Although he warned Alexander Gill to "keep in thy barking Wit, thou bawling Fool" (HS, VIII, 410), Jonson continued to write for the stage. He even seems to have profited from the debacles of 1629 and 1632. The weakest parts of *The New Inn,* as Owen Felltham saw, were the "Jests so nominal" (HS, XI, 339) that Jonson borrowed from the old comedy of humors, and the same criticism could be made of *The Magnetic Lady.* The first three acts of the play are dull, but the last two, with their feverish intrigue and dark secrets from the past, can still hold a reader's attention. In the drama that he wrote during the last few years of his life, Jonson finally abandoned the comedy of humors. His thoughts continued to drift back toward genres that were in vogue during his youth, but the form that he himself had invented no longer held much fascination for him. Instead, he began to experiment with types of drama that he had either rejected in his twenties, or had employed only in the commissions executed for Philip Henslowe between 1598 and 1602.

By spring 1633 Jonson had added two more works to his extensive repertory of plays and entertainments. On May 7 the Revels Office licensed his *Tale of a Tub* for performance, though the Lord Chamberlain also instructed Jonson to remove a character named Vitruvius Hoop from the script, "exceptions being taken against it by Inigo Jones, surveyor of the kings workes."[2] And at the end of the month, when the King visited Newcastle at Welbeck Abbey, the Earl greeted him with Jonson's *Entertainment at Welbeck.*

Both of these works are nostalgic recreations of rustic wedding customs. Jonson based *A Tale of a Tub* on folk observances associated with Valentine's Day and concluded the play with an old-fashioned country wedding, in all of its homespun splendor. We hear of a "greene thing afore the Door," "some fresh hay then, to lay under foot / Some Holly and Ivie to make vine the posts," "Bride-laces," and "Old Father *Rosin,* the chiefe Minstrell here," who will lead the wedding procession wearing "Ribbanding, and Rosemary" and playing the old ballad of Tom Tiler. At the *Welbeck Entertainment,* Father Fitzale's "daughter stale" was "drest like an old *May-Lady,* with Skarfes, and a great wrought Handkerchiefe, with red, and blew, and other habiliments" for her Derbyshire marriage. Six bachelors celebrated her nuptials by running at the quintain—an equestrian game played at rural weddings. The elderly poet immersed himself in

> old Records,
> Of antick Proverbs, drawne from *Whitson-Lord's,*
> And their Authorities, at *Wakes* and *Ales,*
> With countrey precedents, and old Wives Tales.

And he was finally becoming attuned to the folk culture he had formerly scorned. As Barton says, the sixty-year-old author of the *Welbeck Entertainment* and *A Tale of a Tub* sounds like "a man slowly coming to believe that he had once lived in a Golden Age without recognizing it at the time." [3]

Nevertheless, Jonson retained his uncanny ability to adapt his own predilections to the occasion at hand. Newcastle was a devotee of country life and a passionate sportsman who maintained that "there is not better policy for a prince to please his people, than to have many holidays for their ease, and order several sports and pastimes for their recreation, and to be himself sometime spectator thereof." Moreover, during the winter of 1632–33 King Charles had vigorously opposed Chief Justice Richardson's attempts to suppress the annual feasts that the inhabitants of Somerset held on the day of the saint for whom their parish church was named. St. Valentine's Day, the holiday commemorated in *A Tale of a Tub,* was a particularly notorious example of a religious feast that had been adapted to suit the needs of a secular folk culture. As Jonson's malaprop yokels celebrate "*Zin Valentines* day, of all dayes cursin'd, looke you," the mingled heritages of saint and sinner, christening and cursing blithely blend into one another. And the characters' West Country dialect, seemingly out of place in Middlesex County, clearly links them to the current debate over the rural wakes. [4]

A Tale of a Tub gave the Caroline audience a picture of rural sports that mirrored the ideas of King Charles and Bishop William Laud. The magistrates who joined with their Puritan allies in trying to prohibit the Somerset wakes held, reasonably enough, that such festivities led to widespread public drunkenness, wanton acts of violence, and the siring of illegitimate children, who could only increase the sum of human misery. Countering these strictures, Jonson conjures up a Tudor village peopled by innocent rustics who cherish the saint's day because it invests their lives with a modicum of ceremony and order. So long as they cleave to their natural instincts and inherited beliefs, the villagers can never behave in a way that is morally wrong. Left to their own devices, they will invariably act like dyed-in-the-wool conservatives. Constable Turfe wants his daughter to marry John Clay because birds mate on St. Valentine's Day, because Awdrey has drawn John's valentine, because her parents drew one another's valentines thirty years before, because Turfe goes with Clay, and because he recognizes that Squire Tub is above her station. The end of this play does not herald the formation of the "new" society that customarily emerges at the close of a romantic comedy, because none is wanted. As its title suggests, *A Tale of a Tub* depicts a community where, much to everyone's content, nothing ever changes.

This portrayal of a self-governing and innately good rural community also carried an implied critique of the King and his court. When Charles upheld the villagers' right to preserve their traditional recreations, he was not enfranchising them to follow their natural instincts; he was asserting his own sovereignty over their affairs. The King maintained that order flowed down from his court—the political analogue to Plato's form of the good—and into the country. Within the enclosed sphere of the Caroline masque, Jones's machines created an image of nature that was perfectly subservient to the royal will. The newly fashionable genre of the court pastoral similarly depicted Henrietta as a rustic beauty who held sway over a sylvan kingdom of dutiful shepherds and shepherdesses. Both masque and pastoral were antipopular forms that reflected the insularity of the royal household during the era of Personal Rule. Jonson endorses the elitism of court culture at the conclusion of the *Welbeck Entertainment,* when a household official rudely dismisses the Derbyshire locals who have presumed to disport themselves before their sovereign: "You are too blame! Know your disease, and cure it. / Sports should not be obtruded on great Monarchs." [5] But no such disclaimer accompanies *A Tale of a Tub.* The idea of "the country" in this play is radically at odds with the concept that informs the Caroline masque and pastoral. Jonson's rustics instinctively order their existence around antique lore, natural rhythms, and seasonal rites; they possess an earthy folk wisdom that enables them to govern themselves without the intervention of any higher authority. And at the end of the day they perform a wedding entertainment for Awdrey Tub that slyly parodies the elitist court masques which were being danced at the Banqueting House.

Jonson took care to ensure that *A Tale of a Tub* had a sympathetic audience. Instead of selling his play to the King's Men at the Blackfriars Theater, as he had done with his four previous scripts, he took it to Queen Henrietta's Men, who performed at the Cockpit in Whitehall, the "theater royal" that King Charles had recently renovated. A Whitehall audience was more likely than its counterpart at the Blackfriars, which drew a sizable number of clients from the Puritanical city, to give his comedy of 1633 a favorable hearing, and apparently they did, for *A Tale of a Tub* was enough of a success to warrant a court performance on January 14, 1634. But the play was "not likt," according to Sir Henry Herbert, the Master of the Revels, when it was staged there (HS, IX, 163). The courtiers evidently registered the poet's criticism but not his compliment.

Jonson further tried their patience by refusing to obey the spirit of the proviso that the Revels Office had imposed in May. The mock masque in act V, which is provided by an illiterate carpenter named In-and-In Medley, was clearly inserted for the purpose of satirizing Jones, who had plied In-and-In's trade during his youth. In-and-In's masque would not have improved the attractions of Jonson's comedy at the Banqueting House. Jones had jeered *The Magnetic Lady* when it was performed at the Blackfriars Theater in 1632; he had plenty of friends at court; and he had good reason to undercut a play that openly mocked him despite the Lord Chamberlain's instructions to the contrary.

Jonson's spleen toward his former collaborator continued to rankle. A year later, when Newcastle again commissioned his old client to prepare an entertainment welcoming Charles to Derbyshire, Jonson seized the opportunity to insert still another lampoon of Jones into *Love's Welcome at Bolsover*. Colonel Vitruvius, the butt of this work, conveys the same message as his predecessor In-and-In Medley. Jonson reduced the Surveyor of the King's Works to the status of a popular entertainer in order to remind him, and the court, of the folk culture they were renouncing. From a professional standpoint, these slurs at Jones were most ill-advised. Two years earlier Pory noted that Jonson had lost his place at court "for this time" because Jones was exasperated with him; continued attacks on the King's surveyor could only reduce the aggressor's chances of regaining his post. Jonson wrote to Newcastle that the commission to prepare *Love's Welcome at Bolsover* "fell like the dewe of heaven on my necessities." 6 Nevertheless, he could not resist the temptation to pursue his quarrel with Jones in this, the last entertainment he would ever write.

When Jonson's plays failed on the stage his habitual response was to seek out an "understanding" reader who would vindicate him. During the last years of his life Jonson's ideal reader was Sir Kenelm Digby, a poet, adventurer, astrologer, and man of letters who stood foremost among the *virtuosi* of the age. When Sir Kenelm returned from his celebrated privateering raid in the Mediterranean, Jonson warmly applauded his "action done at *Scanderoone;* / Upon my Birth-day the eleventh of *June*" and vowed to write a poem in praise of it. Digby's courtship of Venetia Stanley generated enough amorous intrigues, stormy passions, and high-minded posturing to fill a Hellenistic novel, and when he wrote his "private memoirs" of this love affair, he cast them in the form of a prose romance called *Loose Fantasies*. Digby was also a literary critic who wrote a pioneering commentary on Spenser's *Faerie Queene* and maintained that "divine Spenser's sun no sooner set, but in Jonson a new one rose."[7] The privateering raid, the *roman à clef*, and the exegesis of Spenser's "noble book" were the diversions of a man who was reliving the glories of Elizabethan England at the same time that his client, Ben Jonson, was reimagining the literature of that era.

Jonson especially valued Digby as the guarantor of his own literary reputation. The first part of his "Epigram to My Muse, the Lady Digby, on Her Husband, Sir Kenelm Digby" is a thoroughly conventional tribute to his patron; in the second half of the poem, however, Jonson makes an imaginary journey into the Digby household and describes his reader's reception of the epigram that he has just been writing. Jonson was confident that Digby's response would be favorable,

> For he doth love my Verses, and will looke
>   Upon them, (next to *Spenser's* noble booke,)
> And praise them too. O! what a fame 't will be?
>   What reputation to my lines, and me,
> When hee shall read them at the Treasurers bord,
>   The knowing *Weston,* and that learned Lord
> Allowes them? Then, what copies shall be had,
>   What transcripts begg'd? how cry'd up, and how glad,
> Wilt thou be, *Muse,* when this shall them befall?
>   Being sent to one, they will be read of all. (*Und,* 78.23–32)

These are the words of a housebound poet trying to live vicariously through his art. The epigram at once transports him into Lady Digby's presence and expresses the wish that she will convey his verses to Sir Kenelm, who will submit them to "the knowing *Weston,*" whose approval will ensure their circulation among an ever-widening circle of readers. The poem thus intimates that the poet's continued survival will depend on the good offices of men like Digby and Weston. Before Jonson died he made Digby his literary executor, furnishing him with "true and perfect Copies," in the words of the printer Thomas Walkley, and authorizing him "to dispose thereof at his will and pleasure" (HS, IX, 98).

Lady Venetia Digby, the last of the women whom Jonson referred to as his muse, died on May 1, 1633. Her death plunged Sir Kenelm into a state of acute melancholia. He was especially concerned about Venetia's posthumous reputation. Prior to their marriage, Venetia had born a child out of wedlock to another man, and contemporary gossip, according to John Aubrey, made her out to be a woman of easy virtue. "She was so commonly courted," he wrote, "and that by Grandees, that 'twas written over her lodging one night *in literis uncialibus:* PRAY COME NOT NEER, FOR DAME VENETIA STANLEY LODGETH HERE." Her husband alleged that she had died from drinking excessive quantities of wine mixed with viper's juice, but it was rumored that she had been poisoned by her "viper hus-band who was jealous of her that she would steal a leape." Charles is said to have ordered an autopsy because of these stories; his intervention fur-ther muddied the waters and aggravated Digby's distress. "To avoid envy and scandall," Sir Kenelm moved to Gresham College, where he donned "a long mourning cloake, a high cornered hatt, his beard unshorne, lookt like a Hermite, as signs of sorrowe for his beloved Wife."[8]

Jonson's "Eupheme; or, The Fair Fame Left to Posterity of That Truly Noble Lady, the Lady Venetia Digby" was the last lyric poem, apart from three slight occasional pieces, that he would ever write. The poet consoled Digby by assuring him that his wife had led an exemplary life and was now enrolled among the saints in heaven. The six parts of "Eupheme" that survive (it was originally a ten-part sequence) take up the leading themes of Sir Kenelm's prose letter book "In Praise of Venetia Digby" — *available?* (1633–1635) and restate them in lyric verse. Like his patron, Jonson penned his tribute for the benefit of the three Digby children, the oldest of whom was only eight years old in 1633, but who would one day read

> this last Legacie of Counsell; which so soone as you arrive at yeares of mature Understanding, open you (Sir) that are the eldest, and read it to your Breth-ren, for it will concerne you all alike. Vowed by a faithfull Servant, and Client of your Familie, with his latest breath expiring it,
>
> B.J.

Digby had commissioned many portraits of his wife, including one exe-cuted by Anthony Van Dyck two days after her death; he assured his sons that this legacy would compensate for the shortcomings of his own written memorial. The bereaved husband derived great satisfaction from Van Dyck's portrait and maintained that it was indistinguishable from the im-age of Venetia that he carried in his mind. Jonson of course held other views about the relative worth of visual and verbal artistry. "The Picture of the Body" and "The Picture of the Mind," which he included in "Eu-pheme," both insist upon the superiority of poetry to painting. Although these are the most polished poems in the sequence, Jonson had written them over a decade earlier, before his "mistress" had married his patron, and they exude an air of witty self-assurance that had deserted him by the time he wrote "Eupheme."[9]

The elderly poet who penned his "Elegie on My Muse" ("The truly honoured Lady, the Lady VENETIA DIGBY; who living, gave me leave to call

Sir Kenelm Digby, by Anthony van Dyck, 1636, engraved by Robert van Voerst. Executed while Jonson's grief-stricken patron was living in seclusion at Gresham College.

her so. / Being / Her APOTHEŌSIS, or *Relation to the Saints"*; HS, VIII, 282) for Digby and his children wanted to join Venetia in paradise: "'Twere time that I dy'd too, now shee is dead / Who was my *Muse,* and life of all I sey'd" (*Und,* 84.ix.1–2). Like his friend and patron, Jonson wished to sever the ties of earthly affection and prepare for death.

According to Sir Kenelm, the "wonderfully devout and pious" Venetia

Venetia Stanley, Lady Digby, on Her Death-bed, by Anthony van Dyck, 1633. Anxious about his wife's posthumous reputation, Digby commissioned this work two days after her death. Jonson's "Eupheme," written during the same period, is a verbal portrait of Lady Digby.

had already shown the way to heaven, spending "five or six houres every day upon her knees," and performing countless works of charity. As a result, her husband could take comfort in the prospect of beholding Venetia's resurrected body in paradise. "It is true," he wrote, "that the beatificke vision of the Divinity doth so fill the intellectuall part of the soule, that it not onely satisfieth but aboundeth and runneth over." There they would love one another with the passion of two saints: "If she be a chiefe meanes that I attaine the blisse she enjoyed, shall not I take more comfort in her then in all the Saintes in heaven besides?" Sir Kenelm's beatific vision of a redeemed Venetia Digby consoled her poet as well. Jonson had

long since depicted her body and her mind, but he now believed that neither of these entities ultimately mattered, for

> there is a third, commixt,
> Of *Body* and *Spirit* together, plac'd betwixt
> Those other two; which must be judg'd, or crown'd.

Like Sir Kenelm, he was now convinced that a better Venetia awaited him
in heaven: "You will meet her there, / Much more desir'd, and dearer then
before." Jonson had known the mundane counterpart of this transfigured
Venetia—she was the secular saint commemorated in Digby's letter book.
In the latter part of his "Elegy," Jonson depicts the life of Saint Venetia,
concluding with the vision of the risen Christ that came at the hour of her
death:

> In this sweete *Exstasie,* she was rapt hence. ⎤
> Who reades, will pardon my Intelligence, ⎮
> That thus have ventur'd these true straines upon; ⎮
> To publishe her a *Saint.* My *Muse* is gone.[10]

Poetic immortality had taken on a new meaning for Ben Jonson. "Apotheosis," as his title proclaims, is simply another way of saying "Relation to
the Saints." Maintaining that the poet's loss was the Christian's gain, he
turned his thoughts toward last things and warned his readers to expect
no more verses: "My *Muse* is gone."

The writer of this final elegy is the same Jonson who rehearsed many
"sadd tales" to Nicholas Oldisworth and who was "much aflickted, that
hee had profain'd the scripture, in his playes; and lamented it with hor-
ror." Jonson's death wish had finally evolved into a steadfast religiosity.
Two years previously he had celebrated the transfiguration of Lady Jane
Paulet. In 1634 he paid tribute "To Mrs. Alice Sutcliffe on Her Divine
Meditations"; a year later he contributed another devotional poem, "The
Garland of the Blessed Virgin Marie," to Anthony Stafford's *The Female
Garland.* The strong undercurrent of Mariolatry in these poems suggests
that the author was reverting to the Anglo-Catholic pieties of his late
twenties. His old tie to the Church of Rome could easily have been
strengthened by Digby, a devout Catholic; by Weston, who was believed
to have converted to Catholicism by the time of his death in 1635; and by
Stafford, who had Catholic leanings. The phrases that the elderly Jonson
uses when addressing his patrons are likewise suggestive in this regard. He
pens an "Epistle Mendicant" to Weston; he greets Newcastle with "the
hearty prayers of a Religious Beadsman" in one letter and subscribes another with the words "Your truest beadsman."[11]

Nevertheless, Jonson continued to write secular works of litera-ture until the end of his life. On New Year's Day, 1635, he pre-sented King Charles with a pastoral eclogue based on *Pan's Anniversary*, a masque that he had written for King James fifteen years earlier. Later that year he contributed a commendatory poem to the 1635 quarto of Joseph Rutter's *The Shepherd's Holiday*. He also wrote "An Epigram to My Jovial Good Friend Mr. Robert Dover, on His Instauration of His Hunting and Dancing at Cotswold" for *Annalia Dubrensia* (1636), a collection of poems celebrating the newly revived Cotswold Olympic Games. At about the same time he decided to write a pastoral play of his own. The Prologue to *The Sad Shepherd, or, A Tale of Robin Hood*, his final, unfinished comedy, introduces the author as *"he that hath feasted you these forty yeares."* Since Jonson began writing for the stage in 1597, these words, if taken literally, indicate that he was working on *The Sad Shepherd* in 1637, the year of his death. Lucius Cary, now Lord Falkland, was under this impression, for his funeral elegy on Jonson states that "not long before his *Death*, our *Woods* he meant / To *visit*, and descend from *Thames* to *Trent*," the Trent being the site of *The Sad Shepherd*.[12]

Jonson undertook this project at a moment when pastoral drama, which had flourished under Elizabeth, was enjoying a remarkable revival. The pastoral play first became an important part of the Caroline repertory in 1633 when the Queen, in a breathtaking departure from convention, acted in a court performance of Walter Montague's *The Shepherd's Paradise*. During the pre-Lenten holidays of 1634, when *A Tale of a Tub* was "not likt" at court, their majesties did like revivals of *The Winter's Tale*, *Cymbe-line*, and Fletcher's *Faithful Shepherdess*. Charles and Henrietta valued pastoral because they saw in it a mirror image of the purified court over which they presided. The faithful shepherd's chaste and innocent love re-flected their commitment to marital fidelity; the secluded Arcadian bower was emblematic of their isolation from Europe and the Thirty Years War. In the years ahead, they would also behold a (lost) "pastoral of *Flori-mene*," Rutter's *Shepherd's Holiday*, and Randolph's *Amyntas*.[13]

Although Jonson doubtless hoped that this trend would work to his advantage, his own ideas about pastoral were very different from the ones currently in vogue. The modern English and Italian pastoral poets had erred, Jonson believed, by importing an egregiously literary idiom into allegedly rustic settings. He had grumbled to Drummond in 1619 that "Sidney, Guarini make every man speak as well as themselves, forgetting decorum, for Dametas sometimes speaks Grave sentences" (*Conv*, 611–613). The court pastoral of the 1630s, which set even loftier standards of loquacity, spawned a new generation of polite shepherds who practiced a refined code of etiquette in distant landscapes where Jonson had never traveled. Reacting to this unwelcome development, the Prologue to *The Sad Shepherd* complained "that no stile for *Pastorall* should goe / Current, but what is stamp'd with *Ah*, and O" (53–54).

The Prologue advised prospective spectators that Jonson would be staying closer to home:

> though he now present you with such wooll,
> As from meere *English* Flocks his *Muse* can pull,
> He hopes when it is made up into Cloath;
> Not the most curious head here will be loath
> To weare a Hood of it; it being a Fleece,
> To match, or those of *Sicily* or *Greece*.
> His *Scene* is *Sherwood* . . .

Jonson intended to offer the Caroline audience a version of country life that was radically different from the chaste idylls currently in vogue at Whitehall. He portrays Sherwood Forest as an earthy milieu peopled by good-natured rustics who are comparable, in many ways, to the villagers in *A Tale of a Tub*. Like the country copulatives who cavort their way through Jonson's comedy of 1634, Robin and Maid Marian are flirtatious, sportive types, who feel nostalgic about the

> happy age, when on the Plaines,
> The Wood-men met the Damsells, and the Swaines
> The Neat'ards, Plow-men, and the Pipers loud,
> And each did dance, some to the Kit, or Crowd,
> Some to the Bag-pipe, some the Tabret mov'd,
> And all did either love, or were belov'd.

Although the foresters worry about "the sowrer sort / Of Shepherds"—the Puritans—who "call ours, *Pagan* pastimes, that infect / Our blood with ease, our youth with all neglect," Robin's band of merrymen remains immune to the blight of solemnity and scrupulosity. Indeed it is the absence of any political or religious authorities at all that finally distinguishes their world from that of Squire Tub. Robin and Marian are outlaws; they dwell not in the outskirts of London, but in the remote wilds of Nottinghamshire. Martin Butler has recently argued that several dramatists writing in the decade before the Civil War conceived of rustic outlaw bands as "alternative political bodies, woodland monarchies," which heralded the emergence of a distinctive "country" ideology. "In the absence of parliament when the country as a distinctive political unit did not exist," he writes, these playwrights "were endeavoring to conceptualize the country forcefully and formally as a separate and independent corporate body even while the actual conditions of politics remained court-centered." [14] The author of *The Sad Shepherd* had the same end in view. Jonson's last comedy is both a transplanted Theocritean pastoral and an English Georgic, a final statement of the ideals that he originally articulated in "To Sir Robert Wroth" and "To Penshurst."

Over and against the healthy community composed of Robin and his family, Jonson sets Aeglamour, the sad shepherd for whom the play is named, and Maudlin, the wicked witch who queens it over her family of rustic churls. Aeglamour is Jonson's version of the courtly shepherd who descends from the pastorals of Sidney and Guarini and from the French romances that Henrietta held in such high esteem. True to his kind, Aeglamour whiles away the hours delivering operatic laments for his supposedly deceased love, Earine. Maudlin, his foil and nemesis, personifies the mischievous, uncontrolled energies that threaten to disrupt the fabric of country life. The sorceress is the secret cause of Aeglamour's sadness, for it is she who has spirited Earine away and given her out for dead. The overall scheme of the play thus resembles a rusticated comedy of humors: the overly amorous Aeglamour is played off against the excessively spiteful Maudlin, while Robin defines the norm of wholesome sanity.

Exactly what Jonson would have done with this material is anyone's guess, but the presence of a hermit named Reuben the Reconciler in the cast of characters suggests that he intended to bring the sad shepherd out of his humor and perhaps even to reform Maudlin. Reuben's name sounds like Robin's, and its second syllable, when conjoined with the epithet "Reconciler," qualifies him for membership in the eponymous Tribe of Ben. The founder of the tribe evidently hoped, against very long odds, to assist in healing the cultural disorders that had brought England to the brink of civil war in the summer of his sixty-sixth year. During the same months that King Charles attempted to levy ship money from his unwilling subjects and initiated the first Scot's War, his neglected pensioner was doing what he could to repair the widening rift between court and country.

The other fragment that Jonson left incomplete at the time of his death smacks of even grander aspirations. *Mortimer His Fall* harks back to the Elizabethan chronicle history play, and to the days when Jonson supplied Philip Henslowe with *Richard Crookback* and parts of *Robert II King of Scots*. The current of nostalgia that runs through all of Jonson's late plays continued to draw him back to his point of origin. He now took up a subject that had been treated in Marlowe's *Edward II* and set out to dramatize it, as his self-consciously archaic title would suggest, in the manner of a late medieval *de casibus* tragedy. Yet he also planned to satisfy the formal requirements of classical tragedy. Whereas Marlowe's *Edward II*, like most chronicle histories, depicts a series of events that extends over many years and more than one generation, *Mortimer His Fall,* in keeping with ancient practice and Aristotelian precept, would have focused on the brief interval wherein Mortimer's fortunes changed from weal to woe. The "arguments" that accompany this one-hundred-and-fifteen-line fragment also reveal that Jonson planned to incorporate several choruses and a classical messenger scene in the finished play. The result, one gathers, was to have been a final amalgamation of classical and native tragedy. Needless to say, Jonson's reach now exceeded his grasp, but the spectacle of this aged, paralytic master stirs the imagination, as does the poignant notation that concludes the printed text of *Mortimer His Fall:* "Hee dy'd, and left it unfinished" (HS, VII, 62).

H The nineteenth-century editor William Gifford surmised that *Mortimer His Fall* was "the last draught of Jonson's quill," but that honor could equally well belong to *The Sad Shepherd,* or to *The English Grammar,* or to one of the passages transcribed in *Timber; or, Discoveries Made upon Men and Matter, as They Have Flowed out of His Daily Readings, or Had Their Refluxe to His Peculiar Notion of the Times.* Although books about Jonson, including this one, invariably treat the last-mentioned work as a repository of views that he held throughout his life, the extant text of the *Discoveries* was probably compiled after the fire of 1623; the concluding meditation on dramatic form clearly derives from Daniel Heinsius's 1629 edition of Horace, and another passage is quoted from an edition of Buchler's *Institutio Poetica* published in 1633.[15] It is hard to imagine when Jonson would have stopped transcribing his "discoveries": at the time of his stroke in 1628–29 he had been gathering them for almost thirty years, and confinement is likely to have strengthened this habit.

The *Discoveries* adds another dimension to the story of Jonson's last years. At the same time that he was steeping himself in the native heritage of Elizabethan literature, Jonson was assembling, translating, and commenting on the seminal texts of neoclassical criticism. The *Discoveries,* and especially those parts of it that fall after 1629, reveal that his youthful ambition to grasp the inner logic of literary forms persisted into the last years of his life. In the privacy of his study, Jonson could pursue his life-long quest for formal clarity without fear of rebuff. The comic poet who assured Caroline spectators that he would "steepe their temples, and bathe their braines in laughter" renounced mirth in the pages of his commonplace book: "For, as *Aristotle* saies rightly, the moving of laughter is a fault in Comedie, a kind of turpitude, that depraves some part of a mans nature without a disease." In the penultimate section of his *Discoveries,*

Endings

Jonson translated and transcribed Heinsius's account of the refinement of classical comedy and unequivocally rejected the "old" comedy of Aristophanes: "This is truly leaping from the Stage to the Tumbrell againe, reducing all witt to the originall Dungcart." In his final reflections on "*the magnitude, and compasse of any Fable, Epicke, or Dramatick*," which are also taken from Heinsius, he treats literary artifacts as geometric objects that can be measured and classified in the same way as other natural phenomena. His "*conclusion concerning the Whole, and the Parts*" carries the elderly poet's quest for a grand synthesis to its final resting place: "*For the whole, as it consisteth of parts; so without all the parts it is not the whole; and to make it absolute, is requir'd, not only the parts, but such parts as are true. For a part of the whole was true; which if you take away, you either change the whole, or it is not the whole. For, if it be such a part, as being present or absent, nothing concernes the whole, it cannot be call'd a part of the whole.*" [16]

At first glance, Jonson's continuing rage for order is at variance with his immersion in "*old Records, / Of antick Proverbs, drawne from* Whitson-Lord's," and with his intention to loom the wool of "*meere* English Flocks" in his final comedy. But he had always combined a keen eye for microscopic local details with an equally pronounced affinity for system and method, and, in the final analysis, these two aspects of his genius complement one another. Like his friend Bacon, whose new scientific method was founded on "natural histories" of minute sensory phenomena, Jonson based his literary practice on "language, such as men doe use." In his quest for forms that would enable him to achieve this end, he remained convinced that "*custome* is the most certaine Mistresse of Language, as the publicke stampe makes current money." [17] The regional dialects of *A Tale of a Tub* and *The Sad Shepherd* and the theoretical dicta of the *Discoveries* are equally fitting outcomes of his lifelong search for the foundations of ordinary language.

In the same spirit, the title page of his *English Grammar* (1640) states that he has based it on his "observation of the English Language now spoken, and in use." Jonson meant what he said. He incorporated one hundred and eighteen quotations from twelve different authors, ranging from the fourteenth to the sixteenth centuries, into the fifteen-page section on syntax. A modern grammarian comments that his approach was "quite unique in his own day; one has to go into the eighteenth century before finding anyone systematically giving quotations to illustrate grammatical patterns, and even then it is done mainly with the purpose of taking writers to task, not with that of exemplifying normal usage." Jonson occasionally grumbles about the vagaries of custom. He bemoans the disappearance of inflected verb forms: "For, seeing *time*, and *person* be, as it were, the right, and left hand of a *Verbe;* what can the maiming bring else, but a lamenesse to the whole body." In his account of the alphabet, he seizes an opportunity to voice his nationalistic prejudice against usages imported from France. *Q,* he declares, "is a Letter we might very well spare in our *Alphabet,* if we would but use the serviceable *k.* as he should be, and restore him to the right of reputation he had with our Fore-fathers . . . For, the *English-Saxons* knew not this halting *Q.* with her waiting-woman *u.* after her." [18]

Although Jonson's ideals remained intact, his ability to articulate them perforce declined. Izaak Walton was informed that during Jonson's last years his pensions were "given to a woman that govern'd him, with whome he livd and dyed nere the Abie in west minster . . . nether he nor she tooke much Care for next weike: and wood be sure not to want Wine: of which he usually tooke too much before he went to bed, if not oftner and soner" (HS, I, 182). Clarendon, who knew Jonson personally, writes that "he lived to be very old, and till the Palsy made a deepe impression upon his body and his minde" (HS, XI, 513).

Ben Jonson died on August 16, 1637. He "was buried the next day following, being accompanied to his grave with all or the greatest part of the nobilitie and gentrie then in the towne." Within his own domain—comedy, the short lyric poem, and the masque—the poet whom they honored had bequeathed masterpieces. His best work rivals that of any writer who ever lived. To borrow Henry James's observation about Balzac, "It was not given him to flower, for our convenience, into a single supreme felicity," but he set a standard of literary craftsmanship that has never been excelled. His "sons" and admirers, who promptly assembled a volume of tributes entitled *Jonsonus Virbius* (1638), praised him as the "great instructor" who had taught an entire nation the art of poetry. When the poet Sidney Godolphin characterized Jonson as the *"voice* most eccho'd by *consenting Men,"* he was only giving him his due. Jonson's "To Penshurst" became the model for the country house poem; "Drink to me only with thine eyes" inspired innumerable cavalier lyrics. "Every subsequent royal masque from Charles's reign," write Orgel and Strong, "is a direct elaboration or extension of themes stated in the Jonsonian entertainments of 1631." Dryden would subsequently single out *Epicoene* as the prototype for the English comedy of manners. "These times thus living o're *thy* Models," proclaimed the dramatist William Cartwright, "we / Thinke them not so much *wit* as *prophesie."* [19]

The monument to Jonson in the poet's corner of Westminster Abbey was less imposing but equally eloquent in its way. His burial place was covered by a piece of blue marble, a little over one foot square, that remained blank at the time of his interment. According to Aubrey, a passer-by named Jack Young, "walking there when the grave was covering," gave a stonemason eighteen pence to inscribe it with the words "O RARE BENN: JONSON." Whereas the eulogists who contributed to *Jonsonus Virbius* hailed Jonson as a representative figure, Young, with equal justification, commemorated his uniqueness. Despite his reverence for authority, Jonson stubbornly refused to surrender his individuality to the culturally approved models with which he identified so strongly. Although he advised the aspiring poet to "make choise of one excellent man above the rest, and so to follow him, till he grow very *Hee*," he was also acutely sensitive to the dangers of imitation: "Nay, wee so insist in imitating others, as we cannot (when it is necessary) returne to our selves." "*Tanquam Explorator*," the Senecan motto that he entered on the title pages of his own books, indicates that he regarded himself "as an explorer." In the same spirit, he advised his followers that "I will have no man addict himselfe to mee; but if I have any thing right, defend it as Truth's, not mine." [20]

Jonson's explorations extended into the most painful and embarrassing aspects of his own life. A century later, Samuel Johnson came to value biography above all other genres because it encompasses "what comes near to us, what we can use." [21] Ben Jonson vastly expanded the category

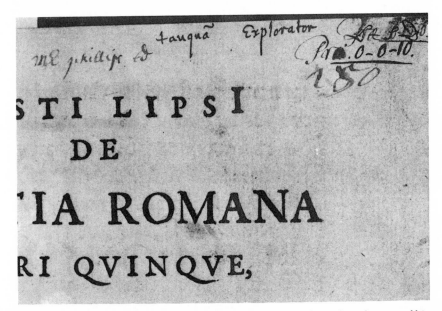

Autograph manuscript of Jonson's Senecan motto. Detail from the title page of his copy of Justus Lipsius, *De Militia Romana*, 1602.

of the usable. The stench of the London streets where he spent his boyhood, the untimely deaths of his daughter and son, the plague of 1610, the drinking bout that made him into a public laughingstock in 1613, the scandalous love affair between his benefactor Buckingham and King James, the obesity of his aging body, the loss of his friend Henry Morison, the stroke that turned him into a paralytic invalid—such were the materials from which he wrought his masterpieces. The moral of Jonson's story is that everything can be of use to us.

Epilogue

Jonson's admirers consoled themselves with the thought that the master lived on in his writings. "Yet if *He* doe not at *his* full appeare," wrote the dramatist John Ford, "survey *him* in *his* WORKES, and know *him* there." This advice proved easy to follow, for Jonson repeatedly addresses his readers in his own voice. The author who speaks to us from within the works is largely concerned with preventing misinterpretations of what he has written. He issues numerous directives that refer his readers to the relevant classical models; he insists that he and he alone has the right to determine the meaning of his poems and plays. Jonson recognized that his claim to be the authoritative interpreter of his own oeuvre would be called into question. When he assures his patron Pembroke, "I have avoided all particulars"—that is, allusions to living persons—he immediately goes on to note that "some will be so readie to discredit me, as they will have the impudence to belie themselves." But such interpretations cannot be valid: "For, if I meant them not, it is so." The contributors to *Jonsonus Virbius* unhesitatingly endorsed Jonson's right to pass judgment on his own works. For Godolphin he remained the "*best Judge* of what was fit." John Vernon, a decidedly lesser son of Ben, confessed that "wee / Did nothing *know*, but what was *taught* by *Thee*." Jonson's voice is so "strong, and yet soe cleare," concluded an anonymous eulogist, that "hee is, his owne Expositor." The only contributor to question this posture of abject dependence was Owen Felltham, who wryly commented that he

> Of whom I write this, has prevented me,
> And boldly said so much in his owne praise,
> No other *pen* need any *Trophie* raise.[1]

Epilogue

Michel Foucault writes that the "coming into being of the notion of 'author' constitutes the privileged moment of *individualization* in the history of ideas, knowledge, literature, philosophy, and the sciences."[2] Jonson's career marks the emergence of this notion within the history of English literature. The codes of reading that he incorporated in his literary works are but a single aspect of his prolonged, and astonishingly successful, effort to establish a proprietary claim to his own writings. Jonson's preoccupation with this goal informs every phase of his professional life. Recall his pioneering attempts to gain control of the scripts he sold to the acting companies; his equally unprecedented supervision of the printing of his plays; the elaborate and innovative process of canon-formation that led to the publication of his authorized *Works;* his inscriptions of his own name into his poems and plays; his projection of his own values onto his patrons; his notorious quarrel with Jones over the authorship of the masques that they prepared together; and, finally, his sponsorship of a coterie of "sons" who reaffirmed their adoptive father's interpretation of his own works.

What motivated Jonson's extraordinary campaign to secure his authorial prerogatives? What needs did it satisfy? Foucault remarks that "historically, this type of ownership has always been subject to what one might call penal appropriation." In other words, "Texts, books, and discourses really began to have authors to the extent that authors became subject to punishment, that is, to the extent that discourses could be transgressive." This generalization aptly describes the circumstances in which Jonson became an author. He entered the literary profession as a writer of outrageously satirical comedies. When his plays came to the attention of the government authorities he was repeatedly interrogated, imprisoned, and, in at least one instance, threatened with bodily mutilation ("the report was that they should then had their ears cutt and noses").[3]

Jonson gives his own view of these tactics in the *Discoveries:* "It is true, I have beene accus'd to the Lords, to the *King;* and by great ones: but it hap'ned my accusers had not thought of the Accusation with themselves; and so were driven, for want of crimes, to use invention, which was found slander . . . And then they may thinke, what accusation was like to prove, when they, that were the Ingineers, fear'd to be the Authors." Jonson insists that his accusers take full responsibility for their interpretations of his work; they, not he, are the authors of the scurrilous meanings they discover in his text. He goes on to argue that these superimposed meanings are inconsistent with the organic unity of the work as a whole: "Nay, they would offer to urge mine owne Writings against me; but by pieces, (which was an excellent way of malice) as if any mans Context, might not seeme dangerous, and offensive, if that which was knit, to what went before, were defrauded of his beginning; or that things, by themselves utter'd, might not seeme subject to Calumnie, which read entire, would appeare most free." In contrast to the piecemeal interpretations of his detractors, Jonson invokes the structural wholeness of the classical text: "*For the whole,* as it consisteth of parts; so without all the parts it is not the whole." By the same token Jonson's assertion that he is himself an author of "works," rather than a malcontent rhymester, rests upon the claim that he possesses the learning and skill to participate in the classical tradition. Any resemblances between the literary artifact and living individuals are coincidental—an unavoidable by-product of "the likenesse of vice and facts." In cases where Jonson had reason to fear that his enemies would perceive such resemblances (*Every Man out of His Humour, Sejanus, Poetaster*), he invoked a vast array of classical authorities, as if to reaffirm in advance the timeless prerogatives of authorship. Inigo Jones understandably complained that Jonson had simply used the ancients to camouflage his own bad intentions: "The good's translation, butt the ill's thine owne." [4] Nevertheless, Jonson's strategy succeeded and won a measure of artistic independence not only for himself, but for Dryden and Pope as well.

Modern critics from Wimsatt and Beardsley to Barthes and Foucault have taught us to see the author as a constricting figure, an unwelcome intruder into the free play of literary interpretation. He is "the principle of thrift in the proliferation of meaning," Foucault maintains, a functional concept "by which one impedes the free circulation, the free composition, decomposition, and recomposition of fiction." [5] This concept arose, however, in a cultural setting where the "free" interpretation of a text could have a chilling effect on artistic expression, and indeed could threaten a writer's very existence. Authors were not the only, or even the most important, factors in the repression of meaning. On the contrary, the institution of authorship created a context in which Jonson's transgressive texts could circulate freely despite official opposition to his work. The role of author helped to enfranchise displaced intellectuals such as himself; its function was to enlarge, rather than to constrain, the sphere of literary discourse.

Four centuries later the author has come to signify the dead hand of the past. If Jonson flourishes today, at a time when authoritarian modes of interpretation appear to be increasingly bankrupt, it is probably because of the powerfully subversive streak that led him to seek the shelter of authorship in the first place. He comes near to us not as a father or a judge, but as a chronic transgressor who lived to tell the tale.

✦ NOTES ✦

✦ ILLUSTRATION CREDITS ✦

✦ INDEX ✦

Notes

In addition to the abbreviations listed on p. xiv, the following abbreviations and short titles appear in the notes:

Bentley   Gerald E. Bentley, *The Jacobean and Caroline Stage*, 7 vols. (Oxford, 1941–1968)

Chamberlain   *The Letters of John Chamberlain*, ed. Norman E. McLure, 2 vols. (Philadelphia, 1939)

Chambers   E. K. Chambers, *The Elizabethan Stage*, 4 vols. (Oxford, 1923)

Dekker   *The Dramatic Works of Thomas Dekker*, ed. Fredson Bowers, 4 vols. (Cambridge, Eng., 1953–1961)

DNB   *The Dictionary of National Biography*, 22 vols. (Oxford, 1908)

JAB   *The Jonson Allusion Book: A Collection of Allusions to Ben Jonson from 1597 to 1700*, ed. Joseph Quincy Adams, Clark Sutherland Northrup, and Martin Wright Sampson (New Haven, 1922)

Kay   W. David Kay, *Jonson, Horace, and the Poetomachia* (Ann Arbor, Mich.: University Microfilms, 1968)

Nashe   *The Works of Thomas Nashe*, ed. R. B. McKerrow, 5 vols. (1904–1910; corrected rpt., Oxford, 1958)

Proclamations   *Stuart Royal Proclamations*, vol. 1, *Royal Proclamations of King James I, 1603–1625*, ed. James F. Larkin and Paul L. Hughes (Oxford, 1973)

Stone   Lawrence Stone, *The Crisis of the Aristocracy, 1558–1641* (Oxford, 1965)

Prologue

1. *Und*, 14, "An Epistle to Master John Selden," line 86; HS, XI, 383–384; Dedication of *Volpone*, HS, V, 18.
2. Freud, *Jokes and Their Relation to the Unconscious*, ed. and trans. James Strachey (London, 1960), p. 233. Where Strachey translates Freud's "Vorstellungsinhalt" as "ideational content," I have substituted the less cumbersome "idea."

3. George E. Vaillant, *Adaptation to Life* (Boston, 1977), p. 385; Horney, *Neurosis and Human Growth,* in *The Collected Works of Karen Horney,* vol. 2 (New York, 1964), pp. 26–27; Kay, p. 30.
4. *Conv,* 234–235. For the title pages of the early quartos, see HS, III, 195, and HS, IV, 24, 197. For early documents relating to Jonson's social status, see HS, I, 217–219, and HS, XI, 572, 579. See below, Chapter 6.

1. *Beginnings*

1. On May 8, 1610, a clerk in the Court of Chancery stated that Jonson was "aged 37. years or thereaboute" (HS, I, 228); a Chancery deposition dated October 20, 1623, gives his age as "50 yeares and upwards" (HS, XI, 582–583); the 1640 folio text of *Und,* 78.14, reads, "Upon my birthday, the eleventh of June" (for the reliability of this reading—it has been questioned—see HS, XI, 100). If restrictively interpreted, the two depositions imply that Jonson's birthday fell between October 1572 and May 1573, but the phrase "and upwards" suggests that it may have been slightly earlier. For expository convenience, I have adopted the traditional birthday of June 11, 1572. Note that the earlier text of *Und,* 9.15, written in January 1619, states that Jonson has "told Six and forty years." Jonson apparently revised the poem after his return to London later that spring: the version published in *The Underwood* gives his age as "Seven and fortie." See Rosalind Miles, *Ben Jonson: His Life and Work* (London, 1986), pp. 280–282; and Mark Eccles's article on Jonson in "Brief Lives: Tudor and Stuart Authors," *Studies in Philology,* 79 (1982), 77–78; *Conv,* 236–239.
2. HS, XI, 508–509; HS, I, 139, 178, 181; Eccles, "Jonson's Marriage," p. 261.
3. J. B. Bamborough, "The Early Life of Ben Jonson," *Times Literary Supplement,* 8 (1960), 225; The London County Council, *Survey of London,* ed. Sir George Gater and Walter H. Godfrey, vol. 18, *The Strand (The Parish of St. Martin-in-the-Fields, Part II)* (London, 1937), pp. 23–25, "The Hartshorn Lane Sewer."
4. Margaret Pelling, "Appearance and Reality: Barber Surgeons, the Body and Disease," in *London, 1500–1700: The Making of the Metropolis,* ed. A. L. Beier and Roger Finlay (London, 1986), p. 87.
5. *Conv,* 240–241; Stone, p. 689; John Sergeaunt, *Annals of Westminster School* (London, 1898), p. 62; Foster Watson, *The Old Grammar Schools* (Cambridge, 1916), pp. 59, 83–92.
6. Stone, pp. 672–724; Mark Curtis, *Oxford and Cambridge in Transition* (Oxford, 1959); J. H. Hexter, "The Education of the Aristocracy in the Renaissance," in *Reappraisals in History,* 2d ed. (Chicago, 1979), pp. 45–70; *Disc,* 65–66.
7. E. Pearlman, "Ben Jonson: An Anatomy," *English Literary Renaissance,* 9 (1979), 368; *Bartholomew Fair,* II.vi.76–77, 79–80.
8. Arthur F. Leach, *Educational Charters and Documents, 598 to 1909* (Cambridge, 1911), p. 501; Sergeaunt, *Annals of Westminster School,* p. 21; *Disc,*

2031–32, 647–668; Dedication of *Volpone*, HS, V, 19; Jonas Barish, *Ben Jonson and the Language of Prose Comedy* (Cambridge, Mass., 1962); *Disc*, 954–956.

9. R. R. Bolgar, "Classical Reading in Renaissance Schools," *Durham Research Review*, 2 (1955), 18–27; Douglas Duncan, *Ben Jonson and the Lucianic Tradition* (Cambridge, 1979).

10. Richard S. Peterson, *Imitation and Praise in the Poems of Ben Jonson* (New Haven, 1981), pp. 57–58.

11. Camden, *Britannia*, trans. Philemon Holland (1610), p. 182; *History of the Most Renowned and Victorious Princess Elizabeth*, ed. Wallace McCaffrey (Chicago, 1970), p. xxii.

12. *A Collection of Curious Discoveries*, ed. J. Ayloffe (London, 1771), as cited in Kevin Sharpe, *Sir Robert Cotton, 1586–1631: History and Politics in Early Modern England* (Oxford, 1979), p. 21; *Ep*, 91, and *The Haddington Masque*, lines 23–29, where Jonson cites Camden.

13. Sharpe, *Sir Robert Cotton*, pp. 195–221.

14. *Ep*, 14.3–4; David Norbrook, *Poetry and Politics in the English Renaissance* (London, 1984), pp. 133, 175–176.

15. *Conv*, 240–241; Bamborough, "The Early Life of Ben Jonson."

16. *Conv*, 242. For a bricklayer's pay, see *Tudor Royal Proclamations*, vol. 3, ed. Paul L. Hughes and James F. Larkin (New Haven, 1969), p. 40; for a soldier's pay, see C. G. Cruickshank, *Elizabeth's Army* (Oxford, 1946), p. 104, and *passim; Conv*, 243–245.

17. Pearlman, "Ben Jonson: An Anatomy," p. 368; more generally, see Ian Donaldson, "Jonson and Anger," in *English Satire and the Satiric Tradition*, ed. Claude Rawson (Oxford, 1984), pp. 56–71.

18. *Conv*, 287–289, 477, 481–482, 290–292, 357–360.

19. Eccles, "Jonson's Marriage"; Peter Laslett, *The World We Have Lost*, 3d ed. (New York, 1983), p. 83; "Statute of Apprentices," in R. H. Tawney and E. Power, *Tudor Economic Documents*, vol. 1 (London, 1924), pp. 339–340.

20. Chambers, IV, 347–349; Dekker, I, 351; Fredson Bowers, "Ben Jonson the Actor," *Studies in Philology*, 34 (1937), 352–406.

21. Dekker, I, 351. For an actor's pay, see Gerald Bentley, *The Profession of Player in Shakespeare's Time* (Princeton, 1984), pp. 24–113; and Mary I. Oates and William J. Baumol, "On the Economics of the Theater in Renaissance London," *Swedish Journal of Economics*, 74 (1972), 157.

22. Gerald Bentley, *The Profession of Dramatist in Shakespeare's Time* (Princeton, 1971), p. 3.

23. Oates and Baumol, "On the Economics of the Theater in Renaissance London," pp. 136–160; F. J. Fisher, "London as an 'Engine' of Economic Growth," in *Britain and the Netherlands*, vol. 4, ed. J. Bromley and E. H. Kossman (The Hague, 1971), pp. 3–16.

24. Bernard Beckerman, *Shakespeare at the Globe* (New York, 1962), pp. 1–23; Stephen Gosson, *The School of Abuse* (1582), p. 188; Alfred Harbage, *Shakespeare's Audience* (New York, 1941), p. 36.

25. Richard Mulcaster, *Positions wherein Those Circumstances Be Examined Necessary for the Training up of Children* (1581), p. 198; Camden, *Britannia,* p. 177.
26. Alfred Harbage, *Shakespeare and the Rival Traditions* (New York, 1952), p. 101; Samuel Schoenbaum, *Annals of English Drama, 975–1700* (London, 1964), *passim;* Thomas Nashe, "To the Gentlemen Students of Both Universities," in Nashe, III, 315; Dekker, I, 351. For biographical details on the playwrights mentioned in this and the following paragraph, see *DNB* and the articles on individual dramatists in Chambers, III.
27. Fenton, *A Form of Christian Policy Gathered out of French* (1574), book III, chap. 7, quoted in Chambers, IV, 195; Sidney, *An Apology for Poetry,* ed. Geoffrey Shepherd (London, 1965), pp. 131, 134.
28. Nashe, III, 311, 324.
29. Harbage, *Shakespeare and the Rival Traditions,* p. 101; Nashe, V, 194; Nashe, III, 220; HS, IX, 166. See also W. David Kay, "The Shaping of Ben Jonson's Career: A Reexamination of Facts and Problems," *Modern Philology,* 67 (1970), 224–237.
30. *The Case Is Altered,* V.xiii.41–49; Anne Barton, *Ben Jonson, Dramatist* (Cambridge, Eng., 1984), p. 41.
31. Wilson, "Morose Ben Jonson," in *The Triple Thinkers,* rev. ed. (New York, 1948), rpt. in *Ben Jonson: A Collection of Critical Essays,* ed. Jonas Barish (Englewood Cliffs, N.J., 1963), p. 63.
32. Stephen Hannaford, "Gold Is but Muck: Jonson's *The Case Is Altered,*" *Studies in the Humanities,* 8 (1980), 11–16; Sigmund Freud, *Collected Papers,* 5 vols., ed. J. Rivière and J. Strachey (New York, 1924–1953), II, 45–50, 164–171; *Conv,* 687–688.
33. *Conv,* 692–693; *JAB,* p. 8; HS, XI, 370. HS gives the date of Fitzgeoffrey's epigram as 1603, but it was published in his *Affaniae: Sive Epigrammatum Libri Tres* (1601). Fitzgeoffrey's reputation as an epigrammatist goes back to 1591, and he could easily have written the one on Jonson, which refers to no play later than *The Case Is Altered,* as early as 1597 (see Kay, "The Shaping of Ben Jonson's Career," p. 227).
34. Nashe, III, 154; HS, I, 217.
35. Chambers, IV, 321–322, 322–323; *Conv,* 257–259; HS, I, 217–218.
36. HS, XI, 307; Glynne Wickham, *Early English Stages: 1300–1660,* vol. 2, part II (London, 1972), pp. 9–29.
37. Dekker, I, 351.

2. The Comedy of Humors

1. Mark Eccles, "Jonson's Marriage," *Review of English Studies,* 12 (1936), 262.
2. HS, XI, 307, 571–573.
3. Chambers, III, 289, 339. For a playwright's pay, see Gerald Bentley, *The Profession of Dramatist in Shakespeare's Time* (Princeton, 1971), chap. 5;

Mary I. Oates and William J. Baumol, "On the Economics of the Theater in Renaissance London," *Swedish Journal of Economics*, 74 (1972), 156–157.

4. Dedication of *Every Man in His Humour* to William Camden in the 1616 folio (HS, III, 301); *Henslowe's Diary*, ed. R. A. Foakes and R. T. Rickert (Cambridge, Eng., 1961), pp. 58–60; Kay, p. 70.

5. *Every Man in His Humour*, I.i.18—all quotations from this play in this chapter are from the 1601 quarto (HS, III, 197–289); Sidney, *An Apology for Poetry*, ed. Geoffrey Shepherd (London, 1965), p. 117; Lucian, *The Dance*, in *Lucian*, vol. 5, ed. and trans. A. M. Harmon (London, 1936), pp. 278–279, as cited in Douglas Duncan, *Ben Jonson and the Lucianic Tradition* (Cambridge, 1979), p. 18.

6. Aristotle, *Poetics*, V.32–34, trans. Ingram Bywater, in *The Basic Works of Aristotle*, ed. Richard McKeon (New York, 1941), p. 1459.

7. Source hunting is pointless with a theory that is so widely diffused. The major classical sources, which were available to Jonson, are Hippocrates' *Of the Nature of Man* and Galen's *Of Temperaments*. For relevant extracts from Sir Thomas Elyot's frequently reprinted *Castle of Health*, see HS, IX, 391–395. For discussion of the origins, transmission, and by-products of the humors, see Gregory Vlastos, "Equality and Justice in Early Greek Cosmologies," *Classical Philology*, 42 (1947), 156–178; R. Klibansky, E. Panofsky, and F. Saxl, *Saturn and Melancholy: Studies in the History of Natural Philosophy, Religion, and Art* (New York, 1964); and Oswei Temkin, *Galenism: Rise and Decline of a Medical Philosophy* (Ithaca, 1973). Passage quoted from *Certain Works of Galens Called Methodus Medendi*, trans. T. Gale (1586), p. 29.

8. See *Every Man out of His Humour*, Induction, 102–117; *Saturn and Melancholy*, pp. 217–240; *Oxford English Dictionary*, s.v. "humour."

9. Hippocrates, *Ancient Medicine*, ed. and trans. W. H. S. Jones (Cambridge, Mass., 1923), pp. 47–53. For additional references see Robert Joly, "Hippocrates of Cos," *Dictionary of Scientific Biography*, vol. 6 (New York, 1972), p. 429 n. 6.

10. Freud, *Jokes and Their Relation to the Unconscious*, ed. and trans. James Strachey (London, 1960), p. 97.

11. *Every Man in His Humour*, ed. Gabrielle Jackson (New Haven, 1969), p. 6; for stage history see HS, IX, 168–185; also Klibansky, Panofsky, and Saxl, *Saturn and Melancholy*, p. 11; Temkin, *Galenism*, pp. 36–38; *Julius Caesar*, V.v.73–75, in *The Complete Works of Shakespeare*, ed. David Bevington, 3d ed. (Glenview, Ill., 1980)—all quotations from Shakespeare in my text are from this edition; *Cynthia's Revels*, II.iii.125–130.

12. H. Jennifer Brady, *Ben Jonson's Works of Judgement: A Study of Rhetorical Strategies in the "Epigrammes"* (Ann Arbor, Mich.: University Microfilms, 1980), p. 7; the title page of Jonson's copy of Puttenham is reproduced in HS, I, 264; Puttenham, *The Art of English Poesy*, ed. R. C. Alston (Menston, Eng., 1968), is a photo facsimile of Jonson's entire copy. See also David McPherson, "Ben Jonson's Library and Marginalia," *Studies in Philology*, 71 (1974), 80.

13. George Vaillant, *Adaptation to Life* (Boston, 1977), p. 51.

14. Kernan, "Acting and Alchemy: The Major Plays of Ben Jonson," *Studies in the Literary Imagination,* 11 (1973), 8.
15. HS, IX, 168; Chambers, II, 6; HS, III, 403, 195.
16. Puttenham, *The Art of English Poesy,* p. 3.
17. Jonas Barish, *Ben Jonson and the Language of Prose Comedy* (Cambridge, Mass., 1962), p. 49, and generally pp. 41–90.
18. *Disc,* 452–455; David Riggs, "The Artificial Day and the Infinite Universe," *Journal of Medieval and Renaissance Studies,* 5 (1975), 177, 184–185.
19. Lester Beaurline, "Ben Jonson and the Illusion of Completeness," *Publications of the Modern Language Association,* 84 (1969), 51–59.

3. Angry Young Man

1. Mark Eccles, "Jonson's Marriage," *Review of English Studies,* 12 (1936), 267; *Middlesex County Records,* ed. John C. Jeafferson, vol. 1 (London, 1886), pp. xxxviii–xlviii; *Conv,* 245–248; *Henslowe's Diary,* ed. R. A. Foakes and R. T. Rickert (Cambridge, Eng., 1961), p. 286; Dekker, I, 356. HS rightly points out that "the law did not recognize duelling" (I, 220); but the *Middlesex County Records* are full of cases in which juries acquitted men charged with murder on the grounds that the other party had initiated the conflict. The image of the Curtain in Booth's "View of the City of London" is discussed in Reginald A. Foakes, *Illustrations of the English Stage, 1580–1642* (Stanford, 1985), pp. 8–9.
2. *Conv,* 249, 250–251; Arnold O. Meyer, *England and the Catholic Church under Queen Elizabeth,* trans. J. R. McKee (London, 1916), p. 371, and *passim;* John Carey, *John Donne: Life, Mind, and Art* (New York, 1981), pp. 15–18.
3. E. Pearlman, "Ben Jonson: An Anatomy," *English Literary Renaissance,* 9 (1979), 369.
4. *Middlesex County Records,* pp. xxxiii–xlvii, esp. p. xlii.
5. HS, XI, 571–572. The relevant regulations pertaining to company apprenticeships are contained in the Tilers' and Bricklayers' 1570 Book of Ordinances (Guildhall Library, MS 4321A). Accounts of cases similar to Jonson's can be found in the Tilers' and Bricklayers' Company Court Minute Book, 1620–1623 (Guildhall Library, MS 3043/2, unfolioed). See minutes for Michaelmas Day, 1620, for March 26, 1621, and for April 23, 1621. For Jonson's payment of quarterage, which has hitherto gone unnoticed, see Guildhall Library, MS 3051/1, Tilers' and Bricklayers' Company Quarterage Book, 1588–1616, unfolioed. I am grateful to Professor Paul Seaver for locating and transcribing these documents.
6. HS, XI, 575; E. A. Wrigley, "Family Limitation in Pre-Industrial England," *Economic History Review,* 2d ser., 19 (1966), 82–109, esp. 104–105; Jean Louis Flandrin, *Families in Former Times: Kinship, Household, and Sexuality,* trans. Richard Southern (Cambridge, Eng., 1979), pp. 194–198, 221–224; John Noonan, *Contraception,* rev. ed. (Cambridge, Mass., 1986), pp. 223–

226, 319; *For*, 11.115–116. For Jonson's antipathy to birth control, see *Ep*, 62; *Und*, 15.95–96; and *Epicoene*, IV.iii.57–61.

7. Thomas R. Forbes, "Life and Death in Shakespeare's London," *American Scientist*, 58 (1970), 511–520.

8. See "The Size and Composition of the Oxford Student Body, 1580–1909," in *The University in Society*, vol. 1, *Oxford and Cambridge from the Fourteenth to the Early Nineteenth Century*, ed. Lawrence Stone (Princeton, 1974), pp. vii, 5–7, 82–83.

9. Mark H. Curtis, "The Alienated Intellectuals of Early Stuart England," *Past and Present*, 23 (1962), 25–43; Bacon, "Of Seditions and Troubles," *The Works of Francis Bacon*, ed. James Spedding, Robert Ellis, and Douglas Heath, 6 vols. (London, 1887–1892), VI, 410; Ellesmere quoted from the "Conference between the Bishops and the Judges before the Privy Council," May 23, 1611, Folger Library, MS, cited in Curtis, "Alienated Intellectuals," p. 42 n. See also Joseph Loewenstein, *Responsive Readings: Versions of Echo in Pastoral, Epic, and the Jonsonian Masque* (New Haven, 1984), p. 78. The bishops' order is discussed in Oscar James Campbell, *Comicall Satyre and Shakespeare's "Troilus and Cressida"* (San Marino, Calif., 1938), p. 1.

10. HS, III, 421; HS, I, 3; HS, IV, 201; Christopher Baker, *Ben Jonson and the Inns of Court: The Literary Milieu of "Every Man out of His Humour"* (Ann Arbor, Mich.: University Microfilms, 1974), pp. 1–39.

11. Philip J. Finkelpearl, *John Marston of the Middle Temple* (Cambridge, Mass., 1969), pp. 32–80; Benjamin Rudyerd, *La prince d'amour* (1660), p. 90; Dekker, I, 382.

12. *Und*, 43, records the loss of "twice-twelve-yeares stor'd up humanitie, / with humble Gleanings in Divinitie" (101–102) in the fire that destroyed the contents of Jonson's study in autumn 1623. It is reasonable to infer that Jonson commenced his study of divinity soon after his conversion to Catholicism in 1598; see Kay, pp. 79–82, and note also the evidence adduced in the following paragraph.

13. *Every Man out of His Humour*, Induction, 73, 217–219, 266–268. See Campbell, *Comicall Satyre*, pp. 57–60; Kay, pp. 141–146; HS, IX, 394–482.

14. *Every Man out of His Humour*, Induction, 201, 203; Prologue, 338–345, 357, 359–360; *Conv*, 681; HS, I, 179—cf. *The Staple of News*, Induction, 61–66.

15. Jackson I. Cope, *The Theater and the Dream* (Baltimore, 1973), pp. 229–236.

16. *Every Man out of His Humour*, Epilogue, 4–5, 8–13; HS, III, 599, 602. John Sweeney, *Jonson and the Psychology of the Public Theater* (Princeton, 1985), pp. 26–29.

4. Search for Patronage and the Poet's Quarrel

1. Chambers, III, 183–200; Joseph Loewenstein, "The Script in the Marketplace," *Representations*, 12 (1985), 101–115; Timothy Murray, "From Foul

Sheets to Legitimate Model: Anti-theater, Text, Ben Jonson," *New Literary History,* 14 (1983), 641–664.

2. Kay, pp. 42–43. Throughout this chapter, I am indebted to Kay's meticulous reconstruction of Jonson's early career, especially of the Poet's Quarrel.

3. Edwin H. Miller, *The Professional Writer in Elizabethan England: A Study of Nondramatic Literature* (Cambridge, Mass., 1959), pp. 137–170; Wilfrid R. Prest, *The Inns of Court under Elizabeth I and the Early Stuarts, 1590–1640* (London, 1972), pp. 1–46, 137–173; Kay, pp. 103–104.

4. Chambers, III, 188–191; G. B. Harrison, "Books and Readers, 1599–1603," *The Library,* 4th ser., 14 (1933), 7–8.

5. *Ep,* 40; *Und,* 25; *For,* 10, 11; *UV,* 5; *For,* 12.79–81; Mark Eccles, "Jonson's Marriage," *Review of English Studies,* 12 (1936), 261; *For,* 12.71, 27–28, 30, 36.

6. The evidence for a connection between Salusbury and Essex is discussed in William Matchett, *The Phoenix and Turtle: Shakespeare's Poem and Chester's Love's Martyr* (The Hague, 1965), pp. 121–123. For Desmond, see HS, XI, 62; for Palmer, HS, XI, 124.

7. Farrant's landlord, cited in Alfred Harbage, *Shakespeare and the Rival Traditions* (New York, 1952), p. 39; *Cynthia's Revels,* Prologue, 1–2. Sources for the remarks about the children's companies in this and the following paragraph are Harbage, *Shakespeare and the Rival Traditions,* pp. 56–57, and *passim;* and Irwin Smith, *Shakespeare's Blackfriars Playhouse* (New York, 1964), pp. 130–154.

8. *Cynthia's Revels,* Prologue, 10–11 (my italics), 15–17; Kay, p. 100.

9. *Cynthia's Revels,* I.i.92–95; Joseph Loewenstein, *Responsive Readings: Versions of Echo in Pastoral, Epic, and the Jonsonian Masque* (New Haven, 1984), pp. 78, 85, and generally pp. 78–92.

10. *Cynthia's Revels,* III.iv.20–21, 95–99; Dekker, I, 325; HS, VIII, 662; HS, XI, 301–302.

11. *Cynthia's Revels,* Prologue, 19–20; Loewenstein, *Responsive Readings,* pp. 81–82; Public Record Office, S.P. 12/278/23, cited in Charlotte C. Stopes, *The Life of Henry, Third Earl of Southampton* (Cambridge, Eng., 1922), p. 236; *Cynthia's Revels,* V.xi.95–97.

12. *Cynthia's Revels,* II.ii.77–78; Dekker, *Satiromastix,* V.iii.188–190, 324–326, cited from the text in Dekker, I; Kay, pp. 100–103.

13. For discussions of the Poet's Quarrel, see Josiah H. Penniman, *The War of the Theaters* (Philadelphia, 1897); Roscoe A. Small, *The Stage Quarrel between Ben Jonson and the So-Called Poetasters* (Breslau, 1899); Alfred Harbage, *Shakespeare and the Rival Traditions,* pp. 90–119; and especially Kay.

14. *Conv,* 284–286; *The Plays of John Marston,* 3 vols., ed. Harvey Wood (Philadelphia, 1938), III, 273; *Satiromastix,* III.iv.21–29; Small, *The Stage Quarrel,* p. 45; Kay, pp. 174, 203–204.

15. *Conv,* 284–285; *Ep,* 49, 68, 100; J. R. Barker, "A Pendant to Drummond of Hawthornden's *Conversations,*" *Review of English Studies,* 16 (1965), 286; Dekker, I, 344; *Ep,* 68.1–4; Kay, pp. 158–251.

16. *The Plays of John Marston*, II, 258, 228, 290; Kay, pp. 226–227.
17. *Poetaster*, IV.vii.41–42; *The Diary of John Manningham of the Middle Temple, 1602–1603*, ed. Robert P. Sorlien (Hanover, N.H., 1976), p. 133.
18. Kay, pp. 125–128; Katherine Maus, *Ben Jonson and the Roman Frame of Mind* (Princeton, 1984), pp. 10–11.
19. Horace, *Odes and Epistles*, ed. and trans. C. E. Bennet (London, 1939), p. 21. For secondary literature on the *recusatio* and for a number of illustrative texts, see R. G. M. Nisbet and Margaret Hubbard, *A Commentary on Horace; Odes, Book I* (Oxford, 1970), pp. 80–83; Gregson Davis, "The Disavowal of the Grand (Recusatio) in Two Poems by Wallace Stevens," *Pacific Coast Philology*, 17 (1982), 92–102; Kenneth Fields, "Your Humble Servant: Strategic Humility in Bradstreet, Dickinson, and Jonson," *Sequoia*, 29 (1985), 34–59.
20. *JAB*, p. 35; *Every Man out of His Humour*, Induction, 268–270; Kay, pp. 178–186.
21. *The Works of Francis Bacon*, ed. James Spedding, Robert Ellis, and Douglas Heath, 6 vols. (London, 1887–1892), VI, 406; *Troilus and Cressida*, I.iii.109–110; *Hymenaei*, lines 208–211, in HS, VII; René Girard, *Violence and the Sacred*, trans. Patrick Gregory (Baltimore, 1977), pp. 62–65, 159–161; René Girard, *To Double Business Bound* (Baltimore, 1978), pp. 136–154; Joel Fineman, "Fratricide and Cuckoldry: Shakespeare's Doubles," in *Representing Shakespeare: New Psychoanalytic Essays*, ed. Murray Schwartz and Coppélia Kahn (Baltimore, 1980), pp. 70–109, esp. 86–87.
22. "To the World," the prefatory epistle to *Satiromastix*, in Dekker, I, 309.
23. *Satiromastix*, I.ii.S.D., 8–14, 116, V.ii.272–273; II.ii.27–35: *Satiromastix* is quoted from the text in Dekker, I, 299–376, and hereafter cited in the text; *Ep*, 73.5–20, 22–23.
24. *Twelfth Night*, I.v.88–90, IV.ii.55, 52–53, III.iv.125–126, V.i.340–341; Bevington, *Complete Works of Shakespeare*, 3d ed. (Glenview, Ill., 1980), p. 393; *The Diary of John Manningham of the Middle Temple*, pp. 48, 265.

5. Early Tragedies

1. *Ep*, 22.5; HS, XI, 575; *Ep*, 22.2; HS, XI, 576.
2. HS, XI, 308; "Apologetical Dialogue," lines 5, 223–225, 237–239, cited from the text in HS, IV, 317–324.
3. Anne Barton, *Ben Jonson, Dramatist* (Cambridge, Eng., 1984), pp. 12–15; HS, XI, 7–8; *Ep*, 40.
4. *The Spanish Tragedy*, ed. Philip Edwards (Cambridge, Mass., 1959), "Additional Passages," lines 12–13. All quotations from *The Spanish Tragedy* are from this edition.
5. *The Spanish Tragedy*, III.xiii.99–101, 106–107; *Hamlet*, II.ii.551, 556–557; Edwards notes this parallel on p. 88. There are, incidentally, a number of striking parallels between *The Spanish Tragedy*, III.xiii (Hieronomo and Bazulto), and *King Lear*, IV.vi (Lear and Gloucester).

6. *Cynthia's Revels,* Prologue, 19–20; *The Spanish Tragedy,* Fourth Addition, 156–161; Barton, *Ben Jonson, Dramatist,* pp. 25–27. See also D. J. Gordon, "Poet and Architect: The Intellectual Setting of the Quarrel between Ben Jonson and Inigo Jones," in D. J. Gordon, *The Renaissance Imagination,* ed. Stephen Orgel (Berkeley, 1975), pp. 77–101.

7. *Ep,* 120, title as in early manuscript but with modern spelling (see HS, VIII, 77); *Conv,* 164–165; *Cynthia's Revels,* Induction, 41; Gerald Bentley, "A Good Name Lost: Jonson's Lament for S. P.," *Times Literary Supplement,* May 30, 1942, p. 276.

8. *Ep,* 120.14–16, 23–24. Quotations are taken from the early manuscript version of the poem (HS, VIII, 77–78).

9. HS, VIII, 665; HS, I, 31 n.; P. W. Hasler, *The House of Commons, 1558–1603,* vol. 3 (London, 1986), "Members, M-Z," p. 520.

10. *Conv,* 261–262; John Nichols, *Progresses of King James I,* vol. 1 (1828), pp. 62–63; F. P. Wilson, *The Plague in Shakespeare's London* (Oxford, 1927), pp. 87–88; Kevin Sharpe, *Sir Robert Cotton, 1586–1631: History and Politics in Early Modern England* (Oxford, 1979), pp. 114–115.

11. Wilson, *The Plague in Shakespeare's London,* pp. 93–96; Paul Slack, *The Impact of Plague in Tudor and Stuart England* (London, 1985), pp. 41–44, 167–169; Walter G. Bell, *The Great Plague in London in 1665* (London, 1924), pp. 312–313, as cited in Cheryl Ross, "The Plague of *The Alchemist,*" *Renaissance Quarterly,* 41 (1989), forthcoming.

12. *Conv,* 263–271; H. Jennifer Brady, *Ben Jonson's Works of Judgement: A Study of Rhetorical Strategies in the "Epigrammes"* (Ann Arbor, Mich.: University Microfilms, 1980), pp. 79, 91 n. 29; Wilson, *The Plague in Shakespeare's London,* pp. 61–64.

13. For the reading of the last line, see L. A. Beaurline, "The Selective Principle in Jonson's Shorter Poems," *Criticism,* 8 (1966), 64–74; Wesley Trimpi, "Ben. Jonson His Best Piece of *Poetrie,*" *Classical Antiquity,* 1 (1983), 145–155.

14. Wilson, *The Plague in Shakespeare's London,* pp. 1–14, 57–58; Thomas R. Forbes, "Life and Death in Shakespeare's London," *American Scientist,* 58 (1976), 512; Wilson, *The Plague in Shakespeare's London,* p. 185. A census made in 1638, and summarized in Roger Finlay, *Population and Metropolis: The Demography of London, 1580–1650* (Cambridge, Eng., 1981), pp. 168–172, lists 1,203 households in the parish of St. Giles, Cripplegate. If we assume an average figure of 4 occupants per household (see E. A. Wrigley and R. S. Schofield, *The Population History of England, 1541–1871: A Reconstruction* [London, 1981], p. 572), the total population of the parish would have been 4,800. Since the population of London doubled between 1600 and 1650 (Finlay, *Population and Metropolis,* p. 51), the figure for 1603 was closer to 3,000. Although these estimates involve a good deal of guesswork, they indicate that the vast majority of those who remained in Cripplegate during the latter half of 1603 died of the plague.

15. Godfrey Goodman, *The Court of King James I,* ed. J. S. Brewer, vol. 1 (1839), p. 31; Nichols, *Progresses,* p. 575.

16. Sharpe, *Sir Robert Cotton*, pp. 114–115, 199–204.
17. *The Diary of Lady Anne Clifford* (London, 1924), p. 8.
18. HS, IV, 351; R. P. Corballis, "The 'Second Pen' in the Stage Version of *Sejanus*," *Modern Philology*, 86 (1978), 273–277.
19. Tacitus, *Annals*, IV.i, as cited in G. K. Hunter, "A Roman Thought," in *An English Miscellany*, ed. B. S. Lee (Cape Town, 1977), p. 110.
20. John G. Sweeney, *Jonson and the Psychology of Public Theater* (Princeton, 1985), p. 55.
21. *Sejanus*, IV.388–389, 92–93, 97–99; II.329–330, 151; V.241–252, 851, 853, 854.

6. The Poet and the King

1. F. P. Wilson, *The Plague in Shakespeare's London* (Oxford, 1927), p. 186; Chambers, IV, 350.
2. The title page of *Sejanus* in the 1616 folio of Jonson's *Works* states that it was "acted, in the yeere 1603. By the K. Majesties Servants." The newly reconstituted King's Men gave their first public performances in April 1604 (Chambers, IV, 350); but they did perform at court on December 26–30, 1603 (Chambers, IV, 168), and I infer that *Sejanus* had its debut at this time. The King's Men presented "one playe" before James at Wilton on December 2, but this is more likely to have been *As You Like It* (see E. K. Chambers, *William Shakespeare: A Study of Facts and Problems*, vol. 2 [Oxford, 1930], p. 329). Moreover, Jonson's first verifiable appearance at court occurs during the holiday season of 1603–4—see *Conv*, 155–158, and HS, XI, 371; a court performance of *Sejanus* gave him a motive for being there (but not for gate-crashing Daniel's masque). For Lord Henry Howard's accusation, see *Conv*, 326–327.
3. G. P. V. Akrigg, *Jacobean Pageant: The Court of King James I* (Cambridge, Mass., 1962), pp. 24–27; Linda Levy Peck, *Northampton: Patronage and Policy at the Court of James I* (London, 1982), pp. 23–30.
4. HS, I, 220; Peck, *Northampton*, pp. 81, 105; *Conv*, 325–326.
5. *The Works of James, King of Britain* (1616), p. 488, as cited in D. J. Gordon, "Hymenaei: Ben Jonson's Masque of Union," *Journal of the Warburg and Courtauld Institutes*, 8 (1945), 121; *Ep*, 5.3–4; HS, VIII, 28.
6. *Basilikon Doron*, ed. James Craigie, 2 vols. (Edinburgh, 1944–1950), II, 17; John Nichols, *The Progresses of King James I*, vol. 1 (1828), p. 148; *Basilikon Doron*, I, 207; Kevin Sharpe, *Sir Robert Cotton, 1586–1631: History and Politics in Early Modern England* (Oxford, 1979), pp. 114–115; Nichols, *Progresses of King James I*, I, 325 n. 1; Carolyn Greenstein, *The Poet and the King: Solus Rex et Poeta non Quotannis Nascitur* (Ann Arbor, Mich.: University Microfilms, 1971), pp. 12–13, 75–77; Graham Parry, *The Golden Age Restor'd: The Culture of the Stuart Court* (Manchester, 1981), pp. 1–39.
7. *The Eclogues of Vergil*, trans. H. J. Rose (Berkeley, 1942), p. 192, as cited in Greenstein, *The Poet and the King*, pp. 96–97; *The King's Entertainment in*

Passing to His Coronation, lines 292, 341, 346–347. Parry, *The Golden Age Restor'd,* discusses the iconography of the Fenchurch arch on pp. 4–7.

8. Dekker, II, 294, 296, and generally 253–303; Greenstein, *The Poet and the King,* pp. 90–94; Parry, *The Golden Age Restor'd,* pp. 3–21.

9. Arthur Wilson, *The History of Great Britain, Being the Life and Reign of King James I* (London, 1653), p. 12; David Bergeron, *English Civic Pageantry* (London, 1971), p. 66.

10. "Panegyre," 63–64; James D. Garrison, *Dryden and the Tradition of Panegyric* (Berkeley and Los Angeles, 1975), pp. 83–91; Jonathan Goldberg, *James I and the Politics of Literature* (Baltimore, 1983), pp. 120–123.

11. Jenny Wormald, "James VI and I: Two Kings or One," *History,* 68 (1983), 187–209; *A Royalist's Notebook: The Commonplace Book of Sir John Oglander,* ed. Francis Bamford (London, 1936), pp. 196–197, as cited in D. H. Willson, *King James VI and I* (London, 1956), p. 165.

12. *King's Entertainment,* lines 253–257; Dekker, II, 255; *King's Entertainment,* lines 263–267.

13. *Conv,* 82–88; HS, IV, 349, 350; HS, I, 221. See also Mark Eccles, "Jonson's Marriage," *Review of English Studies,* 12 (1936), 268–271; HS, XI, 576–577; and Chapter 7, note 14, below.

14. Neil Cuddy, "The Revival of the Entourage: The Bedchamber of James I, 1603–1625," in *The English Court,* ed. David Starkey (London, 1987), pp. 173–225.

15. Dekker, I, 353.

16. Louis A. Montrose, "Gifts and Reasons: The Contexts of Peele's *Arraynge-ment of Paris,*" *ELH,* 47 (1980), 433–461.

17. Stone, p. 475; John Hacket, *Scrinia Reserata: A Memorial of John Williams* (1692), p. 225.

18. Bacon, "Of Masques and Triumphs," in *The Works of Francis Bacon,* 6 vols., ed. James Spedding, Robert Ellis, and Douglas Heath (London, 1887–1892), VI, 467; *Althorpe Entertainment,* lines 269–273.

19. See, for example, HS, VII, 169, 181; HS, X, 491.

20. Samuel Daniel, *Complete Works,* 5 vols., ed. A. B. Grosart (1885; rpt. New York, 1963), III, 195.

21. *The Masque of Blackness,* lines 155–156, 175, 189–190, 194–95, 254–255.

22. Ibid., lines 100, 102, 106–108, 291–292; Chambers, *William Shakespeare,* II, 330–332; Joseph Loewenstein, *Responsive Readings: Versions of Echo in Pastoral, Epic, and the Jonsonian Masque* (New Haven, 1984), pp. 96–102, esp. pp. 99–100.

23. Stone, pp. 664–665; *The Diary of Lady Anne Clifford* (London, 1924), pp. 16–17.

24. See Historical Manuscripts Commission, 9 *Salisbury,* VII (1899), 392; Stone, p. 665; G. P. V. Akrigg, *Jacobean Pageant* (Cambridge, Mass., 1962), p. 107; Public Record Office, S.P. 12/278/23, cited in Charlotte C. Stopes, *The Life of Henry, Third Earl of Southampton* (Cambridge, Eng., 1922), p. 236.

25. *Dudley Carleton to John Chamberlain, 1603–1624: Jacobean Letters,* ed. Maurice Lee (New Brunswick, N.J., 1972), p. 55; HS, X, 448.

26. Greenblatt, "Invisible Bullets: Renaissance Authority and Its Subversion," *Glyph*, 8 (1980), 41.
27. *The Masque of Blackness*, lines 358–359; Castiglione, *The Book of the Courtier*, trans. George Ball (London, 1967), p. 119.

7. Eastward Ho, *Prison*, and Volpone

1. Stone, pp. 71–82; HS, IV, 445–449; *Eastward Ho*, III.iii.41–48.
2. Chapman's letter to Suffolk, in *Eastward Ho*, ed. R. W. Van Fossen (Manchester, 1979), pp. 218–219; James was on progress for most of the summer of 1605—see John Nichols, *The Progresses of King James I*, vol. 1 (1828), pp. 517–518; HS, I, 195.
3. Chambers, I, 325; *Nugae Antiquae*, ed. H. Harington, vol. 1 (1804), p. 345.
4. Chambers, I, 325; HS, I, 181.
5. *Conv*, 273–274; HS, I, 198; *Conv*, 276–277; G. P. V. Akrigg, *Jacobean Pageant* (Cambridge, Mass., 1962), pp. 48–55.
6. HS, I, 195, 197, 200; HS, I, 193–200 *passim*.
7. *Eastward Ho*, ed. R. W. Van Fossen, p. 218; HS, I, 193–194.
8. *Eastward Ho*, ed. R. W. Van Fossen, p. 219; *Ep*, 127.4–5, 6–8.
9. *Conv*, 250; *UV*, 7; Theodore A. Stroud, "Ben Jonson and Father Thomas Wright," *ELH*, 14 (1947), 274–282; "Father Thomas Wright: A Test Case for Toleration," *Biographical Studies, 1534–1629*, I (1951–52), 187–219; HS, I, 202.
10. *The Political Works of James I*, ed. C. H. McIlwain (New York, 1965), pp. 285, 282, as cited in Jennifer Brady, "Jonson's 'To King James': Plain Speaking in the *Epigrammes* and the *Conversations*," *Studies in Philology*, 82 (1985), 394–396; *Ep*, 35.5–6, 8, 9–10.
11. *Ep*, 43.1–2, 5–6, 8–9.
12. *Ep*, 63.3–4; *Ep*, 64.17–18.
13. *Ep*, 60; *Ep*, 67.6, 7–8, 12; *Cynthia's Revels*, Prologue, 14.
14. The Simpsons ask, "Did Jonson pay more than one visit to Aubigny—a shorter one about 1604 and a longer one in 1613–18?" I maintain that he did; see below, Chapter 10. The Simpsons were confused by the 1606 citation for recusancy (HS, I, 220–223; XI, 576–577) because they did not realize that Jonson was answering two quite distinct questions. When he said that he and his wife had been going to their parish church for the previous six months, he was talking about *attendance*. When he said that his wife "for anything he knowethe hath gon to Churche and used always to receive the Communion," he referred to her "Easter duty." If we assume that the Jonsons had been separated between February 1603 and the summer of 1605—as Manningham's *Diary*, *Conv*, 261–262, and *Conv*, 86–88, would suggest—the two answers are perfectly congruous with each other. The myth that Jonson spent his "5 yeers" with Aubigny (*Conv*, 254) between 1602 and 1607 has persisted because scholars have neither grasped the fact that Manningham used old style dating; nor realized that Aubigny would not have obtained his Blackfriars mansion prior to 1604, after the plague had subsided; nor under-

stood the 1606 citation for recusancy. For regulations concerning attendance at Holy Communion, see *Book of Common Prayer, 1559: The Elizabethan Prayer Book*, ed. John E. Booty (Charlottesville, Va., 1976), p. 268; *Visitation Articles and Injunctions of the Period of the Reformation*, vol. 3, *1559–1575*, ed. W. H. Frere, Alcuin Club Collections, 16 (London, 1910), pp. 93, 260, 275; J. P. Bolton, "The Limits of Formal Religion: The Administration of Holy Communion in Late Elizabethan and Early Stuart London," *London Journal*, 10 (1984), 135–154, esp. p. 138.

15. HS, X, 465; Vernon Snow, *Essex the Rebel: The Life of Robert Devereaux, the Third Earl of Essex* (Lincoln, Nebr., 1970), p. 29.

16. HS, X, 466; *Hymenaei*, lines 250–252; D. J. Gordon, "*Hymenaei*: Ben Jonson's Masque of Union," *Journal of the Warburg and Courtauld Institutes*, 8 (1945), 107–141.

17. Essex had knighted Sir Robert Carey, Sir William Constable, Sir Robert Drury, Sir Richard Houghton, Sir Carey Reynolds, Sir William Woodhouse, Lord Willoughby, and the Earl of Sussex, all of whom vied on behalf of Opinion. See "List of Masquers and Tilters," HS, X, 428–438; and *DNB*, s.v. Carey, Robert; Radcliffe, Robert; and Bertie, Robert.

18. Lines 37–40 of the letter written to Salisbury from prison (HS, I, 195) and lines 50–54 of the prefatory epistle to *Volpone* (HS, V, 18) both derive from Erasmus's prefatory epistle to Martin Dorp: see HS, IX, 683–684.

19. Douglas Duncan, *Ben Jonson and the Lucianic Tradition* (Cambridge, 1979), pp. 9–25.

20. *Desiderii Erasmi Roterodam: Opera Omnia*, ed. J. LeClerc (1703–1706), I, 243–246, as cited and translated in Duncan, *Jonson and the Lucianic Tradition*, pp. 28–29.

21. *Volpone*, I.i.16–17; Duncan, *Jonson and the Lucianic Tradition*, pp. 148–149.

22. *Volpone*, ed. Alvin Kernan (New Haven, 1962), pp. 214–216; *Volpone*, II.ii.34–47, 49, 50–51, 65.

23. *Volpone*, II.ii.72–73; Duncan, *Jonson and the Lucianic Tradition*, p. 154; *Volpone*, II.ii.149–156, 94–95, 160–161, 167–168, 168–170, 179–181.

24. *Volpone*, II.ii.149–150. For the latent psychological metaphor, see *Oxford English Dictionary*, s.v. "sublimate," 2(b).

25. *Volpone*, V.i.5–6, 13, 14–16; V.xii.124.

26. Chambers, IV, 350; *Conv*, 185–187; Alvaro Ribero, "Sir John Roe: Ben Jonson's Friend," *Review of English Studies*, 24 (1973), 153–164; *Ep*, 32.7; *Ep*, 33.5–6.

27. *For*, 5.1–2; *For*, 9.1–2; *Ep*, 98.9; Thomas M. Greene, "Ben Jonson and the Centered Self," *Studies in English Literature*, 10 (1970), 325–348.

28. HS, VII, 238; Scott McMillin, "Jonson's Early Entertainments: New Information from Hatfield House," *Renaissance Drama*, n.s., 1 (1968), 153–166; HS, X, 401; HS, XI, 586–587.

29. See D. J. Gordon, "Roles and Mysteries," in *The Renaissance Imagination*, ed. Stephen Orgel (Berkeley, 1975), pp. 3–23.

8. Man about Town

1. Sidney, *An Apology for Poetry,* ed. Geoffrey Shepherd (London, 1965), p. 117.
2. Bacon, "Of Praise," *The Works of Francis Bacon,* ed. James Spedding, Robert Ellis, and Douglas Heath, 6 vols. (London, 1887–1892), VI, 502; *Ep,* 65.3, 2, 12–14, 15–16.
3. *The Masque of Beauty,* lines 5–8, 128–129, 372, 394–395.
4. HS, X, 456–458; trans. from Antoine Le Fevre de La Boderie, *Ambassades . . . en Angleterre,* vol. 3 (Paris, 1750), pp. 12–13.
5. *DNB,* s.v. Hay, James, and Sanquhar, Robert; see Stone, p. 626. HS, X, 435, identifies the dancer named "Sir Jo. Kennethie" with the sixth Earl of Cassils, but he was only twelve or thirteen years old in 1608: see *The Complete Peerage,* vol. 3, ed. Vicary Gibbs and H. Arthur Doubleday (London, 1913), p. 76. The Sir John Kennedy who married Elizabeth Brydges in 1603 is described in Stone, pp. 625–626.
6. *The Haddington Masque,* lines 30, 252, 283, 280; D. J. Gordon, "The Imagery of Ben Jonson's *Masques of Blackness* and *Beauty*," in *The Renaissance Imagination,* ed. Stephen Orgel (Berkeley, 1975), pp. 134–156.
7. Stone, pp. 625–626, 102; G. P. V. Akrigg, *Jacobean Pageant* (Cambridge, Mass., 1963), p. 53; see also works cited in note 5 above.
8. D. H. Willson, *King James VI and I* (London, 1956), pp. 249–257; Akrigg, *Jacobean Pageant,* pp. 625–626.
9. *The Masque of Queens,* lines 2, 13, 111–112, 132, 133–134.
10. Ibid., lines 362, 360, 399, 670–678, 422–423, 427–428; Joseph Loewenstein, *Responsive Readings: Versions of Echo in Pastoral, Epic, and the Jonsonian Masque* (New Haven, 1984), p. 117.
11. *Und,* 49.1–2; R. C. Bald, *John Donne: A Life* (New York, 1970), pp. 177–179; *The "Conceited Newes" of Sir Thomas Overbury and His Friends,* ed. James E. Savage (Gainesville, Fla., 1968), pp. xxiii–lxii.
12. *Und,* 49.7, 8, 16–17, 32, 35–36; *Conv,* 646–648.
13. *UV,* 9; HS, VIII, 372; *UV,* 9.3, 7; HS, VIII, 372.
14. Mark Eccles, "Jonson's Marriage," *Review of English Studies,* 12 (1936), 267–268.
15. Ian Donaldson, *The World Upside-Down: Comedy from Jonson to Fielding* (Oxford, 1970), pp. 37–45; Leo Salingar, "Farce and Fashion in *The Silent Woman,*" *Essays and Studies,* 20 (1967), 40–44.
16. *Epicoene,* III.v.43–44, 44–52; Donaldson, *The World Upside-Down,* p. 38.
17. Donaldson, *The World Upside-Down,* p. 38.
18. Arthur Wilson, *The History of Britain* (1653), as cited in HS, X, 11; Leo Salingar, "Farce and Fashion in *The Silent Woman,*" pp. 40–44, 45; Scott McMillin, "Jonson's Early Entertainments: New Information from Hatfield House," *Renaissance Drama,* n.s. 1 (1968), 166; Lawrence Stone, "Inigo Jones and the New Exchange," *Archaeological Journal,* 114 (1957), 116, quotes from unpublished manuscripts at Hatfield House that supply the outline of Jonson's lost *Entertainment at Britain's Burse.*

19. *Epicoene*, I.iii.33–35, III.iii.69, I.i.73–76.
20. Salingar, "Farce and Fashion in *The Silent Woman*," p. 42.
21. *Epicoene*, Prologue, 1–2, 4–6, 7, 8–9, 10–15; HS, XI, 517.
22. Jonas Barish, *Ben Jonson and the Language of Prose Comedy* (Cambridge, Mass., 1962), p. 184.
23. HS, VIII, 370; *UV*, 8.1–2; Bald, *John Donne*, pp. 158–159; *Ep*, 94; I. A. Shapiro, "The Mermaid Club," *Modern Language Review*, 49 (1950), 6–17; Danby, *Elizabethan and Jacobean Poets: Studies in Sidney, Shakespeare, Beaumont, and Fletcher* (1952; rpt., London, 1965), p. 161.

9. Reluctant Patriot

1. J. W. Williamson, *The Myth of the Conqueror, Prince Henry Stuart: A Study of Seventeenth Century Personation* (New York, 1978), p. 40; Roy Strong, *Henry, Prince of Wales and England's Lost Renaissance* (London, 1986), p. 54; HS, VII, 281.
2. Williamson, *Myth of the Conqueror*, pp. 1–108, esp. p. 61; Strong, *Henry, Prince of Wales*, pp. 7–70.
3. *The Speeches at Prince Henry's Barriers*, lines 10–11, 40, 63 (marginal stage direction), 83–85, 167–168, 175–176, 173–174, 187–190, 193–194; Williamson, *Myth of the Conqueror*, pp. 90–95; Norman Council, "Ben Jonson, Inigo Jones, and the Transformation of Tudor Chivalry," *ELH*, 47 (1980), 259–295. For commentary on St. George's Portico, see Strong, *Henry, Prince of Wales*, pp. 149–150.
4. *The Alchemist*, Prologue, 5–11; Rosalie Colie, *Paradoxia Epidemica* (Princeton, 1967).
5. F. P. Wilson, *The Plague in Shakespeare's London* (Oxford, 1927), p. 54; Chambers, IV, 351; HS, IX, 224; *The Alchemist*, ed. F. H. Mares (London, 1967), p. lxiii.
6. *The Alchemist*, Argument, 1–12; Cheryl Ross, "The Plague of *The Alchemist*," *Renaissance Quarterly*, 42 (1989), forthcoming.
7. Chambers, III, 123; R. L. Smallwood, "'Here, in the Friars': Immediacy and Theatricality in *The Alchemist*," *Review of English Studies*, 57 (1981), 142–160.
8. Clifford Geertz, *The Interpretation of Cultures* (New York, 1973), p. 432; Wilson, *The Plague in Shakespeare's London*, pp. 49–54; *Proclamations*, pp. 193–195.
9. *The Alchemist*, Prologue, 17–18, 15–16, 23–24.
10. William Blissett, "The Venter Tripartite in *The Alchemist*," *Studies in English Literature*, 8 (1968), 323–334; Allan Dessen, *Jonson's Moral Comedy* (Evanston, Ill., 1971), pp. 105–137; Robert N. Watson, *Ben Jonson's Parodic Strategy: Literary Imperialism in the Comedies* (Cambridge, Mass., 1987), pp. 113–138; *The Alchemist*, I.ii.52–53, I.iii.36–38, II.vi.63–64, V.v.76–78, III.i.109.
11. Alvin Kernan, *The Playwright as Magician: Shakespeare's Image of the Poet*

in the English Public Theater (New Haven, 1979), p. 134; *Romeo and Juliet,* II.ii.2–3; *The Alchemist,* II.iii.162–163, II.v.20–21.

12. Frances Yates, *Shakespeare's Last Plays: A New Approach* (London, 1975), pp. 105–137; John S. Mebane, "Renaissance Magic and the Return of the Golden Age: Utopianism and Religious Enthusiasm in *The Alchemist*," *Renaissance Drama,* 10 (1979), 117–140; Keith Thomas, *Religion and the Decline of Magic* (New York, 1971), pp. 245, 249; *Conv,* 306–310.

13. See especially "On the Famous Voyage" (*Ep,* 133), *The Devil Is an Ass, The Magnetic Lady, Mercury Vindicated from the Alchemists at Court,* and *The Fortunate Isles.*

14. Graham Parry, *The Golden Age Restor'd: The Culture of the Stuart Court* (Manchester, 1981), p. 74; *Oberon,* line 65 (italics added); marginal gloss, HS, VII, 343; *Oberon,* lines 291, 418–419.

15. *Proclamations,* pp. 245–250.

16. HS, IX, 240; *Catiline,* I.ii.423, III.ii.369, IV.ii.246–247; Barbara N. DeLuna, *Jonson's Romish Plot: A Study of "Catiline" and Its Historical Context* (Oxford, 1967), pp. 37–42, 62–65, 173–174.

17. *Disc,* 899–890; *Catiline,* III.i.397–398, 399–400 (italics added); Michael J. Warren, "Ben Jonson's *Catiline:* The Problem of Cicero," *The Yearbook of English Studies,* 3 (1973), 71–72.

18. Quentin Skinner, *Machiavelli* (New York, 1981), pp. 3–4, 43–47; *Ep,* 59.1; *Life Of Cicero,* in *Fall of the Roman Republic, Six Lives by Plutarch,* trans. Rex Warner, cited in Howard Norlund, "The Design of Ben Jonson's *Catiline,*" *Sixteenth Century Journal,* 9 (1978), 73.

19. "To the Reader in Ordinairie," HS, V, 432; Bentley, IV, 608; Gerald Bentley, *Shakespeare and Jonson: Their Reputations in the Seventeenth Century Compared,* vol. 1 (Chicago, 1945), pp. 109–112.

20. *Conv,* 353–354, 325; Ethel C. Williams, *Anne of Denmark* (London, 1970), pp. 133–142.

21. HS, V, 431; *For,* 14.1–10; Lisle Cecil John, "Ben Jonson's 'To Sir William Sidney on His Birthday,'" *Modern Language Review,* 52 (1957), 168–176; HS, V, 289–290; *The Poems of Lady Mary Wroth,* ed. Josephine Roberts (Baton Rouge, La., 1983), pp. 24–25. See below, Chapter 11.

22. Neil Cuddy, "The Revival of the Entourage: The Bedchamber of James I, 1603–1625," in *The English Court,* ed. David Starkey (London, 1987), pp. 206–211.

23. *Ep,* 102.13–15; *For,* 2.45–46; *For,* 3.1–4; *For,* 14.41–42; *For,* 2.97–98.

24. HS, XI, 575; *For,* 13.1–2, 99–107, 95–96.

25. Leah Marcus, *The Politics of Mirth: Jonson, Herrick, Milton, Marvell and the Defense of Old Holiday Pastimes* (Chicago, 1986), pp. 29–30; HS, X, 519–522, 532–533; HS, VII, 377.

26. *Love Restored,* lines 56–59, 70, 87–88, and 70–143 *passim;* Marcus, *The Politics of Mirth,* p. 34.

27. J. C. A. Rathmell, "Jonson, Lord Lisle, and Penshurst," *English Literary Renaissance,* 1 (1971), 258, 256, and generally 250–260; *For,* 2.1–5, 45–46.

28. Roger Howell, *Sir Philip Sidney: The Shepherd Knight* (Boston, 1968), p. 18; Don Wayne, *Penshurst* (Madison, 1984), p. 101, and generally pp. 96–105.

29. Rathmell, "Jonson, Lord Lisle, and Penshurst," pp. 252–253; John Nichols, *The Progresses, Processions, and Magnificent Festivities of King James I*, vol. 2 (London, 1828), p. 445 n. 2; *For*, 2.76–80, 85.

10. The Broken Compass

1. Stone, p. 700; *Volpone*, IV.i.23.

2. Roger Ascham, *The Schoolmaster*, ed. Edward Arber (1870), p. 71; Stone, pp. 699, 698; *Conv*, 296.

3. HS, XI, 581; HS, I, 65–67; L. A. Beaurline, *Jonson and Elizabethan Comedy* (San Marino, Calif., 1978), pp. 226–230; *Und*, 43.103–104.

4. *Conv*, 298–302; HS, I, 65; HS, XI, 581, 582.

5. David McPherson, "Ben Jonson Meets Daniel Heinsius," *English Language Notes*, 44 (1976), 105–109.

6. *Und*, 43.129–136; *Conv*, 254–255; Mark Eccles, "Jonson's Marriage," *Review of English Studies*, 12 (1936), 257–258.

7. *UV*, 10; Coryate, *Greetings from the Court of the Great Mogul* (1616), p. 137.

8. Michael Strachan, *The Life and Adventures of Thomas Coryate* (London, 1962), pp. 269–292.

9. *UV*, 19; *UV*, 17; *Und*, 14; *Und*, 46; HS, IV, 201; I. A. Shapiro, "The Mermaid Club," *Modern Language Review*, 45 (1950), 6; Strachan, *Thomas Coryate*, pp. 144–145.

10. Kevin Sharpe, *Sir Robert Cotton, 1586–1631: History and Politics in Early Modern England* (Oxford, 1979), pp. 35, 76, 205; *Conv*, 198–201; HS, XI, 383–384; *Und*, 24; *Und*, 14; *UV*, 13–15; trans. from HS, XI, 134–135.

11. HS, X, 213; HS, I, 204; R. C. Bald, *John Donne: A Life* (New York, 1970), pp. 196–197, identifies the recipient of the letter in HS, I, 204, as Henry Goodyear; *Tempe Restored*, lines 49–50, quoted from Stephen Orgel and Roy Strong, *Inigo Jones: The Theater of the Stuart Court*, vol. 2 (Berkeley, 1973), p. 480; *Bartholomew Fair*, V.iii.116–117, V.i.15–16.

12. *Bartholomew Fair*, V.v.4–5, 8–9; Robert Milles, *Abrahams Sute for Sodom* (1612), sig. Dov, as cited in Millar MacLure, *The Paul's Cross Sermons: 1534–1642* (Toronto, 1958), p. 140, p. 182 nn. 36, 37. On pp. 3–4 MacLure discusses the early painting of Paul's Cross, reproduced in my text.

13. Beaurline, *Jonson and Elizabethan Comedy*, pp. 226–230; *Bartholomew Fair*, V.v.34–35; *Disc*, 50–51, 60–64 (trans. Debora Shuger); Debora Shuger, "Hypocrites and Puppets in *Bartholomew Fair*," *Modern Philology*, 82 (1984), 71–74; *Bartholomew Fair*, V.v.98–100, 104–105, 116–117.

14. *Bartholomew Fair*, I.iii.143–144; *Und*, 14.39–46; Wesley Trimpi, *Ben Jonson's Poems: A Study of Plain Style* (Stanford, Calif., 1962), pp. 144–147; Paul R. Sellin, *Daniel Heinsius and Stuart England* (Leiden, 1968), pp. 103–107; *Conv*, 605; *The Duello*, sig. A2v.

15. John Selden, *Table Talk* (London, 1890), p. 7; HS, XI, 384.
16. William Bouwsma, "Lawyers in Early Modern Culture," *American Historical Review*, 83 (1973), 305; Bacon, "Of Religion," in *The Works of Francis Bacon*, ed. James Spedding, Robert Ellis, and Douglas Heath, 6 vols. (London, 1887–1892), VI, 543–544; Selden, *Table Talk*, pp. 121, 142, 143, 144.
17. *The Autobiography and Correspondence of Sir Simonds D'Ewes*, vol. 2 (London, 1845), p. 333; for the Essex divorce case and its aftermath, see Beatrice White, *Cast of Ravens: The Strange Case of Sir Thomas Overbury* (New York, 1967).
18. *A Complete Collection of State Trials and Proceedings for High Treason and Other Misdemeanors*, vol. 2 (London, 1809), pp. 788, 858; Chamberlain, II, 461.
19. *A Challenge at Tilt*, lines 60–61, 101–107, 166–167 (italics added).
20. HS, VIII, 384; UV, 18.1–2, 3–4, 5–6, 14, 23–24; HS, XI, 138.
21. *Und*, 14.31–33; *Conv*, 578–579. For the iconography of Jonson's broken compass, with specific reference to the image in Corrozet's *Hecatongraphie*, see Beaurline, *Jonson and the Rhetoric of Elizabethan Comedy*, pp. 298–312.
22. DNB, s.v. Selden, John.
23. Dekker, I, 321; *Every Man out of His Humour*, IV.iv.25–26; *JAB*, p. 81; *Und*, 9.
24. Bentley, I, 176; Bentley, III, 299–302; *Conv*, 164–165; *Bartholomew Fair*, V.iii.88.
25. *Bartholomew Fair*, Prologue, 2, 4, 6–7; Ian Donaldson, *The World Upside-Down: Comedy from Jonson to Fielding* (Oxford, 1970), pp. 46–77; Leah Marcus, *The Politics of Mirth: Jonson, Herrick, Milton, Marvell and the Defense of Old Holiday Pastimes* (Chicago, 1986), pp. 38–63.
26. Jonathan Haynes, "Festivity and the Dramatic Economy of *Bartholomew Fair*," *ELH*, 51 (1984), 659; *Bartholomew Fair*, Induction, 76–78, 98, 81–82.
27. R. B. Parker, "The Themes and Staging of *Bartholomew Fair*," *University of Toronto Quarterly*, 39 (1970), 296–297; Mikhail Bakhtin, *Rabelais and His World*, trans. Helene Iswolsky (Cambridge, Mass., 1968), pp. 368–436; *Bartholomew Fair*, II.ii.106, II.v.95–97; Ian Donaldson, *The Poems of Ben Jonson* (Oxford, 1975), p. 84, note on lines 193–194 of "The Famous Voyage"; Michael Field, *Alternate Design: A Study of the Interaction of Theme and Structure in Ben Jonson's Poetry* (Ann Arbor, Mich.: University Microfilms, 1976), pp. 29–40.
28. *Bartholomew Fair*, II.v.77 and 63, III.vi.34–37, II.ii.44–45; Bakhtin, *Rabelais and His World*, pp. 329–336.
29. *Bartholomew Fair*, ed. E. M. Waith (New Haven, 1963); Parker, "The Themes and Staging of *Bartholomew Fair*," pp. 293–296.
30. Jackson I. Cope, "*Bartholomew Fair* as Blasphemy," *Renaissance Drama*, 8 (1965), 127–152; Shuger, "Hypocrites and Puppets in *Bartholomew Fair*"; *Bartholomew Fair*, III.iii.2–3 and 9–13, V.ii.5–6, V.vi.99–101.
31. *Bartholomew Fair*, IV.i.54 and 58–59, V.ii.129–130; Haynes, "Festivity and

the Dramatic Economy of Jonson's *Bartholomew Fair*," p. 655; Stephen J. Greenblatt, *Renaissance Self-Fashioning: From More to Shakespeare* (Chicago, 1980), p. 228; *Bartholomew Fair,* V.ii.118.

11. The Making of a Jacobean Poet

1. Bacon, "Of Great Place," in *The Works of Francis Bacon,* ed. James Spedding, Robert Ellis, and Douglas Heath, 6 vols. (London, 1887–1892), VI, 401; Edward Hyde, Earl of Clarendon, *The History of the Rebellion,* vol. 1 (Oxford, 1888), p. 73; *Ep,* 102.9–10, 19.

2. For contemporary accounts of Villiers's rise, see J. Rushworth, *Historical Collections,* vol. 1 (1721), pp. 456–457; Sir William Sanderson, *Aulicus Coquineriae; or, A Vindication* (1650); Sir Henry Wotton, *A Short View of the Life and Death of George Villiers, Duke of Buckingham,* Harleian Miscellany, 8 (1811), 614. See also Roger Lockyer, *Buckingham* (London, 1981), pp. 16–24, and contemporary sources cited in his notes; Brian O'Farrell, *Politician, Patron, Poet: William Herbert, Third Earl of Pembroke, 1580–1630* (Ann Arbor, Mich.: University Microfilms, 1984), pp. 74–77.

3. *The Golden Age Restored,* lines 9–12, 107–108, 110, 126–128.

4. Ibid., lines 12, 163–168; *Proclamations,* p. 324; HS, X, 553.

5. *A Complete Collection of State Trials and Proceedings for High Treason and Other Misdemeanors,* vol. 2 (London, 1809), pp. 911–950.

6. *State Trials,* II, 931; *Mercury Vindicated from the Alchemists at Court,* lines 134–136, 183–184.

7. HS, I, 231–232. Jonson never held the office of Poet Laureate: see Edmund K. Broadus, *The Laureateship* (Oxford, 1921), pp. 40–44.

8. Johann Gerritsen, "Stansby and Jonson Produce a Folio: A Preliminary Account," *English Studies,* 40 (1959), 52–55; T. H. Howard-Hill, "Towards a Jonson Concordance: A Discussion of Texts and Problems," *Research Opportunities in Renaissance Drama,* 15–16 (1972–73), 17–32.

9. Elizabeth Eisenstein, *The Printing Press as an Agent of Change* (Cambridge, Eng., 1979); Richard C. Newton, "Jonson and the (Re-)Invention of the Book," in *Classic and Cavalier: Essays on Jonson and the Sons of Ben,* ed. Claude J. Summers and Ted-Larry Pebworth (Pittsburgh, 1982), pp. 31–58; HS, IX, 45–52. See also HS, IX, 15–16; for the iconography of Jonson's frontispiece, see Margery Corbett and Ronald Lightbown, *The Comely Frontispiece: The Emblematic Title-Page in England, 1550–1660* (London, 1979), pp. 149–152.

10. Joseph Loewenstein, *Responsive Readings: Versions of Echo in Pastoral, Epic, and the Jonsonian Masque* (New Haven, 1984), pp. 84–85; HS, IV, 194.

11. HS, III, 403; for revisions of individual plays, see the textual introductions in HS, vols. 3, 4, and 5 (page references are given in HS, IX, 45 n. 1); Newton, "Jonson and the (Re-) Invention of the Book," pp. 37–38.

12. *Every Man in His Humour,* ed. Gabriel B. Jackson (New Haven, 1969), pp. 221–239.

13. HS, V, 431; HS, VIII, 25–26; O'Farrell, *Politician, Patron, Poet,* p. 89.

14. J. W. Saunders, "The Stigma of Print: A Note on the Social Bases of Tudor Poetry," *Essays in Criticism,* I (1951), 139–154; *For,* 10.29.

15. *Ep,*14.1–3, 13–14; *Ep,* 23.9–10; *Ep,* 43.8; *Conv,* 154; *Ep,* 55.3–4.

16. *Ep,* 101.1, 5–6, 13–20, 23, 36, 35; *Conv,* 258; Joseph Loewenstein, "The Jonsonian Corpulence; or, The Poet as Mouthpiece," *ELH,* 53 (1986), 491–519; Mark Eccles, "Jonson and the Spies," *Review of English Studies,* 13 (1937), 285–297.

17. *Ep,* 102.1–2; Friedberg, "Ben Jonson's Poetry: Pastoral, Georgic, Epigram," *English Literary Renaissance,* 4 (1974), 117–118; *Ep,* 92.18–19; *Ep,* 102.7–8, 19–20.

18. O'Farrell, *Politician, Patron, Poet,* pp. 51–87, 213–214, 220.

19. HS, II, 341; Wilson, "Morose Ben Jonson," in *The Triple Thinker* (New York, 1928), rpt. in *Ben Jonson: A Collection of Critical Essays,* ed. Jonas Barish (Englewood Cliffs, N.J., 1963), pp. 60–74.

20. *Ep,* 128.12–14; *Ep,* 133.73–76; *For,* 11.3–4; HS, VIII, 664, XI, 302; Richard Peterson, *Imitation and Praise in the Poems of Ben Jonson* (New Haven, 1981), pp. 9–10.

21. *For,* 1; *For,* 7–9; *Conv,* 364–368; *For,* 7.9–10.

22. *For,* 9.1–8; William Empson, *Seven Types of Ambiguity,* 3d ed. (London, 1956), p. 242; Marshall van Deusen, "Criticism and Ben Jonson's 'To Celia,'" *Essays in Criticism,* 7 (1957), 95–103; Richard Newton, *Foundations of Jonson's Poetic Style: "Epigrammes" and "The Forest"* (Ann Arbor, Mich.: University Microfilms, 1976), pp. 405–406 and generally pp. 397–409.

23. *For,* 14.17–18, 39–40; *For,* 12.93–94, 99–100, 92–93; HS, VIII, 116. Jonathan Z. Kamholtz, "Ben Jonson's Green World: Structure and Imaginative Unity in *The Forest,*" *Studies in Philology,* 78 (1978), 170–193.

24. *For,* 15.1–4, 17–22; William Kerrigan, "Ben Jonson Full of Shame and Scorn," *Studies in the Literary Imagination,* 6 (1973), 199–218.

25. HS, I, 30; *Ep,* 45.5–6; *For,* 15.23–26. I am indebted to an unpublished paper by Theresa McKenny for the reading of the final line.

26. *Disc,* 2465–66; HS, IX, 13; HS, XI, 516.

27. *Coleridge's Miscellaneous Criticism,* ed. T. M. Raysor (London, 1936), p. 47; T. S. Eliot, *Selected Essays* (London, 1932), p. 127; *Disc,* 2410–11; *UV,* 26.

12. *"Our Wel Beloved Servant"*

1. Anne Barton, *Ben Jonson, Dramatist* (Cambridge, Eng., 1984), p. 220.

2. Ibid.

3. *The Devil Is an Ass,* II.ii.13–14, 19, 126–128; II.v.11.

4. *Conv,* 287–289, 290–294, 476–480; *The Devil Is an Ass,* II.vi.94–113, and *Und,* 2.iv.11–30.

5. *Every Man in His Humour,* Prologue, 24, 14; *The Devil Is an Ass,* V.viii.169–170; Douglas Duncan, *Ben Jonson and the Lucianic Tradition* (Cambridge, 1979), pp. 226–228.

6. *The Devil Is an Ass*, V.v.49–51; G. L. Kittredge, "King James I and *The Devil Is an Ass*," *Modern Philology*, 9 (1911), 195–209.

7. *The Devil Is an Ass*, II.i.45–46; Chamberlain, II, 288; *Conv*, 414–415; Leah Marcus, *The Politics of Mirth: Jonson, Herrick, Milton, Marvell and the Defense of Old Holiday Pastimes* (Chicago, 1986), pp. 91–94, 101–105.

8. *The Tempest*, Epilogue, 1–2; *The Devil Is an Ass*, Epilogue, 1–2; Robert N. Watson, *Ben Jonson's Parodic Strategy: Literary Imperialism in the Comedies* (Cambridge, Mass., 1987), pp. 206–207.

9. HS, I, 231; *JAB*, p. 94.

10. *Proclamations*, pp. 323–324, 357; *The Political Works of James I*, ed. Charles McIlwaine (Cambridge, Mass., 1918), p. 343.

11. *Political Works of James I*, p. 343.

12. *Christmas His Masque*, lines 14–17, 174; Marcus, *Politics of Mirth*, pp. 77–81.

13. *Christmas His Masque*, lines 133–137, 144–149, 193, 253, 264, 265–267; Marcus, *Politics of Mirth*, pp. 81–83.

14. *Political Works of James I*, pp. 343–344; Marcus, *Politics of Mirth*, pp. 69–76; Anne Lake Prescott, "The Stuart Masque and Pantagruel's Dreams," *ELH*, 51 (1984), 407–420.

15. HS, X, 568; *The Vision of Delight*, lines 201–204; Jonathan Goldberg, *James I and the Politics of Literature* (Baltimore, 1983), pp. 61–62.

16. *The Irish Masque*, lines 177–180; HS, X, 428–429; Arthur Wilson, *The History of Great Britain* (London, 1653), p. 105.

17. *Althorpe Entertainment*, lines 261–266; UV, 47; HS, I, 180.

18. *Pleasure Reconciled to Virtue*, lines 218–223, 231, 269–272, 333; Stephen Orgel, *The Jonsonian Masque* (Cambridge, Mass., 1965), pp. 175–180.

19. Trans. from HS, X, 583; HS, X, 576.

20. HS, X, 566; *Pleasure Reconciled to Virtue*, line 15; Stone, pp. 555–562; for the account of Hay in this and the following paragraph, see *DNB*, s.v. Hay, James.

21. Mayerne, cited in D. H. Willson, *King James VI and I* (London, 1956), p. 455 n. 11; Tillières, quoted in Dale Randall, *Jonson's Gypsies Unmasked* (Durham, N.C., 1975), p. 172.

22. *For the Honour of Wales*, lines 5, 35–40, 60–62, 312.

23. *Conv*, 682–684; *Pleasure Reconciled to Virtue*, line 45; *Und*, 9.17; *Und*, 56.11; Robert M. Adams, "On the Bulk of Ben," in *Ben Jonson's Plays and Masques*, ed. R. M. Adams (New York, 1979), pp. 482–492; Joseph Loewenstein, "The Jonsonian Corpulence; or, The Poet as Mouthpiece," *ELH*, 53 (1986), 491–519.

24. *Conv*, 615–616; *Disc*, 622–624; *Conv*, 174, 180, 196, 371–372; *Disc*, 587–588, 611–612, 617–619; *Conv*, 566, 50–51.

25. *Conv*, 420–423, 64–65, 611–612, 393–398, 402–403, 89–91.

26. *Conv*, 649–650, 661–678; *Und*, 86.6; *The Greek Anthology*, trans. George Burgess (London, 1852), p. 144, as cited in Anne Ferry, *All in War with Time* (Cambridge, Mass., 1975), p. 277.

27. *DNB*, s.v. Corbet, Vincent; HS, XI, 54; *Und*, 12.8–11, 29–30.

13. Celebrity and Decline

1. E. M. Portal, "The Academy Roial of James I," *Proceedings of the British Academy,* 7 (1915–16), 189–208; trans. from HS, I, 234–235; *Conv,* 234–235, 312–313; C. J. Sisson, "Ben Jonson of Gresham College," *Times Literary Supplement,* September 21, 1951, p. 604; HS, XI, 582–585; but see also Paul Sellin, *Daniel Heinsius and Stuart England* (London, 1968), pp. 152–153.

2. Roy Strong, *The English Icon: Elizabethan and Jacobean Portraiture* (London, 1969), p. 27; Roy Strong, *Tudor and Jacobean Portraits,* vol. 1 (London, 1969), pp. 13–14, 183–184; K. K. Yung, *National Portrait Gallery: Complete Illustrated Catalogue, 1856–1979* (London, 1981), pp. 105, 34; HS, V, xii–xiii.

3. *Conv,* 371–372; Chamberlain, II, 436.

4. S. R. Gardiner, *History of England, 1603–1642* (London, 1895), III, 261–398; Menna Prestwich, *Cranfield, Politics and Profits under the Early Stuarts* (Oxford, 1966), pp. 330–344, esp. pp. 341–342.

5. As cited in *Proclamations,* p. 496; *Proclamations,* pp. 495–496.

6. Sara Pearl, "Sounding to Present Occasions: Jonson's Masques of 1620–25," in *The Court Masque,* ed. David Lindley (Manchester, 1984), pp. 60–61.

7. *News from the New World Discovered in the Moon,* lines 172, 18–19, 21–22, 42–43, 174–175.

8. Ibid., lines 300, 349–352; Stephen Orgel and Roy Strong, *Inigo Jones: The Theater of the Stuart Court* (Berkeley, 1973), p. 13.

9. *Pan's Anniversary,* 9–10, 160, 192–193; Joseph Loewenstein, *Responsive Readings: Versions of Epic in Pastoral, Echo, and the Jonsonian Masque* (New Haven, 1984), pp. 126–134.

10. G. P. V. Akrigg, *Jacobean Pageant: The Court of King James I* (Cambridge, Mass., 1963), pp. 224–225.

11. Dale Randall, *Jonson's Gypsies Unmasked* (Durham N.C., 1975); John Timpane, *The Romance of the Rogue* (Ann Arbor, Mich.: University Microfilms, 1980), pp. 111–128, 266–300; *The Gypsies Metamorphosed,* lines 1022–23.

12. Roger Lockyer, *Buckingham* (New York, 1981), pp. 101–103, 22; Jonathan Goldberg, *James I and the Politics of Literature* (Baltimore, 1983), pp. 143–146; *The Gypsies Metamorphosed,* lines 15, 23–24.

13. HS, XI, 387–389; Randall, *Jonson's Gypsies Unmasked,* pp. 76–78; *The Gypsies Metamorphosed,* lines 1124–25.

14. Randall, *Jonson's Gypsies Unmasked,* p. 81; HS, X, 633; *JAB,* p. 122.

15. Prestwich, *Cranfield,* pp. 330–344; *The Gypsies Metamorphosed,* lines 596–597.

16. *The Masque of Augurs,* lines 85, 11–12, 38–39, 86–87, 100–103, 254.

17. *Proclamations,* pp. 496, 520; W. Todd Furniss, "Ben Jonson's Masques," in *Three Studies in the Renaissance* (New Haven, 1958), p. 115.

18. *Time Vindicated to Himself and to His Honors,* line 73; HS, X, 653; *Calendar of State Papers, Domestic Series, James I, 1619–23,* p. 268.

19. HS, X, 653; *Time Vindicated to Himself and to His Honors,* lines 164–166, 172, 174, 96, 122–123, 126, 128–129.

20. Sara van den Berg, "'The Paths I Meant unto Thy Praise': Jonson's Poem for Shakespeare," *Shakespeare Studies,* 11 (1978), 207–218; W. W. Greg, *The Shakespeare First Folio* (Oxford, 1955), pp. 18–21.

21. A. C. Partridge, *Orthography in Shakespeare and Elizabethan Drama* (Lincoln, Nebr., 1955), pp. 130–140; J. Dover Wilson, "Ben Jonson and Julius Caesar," *Shakespeare Survey,* 2 (1949), 36–43. Shakespeare's supposed blunder was still on Jonson's mind three years later: see *The Staple of News,* Induction, 35–37.

22. *UV,* 26.7, 9, 11, 19–20, 29–30, 31, 33–40; van den Berg, "'The Paths I Meant unto Thy Praise,'" p. 210; *UV,* 26.47–48, 55–56, 77, 78.

23. HS, V, 291; *Disc,* 2409–34; John Dryden, *Essays,* ed. W. P. Ker, vol. 2 (London, 1900), p. 18.

24. Harry Levin, "An Introduction to Ben Jonson," in *Selected Works of Ben Jonson,* ed. Levin (New York, 1938), rpt. in *Ben Jonson: A Collection of Critical Essays,* ed. Jonas Barish (Englewood Cliffs, N.J., 1963), p. 40.

25. Thomas Grenville inserted a print of this engraving into the British Library folio copy of Jonson's *Works* (1616), but the portrait was engraved not earlier than 1622. See Margery Corbett and Michael Norton, *Engraving in England in the Sixteenth and Seventeenth Centuries, Part III: The Reign of Charles I* (Cambridge, Eng., 1964), p. 57; HS, III, ix–x.

26. *Und,* 20.5; *Und,* 21; *Und,* 2.i–x (citations of *Charis* are given by poem, section, and in some cases line numbers); *Und,* 47; *Und,* 43; *Und,* 42. Although many of the poems in *Und* give no indication of when they were written, the first two-thirds of the collection does include a sizable body of verse that falls between the 1616 folio and the stroke that afflicted Jonson in 1628. The fifteen poems that either certainly, or very probably, were written before the stroke are: 2, 3, 9, 12, 13, 16, 35, 42, 43, 44, 47, 48, 51, 52, 56. The break between the earlier (largely Jacobean) and the later (Caroline) sections of *Und* is unmistakable. None of the first fifty-seven poems in the numbered sequence of *Und* can confidently be assigned a date later than 1627; but virtually all of the poems from 58 to the end of the sequence were written between 1628 and 1635.

27. *Und,* 2.i.7–12; *Und,* 9.9–10; *Und,* 56.9–10, 13–14; *Und,* 52.2–3.

28. *Und,* 2.ii.30; 2.iv.21–24; HS, VIII, 136; Paul M. Cubeta, "'A Celebration of Charis': An Evaluation of Jonson's Poetic Strategy," *ELH,* 25 (1958), 173; Wesley Trimpi, *Ben Jonson's Poems* (Stanford, 1962), p. 218.

29. *Und,* 42.1–6, 11–12, 29, 32.

30. HS, XI, 54–57; *Ben Jonson's Poems,* ed. Ian Donaldson (Oxford, 1975), p. 205; Hugh McLean, "Ben Jonson's Poems: Notes on the Ordered Society," in *Essays in English Literature from the Renaissance to the Victorian Age Presented to A. S. P. Woodhouse,* ed. Millar McLure and F. W. Watt (Toronto, 1964), p. 50.

31. Samuel Johnson's *Dictionary,* as cited in Lawrence Stone, *The Family, Sex, and Marriage in England, 1500–1800* (New York, 1979), pp. 95–99; D. H. Rawlinson, "Ben Jonson on Friendship," *English,* 29 (1980), 203–217.

32. HS, VIII, 653–657; HS, XI, 296–297; HS, VIII, 657; HS, XI, 390.

33. *Und*, 47.16–17, 38, 31, 35–36, 39, 43, 48, 50; Pearl, "Sounding to Present Occasions," p. 62.

34. Richard S. Peterson, *Imitation and Praise in the Poems of Ben Jonson* (New Haven, 1981), pp. 112–157; *Und*, 14.1–2; *Und*, 47.73–78; Stanley Fish, "Author-Readers: Jonson's Community of the Same," *Representations*, 7 (1984), 56.

35. *Und*, 43.89–104, 1, 15; George B. Johnston, "Notes on Jonson's 'Execration upon Vulcan,'" *Modern Language Notes*, 46 (1931), 150–153. I am indebted to Christopher Highley for this reading of *Und*, 43.

36. *Und*, 43.88; HS, XI, 406–412; "Invective of Mr. George Chapman," 117–120, in *The Poems of George Chapman*, ed. Phyllis Bartlett (London, 1941), p. 477.

37. *Neptune's Triumph for the Return of Albion*, line 54.

38. Chamberlain, II, 515–516.

39. Ibid., 527; HS, X, 658; Chamberlain, II, 538; *Calendar of State Papers, Venetian*, XVIII, 192. These passages are cited in Jerzy Limon, *Dangerous Matter: English Drama and Politics in 1623/24* (Cambridge, Eng., 1986), pp. 21–22.

40. *Neptune's Triumph*, lines 54, 58–60, 233, 245, 65, 247; *Hymenaei*, lines 18–19.

41. *Neptune's Triumph*, lines 361–362, 510–513; Limon, *Dangerous Matter*, pp. 35–36.

42. Chamberlain, II, 538–539, as cited in Limon, *Dangerous Matter*, p. 23.

43. *Neptune's Triumph*, lines 34–35.

14. Return to the Playhouse

1. *Calendar of State Papers, Venetian*, XIX (1625–26), 21, as cited in Kevin Sharpe, "The Image of Virtue," in *The English Court*, ed. David Starkey (London, 1987), p. 228; Chamberlain, II, 606; Lucy Hutchinson, *Memoirs of the Life of Colonel Hutchinson* (London, 1906), p. 69; *Stuart Royal Proclamations*, vol. 2, ed. James Larkin (Oxford, 1983), 37–39; F. C. Dietz, *English Public Finance, 1554–1641* (New York, 1964), pp. 223, 228, as cited in Sharpe, "The Image of Virtue," p. 236. Bentley, VII, 58–77.

2. *The Staple of News*, III.ii.301; Bentley, IV, 629–630.

3. *The Staple of News*, III.ii.21, 26, 28–31; Sara Pearl, "Sounding to Present Occasions: Jonson's Masques of 1620–25," in *The Court Masque*, ed. David Lindley (Manchester, 1984), pp. 73–74.

4. *The Staple of News*, 4th Int., 4–9; *Conv*, 636; Calvin Thayer, *Ben Jonson: Studies in the Plays* (Norman, Okla., 1963), pp. 188–189; *The Staple of News*, 4th Int., 9–10.

5. *The Staple of News*, Induction, 62–64; 1st Int., 84; 2d Int., 1–2; 4th Int., 81–85.

6. "To the Readers," 2–7; Bentley, IV, 632; *The Staple of News*, II.v.42–43; 2d Int., 27–28, 31–32.

7. *Und,* 71.4–5, 6; HS, XI, 585; HS, I, 242, 179; HS, XI, 576.

8. *Und,* 44.23–26, 47, 51–60, 64, 86, 87–88; George Parfitt, "History and Ambiguity: Jonson's 'A Speech According to Horace,'" *Studies in English Literature,* 19 (1979), 85–92.

9. Stone, p. 239; *Conv,* 27–28; *UV,* 30.69–70.

10. HS, I, 242–244; Anne Barton, *Ben Jonson, Dramatist* (Cambridge, Eng., 1984), pp. 315–317.

11. Margaret, Duchess of Newcastle, *The Life of William, Duke of Newcastle,* ed. C. H. Firth (London, 1886), p. 104; Geoffrey Trease, *Portrait of a Cavalier: William Cavendish, First Duke of Newcastle* (New York, 1979), p. 55.

12. *UV,* 22; HS, VII, 765–778; *UV,* 28; *Und,* 53; HS, XI, 89–90.

13. HS, XI, 91–92; *The New Inn,* I.vi.120–121, 123, 132–133; I.iii.57, 47–48, 51; Sir Philip Sidney, *An Apology for Poetry,* ed. Geoffrey Shepherd (London, 1965), p. 119; Anne Barton, "Harking Back to Elizabeth: Ben Jonson and Caroline Nostalgia," *ELH,* 47 (1981), 722; Barton, *Ben Jonson, Dramatist,* pp. 258–284.

14. Kathleen Lynch, *The Social Mode of Restoration Comedy* (New York, 1926), pp. 43–79; Alfred Harbage, *Cavalier Drama* (New York, 1936), pp. 28–32; Annabel Patterson, *Censorship and Interpretation: The Conditions of Writing and Reading in Early Modern England* (Madison, Wisc., 1984), pp. 159–176.

15. *The New Inn,* I.v.52–53; III.ii.205–206, 236–238; V.i.26–27.

16. *The New Inn,* Prologue, 1–2, 3–4; I.iii.128; I.iv.13–14; I.iii.96, 109–110, 111–115; II.iv.4, 17–18; Robert N. Watson, *Ben Jonson's Parodic Strategy: Literary Imperialism in the Comedies* (Cambridge, Mass., 1987), p. 213; Thayer, *Ben Jonson,* pp. 201–202.

17. *The New Inn,* V.v.92; I.v.61–64; I.iii.132–136; I.iii.4–5; V.v.92–100; HS, XI, 387–389; *UV,* 45, and HS, XI, 162; Thayer, *Ben Jonson,* p. 230.

18. HS, IX, 252; HS, VI, 395, 397; HS, XI, 339.

15. *"Come Leave the Lothed Stage"*

1. HS, XI, 339, 345, 335, 343, 334.

2. For biographical details on Cary and Morison, see Kenneth B. Murdock, *The Sun at Noon: Three Biographical Sketches* (New York, 1939); Kurt Weber, *Lucius Cary, Second Viscount Falkland* (New York, 1940).

3. "An Elegy on Sir Henry Morison, by Lucius Cary, Viscount Falkland," ed. Kenneth B. Murdock, in *Harvard Studies and Notes in Philology and Literature,* 20 (1935), 29–30, lines 34–35, 200–201, 217–218, 221–222, 357–358. The poem is discussed in the introduction to Murdock's edition and in Richard S. Peterson, *Imitation and Praise in the Poems of Ben Jonson* (New Haven, 1981), pp. 195–199.

4. For a thorough account of the classical models that Jonson employs, see Peterson, *Imitation and Praise in the Poems of Ben Jonson,* pp. 195–232.

5. *Und,* 70.1–2, 9–10; John M. Major, "A Reading of Jonson's Epitaph on Elizabeth L. H.," *Studies in Philology,* 73 (1976), 62–86.

6. Seneca, *Epistulae Morales,* ed. and trans. Richard M. Gummere, vol. 3 (Lon-

don, 1953), p. 5; *Und,* 70.21–22, 31–32, 43–44, 45, 48–52, 53, 55–56; *Ep,* 45.7–8; *Und,* 70.62–64.

7. *Und,* 70.65–74; Seneca, *Epistulae Morales,* III, 7; cited from *Ben Jonson's Poems,* ed. Ian Donaldson (Oxford, 1975), p. 236.

8. *Und,* 70.75–78, 81–86; *Und,* 45.9–10; for the relationship between "On My First Son" and the Cary-Morison ode, see Mary I. Oates, "Jonson's 'Ode Pindaricke' and the Doctrine of Imitation," *Papers on Language and Literature,* 11 (1975), 134.

9. *Conv,* 1–3; Sidney, *An Apology for Poetry,* ed. Geoffrey Shepherd (London, 1965), p. 118.

10. HS, XI, 403; *The Life of Edward, Earl of Clarendon,* vol. 1 (Oxford, 1760), p. 32.

11. *Und,* 64.7–10, 21–22; Quentin Bone, *Henrietta Maria, Queen of the Cavaliers* (Urbana, Ill., 1972), p. 73; *Und,* 65.13–14.

12. HS, XI, 585; Michael Van Cleave Alexander, *Charles I's Lord Treasurer: Sir Richard Weston, Earl of Portland (1577–1635)* (London, 1975), p. 133; Stone, p. 422; *Und,* 68.1–2, 12–14; *Und,* 57.11–21.

13. *Inigo Jones: The Theater of the Stuart Court,* ed. Stephen Orgel and Roy Strong, 2 vols. (Berkeley, 1973), I, 12; *Tempe Restored,* quoted from *Inigo Jones,* ed. Orgel and Strong, I, 2, 50; John Owen, *Certain Epigrams* (1628), p. 31, as cited in Kevin Sharpe, "The Image of Virtue," in *The English Court,* ed. David Starkey (London, 1987), p. 258; *Letters of Queen Henrietta Maria* (London, 1857), pp. 14–15; Public Record Office, LC5/180, p. 1, as cited in Sharpe, "The Image of Virtue."

14. HS, VII, 733; *Tempe Restored,* quoted from *Inigo Jones,* ed. Orgel and Strong, II, 2.

15. HS, XI, 102–103; *Und,* 83.1–6, 52, 54, 55–56, 67–68, 99–100.

16. *JAB,* p. 168; HS, I, 240, 213.

17. HS, I, 213; John Webster, *The White Devil,* ed. J. R. Brown (London, 1960), IV.ii.110–112 and note; Ian Donaldson, "Jonson's Magic Houses," in *Essays and Studies,* ed. G. A. Wilkes (London, 1986), pp. 60–61; *Volpone,* V.xii.124.

18. *Und,* 71.1–4, 9, 11–12, 14–15.

19. HS, I, 103; *Und,* 73–75; HS, XI, 406 and *UV,* 37; HS, I, 212; *JAB,* pp. 194–195; HS, I, 241; Frances Teague, "Ben Jonson's Poverty," *Biography,* 2 (1979), 260–265.

20. *JAB,* p. 168; *UV,* 34.49–50; *Und,* 77.6–7, 25–28; D. J. Gordon, "Rubens and the Whitehall Ceiling," in *The Renaissance Imagination,* ed. Stephen Orgel (Berkeley and Los Angeles, 1975), pp. 24–50; Roy Strong, *Van Dyck: "Charles I on Horseback"* (New York, 1972); Alexander, *Charles I's Lord Treasurer,* pp. 37–38, 168–169, 179.

16. Endings

1. *The Magnetic Lady,* I.ii.33–34; Anne Barton, *Ben Jonson, Dramatist* (Cambridge, Eng., 1984), p. 296.

2. Bentley, IV, 632.

3. *A Tale of a Tub*, I.iii.17, 26–27; I.iv.20, 34, 37, 39; Mary C. Williams, "*A Tale of a Tub*: Ben Jonson's Folk Play," *North Carolina Folklore Journal*, 22 (1974), 161–168; *The King's Entertainment at Welbeck*, lines 244–246; *A Tale of a Tub*, Prologue, 7–10; Barton, *Ben Jonson, Dramatist*, p. 337.

4. Margaret Cavendish, Duchess of Newcastle, *The Life of William Cavendish, Duke of Newcastle*, ed. C. H. Firth (London, 1886), p. 237; John Brand, *Observations on the Popular Antiquities of Great Britain*, ed. Sir Henry Ellis, vol. 2 (London, 1900), pp. 143–153, 163–164; Leah Marcus, *The Politics of Mirth: Jonson, Herrick, Milton, Marvell and the Defense of Old Holiday Pastimes* (Chicago, 1986), pp. 133–134; *A Tale of a Tub*, I.ii.2.

5. Martin Butler, *Theater and Crisis, 1632–1642* (Cambridge, Eng., 1984), pp. 251–253; *Welbeck Entertainment*, lines 304–305.

6. Marcus, *Politics of Mirth*, p. 132; *JAB*, p. 168; HS, I, 212.

7. *Und*, 78.13–14, 18; Digby, *Observations on the 22. Stanza in the 9th Canto of the 3rd. Book of Spenser's Fairy Queen* (London, 1643), quoted in R. T. Petersson, *Sir Kenelm Digby: The Ornament of England, 1603–1665* (Cambridge, Mass., 1965), p. 92.

8. *Aubrey's Brief Lives*, ed. Oliver L. Dick (Ann Arbor, 1957), pp. 98–102; see also Petersson, *Sir Kenelm Digby*, pp. 101–105.

9. *Und*, 84.viii.4–9; Vittorio Gabrieli, "A New Digby Letter-Book: 'In Praise of Venetia,'" *The National Library of Wales Journal*, 9 (1955), 121, 129; Vittorio Gabrieli, *Sir Kenelm Digby; Un inglese italianato nell'eta della controtriforma* (Rome, 1957), p. 246; HS, XI, 103.

10. Gabrieli, *Sir Kenelm Digby*, p. 262; Gabrieli, "A New Digby Letter-Book," pp. 147, 139; *Und*, 84.ix.53–55, 108–109, 225–228.

11. HS, I, 181–182; *Und*, 83; *UV*, 40, 41; *DNB*, s.v. Digby, Kenelm; Michael Van Cleave Alexander, *Charles I's Lord Treasurer: Sir Richard Weston, Earl of Portland (1557–1635)* (London, 1975), pp. 29–30; HS, XI, 159–160; *Und*, 71; HS, I, 211–212.

12. *Und*, 79; *UV*, 42, 43; *The Sad Shepherd*, Prologue, 1; HS, XI, 436.

13. Bentley, IV, 917–920; HS, IX, 163; Annabel Patterson, *Censorship and Interpretation: The Conditions of Writing and Reading in Early Modern England* (Madison, Wisc., 1984), pp. 171–175; Bentley, V, 1334, 1030, 970–971.

14. *The Sad Shepherd*, Prologue, 9–15; I.iv.42–47, 18–19, 36–37; Butler, *Theater and Crisis*, pp. 261–262, 260–279.

15. HS, VII, 53; HS, VIII, 561; Paul R. Sellin, *Daniel Heinsius and Stuart England* (London, 1968), pp. 149–153; *Ben Jonson*, ed. Ian Donaldson (Oxford, 1985), p. 755.

16. *The Magnetic Lady*, II, Chorus, 46–47; *Disc*, 2631–33, 2675–77, 2677–78, 2805–11.

17. *A Tale of a Tub*, Prologue, 7–8; *The Sad Shepherd*, Prologue, 10; *Every Man in His Humour*, Prologue, 21; *Disc*, 1926–27.

18. HS, VIII, 463; N. E. Osselton, "Ben Jonson's Status as a Grammarian," *D. Q. R.*, 12 (1982), 207; HS, VIII, 515, 488–491.

19. Wayne H. Phelps, "The Date of Jonson's Death," *Notes and Queries,* 27 (1980), 146–149; Sir Edward Walker quoted from *JAB,* p. 99; Henry James, *The Future of the Novel: Essays on the Art of Fiction,* ed. Leon Edel (New York, 1956), p. 103; HS, XI, 431, 450; *Inigo Jones: The Theater of the Stuart Court,* ed. Stephen Orgel and Roy Strong, 2 vols. (Berkeley, 1973), p. 58; HS, XI, 516–519, 455.
20. HS, I, 179–180; *Disc,* 2469–70, 1095–96, 154–156.
21. James Boswell, *Journal of a Tour to the Hebrides,* ed. Frederick Pottle and Charles Bennett (New York, 1936), p. 55.

Epilogue

1. HS, XI, 466; HS, VIII, 26; HS, XI, 450, 449, 462.
2. "What Is an Author?" in *The Foucault Reader,* ed. Paul Rabinow (New York, 1984), p. 101.
3. *The Foucault Reader,* p. 108; HS, I, 140.
4. *Disc,* 1333–41, 1351–58, 2805–6; HS, VIII, 25; HS, XI, 385.
5. *The Foucault Reader,* pp. 118–119.

Illustration Credits

Illustration Credits

Illustration Credits

Index

Boldface type indicates page on which illustration appears.

Index

Index

Heroologia, 258
Heywood, Thomas, 26, 37
History of the World (Raleigh), 193
History of Tithes, The (Selden), 198
Histriomastix (Marston), 72, 79, 80
Hobbes, Thomas, 188
Hock Tuesday play, 291
Holidays, 246–248
Holland, Hugh, 16, 193
Holme, William, 64, 65
Hood, Robin, 343–345
Horace: Jonson and, 45, 46, 73, 78, 91,
    222–224, 259; on poetry, 45, 65, 115;
    Ovid and, 75, 76, 77; Dekker on, 81;
    motto from, 222, 223
Horney, Karen, 4
Hoskins, John, 192
Hoskins, Richard, 56, 57
Howard, Henry, Earl of Northampton, 97,
    106, 141, 179, 219
Howard, Lady Frances, 133, 201, 202, 204
Howard, Thomas, Earl of Nottingham, 106
Howard, Thomas, Earl of Suffolk, 106,
    117, 125, 230
Hull, John, 270
"Humble Petition of Poor Ben . . . ,"319
Humorous Day's Mirth, An (Chapman), 38,
    45
Humors, theory of, 3, 38–39, 41, 140
Hutchinson, Lucy, 295
Hymenaei, 133–134, 142, 199, 204, 226

Infanta, Princess, 274, 289, 291, 298
Inns, theater and, 304
Inns of Court, 17, 56, 57, 84, 93, 193
"Invective . . . against Mr. Ben Jonson"
    (Chapman), 288
"Inviting a Friend to Supper," 230, 283
Isle of Dogs, The (Jonson and Nash), 32,
    34, 51, 56, 57, 74, 76, 231

James I, King, 108, 111, 112, 166, 199,
    244, 246, 252; enters England, 93, 112;
    patronage under, 97, 98, 117; court
    of, 106, 123, 148, 175, 186, 220, 249–
    252, 273–274; poetry of, 107; themes of
    his monarchy, 109, 148, 156; court
    masques and, 117, 118, 119, 181; *East-
    ward Ho* and, 123; assassination at-

tempt on, 128–129; epigrams to, 130;
    Prince Henry and, 165; insolvency of,
    182–183, 273; hunting excursions, 185;
    Carr and, 202; Jacobean ideology and,
    209; *Bartholomew Fair* and, 213; ex-
    travagance of, 247, 250–253; decline of,
    264; proclamation of 1620, 266; birth-
    day masque, 267; Buckingham and,
    267, **268**, 270; homosexuality of, 270;
    edicts of, 274; and absolutism, 290;
    death of, 295; attitude toward women,
    302
Jones, Inigo, 324; rivalry with Jonson, 2,
    321–323, 325–326, 337, 353; masques
    and, 147, 150, 157, 182, 219, 321; Jon-
    son on, 193, 329, 334; visual imagery of,
    321. *See also specific productions*
Jonson, Ann. *See* Lewis, Ann (Mrs. Ben
    Jonson)
Jonson, Ben, 263, 281; psychology of, 2,
    31, 45, 88, 94–95, 138; sex life of, 3, 19,
    44, 54, 134, 145, 153–154, 242; as tutor,
    188, 206; library of, 193, 258, 288;
    physical appearance of, 206–207, 254,
    259, **263**, 281, 282, 307; pensions of,
    220–221, 245, 295, 319, 326, 348; ac-
    cused of sedition, 32–33, 76, 80, 106,
    231, 244, 352; abandons stage, 245, 264;
    honorary degree of, 262; financial diffi-
    culties of, 273, 283, 298, 308, 319, 325,
    327; "Ben" persona, 279, 282; failing
    health of, 298, 307, 331, 348; death of,
    330, 348; monument to, 348; historical
    role of, 352. *See also specific contempo-
    raries, family members, patrons, sources,
    works*
Jonson, Ben (first son), 20, 89, 96, 315
Jonson, Ben (third son), 145, 180
Jonson, Joseph (second son), 54, 86, 89,
    96–97
Jonson, Mary (first daughter), 54, 86
Jonsonus Virbius, 348, 349, 351
Julius Caesar (Shakespeare), 13, 100, 276

Kamholtz, Jonathan, 236
Kelley, Edward, 173
Kemp, Will, 84
Kennedy, John, 149, 371
Kernan, Alvin, 45, 137
King's Entertainment, 111

Index